BUSES, COAC
and... PEOPLE

Saturday 17 April, 1993, 7.30pm, near Maccynlleth and this bus stop flag is silhouetted against the clear Welsh evening sky.

Route S18 ran from Maccynlleth to Dinas Mawddwy on a rather mixed timetable, reflecting market days – Monday to Friday two daily trips, supplemented by two more on Tuesday and Wednesday, but on Saturday five round trips were run.

Route S22 ran from Maccynlleth via Carno to Drenewydd again on a mixed, but different, frequency with four trips Monday to Friday, one extra Tuesday, but ten round trips on Saturday. As was traditional no Sunday services ran.

700 known as Traws-Cambria (now Traws Cymru) operated from 1979 with departures from Cardiff through Brecon, Llandrindod Wells, Maccynlleth, Porthmadog to Bangor. Initially reasonably successful within three years Crosville found that in wintertime they were losing money and reduced the service to Friday to Monday only. Many changes have followed in recent years that are far too complex to detail here.

BY DAVID GLADWIN

Published by Adam Gordon

VOLUME 1 – THE EARLY DAYS – and beyond!

It has always been our intention that this should be volume one of two, although both books are self contained. Volume two will continue the story of Buses, Coaches and People from 1945 to 1995, but because motor-bus traffic flows on like a never-ending river inevitably there is some crossover in photographs and text between the two cut-off years. We also have hundreds of colour images all scanned and ready to publish, but without any clue as to the potential demand for a third full colour printed volume we are being cautious about the expenditure on that venture. Feedback from readers of this first volume would be invaluable! Contact details are below.

ACKNOWLEDGEMENTS

The gestation of this book came about 25-30 years ago but various aspects of life intervened, some personal, but on the writing front included were my 'Steam Tram' series for Adam Gordon and research work for a University study.

Unfortunately this time lag does mean a number of my contemporaries who had helped with advice and identification of photographs are no longer with us, and even some 'family' photographs are inherited with no one left to identify dates, etc, with any real accuracy.

However I am pleased to thank (in alphabetical order) Allan C. Baker, Les Baynham, Gavin Booth, Alan Brotchie, Mrs P. Edwards (for L.A. 'Teddy' Edwards), Mrs Dorothy Frewin (for Foster Frewin), David Grimmett, Peter Hammond, Geoff Harper, Gerald Hartley, David Harvey, George Hearse, Tom Henshaw, Stephen Howarth, Leslie Ives, Nick Kelly, Colin Laidler, Geoff Lumb, Mrs Siobhan Maksymiw, Roy Marshall, Geoff Mills, Ms Bev. Newman, Christopher Sims, Roger A. Smith, George Toms, Keith Turns, Peter Waller.

Members of The Omnibus Society , Omnibus Society Library Staff, the Editor, 'Omnibus' Magazine, London Historical Research Group, Provincial Historical Research Group, PSV Circle, Kithead Trust. The Editors of *Commercial Motor, Route One, Bus & Coach Preservation, Classic Bus.* Ian Allan Publishing, Rt. Hon. the Lord Iliffe. David Gladwin

Publisher's note: Research has brought to light many contemporary and rare photographs and other illustrations of varying quality. They are reproduced after careful scanning and enhanced as far as possible. Every attempt has been made by the author and the publisher to secure the appropriate permissions for materials reproduced in this book. If there has been any oversight we will be happy to rectify the position in future editions, to which end a written submission should be made to the Publisher.

ISBN 978-1-910654-08-8
Publication no. 112
Published in 2016 by Adam Gordon, Kintradwell Farmhouse, Brora, Sutherland KW9 6LU
Tel: 01408 622660
E-mail: adam@ahg-books.com

Printed by: 4edge Ltd, 7 Eldon Way, Hockley SS5 4AD
Production by: Trevor Preece, 2 Sella Bank, The Banks, Seascale, Cumbria CA20 1QU
E-mail: trevor@trpub.net or trevor@trpub.uk

CONTENTS

A comprehensive
index will be
published in
Volume 2

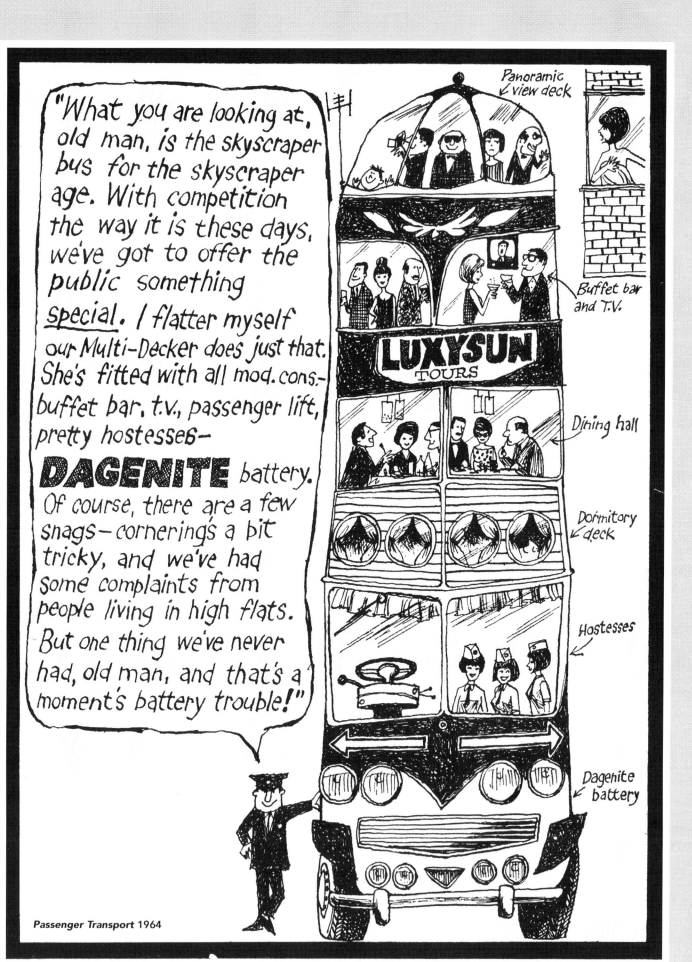

AUTHOR'S NOTE

Back a long time, a Swiss with the nickname of Le Corbusier, laid down his five points of architecture:

1. His house should be on stilts.
2. The interior should not depend on the outer skin.
3. There should be an open floor plan.
4. There should be 'long strips of ribbon windows'.
5. There should be a roof garden.

Regard then a double-decker bus – the stilts are tyres, the seats are normally bolted to the floor, this 'floor plan' can be adjusted according to demand, ribbon windows we have and for a 'roof garden' substitute either an open top or a Lincrusta ceiling.

An operator might look at his double-decker with a more prosaic eye, but it cannot be denied there is a strong connection between the ideal building and the ideal bus. The one should house as many people as possible on a small footprint while giving them room to live; a bus should seat as many passengers as possible while giving them leg and shoulder room.

The logical derivation of this dream machine is the rear engined 'Transbus Enviro 400', with a 2-axle Volvo or Scania chassis, seating between 64 and 90 passengers in air-conditioned quiet comfort. Conversely at most museum open days you can ride in the ultimate Le Corbusier dream machine, a neat Atlantean, Fleetline, or the Enviro's predecessor, the Dennis Dominator.

Many enthusiasts in the bus and coach world love their vehicles for what they are, especially the older ones with polished wood interiors, fancy seashell-shaped light shades, a beautifully veneered sliding roof – even if it no longer slides – shining chrome, even such minutiae as the cigarette stubbers on the back of seats or those horrible little window catches that happily nipped thousands of fingers. Or, if a 'pure' bus, the degree of light in the saloon or those mysterious creaks and groans that have always been such a part of the upper deck travel. The moquette of the seats downstairs may be redolent of school child days and the odd cigarette burn in the leather upstairs tells its own tale.

But all of this and more has required people to give the machine its own patina – notice, for example, how the chrome of the handrails is dulled by a million scratches from the rings on the fingers of girls, and how the chrome has worn away from the knobs on the ends of seats exposing the basic brass, chrome worn off those banes of a conductor's life as once more his hip bounces off them, or the way the cord of the bell dinger sags between the eyelets holding it to the ceiling. In 'The Automobile' magazine much play is made of the recent trend towards 'oily rag' non-restorations. Instead of a re-spray with new leather on the seats, new flooring and the like, now conservation is the watchword, an oily rag over the paintwork to restore a gleam but not gloss, leather food to strengthen the seats but leaving the sags of people still in place, woodwork not stripped and re-varnished but buffed up by human sweat, instruments made to work but not to have new flashy chrome – in other words for the car, van, lorry, bus or whatever to reflect the lives of the people that have owned it.

By and large bus and coach people are not bad at showing their vehicles, although there is a sad trend to arrive on the site, lock up the vehicle and leave it, without any placard or notice to tell the paying public what they are looking at; which is probably all they need. Conversely, many who show their vehicles are only too happy to tell the story of its life and so on; vital if the younger generations are to take an interest.

So, this volume will show, in a vaguely chronological order, people – people working, people building, people travelling or just ambling about in, on or near buses.

COUNTRY BUS PUR SANG

TO 4460 belongs to E. & H. Frakes 'Ella Services', one of the many operators who had to cease when regulations were tightened, but their apple green Chevrolet (one of two) poses a number of questions. The bodywork as far as the windscreen is attractive in a functional sort of way, but was it second-hand to this chassis? The frontal aspect looks like an odd-job run off with a bit of 2" x 2" timber and plywood, while the bracketry holding it together looks like something the local blacksmith knocked up. It has the routine split windscreen and, of course, no windscreen wiper. I once drove a contemporary machine for a friend, this had the latest idea for the period – the wiper could be persuaded to run horizontally across the windscreen by winding a handle, returning via a spring.

Generally it is accepted and was known that preparations for war started in the mid 1930s and accelerated before the actual outbreak. We have to assume that located in Newcastle upon Tyne the Northern General Transport Co. was well aware of this, but tapped into the extra money being earned by those in the armaments industry with their 146-page *'luxury coach tours'* brochure for 1939. This rather delightful screed which well belies the impression of the dour North East was illustrated by Shirley Grey and written by 'Vagabond' (Frederick A. Wills). We have tried to trace this couple but without any luck; their books are as attractive as you see below.

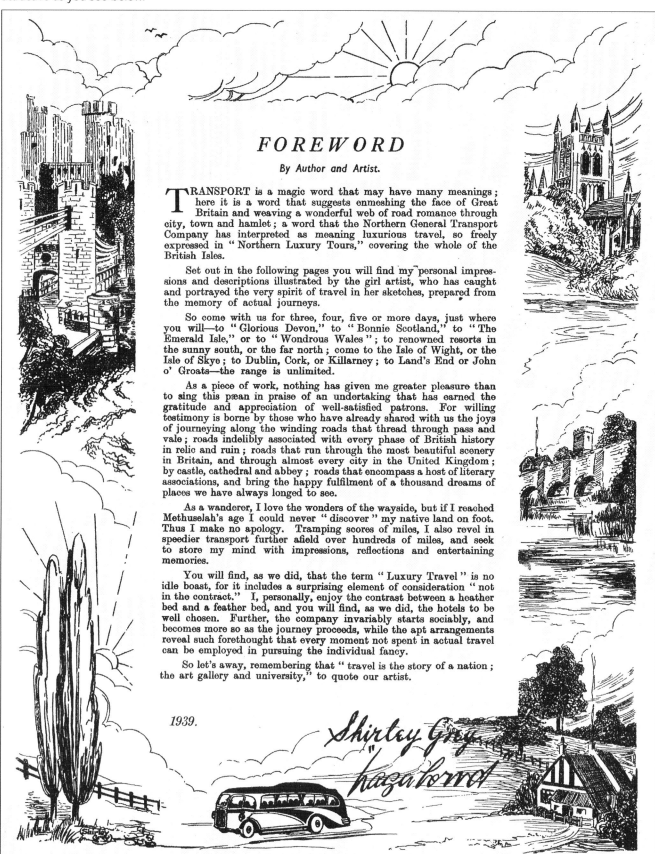

FOREWORD

By Author and Artist.

TRANSPORT is a magic word that may have many meanings; here it is a word that suggests enmeshing the face of Great Britain and weaving a wonderful web of road romance through city, town and hamlet; a word that the Northern General Transport Company has interpreted as meaning luxurious travel, so freely expressed in " Northern Luxury Tours," covering the whole of the British Isles.

Set out in the following pages you will find my personal impressions and descriptions illustrated by the girl artist, who has caught and portrayed the very spirit of travel in her sketches, prepared from the memory of actual journeys.

So come with us for three, four, five or more days, just where you will—to " Glorious Devon," to " Bonnie Scotland," to " The Emerald Isle," or to " Wondrous Wales "; to renowned resorts in the sunny south, or the far north; come to the Isle of Wight, or the Isle of Skye; to Dublin, Cork, or Killarney; to Land's End or John o' Groats—the range is unlimited.

As a piece of work, nothing has given me greater pleasure than to sing this pæan in praise of an undertaking that has earned the gratitude and appreciation of well-satisfied patrons. For willing testimony is borne by those who have already shared with us the joys of journeying along the winding roads that thread through pass and vale; roads indelibly associated with every phase of British history in relic and ruin; roads that run through the most beautiful scenery in Britain, and through almost every city in the United Kingdom; by castle, cathedral and abbey; roads that encompass a host of literary associations, and bring the happy fulfilment of a thousand dreams of places we have always longed to see.

As a wanderer, I love the wonders of the wayside, but if I reached Methuselah's age I could never " discover " my native land on foot. Thus I make no apology. Tramping scores of miles, I also revel in speedier transport further afield over hundreds of miles, and seek to store my mind with impressions, reflections and entertaining memories.

You will find, as we did, that the term " Luxury Travel " is no idle boast, for it includes a surprising element of consideration " not in the contract." I, personally, enjoy the contrast between a heather bed and a feather bed, and you will find, as we did, the hotels to be well chosen. Further, the company invariably starts sociably, and becomes more so as the journey proceeds, while the apt arrangements reveal such forethought that every moment not spent in actual travel can be employed in pursuing the individual fancy.

So let's away, remembering that " travel is the story of a nation; the art gallery and university," to quote our artist.

1939.

Shirley Grey

CHAPTER 1
INTRODUCTION

It is a physical impossibility to tell the whole story of buses, coaches and people in one book and I have, therefore, gone down the other path taking a series of snapshots of how vehicles evolved over around 120 years. When we look at these photographs we can see that the very landscape, as well as the clothing and general appearance of people, has altered almost beyond comprehension.

I am not entirely convinced that all the changes are for the better, as to take an agricultural view in harvest we worked seven days a week (religion's hold was already weakened in our area) and there was, to some extent, a camaraderie about the whole thing, the synchronicity between the fetching of the stooks of hay, the pitching up to the man on the haystack and the skill as our Mr Nunn worked the sheaves into the shape he wanted. Life was to quite a degree crude, our lavatory was the back of the hedge and some men stunk, and since water was scarce (plenty for the thrashing engine little for us!), for those two or three weeks washing was hardly de rigueur for the men (unfairly, it was for us kids when we got home), but after the Harvest Fair a day out in coaches was organised for almost the whole of the village – Southend-on-Sea was favourite!

Now, though, the entire hay crop is cut, sorted and placed in black bales (for silage) or big rolls, by one man – often a contractor – driving a monstrous tractor or combine. His companionship is his music, mobile phone and satnav. He goes to Spain for his holidays.

In a few villages the last of the older, small operators hang on, but in the towns and cities not only are the vehicles almost unrecognisable, but the comfortable familiar municipal garage has been replaced by yet another supermarket or by 'ticky-tacky' houses whose lives do not revolve around the 'bus but their cars. Two examples of this change happened to places where I once worked, once for a municipal and the second a smart private operator. The municipal's garage had, in its day, served horse trams, steam trams, then the new electrics, culminating in diesel buses serving a 'back-bone' route. Alas the powers-that-be decided to sell it for re-development, with most of the staff drifting off – at least half going to British Rail – and eventually the area became an expensive, up-market-gated area; the other, private operator working in as Keith Turns put it, in his *The Independent Bus*, the Marginal West Midlands inheriting the services of Cecil and Sylvia Marks, the gloriously named 'Pride of the Pyke' utilising the local dialect work 'Pyke' (probably derived from Turnpike) with pride.

In 1967 'our' operator bought the company, its licences and the garage, with a good patch of land, but so far had traffic fallen away that, initially, the new company only had two vehicles with the owner doing the driving assisted by part-time staff, although in less than a decade a fine network of bus and express coach routes were in operation, together with a very profitable travel bureau. By 1980 it was difficult to see where this company moved – stage carriage (bus) work only accounted for less than 10% of the business, and the always unstable contract movements over 50%, including high dependency on work to 'The Austin', Longbridge. Given an offer they could not refuse the company was sold in 1983

and where once we drove coaches, now the latest Audi and Mercedes cars live!

Hundreds, if not thousands, more operators have come and gone, many without even a photograph to record their passing, but for others we can at least look at the illustrations and join in their dreams. The whole story is riddled with the financial woes of not only operators but the outside world, time and time again. Obviously, bus and coach work has always been susceptible to employment or lack thereof – when mills, steelworks, collieries and factories closed down in the 1920s, not only did day travel decline, but contract work, especially in mining districts, was promptly cancelled. Markets suffered as wives no longer had the cash in their handbags to shop as long or as often as they had done and often the bus fare simply was not there. The finest description of the state of a one-industry town (in this case a shipyard) was described by Nevil Shute in '*Ruined City*' where the trams stopped, Woolworths (then a barometer of the health of an area) closed, and just for once the town was clean, for the loss of the shipyard closed the local mines and chimneys lay idle while trains laden with steel no longer ran along the rusted tracks. Although not mentioned in his text, the local thriving 'bus company reduced his fleet from 22 (12 on contract work) to 5, three of them on 'schools' barely covering the cost of running them, and his drivers, conductors, mechanics, even the little office girl, were gradually laid off, adding to the unemployment. And, of course, now in the 21st century we see the same cycle occurring but worse in some ways, for the old staples of the Market Day bus and the Cinema bus are almost finished, and it has been said, I think with justification, that if you cancelled school transport and the 'free' (but paid for out of the taxes) pensioners passes and travel passes for the unemployed, half the buses on the road would stop overnight.

It is true there are now new traffics – airport work, express coaches for students at unbelievable low fares, the National Express network, and specialised 'dedicated' routes – but almost all of these are in the purlieu of the big operators, very few of whom are British owned.

To me the saddest part of modernisation is the lack of the human interface – the link between the conductor or the driver and their passengers. In a country district like mine many, perhaps 'old fashioned', passengers will thank the driver, but it is no more than a courtesy as the bus operator tends to change the drivers working day-to-day, so in a week you may see three drivers following their rosters up or down. If you ask the management why, we can only try to explain the problem of driver's hours and his (or her) requirement for a 'personal needs' break.

This book is split into rough chronological order but, it is a big but, where the story of an individual operator means we span decades, then we start at, for example, 1922 and may run up to 1952. Photographically this can be very interesting to show the evolution of the vehicles used; although there was a famous operator who started with a Bedford-Duple in the 1930s and remained faithful to Bedford to the very end, always with Duple bodywork; when he could no longer get this combination within 5 years he just put his vehicles away and ceased operating.

The decision was made quite early on to separate the colour illustrations from the monochrome, partly on the grounds of expense but mainly because they rarely seem to mix very well; monochrome was the medium used by photographers of the period who understood the importance of the play of light and shadow. A handful of the illustrations are below par but are quite irreplaceable or unique. Where relevant we have included timetables, although there just is not enough space to put in more than a few, and even less maps. Horse-drawn coaches and buses do not occupy many pages for a number of reasons, not least that, although we were allowed to ride our farm horses, that is my total physical knowledge of four-legged motors.

Conversely our illustrations go right back to the dawn of motoring vehicles, including some unusual aspects of steam coaches; typically one report in the text dated 1898 covers the Panhard 'bus for 13 persons but which predicted that "lines of steam omnibuses will be the railways of the future", accompanied by a delightful engraving of a De Dion 12-seated 'bus. I think for an onlooker the middle 1920s must have been the most exciting time, as vehicles progressed from the char-à-banc to a bus or coach which would be recognisable today.

Many long years ago a German colleague (an ex-POW) told me about his introduction to char-à-bancs. He was a young officer during the invasion of France, with his steed a Panzerkampfwagen II mounting a 2cm KwK20 L/55 cannon. Early on they were mauled by a batch of French Somua and Char B tanks and had become worried as their 2cm gun only raised sparks from the French armour (drily, he mentioned "I expect they had headaches") while the French cannon ruined their armour.

In the distance they saw a row of Char B tanks sitting on railway transporters with their guns fore and aft and the crews sitting around having baguettes and coffee. On seeing his Panzer a white flag appeared. It seemed their petrol was on another train, their ammunition on a third and, anyway, they were reservists who had never trained on the Char B. Within 10 minutes the French crews were wearing civilian clothes and had wandered off. He had no facilities or inclination for taking prisoners. "So", said my colleague "French men sitting on 'bancs' on Char Bs – there is your char-à-bancs." (Benches in tanks).

A Hereford newspaper took a slightly different view of the word under the heading "That word char-à-bancs":

"When the man in the street becomes embroiled in the controversy as to the correct pronunciation of the word spelt c-h-a-r-a-b-a-n-c-s there may well develop a certain hesitation in using the term, lest in "opening our mouth we put our foot in it". What with 'charabang', 'char-abanc' (the first syllable sounded as in charwoman), 'charrybang', the lady who called it a 'charabong' and the dictionary which gives the pronunciation as 'shar-ashan" – all evolutions of a scheme of more or less higher education, some of us are beginning to feel that in early youth our scholarly equipment must have been sadly neglected, or else the term was never meant to be interpreted in English. In which case, why not an anglicised equivalent?

"The A.A. have addressed a letter to all members of the industrial vehicle section of the Association anent the outcry against the motor char-à-bancs. They point out that it is not the char-à-bancs so much as the manner in which it is handled that is the cause of the trouble, and the Association suggests that owners should issue instructions to their drivers to give other road users every consideration."

It is only when we begin to delve in the archives that we can grasp how popular the char-à-banc really was, and how quickly after the end of the first war it became the accepted mode of transport. For example:

"At the end of the month the Oldham Equitable Co-operative Society will be organising a week's motor tour through Scotland, following much of the route of the early Reliability Motor Trials, for £11 5s., including hotel accommodation. This society has two Karrier, an A.E.C., and a Guy char-à-bancs and will doubtless hire others to carry its large party for the Wakes Week."

Elsewhere the Co-op societies were on the forefront of coaching – Rochdale's Pioneer had a Thornycroft, the Provident two Dennis and three Leylands, Eccles two Halleys and a Fiat, Ashton-under-Lyme and Crompton a Leyland apiece, Wigan took to the Dennis, while the Manchester and Salford Co-operative Society favoured the rugged Pagefield. "It is safe to conjecture that before next season (i.e. 1921) at least another 70 co-operative societies in Lancashire will be running char-à-bancs." But there was a distaff side to all this activity; in 1921 this appeared in the *Hereford Journal*, not then a paper known for hysterical outbursts:

THE CONDUCT OF MOTOR COACH PARTIES

The rowdy conduct of certain classes of motor coach trippers this season has become so pronounced that steps are now being taken to prevent a recurrence of this undesirable behaviour. The proprietors of motor coaches are the first to realise the damage to their business that this kind of conduct entails, but unless universal action is taken any individual attempt at suppressing this rowdyism will simply result in loss of business to the individual concerned.

Another feature of the case with which the proprietor is intimately concerned is the difficulty of collecting his passengers at night. Parties stay out late in some distant town and often do not reach home till midnight. The driver, who is generally paid a weekly wage, naturally does not turn up at the garage till late next morning and when, quite possibly, the coach has to go out again. The result is that the examination of the vehicle is either neglected or skimped, for the driver is only able to spend a few minutes instead of a few hours on its care and maintenance. The proprietor suffers in consequence and two courses are open to him. One is to employ a relief driver, the other to enforce an earlier and more orderly return on the part of his passengers. He is loath to take the latter course, as it will inevitably result in the same business going elsewhere to proprietors who are less particular.

The only cure seems to lie in the introduction of local legislation to deal with these special cases. Such legislation has already been introduced in some parts of the country and there seems to be a feeling amongst proprietors that it might be extended with advantage.

This advertisement is by Worthington Coaches of London.

MANCHESTER COACH OWNERS' NEW WORRY

Statistics show just how crowded some roads were and it is difficult to see just how many of these companies paid their way. For example, London to Brighton in the summer of 1929, there were twelve operators, some, like Southdown, running hourly – all this on a line where the railways contested vigorously. Fourteen coaches ran daily between Cambridge and London. Bournemouth was served by twelve operators each weekday from London, giving I suppose, 25 separate coaches each holding 24-30 – 600 to 750 seats; at a time when unemployment was just beginning to bite and most would-be passengers that had work were busy toiling in their factories, mills or other industrial plant; whether we like it or not the majority of coach passengers were, and are, drawn from (what was called) the working classes, students and pensioners.

1929 and an argument has never really been settled. In certain circumstances – so called 'executive coaches' – where journeys could be overnight or the clientèle well primed with alcohol and unable to last too long – then on board lavatories made sense. In the heyday of coaches there were 'facilities' at regular intervals though, I am afraid, they varied between quite decent and dreadful! From a *Bus & Coach* editorial.

"Talking to long-distance people, I have recently heard very divided opinions regarding the value of lavatory and buffet equipment. Those 'against' say that passengers, especially women, do not like to use a lavatory on a coach, and much prefer a short break in the journey for refreshments. Other owners are equally emphatic that these objections do not exist, and that the facilities are appreciated.

Personally, I favour scheduled halts. Attractive wayside cafes are springing up along all the main roads, and a ten or fifteen minutes' stop at one of these for morning coffee or afternoon tea is an excellent idea, and one that appeals to women especially. Yes, if I were putting a long-distance car on the road, the room occupied by lavatory and buffet would be utilised to give an inch or two extra between each seat."

The relevant sections of the Road Traffic Act of 1930 has been best summed up by Graces Guide, as follows:

Central regulation of UK coach services
Introduction of a 30 mile an hour [48km] speed limit for buses and coaches
Issue of public service vehicle licences
Rules regarding the conduct of drivers, conductors and passengers on public service vehicles
Limitation of hours of continuous driving

Car owners gained and lost; speed limits were dropped; various driving offences were introduced including driving while under the influence of drink and drugs; compulsory third party insurance; licensing of drivers after a driving test; construction, weight and equipment of motor vehicles the emergence of the printed Highway Code etc.

The fact was that from 1928 onwards "The Combine" was already consuming many independent companies, the might of B.E.T. plus Tillings and the four mainline railway companies who were awash with cash to ensure they reached a monopoly position – their investments had to be protected. The odd thing is that the 1930 Act was forced through by a hard-line lifelong socialist, Herbert Morrison,

---

In granting permission for the operation of additional express bus services, Manchester Watch Committee has introduced a new condition in licences which is causing serious concern to motor coach owners who have street stands and booking offices in the centre of the city. It is understood that in future licences will only be granted on condition that passengers are loaded at a garage and not at their city booking office, as is at present the case. Manchester Owners have always taken the view that it is a public convenience for passengers to join outward-bound coaches in the central part of the city as here are located the various inquiry and booking offices.

If the new condition is enforced the business will in all probability be transferred to less convenient premises. We believe that representations are being made with the object of obtaining some modification in the new regulation.

NORRIS, HENTY & GARDNERS LTD OF PATRICROFT, MANCHESTER
ROAD TRANSPORT ENGINE DATA

Engine	Swept Volume		B.H.P.	R.P.M.	Maximum Torque		Approximate Weight lb.
	Cu. In.	Litres			lb. ft.	r.p.m.	
4LK	232	3.8	57	2,100	161	1,100	775
4LW	340	5.6	75	1,700	237	1,300	1,090
4HLW	340	5.6	75	1,700	237	1,300	1,130
5LW	426	7.0	94	1,700	300	1,300	1,250
5HLW	426	7.0	94	1,700	300	1,300	1,295
6LW	511	8.4	112	1,700	358	1,300	1,440
6HLW	511	8.4	112	1,700	358	1,300	1,490
8LW	680	11.2	150	1,700	478	1,300	1,850

The famous 'Gardner' engine ruled supreme in the world of diesel engines for many decades, and for sheer flogability has never been surpassed. This table shows the 1954 range.

This is from a trade magazine dated April 1929, one result was the building of a number of city termini, some satisfactory and some which by the 1950s were getting pretty dreadful and deteriorating thereafter – Digbeth, Birmingham, with permanent stink of diesel and early morning coughs from the sparrows, Victoria coach station, London, with a demented merry-go-round of vehicles coming and going – one ten minutes late and total chaos could ensue – not through any fault of the inspectors but just too many vehicles. Manchester's horror was Lower Mosley Street, which for whatever reason tended to make me an unhappy driver. Blackpool – ever our favourite as hundreds of coaches descended upon this one area, but somehow it was all sorted out – well nearly always!! Trips to the seaside depended on the foresight of their councils – Weston-super-Mare once had a dedicated coach station on the old railway yard in Locking Road which was ideal although the road to it (the old A370) was narrow and always congested. One practice we liked was to drop the passengers off at a suitable point and then park up in another operator's yard, but if the weather changed the passengers took a dim view of waiting on the Prom!

The sad part is that letters in trade magazines today speak of vicious and bumptious Traffic Management Officers (Wardens to us) who delight in giving out tickets even when the parking bay has been paid for in advance. I ran in to this relatively recently when we took a party of disabled in a minibus to a Welsh seaside resort and got 'booked' when dropping them off at the hotel prior to parking elsewhere as the woman reckoned the disabled persons 'Blue Badge' issued in England, did not apply in Wales. This ticket was cancelled later but it was embarrassing – and stupid.

pacifist in the first world war, and War Minister in the second; not a man that some first world war veterans running bus and coach companies would appreciate. But they had no choice!

The 1930 Act was, basically, for the benefit of the big boys – hardly a socialist operation – and although, where it was possible, many independents were protected, as operators of their stage carriage services, by its very nature the Act constrained any efforts to expand or vary their routes to meet changing traffic flows. Our local route still follows the old main road, ignoring the by-passes (where housing has grown up) which were opened in 1969. The independent that ran it for years never wanted to change, and the big operator of today probably finds it easier to let sleeping dogs lie, although our daily services have shrunk from seven (1980s) to four today.

Often overlooked in this battle between railway and privately owned companies was that the 'fat cats' of the 1930s often had their money invested in railway stocks; they closed ranks.

Clearly, in the more remote parts of the country some sensible evasions of the Act took place; our 'cinema' bus was regularly overcrowded with girls either sitting on laps or in the isle – the Trent inspector used to conveniently go for a can of tea at the right time. Similarly, when on hire to Ribble for the Blackpool run, we used our 'big' Albions (licensed for summer use only), no-one was surprised to see, although we were the 10th or 11th relief vehicle, that mill girls ended up sitting in the aisle upstairs – not wanting to be separated from their friends. Another trick one of my employers had was to have a fleet of six Leyland Leopards with similar Duple bodies and when one's tyres were tired or a mechanical ailment became apparent, registration plates, tax discs etc. were swopped over – even most drivers did not seem to notice the difference!

Wright Brothers had one of the worst operating areas in the country.

Keith Turns, in his "The Independent Bus", writing in 1974, tells us that Nenthead is the highest village in England, has three times the rainfall of Manchester and a climate approximating to the Faroes. "Nestling around the 1500ft level, snow has been known in June, and is common in May". Wright's routes, as shown both in their permits and on the map, must have been impossible to work in the 1930s. Keith describes the Hexham to Penrith route, started in 1925, as "44 miles of some of the toughest main road in England, including an alpine-type zigzag down into the West Allen Valley, and the crossing of Hartside, at 1889ft, the highest A class road pass in England." Small wonder initially it was a summer-only operation, as even now these roads can be lonely – remember no mobiles and precious few telephones of any type then.

Trying to find extra work another route was essayed – that on Market Days from Alston to Haltwhistle. Narrow roads, 1 in 3½ hills, and bends so sharp as to need reversal, ensured this ceased after six months.

Employment locally steadily ran down and with it coach and bus services. This decline, not only of Nenthead but of the whole area, can be seen in population figures. Even so, Nenthead suffered less than others.

	1861	1871	1881	1951	1961
Nenthead	2040	1811	1419	639	350
Alston	1700	1516	1360	1299	1360

In the 1930s the 'main line' to Hexham shrunk to a market journey from Alston via Nenthead and Carrshield to Hexham; still the highest bus service in England "although reaching a mere 1,999 ft."

But in 1929 the editor of *Bus & Coach* rambled over a number of items, these three being most important, inasmuch as they draw attention to a problem which still exists if we substitute buggies, wheelchairs, or backpacks for parcels.

THROUGH PASSENGERS' EYES
by Wanderer
who comments from the passengers' point of view.
Letters from readers are invited

I am beginning to be afraid of mentioning the word "luggage" lest somebody should accuse me of monotony. However, this is a new aspect of the position, so here goes! A reader speaking on the telephone asked me why, seeing that the roof of a coach was good enough for passengers' luggage, should not ordinary parcels accepted by a company as common carriers be also slung on the roof? Except to say that so far as I know it simply isn't done, I will leave the matter.

Earlier this year a correspondent who signed his letter "L.M.M." complained that in several service buses in which he had travelled passengers' space was taken up by parcels being carried by the companies concerned. He also said that in some instances parcels were strewn about the bus gangways and hampered the free movement of passengers.

It is interesting to note how a South Wales firm have overcome the luggage difficulty raised in "L.M.M.'s" letter. On a 36-seated body there are arranged, in place of the back row of seats, two luggage racks running the full width of the body. These racks, with the space beneath the lower one, give plenty of room for luggage without hampering the movement of passengers.

Whilst at the Commercial Vehicle Show I spent a good deal of time examining the buses and coaches exhibited there to see how body builders are tackling the problem of passengers' luggage. Candidly, I was disappointed. Roof boxes predominated, and although some of these were carefully designed to provide the maximum of weather protection the majority struck me as being rather poor. Likewise many of the side net-racks were more ornamental than useful. Some of them would not accommodate a bowler hat, while others would obviously "spill" when the coach swayed on corners. One or two were reasonably wide and deep, but of course the position with regard to side racks has been complicated by the growing use of sunshine roofs. Several coaches had luggage accommodation in the boot, but it was limited, and such space can only be used really advantageously when suitcases of a special size are standardised. It would certainly appear that satisfactory luggage space can be provided only at the cost of reduced seating accommodation, but perhaps some designer will have a real brain-wave before long!

Bus & Coach, December 1929

By 1934 the Trades Unions had become well aware that the new Transport Act had given them powers hitherto unknown, especially as more and more municipals and B.E.T. companies alike were abandoning tramways (which the Act did not cover) and replacing them with buses, petrol, diesel or electrically powered. Although the bus driver could work a straight 8-hour day this was not only unhealthy but an uneconomic use of the man. Eventually, of course, the practice of double (split) shifts and that ultimate evil, the triple shift, was developed.

TRANSPORT WORLD EDITORIAL
MAY 17, 1934
TIME AND DUTY SCHEDULES

For many years tramway managers were troubled with the long spreadover which was incumbent upon car crews on account of the peak load periods. The concession of the eight-hour day enforced a solution of the problem at varying degrees of expense for extra staff. With the development of omnibus services the trouble, together with the new one of speed, has passed to that department. The questions of the hours of duty and of speed in the provinces are now receiving attention from the men's union, who complain that the eight hours have to spread over twelve to fourteen hours a day. It would be easy to remedy that complaint if an omnibus undertaking, with its higher cost of operation, could carry a larger staff and find a full eight hours' work for each man. Another remedial measure would be available if the Road Traffic Act permitted omnibus drivers to serve for eight hours continuously. That is the case with tramcar motormen, who do not come under the Act. In view of the more arduous nature of the omnibus driver's task, and the fact that it entails greater risks for other road users, that course is not likely to be adopted. The straight shift has a great attraction for many motormen, but its effect upon their health should be solely watched. In a short time now the period for reviewing the results of increasing the speed of the London omnibuses will be at hand, and as the management has consented to the report being communicated to the union, some useful data will be available for comparison with provincial systems. In the meantime the union is seeking to interest managers and transport committees in the questions of hours and speed. If all the area representatives manage that task as satisfactorily as Mr T. McLean, the secretary of the North-Western area, did recently at Wallasey, a useful service will be rendered to both the employers and the employees. Alderman J.G. Storey, chairman of the Corporation Bus Committee, Alderman S.P. Brick, deputy chairman and other members of the Committee, were present at the meeting. All were sympathetic in the desire to remedy grievances where possible, and they had the pleasure of hearing a tribute paid to the Corporation for the generous manner in which the employees had been treated during the process of changing over to omnibuses. Mr McLean's observations regarding speed embraced the country generally. The schedules, he complains, are producing neurasthenia through the men taking risks which they ought not to be called upon to take. This is due, he alleges, not only to the time schedules, but to the fact that the omnibuses are not in all cases capable of what is required of them. Where this contention applies, no time should be lost in taking advantage of the technical developments which have been made by manufacturers in recent years and in providing vehicles of the requisite efficiency.

Thankfully at this juncture the eight-hour day hardly applied to coach operations and this text drawn from *The Transport World* 17 January 1935, tells us exactly where the world of coaching stood just five years before the outbreak of war – a short space of time for operators whether small or large to consolidate their positions prior to the total breakdown of 1939-1945.

THE OUTLOOK FOR MOTOR COACHES

The unlooked-for continuance of the startling concessions in cheap travelling on the four group railways has led in some quarters to a despondent view being taken of the prospects of motor coach traffic. What the operators have to do is to devise means of meeting the penny-a-mile return tickets and the three-farthings-a-mile rate for night travel which the L.M.S. and L.N.E.R. lines now offer. Short of deleting from the Road Traffic Act provisions that force the Traffic Commissioners to administer it in favour of the railways, there are directions in which an effort can be made to meet the new challenge. It should not be impossible to devise an alliance between the small operator and the combines somewhat on the lines of the companies associated with the railways. Even then more energy must be imparted to the business all round. In winter there are few towns not served by long-distance coaches running to London. It is difficult, however, for the public to ascertain particulars of the services. Not many are aware of the addresses of the stations situated on the borders of inner London, and not many prospective passengers are inclined to pay several pence for timetables. As is the case with the cheap facilities of the railways, advertising must be regular. A vast public is still unaware of any difference between the coach and an omnibus, and that the former continues in service throughout the winter, with its interior comfortably heated and offering seats not to be excelled in a first-class railway car. Intensive publicity is called for more than ever now that coaches are debarred from entering central London except on Saturday afternoons and Sundays. Provincial coaches are rarely seen except at the termini already referred to. Adequate organisation of suburban agencies might provide a set-off to that drawback, and attention should now be given to a possible revision of suburban picking-up points which have been imposed by the Traffic Commissioners. Operators, too, must cease to oppose one of their number when a firm purchase another business in order to obtain the advantage of picking-up places north or south of the Thames. Patrons prefer a through service; fewer will travel if forced to use a feeder coach to reach a main route. Fortunately there is one direction, at least – that of duplicate restriction – in which operators show no inclination to submit to unfair treatment. Sufficient facts should now have been accumulated to enable the industry to go to the Minister of Transport and ask for less severe applications of restrictions admittedly imposed solely in the interest of the railways. Failing success, Parliamentary opposition must be organised against this and other grievances.

A report in a trade magazine dated 1931 explains to some degree why bus manufacturers and, more importantly, their customers, were apparently quite sluggish in their uptake of diesel – or compression ignition – engines.

IN OUR OPINION
DIESEL-ENGINED PASSENGER VEHICLES

So far as we are aware, no passenger vehicle fitted with a diesel engine has yet been put into regular service in this country, though at least one has been in experimental operation. Like others who have investigated the possibilities of the compression ignition engine for road transport, we believe that it is only a matter of time before designs will have sufficiently advanced to render this class of power unit suitable for passenger-carrying machines. There remain, indeed, few difficulties to be overcome before the present supremacy of the spirit-burning motor will be seriously challenged by those using heavy oil fuel.

These views have already been expressed by several of our correspondents, and obtain authoritative confirmation in an article appearing in the present issue, contributed by Mr George J. Shave, operating manager and chief engineer of the London General Omnibus Co., Ltd. In surveying the present position with regard to the use of heavy oil fuels, by vaporisation with ignition by applied heat, and by direct injection into the combustion spaces and ignition by the heat of compression, Mr Shave expresses the definite opinion that the latter will prove the ultimate solution of the problem. This is distinctly encouraging to all those interested in the development of the full diesel type of power unit as applied to road transport, and it is therefore to be regretted that it is a matter with which so few in this country are at present concerned. "We should like to see an increase in the number of British manufacturers who have given attention to this question, either by introducing compression ignition engines of their own design or subjecting existing types to thorough tests on the bench and in road service. There are also many motor transport users in a position to carry out independent investigations. At present the principal defects of engines operating on the diesel cycle affect passenger carriers more adversely than goods transport vehicles. We may, therefore, expect the latter to serve as a valuable trial ground where heavy oil-burning engines will be thoroughly tried out before being widely used for passenger-carrying machines."

The biggest and most long-lasting effect of the later 1930s was the virtually total substitution of the diesel engine in buses for the trusted, but expensive to run, internal combustion equivalent.

Trade magazines of the period mention the phenomenal growth as by December 1933, from a virtually nil figure two years earlier, 910 oil-engined omnibuses were in operation with orders for another 500 (at least) in hand. A contemporary writer notes:

"... and it is significant that several of the chief manufacturers are prepared to undertake annual maintenance of the engine for .54d per mile. Not the least interesting information is that the improved braking, which is a feature of the oil engine, gives in Manchester an improvement of 20 per cent in the life of brake liners. Manchester's operating costs are remarkable; for the week ended December 24, 1933, the saving was nearly £770 per week, or 2.13d per mile. Means are indicated for overcoming exhaust smoke trouble and dilution of lubricating oil. The drivers enjoy better health owing to the absence of carbon monoxide in the exhaust, and their work is rendered easier as the pulling power of the engine is greater at the lower speeds, making gear-changing less necessary on hills and after having slowed down in the traffic".

This is the first comment I have seen, other than from drivers, of carbon monoxide poisoning, but I suppose it was

inevitable given indifferent maintenance and the hours spent in those cramped cabs.

A side-effect not expected among early diesels was one known to the owners of 'one-pop' semi-diesels, that of the high compression forcing carbon and iron dust past the piston rings into the sump. Incandescent and graphitic in nature it did the oil in the sump, and hence the working parts, no good whatsoever. Injectors (sprayers for a Gardner engine) needed to be cleaned of sooting every 3,000 miles, but for indirect injection 7,000 was right.

"The life of the moveable parts is, on the average, equal to half that of the corresponding parts of the petrol engine. This is so particularly with the cylinders and pistons and partly also with the ball bearings and crankshafts."

And one final set of statistics but with a twist. The emphasis today is on 'green' with clean engines, battery cars, and

MANCHESTER CORPORATION TRANSPORT DEPARTMENT
COMPARISON OF FUEL AND LUBRICATING OIL COSTS OF COMPRESSION IGNITION AND PETROL ENGINE BUSES.
Price of fuel oil = 4.5d. per gallon (including tax). 1d. per gallon tax on oil commenced on April 25, 1933.

Week Ended	No. of Compression Ignition Buses in Stock	Mileage	COSTS PER BUS MILE		TOTAL COST PER BUS MILE. Fuel and Lubricating Oil	Total Compression Ignition costs for fuel and lubricating oil	Fuel and Lubricating Oil costs if petrol engine buses had been operated.	SAVING		Price of Petrol (including tax).
			Fuel	Lubri-cating				Per Week	Per Mile	
1932			d.	d.	d.	£ s. d.	£ s. d.	£ s. d.	d.	s. d.
April 3	26	21,364	0.409	0.232	0.641	57 0 7	226 4 0	169 3 5	1.900	0 10⁷/₈
Oct 2	36	24,520	0.404	0.179	0.583	59 12 11	325 13 9	266 0 10	2.604	1 1³/₄
1933										
April 2	67	49,925	0.398	0.146	0.544	113 1 5	651 7 10	538 6 5	2.587	1 1¹/₂
Dec 24	103	86,513	0.534	0.133	0.667	240 7 0	1,010 5 1	769 18 1	2.136	1 0

ORDERS FOR OIL-ENGINED OMNIBUSES
200 MORE OIL BUSES FOR LONDON.

Chief among the orders announced by the Associated Equipment Co., Ltd., during the week ended January 9, was a repeat order from the London Passenger Transport Board for 200 Regent double-deck omnibuses fitted with the A.E.C.-Ricardo oil engine. Another notable order was for 40 single-deck Regals from the Scottish Motor Traction Co., with similar engines.

LEEDS ORDERS 40 A.E.C. OIL-ENGINED BUSES.

Leeds Transport Committee has placed the following contracts: 40 A.E.C.-Ricardo oil-engined chassis, with fluid flywheel transmission, for double-deck buses, Associated Equipment Co., Ltd.; 30 double-deck bodies, Chas. H. Roe (1923), Ltd.; five metal double-deck bodies, Metropolitan-Cammell-Weymann Motor Bodies, Ltd.; five metal double-deck bodies, English Electric Co., Ltd. The total cost is £63,175.

BIRMINGHAM ORDERS 135 DAIMLER CHASSIS

Birmingham Corporation during the past month has placed an order for 135 fluid flywheel omnibus chassis with the Daimler Company, Ltd., of Coventry. This is said to be the largest single order for omnibuses ever placed outside London. The new vehicles are to be of the C.O.G. 5 type, fitted with five-cylinder Gardner oil engines and a four-speed pre-selector gear-box. Of the total, 100 are intended for use with double-deck bodies. When this contract is completed Birmingham will have 275 fluid flywheel omnibuses in service, out of a total of about 500.

Orders for new omnibus bodies have been placed as follow:—

Metropolitan-Cammell Carriage, Wagon & Finance Co., Ltd., 50 double-deck and 20 single-deck bodies.

Birmingham Carriage & Wagon Co., 50 double-deck bodies; Strachans, of Acton, 15 single-deck bodies.

GLASGOW OMNIBUS CONTRACTS.

At a meeting of Glasgow Corporation on December 12, it was decided to revise the allocation of the contracts for the 110 new oil-engined omnibuses. The transport Committee's recommendations, already published in THE TRANSPORT WORLD, were that orders for 60 complete vehicles should go to Leyland Motors, Ltd., for 50 chassis to Albion Motors, Ltd. (of which 30 were to be fitted with Beardmore engines and 20 with Gardner engines), the 50 bodies to be built by F. D. Cowieson & Co.

The Corporation decided that all the bodies should be constructed by F. D. Cowieson & Co., a local firm, which will add to the total cost by about £4,000. The other proposals were adopted.

The following are the contract prices:—

Leyland, £825 for chassis and engine	£49,500
Albion, £770 for chassis with Beardmore engine ..	23,100
Albion, £809 for chassis with Gardner engine ..	16,180
F. D. Cowieson & Co., £725 10s. for each bus body	79,805
	£168,585

In *The Transport World* 17 January 1935; this item appeared as part of the editorial to show how sales of the compression-ignition (diesel) engine were accelerating; within a year or two only seaside towns with their particular clientèle and some coach operators would put up with high fuel costs in exchange for smooth running and quiet.

push-bikes the chosen method of transport, seemingly regardless of cost – locally they are 'pushing' a battery-hybrid car, pointing out that with the government subsidy it costs no more than a petrol engine variant until you dig deeper when an extra, not inconsiderable, amount of money is to be paid monthly to rent the batteries. It is fashionable to blame all the world's ills upon 'old fashioned' methods of working but even in 1935 General Managers of bus firms were working to ameliorate this – the cleanest vehicle of all – the trolleybus – was one answer, the tram outmoded, but let these statistics and R. Stuart Pilcher of Manchester tell the true story.

The Construction and Use Regulations of January, 1931 Paragraph 17: "Every motor vehicle shall be so constructed that no avoidable smoke or visible vapour is emitted therefrom," and *Paragraph 67: "Every motor vehicle shall be maintained in such condition and shall be so driven and used on a road that there shall not be emitted therefrom any smoke, visible vapour, grit, sparks, ashes, cinders or oily substance, the emission of which could be prevented or avoided by the taking of any reasonable steps or the exercise of reasonable care or the emission of which might cause damage to other persons or property or endanger the safety of any other users of the road in consequence of any harmful content therein."* It is therefore clear that any objectionable exhaust smoke or excessive noise from public service vehicles is exposed to the risk of prosecution. On this account, the question of the elimination of exhaust smoke is of prime importance.

Diesel engines may have defects and may cause trouble in different directions but if there is black smoke from the exhaust the buses are prohibited from running. I therefore consider that if these engines are to continue their success, it is essential that they should operate free from objectionable exhaust smoke.

The extent of the nuisance varies according to weather conditions. Objectionable fumes are most prevalent during periods of damp foggy weather and when there is an absence of wind. They are particularly objectionable in 'one-way' streets with dense traffic when the exhaust pipe puffs the exhaust over the side walk and on to pedestrians. Apart from the question of possible prosecution, it is recognised by all operators that in the public interest exhaust smoke must be avoided."

One side effect of the 1939-1945 war was a revival of the petrol engine in coaching in the shape of the Bedford OB and in bus work the Bedford OWB. In truth, by the time I knew these vehicles in the 1950s they were almost interchangeable, especially as one of our local operators substituted a Perkins diesel for his Bedford original – slow, noisy, vibrating and not cheap to buy, its saving grace was that it ran on almost anything, although the rumours we heard about a mixture of paraffin and used sump oil may not have been entirely based on fact!

The 1950s provided probably the greatest golden age for both bus and coach work, whether in chassis supply, body building or the operation of all classes of vehicles, but this was all handicapped by a lack of materials. Such was the shortage of timber that one of the largest importers, Glikstens, talked of a three-year wait for some hard woods. It is surprising how much timber was then involved in coach bodies *"[it] is of all wood construction, braced with fish-plates"* with a number of company's builders as well as suppliers actually boasting of this. The theory, at least, was that the body being flexible this could ameliorate the vibrations inherent in some chassis, particularly where the engines were bolted solid to the frame. But this could be a snare and a delusion as the vibration could make the separate panels of the body come loose and the resultant leaks rapidly rotted the ash woodwork.

M.W. Lloyd in *"Historic Commercial"*, 1976, wrote about trying to preserve a rather special coach bodied, however, by a second-string body-builder, Dutfield, on an unusual Commer Avenger in 1950! He purchased this for preservation in 1968 when *"I found the Dutfield-bodied Commer parked forlornly outside the garage, its Certificate of Fitness expired, and awaiting its fate. Enquiries revealed that although a local man was contemplating using it as a mobile shop ... it would probably end its days in the yard of the local scrap man"*. It had been used in body builder's publicity material and was fitted with radio!! Eventually Mr Lloyd purchased the machine and the fun began, as he only had a motorcycle (Class G as was) licence and insurance was awkward. Left on a farm *"... rather sadly, and with something of a conscience, I had to leave the* coach to her fate and the elements were not kind to her, in fact much of her timber rotted badly (partly because of leaks in the bodywork which Mr. House [the original owner] subsequently told me he had never been able to repair successfully)..."

Some companies were forced to diversity as their main market – that of luxury bespoke car bodies disappeared – and generally they did rather well, although craftsmanship came at a price, especially as designs of the base vehicles were in a state of flux and became outdated very quickly. Two firms in this class were Gurney Nutting, who closed down in 1954, and Windover with some elegant designs produced in quite good quantities including Sheffield United Tours, who purchased 78 coaches, and during their heyday (1948-1952) 28 Fodens were bodied for a number of companies, including 8 for Biss Bros. of Bishops Stortford.

Other companies had very patchy records. Associated Coach Builders produced a few excellent machines, and a couple of not-so-good, one of which went to T.G. Smith (Eagle Coachways) of Trench in 1947. DUX 654/655 had Daimler CVD6 chassis and ACB 33-seat bodies. The chassis of 654 lasted until July 1963 and 655 until August 1966 not, however, before 654 had a replacement ACB body ex a Dennis Lancet in June 1959, while 655 almost unbelievably was re-bodied by Metalcraft in March 1948 – when the ACB body was just one year old. When withdrawn 654 was immediately scrapped and 655 went to another operator for contract work. An ephemeral London firm was that of West-

This 31 Seater Full Luxury Observation Coach on a Foden Oil Engine Chassis is a typical example of James Whitson coach building.

Built first bodies in 1946, this is from a 1951 advertisement, but they stopped building PSVs mid-1950s.

Nor who supplied a coach body on a Maudsley Marathon in 1947. It was laid up with excessive leaks and rattles until scrapped in 1952. Quite a number of these firms lived in leased accommodation, often war dispersals buildings owned or used by the RAF, who then seemed not to worry who did what with them – at one aerodrome where we were located for 'emergency landings only', not only did the farmer let his sheep graze on the land – and the grass runway – but No. 6 Quonset housed three men who, in a very desultory way, were building new bodies on ex-WD lorry chassis. Having little cash every week (until they sold one) they had to wait for timber supplies or other materials including driver's seats. Once paid for a sale, deliveries speeded up for a few weeks. They had been producing wooden parts for Wellington Bombers when orders were cancelled overnight and had boxes of specialised turned

wood sections against each wall. Had the work been offered I am certain they would have built a coach body or two!

At one time I did try to tot up the number of builders with very small outputs and got to sixteen I could confirm, varying from one to ten bodies – one trouble was that not only were these bodies physically ephemeral but although no records exist, any photographs cannot easily be identified – many of them were half-cab and based on the classical Duple "A" body. In a relatively new book (2013) by James Taylor, "A-Z of British Bus Bodies" he has tried to detail all known manufacturers in over 160 pages, listing concerns known and almost unknown, while another author, Colin Peck, in the same year had "Wooden-Bodied Vehicles" published, which for perfectly sound financial reasons has to include re-bodying car and lorry chassis, but usefully does point out the pitfalls of trying to restore wooden and composite bodied buses and coaches.

34

CHURCHILL COACHWORK NORWICH

Presenting the **34-SEATER FULL LUXURY COACH**
on Under-floor engine Commer Avenger Chassis.
(36 SEATER SERVICE) Patent Applied for.

We cordially invite YOU to inspect our modern factory to
see for yourself that only the finest materials and highest-
skilled labour are used throughout. You will meet good
old-fashioned courtesy and pride of workmanship.
LEYLAND, BEDFORD, AUSTIN, COMMER, FORD, MORRIS.
Prices, photographs and specifications sent on request per return.

New Vehicles delivered in 6 to 8
weeks from receipt of chassis. Our
special coach repair section can deal
with any body repairs including
re-painting and re-trimming.

CHURCHILL COACHWORK
PERFECTION

CHURCHILL CONSTRUCTORS LTD.
MOUSEHOLD, NORWICH.
TELEPHONE -- NORWICH 25271

ANOTHER BATCH of AVENGERS for the **HOME** MARKET

This 1950 two-page advertisement from Churchill Constructors appeared in 1950 when
they were at their apogee. Established in 1946, by the end of 1953 they were no more.

Naturally ... a good production★

BELLHOUSE, HARTWELL & CO., LIMITED

chose

Planet

CURVED WINDSCREENS
for the "LANDMASTER"
MARK IV

★ Photograph shows the latest
lightweight "Landmaster"
Mark IV on the Castle set of
Metro-Goldwyn-Mayer's
colourful "Knights of the
Round Table".

Percy Lane LTD

PERCY LANE LTD.,
PLANET WORKS, ERDINGTON,
BIRMINGHAM, 24.

Bellhouse
Hartwell had
their works at
Pemberton near
Wigan. This is
one of their
finest products,
the 'Landmaster'
also known to
our crew and
passengers alike
as 'Sabrina' or
'Marilyn'. The
company ceased
building PSV
bodies in July
1955, but were
still trading until
2002.

CHAPTER 2
FOUR LEGS GOOD
FOUR WHEELS NOT (VERY)

Steam coaches were, alas, an evolutionary dead-end, the governments of their time setting their horse-shaped brains against such new fangled machinery much as they were later to inveigh against steam trams. The odd thing is that many of these 'elected representatives' later had shares in railway companies. Some of the steam coachmen were in spirit true predecessors of the motor coach operators I am proud to have known – a typical steam man was Lt Col. Macerone who was never content with a horse's speed and endurance and who in 1832 pawned his last watch to buy a sack of coke for a drive out to Windsor.

Famous names, among them Richard Trevithick, William Murdock, Joseph Bramah, Goldsworthy Gurney, James Nasmyth and James Napier were among the pioneers of steam road transport, but what does one do when faced, as was Sir Charles Dance running four trips daily between Gloucester and Cheltenham at 12mph (running in all 4,000 miles) with piles of stones placed maliciously on the turnpikes' surfaces. Curiously this sabotage by horse-heads also stopped stage-coaches: "The Champion, from London, a fine four horse coach, was brought up, and in whipping to get through broke the harness to pieces." These stones, though, were eventually to literally break up Dance's steam coaches.

"Thus in days of yore"

This begins a famous story which goes on to extol the glory of a summer's day on top of a Mail Coach thundering along the Turnpike. In reality it was a dirty cruel game that relied upon the coachman flogging his horses unmercifully to maintain time. Small wonder we have note of their dropping dead as they were changed en route and as the railways took a grip on the most paying routes the quality of the feed declined forcing the horses into worse conditions. In this article from the *Hereford Journal*, 4 October 1924, the writer is speaking from his heart and in some ways sets the scene for the contents of this book. Please turn to the next page...

Walter Hancock was probably the most successful (commercially) of all the early steam vehicle builders. Automaton was the last, built in 1835 and, in truth, was a hybrid between a chara and a toast-rack, seating 22 but requiring a three-man crew (driver, engineer and a stoker). London to Cambridge, October 1839, saw Automaton take four and a half hours for the 52 miles and in July 1890 the Stratford (London) Cricket Club XI plus 21 spectators were taken successfully on a private hire trip to a game in Epping Forest.

STRETFORD LOCAL BOARD.
LIST OF FARES.

	ONE-HORSE COACH.	TWO-HORSE COACH.
One or two passengers, per mile - - - - - - -	9d.	1s.3d.
For every third or lesser portion of a mile - - -	3d.	5d.
One or two passengers, per hour - - - - -	2s.	3s.6d.
For every quarter or lesser portion of an hour - - -	6d.	10½d.
Three or more passengers, per mile - - - - -	1s.	1s.3d.
For every third or lesser portion of a mile - - -	4d.	5d.
Three or more passengers, per hour - - - - -	2s.6d.	3s.6d.
For every quarter or lesser portion of an hour - - -	7½d.	10½d.
If kept waiting, for every fifteen minutes at any one place -	6d.	9d.

DOUBLE FARES FROM 12 p.m. TO 6 a.m.
No extra charge for a reasonable quantity of luggage.

THE GOOD OLD DAYS

Journey By Coach From London to Hereford
INCIDENTS RECALLED
Hereford Journal, 4 October 1924

There are people in Hereford who grumble about the cost of a railway journey to London and back and the time that the journey each way occupies.

The ordinary single fare nowadays is 18/-, and the journey between the two cities can be made in a little over 4 hours. But in the "good old days" the fare by coach was 30/- each way and an "outside" seat at that, too, so that the traveller was exposed to the weather, including the snow and cold of winter and the rain of summer, if ever in those times they had such a "summer" as this generation has lately enjoyed!

Travelling on the top of a coach, rumbling along in the fierce sunlight of an "old-fashioned" summer, might also have had its drawbacks.

The "Joys" of the Road

However, it was recalled some years ago by an old Herefordian that he would never forget his first journey from London to Hereford, when he came to visit his grandfather. That was in 1835. He wrote: "It was in January, and I came here in Botley's day-coach "Mazeppa!" We started at 5am in the dark from the "Bolt-in-Tun", Fleet Street. We got to Oxford at 1.30 and after dinner travelled through Witney, Burford and Northleach, and we were coming over the Wye Bridge at 11pm."

Just imagine! Eighteen to nineteen hours outside a coach on a January day and we did have cold weather then; such snow and frost as we do not suffer in these days of well drained and warmer land.

Outrageous Tips

Besides the fare there were other expenses to which the traveller of the present day is not subject or, at any rate, which press very lightly upon him. I refer to "tips", or "pecuniary honorariums" as barristers term their fees. On the journey there were four coachmen, besides the guard, the coachmen driving in turn and each leaving the coach at the end of his tenure of the reins.

"Please remember the coachman", said each, at the psychological moment, and that meant a shilling a time, or an extra four shillings on the fare, whereas the modern traveller's financial compliments need not amount to more than the smallest silver coin of the realm whenever he requires the temporary services of a porter.

More Expense

This, however, was not all that the passenger of pre-railway days had to pay. There would be three or four shillings for the guard. That payment was usually a good investment, as that official would then see to the comfort of the passenger, put straw round his (the passenger's) legs to keep them warm, and so on. There was no heating of the coaches like railway carriages are now, of course, but the old coaches were not even furnished with those galvanised iron receptacles of hot water which were formerly placed in train compartments for the passengers to place their feet upon.

Swallow Scalding Soup

One could get more comfort inside the coach, but then the fare was nearly double. The interior, however, was dull, not to say dark, and stuffy and ill-ventilated, and if crowded, the outside was preferable.

In those days there was no serving of lunch, or hot dinner, or tea as on the main-line trains of today. The coach would pull up at some wayside hostelry, there would be a change of horses and the passengers would be expected to swallow scalding hot soup in the brief interval. Charges for lunch or an ordinary dinner were high, as much as three to four shillings.

A Delightful Thing

There were, however, times when to ride along the country roads on the top of a coach was even more pleasurable than is travelling in a luxuriously appointed first class saloon of an express train at the present day– on a beautiful sunny spring morning, for instance. There was the romance of the high road, of which Byron sang in his "Don Juan":

> "What a delightful thing's a turnpike road!
> So smooth, so level, such a mode of sharing
> The earth, as scarce the eagle in the broad
> Air can accomplish, with his wide wings waving."

The English main roads, in those days, be it remembered, were as they are now, the best in the world. More than a century has passed since MacAdam, who dwelt in the neighbourhood of the most frightful roads, hit on the fortunate idea that could a road be strewn with a quantity of small stones it might be kept dry and hard, and free from ruts. People smiled at his idea, but he realised £10,000 in one year alone by superintending the several post-roads constructed upon his own plan.

Byron and the Future

It would be interesting to surmise what Byron with his idea of the high speed of vehicles in his day, and MacAdam with his notions of the perfect road, would think of motor cars, not to mention railways and aeroplanes, and of the present roads could they visit the highways of today.

Unless handling horses is a hobby it is difficult to realise how skittery these animals can be – in certain circumstances they will shy at a piece of paper fluttering, or a line of washing cracking in the wind, and even a railway locomotive bashing over the points could make a horse rear and kick as much as they would on seeing a tram or omnibus.

And of course the bulk of horses in daily use during Victorian days were not heavy, relatively placid, carthorses, but cobs or general purpose sturdy little ponies whose breaking for harness may have been handled with extreme cruelty, and their subsequent care and feeding may have left much to desire: 'uncaring' was a common epithet given to hostlers.

This particular report appeared in the *Glasgow Mail* at the end of August 1889 and is included to show how the simplest action could affect a horse drawn vehicle:

ALARMING ACCIDENT IN THE TROSSACHS. A COACH SUSPENDED OVER A RAVINE.

News of an alarming accident which on Monday last befell the four-horse coach that runs between the Trossachs and Aberfoyle has just been permitted to come to light. On that day the coach left the Trossachs at the usual time, and arrived at Aberfoyle without mishap. The return journey was started upon about half-past 12, the coach containing a good complement of tourists, among whom was a company of American gentlemen on a visit to this country. All went well until half of the journey had been accomplished, when the horses shied at two bicycle riders who were seated beside their machines on the side of the road. On the opposite side of the road from that on which the men were seated there is a ravine some 20ft or 30ft deep. The driver of the coach endeavoured to pacify the animals, but they grew more restive still, with the result that the coach was ultimately upset at the edge of the road and the passengers thrown out. The coach was then backed by the struggling horses over the side of the road, and had it not been for a projecting branch of a birch tree, coach and horses, if not some of the passengers, would have gone to the bottom of the ravine. Three of the American gentlemen were injured, as was the driver, but none of them seriously. Aided by the passengers the driver managed to get the coach on the road again, where it was righted, the passengers re-embarked and the coach proceeded on its way. The part of the road at which the accident occurred is somewhat narrow and curves. It was the coming suddenly in view of the bicyclists that caused the horses to shy. The injured gentlemen were attended to at the Trossachs Hotel.

CITY CHAT

The lively bus competition on the cable tramway routes reminds the older inhabitants of Handsworth of the time when the bus company was first formed in opposition to a number of old and faded conveyances plying between Birmingham and that suburb. The colours – red and green – distinguished the old from the new, and this form of competition caused an unusual stir in those old times. It was long before the days of properly licensed and duly registered drivers, and the consequences may be easily imagined. A system of careless and furious driving became the fashion, and accidents were innumerable. It was purely and simply a system of running one another down at any risk. A man named "Long Tom" was the chief of the private drivers, and he became a notorious figure at the Villa Cross by reason of his enterprises. Furious driving was then an offence against the bye-laws, and "Long Tom" was fined week after week, and eventually the magistrates sent him to prison. The drivers on both sides were fined again and again, and it was simply by the persistent action of the police that anything like careful driving was obtained. "Long Tom" has long since retired from active work, but the spice of opposition is still strong within him, and during the past week he has been seen "wielding the colours" on behalf of the company.

Birmingham Times, November 22, 1889

"Long Tom", the hero of the severe competition which took place many years ago on the Handsworth route between the old omnibuses and the first properly organised company, still lives to exult in the revival of road racing. That worthy was brought up and fined week after week, and at length was sentenced to a term of imprisonment. He is now a veteran of veterans, but his heart is still in the fray, and he is to be seen daily cheering and encouraging the drivers of Freeman's 'buses to take the lead and distance their opponents.

Birmingham Mail, November 23, 1889

CHAR-À-BANC TRAVEL IN LATE-VICTORIAN TIMES

This photograph (about 1890) is of a four-in-hand chara-banc with five bench seats, which on this occasion is carry-ing a mixture of about 20 adults and children. Since they are outside a family hotel (notice the chambermaid looking out of the window) these tourists are either off for a cay's outing or being taken to the railway station, they could not have travelled great distances like this. Luggage in either case would have gone on a separate wagon. The great period of coaching was much earlier in history – 1750-1840, with the Golden Age of the fast day coaches so beloved by contem-porary Christmas card illustra-tors, surviving for the last twenty. By 1840 the railways had taken passengers and the Royal Mail away. and most coaches were restricted to public urban transport.

This is a genuine salted paper print reproduced from a 19th century Victorian image according to Fox Talbot's origi-nal photogenic drawing process. It has been chemically fixed and archivally mounted for permanence. Nevertheless the original would not take kindly to being left in bright sunlight.

On and after September 1st, 1878, until further notice,
S. ANDREWS' OMNIBUSSES

Will run between Cardiff and the undermentioned places (unless unavoidably prevented), as under :—

CARDIFF AND PENARTH.

From Bus Office, Penarth.		From St. Mary Street, Cardiff.		SUNDAYS.	
				From Penarth	From Cardiff.
5 30	3 40	6 10	4 20	9 30	10 20
8 20	4 10	9 10	5 0	10 10	12 50
9 20	4 50	10 10	5 40	1 30	2 20
10 20	5 30	11 10	6 20	2 0	2 50
11 10	6 5	12 0	7 0	3 0	3 45
11 50	6 40	12 40	7 30	4 0	4 45
12 30	7 25	1 20	8 10	5 0	6 0
1 5	7 55	1 55	8 40	6 0	6 45
1 50	8 20	2 40	9 5	7 0	7 45
2 30	9 0	3 20	9 40	8 0	8 50
3 10		3 50		8 50	9 40

Excursion Parties can be accommodated at any time.

Fares :—For 5.30 a.m. from Penarth, 1s. ; Cardiff to Cogan, Llandough and Dynas Powis Roads, 4d. ; Penarth, 6d ; Return Tickets, 9d, available for day of issue only

ST. MARY STREET AND ROATH.

From Elm-street, Roath.				From Royal Arcade, St. Mary-street.			
9 0	12 40	4 0	7 20	9 20	12 50	4 10	7 30
9 20	1 0	4 20	7 40	9 40	1 0	4 20	7 40
9 40	1 10	4 30	7 50	10 0	1 20	4 40	8 0
10 0	1 20	4 40	8 0	10 10	1 30	4 50	8 10
10 20	1 40	5 0	8 20	10 20	1 40	5 0	8 20
10 30	1 50	5 10	8 30	10 40	2 0	5 20	8 40
10 40	2 0	5 20	8 40	10 50	2 10	5 30	8 50
11 0	2 20	5 40	9 0	11 0	2 20	5 40	9 0
11 10	2 30	5 50	9 10	11 20	2 40	6 0	9 20
11 20	2 40	6 0	9 20	11 30	2 50	6 10	9 30
11 40	3 0	6 20	9 40	11 40	3 0	6 20	9 40
11 50	3 10	6 30	9 50	12 0	3 20	6 40	10 0
12 0	3 20	6 40	10 0	12 10	3 30	6 50	10 20
12 20	3 40	7 0		12 20	3 40	7 0	
12 30	3 50	7 10		12 40	4 0	7 20	

FARES, TWOPENCE.

CARDIFF AND LLANDAFF.

From Black Lion Inn, Llandaff.			From Bus-office, 34, High-st., Cardiff		
9 5	3 5	7 5	9 35	3 5	7 5
10 5	3 35	7 35	10 35	3 35	7 35
11 5	4 5	8 5	11 35	4 5	8 5
12 5	4 35	8 35	12 35	4 35	8 35
1 5	5 5	9 5	1 5	5 5	9 5
1 35	5 35	9 35	1 35	5 35	
2 5	6 5		2 5	6 5	
2 35	6 35		2 35	6 35	

Fares to Llandaff, 4d. ; to Severn Road, Canton, 2d.

PRIVATE OMNIBUSES FOR FAMILY PARTIES

TRAVELLING BY

GREAT WESTERN RAILWAY.

The Great Western Company provide Omnibuses to and from the PADDINGTON STATION, capable conveying SIX PERSONS INSIDE and TWO OUTSIDE, with the usual quantity of luggage.

To avoid disappointment, these vehicles should be ENGAGED BEFOREHAND, and should there at any time b more orders than can be executed with the number of vehicles at disposal, such orders will be dealt with according to priority.

Parties LEAVING LONDON and requiring to proceed to PADDINGTON STATION from their Residences or Hotels should give TWELVE HOURS' NOTICE, addressed to the Station Master, Paddington Station, W., stating the date, and likewise the train by which they intend to leave Paddington.

Parties intending to PROCEED TO LONDON from Country Stations should give 24 hours' notice, either at the Station from which they will start, or to the Station Master, Paddington, W., stating the date and likewise the train by which they intend to travel, and their destination in London. Parties travelling to London and desiring to engage an Omnibus, but not having previously ordered one, should request the Station Master at Swindon, Oxford or Didcot as the case may be, to telegraph to Paddington Station for an Omnibus to be in readiness, when every endeavour will be made to provide one.

The Charge for the use of an Omnibus within a 4 mile radius of Paddington Station will be ONE SHILLING PER MILE, driver and luggage included. Minimum charge THREE SHILLINGS. Sixpence per mile extra will be charged outside the radius. When the distance or the quantity of luggage is too great for one horse, and two horses become necessary, the charge for any distance will be Two Shillings per Mile, with a minimum charge of Six Shillings.

Although later in origin than the text entries the Lynton and Lynmouth Railway is a truly ingenious example of Victorian thinking and expertise. Located in North Devon this unique solely water powered funicular was opened Easter Monday 7 April, 1890 and can carry 40 passengers in each car, raising them up the 862 feet (282.8 metres) of track on a 58% incline, saving both a long and wearisome climb and the stresses on animals previously used. *(Trevor Preece)*

Great Western Railway: Coaches in Broad Gauge Days

My apologies for the condition of this document – it was in a rummaging pile at a local 'antiques fair' with 10p or 20p per item. I do not know the source, or indeed the age. The Mansion House line was opened in 1871 and the text refers to travelling by "Broad gauge" which went in 1892. However of more interest to us are a number of notes relating to Omnibuses.

We have also reproduced a portion of one and a quarter pages on *"Coaches, Omnibuses from the Company's stations"*, around 90 entries in all. One for Wantage Road is interesting as the entry shows "Steam Car" to Wantage, although this was a roadside tramway. It will be seen that the railway's 'omnibuses' have very little connection with what we now call omnibuses, but they were a relatively expensive form of transport limited by the strength and endurance of horses.

2

ILFRACOMBE.

COACHES run three times each way daily (Sundays excepted), viz.: from Barnstaple at 1.20, 3.40 p.m., 5.35 p.m., upon the arrival of the 5.30 a.m., 9.0 a.m. and 11.15 a.m. trains from Paddington, returning from the Clock Tower Office, Ilfracombe, daily (Sundays excepted) at 7.0 a.m., 9.25 a.m. and 1.40 p.m. in time for trains leaving Barnstaple at 8.55 a.m., 11.25 a.m. and 3.40 p.m., due at Paddington at 2.45 p.m., 6.0 p.m. and 10.20 p.m.

LYNTON.

A Coach leaves the Royal Castle Hotel, Lynton, daily (Sundays excepted) at 8.0 a.m., in time for train leaving Minehead at 11.45 a.m., due at Paddington at 6.0 p.m., returning from Minehead to Lynton daily (Sundays excepted) at 3.25 p.m., after arrival of 9.0 a.m. Train from Paddington.

From Monday, July 2nd to Saturday, July 28th, an additional Break will run as follows; from Minehead at 9.45 a.m. on Mondays, Wednesdays, and Fridays, after arrival of 6.15 a.m. train from Bristol. From Lynton at 4.30 p.m. on the same days in time for train leaving Minehead at 8.35 p.m., due at Paddington at 4.35 p.m. following morning.

From Monday, July 30th, to September 29th, this Break will run daily (Sundays excepted).

BARNSTAPLE.

An Omnibus runs between the Great Western and London and South Western Railway Stations at Barnstaple, meeting those Companies' Trains as follows, viz.:—From Great Western Trains due at Barnstaple at 9.50 a.m., 1.15 p.m., 3.35 p.m. and 5.30 p.m., conveying Passengers to the Barnstaple Quay and Junction Stations. From London and South Western Trains due at Barnstaple Quay Station at 7.51 a.m., 10.51 a.m., 3.10 p.m. and 5.14 p.m. Also from London and South Western Trains due at Barnstaple Junction Station at 7.53 a.m., 10.57 a.m., 3.13 p.m. and 5.8 p.m., conveying Passengers to the Great Western Station. Fares—6d. each adult ; 3d. each, children.

COACHES, OMNIBU[SES]
RUNNING TO AND FROM THE COMPANY'S

The Company do not hold themse[lves] responsible for these Conveyances as they are not under their control neither for the accuracy of the information wi[th] although every care is taken to ensure the announcements b[e]ing reliable.

STATION.	PLACE.	DAYS ON WHICH CONVEYANCE RUN.	LEAVE STATION FOR PLACE.	LEAVE PLACE FOR STATION.	ARR[IVE]
ABERNANT	Aberdare		From all Trains	For all Trains.	
ABERYSTWITH	Devil's Bridge		9.30 a.m		
Do.	Cardigan	Each week day	4.0 p.m.		1.0 p.
AWRE JUNCTION	Blakeney		From all Trains 7.0 a.m.	For all Trains.	
BARNSTAPLE	Ilfracombe (see page 2)	Each week day	1.20, 3.40 p.m. and 5.35 p.m.	7.0 a.m.9.25 a.m.and 1.40p.m.	8.50,11.20 a.m.,3.35 p.m.
Bath	Weston (near Bath)	Daily, Sundays excepted	12.15 p.m., 2.40 p.m., 7.25 p.m.	11.0 a.m., 2.0 p.m., 6.0 p.m.	11.20 a.m., 2.30 p.m., 6.30 p.m.
Do.	Coombe Down	Do.	11.35 a.m., 4.20 p.m.	9.20 a.m., 1.40 p.m.	10.15 a.m., 2.35 p.m.
BODMIN ROAD	Bodmin		From all Trains	For all Trains.	
Do.	Camelford and Boscastle	Daily	5.49 a.m.	Camelford, 3.30 ; Boscastle, 2.30	6.10 p.m.
Do.	Wadebridge	Week days	5.49, 8.55, 12.55 and 6.20 p.m.	7.0, 9.45 a.m., 1.0, 4.20 p.m.	5.50 a.m., 12.0, 3.20, 6.10 p.m.
		Sundays	5.49 a.m.	4.20 p.m.	6.10 p.m.
Do.	Padstow	Week days	5.49, 12.35 and 6.20 p.m.	5.30, 8.10 a.m., 3.0 p.m.	5.50 a.m., 12.0, 6.10 p.m.
		Sundays	5.49 a.m.	3.0 p.m.	6.10 p.m.
BRIDPORT	Beaminster	Week days	3.0 p.m.	10.30 a.m.	11.40 a.m.
Do.	Lyme Regis & Charmouth	Do.	3.30 p.m.	10.0 a.m.	11.35 a.m.
BRUTON	Wincanton				
BRISTOL (Talbot)	Ashton	Do.	12.0 noon, 5.0 p.m.	9.0 a.m., 2.0 p.m.	10.0 a.m., 3.0 p.m.
BRISTOL (Hope & Anchor)	Blagdon	Mon., Thurs., Sat.	4.30 p.m.	8.0 a.m.	11.0 a.m.
BRISTOL (Castle and Bull)	Frenchay and Hambrook	Week days	4.30 p.m.	9.30 a.m.	11.0 a.m.
BRISTOL (Rummer Office)	Henbury and Shirehampton	Do.	11.30 a.m., 4.0 p.m.	9.30 a.m., 2.0 p.m.	11.0 a.m., 3.30 p.m.
CAMBORNE	Helston	Each week day	10.0 a.m., 5.0 p.m.	10.0 a.m., 5.0 p.m.	12.0 noon, 7.0 p.m.
CASTLE CARY	Lydford, Keinton Somerton	Thurs. and Sat.	5.0 p.m.	8.0 a.m.	9.40 a.m.
Do.	Barton, St. David	Thursdays	5.0 p.m.	8.0 a.m.	9.40 a.m.
CHEDDAR	Cheddar Cliffs	Daily during Summer months	From all trains	For all trains.	
CHIPPENHAM	Badminton and Castle Coombe	Daily, Sundays excepted	2.30 p.m.	9.10 a.m.	10.40 a.m.
Do. (from G. W. Hotel)	Sherston and Grittleton	Mondays & Fridays	3.30 p.m.	8.0 a.m.	10.30 a.m.
Do. (from Black Horse)	Hawkesbury and Upton Chipping Sodbury & Castle Coombe.	Mon., Wed. & Fri.	3.30 p.m.	7.15 a.m.	12.0 noon.
CIRENCESTER	Fairford	Daily	3.50 p.m.	10.10 a.m.	12.0 noon.
ULHAM	Dorchester (Oxon)	Mon. and Thurs.	4.0 p.m.	8.0 a.m.	9.0 a.m.
[DA]RTMOUTH	Kingsbridge	Tues.,Thurs.&Sats.	4.30 p.m.	9.0 a.m.	12.0 noon.
Do.	Do.	Each week day	9.30 a.m.	3.30 p.m.	6.45 p.m.
[DE]VIZES	Potterne, Market Lavington, West Lavington	Do.	From Elm Tree Hotel at 2.30	9.30 a.m. from Market Lavington; West Lavington, 9.35 a.m.; Potterne, 10.0 a.m.	10.45 a.m.
Do.	Potterne, Market Lavington, West Lavington	Thursdays	From Crown Hotel at 2.15	10.0 a.m. from Market Lavington; West Lavington 10.10 a.m.; Potterne, 10.55 a.m.	11.30 a.m.
[DO]LGELLY	Harlech	Each week day	10.0 a.m.	3.0 p.m.	
[F]ALMOUTH (Strand)	Helston	Each week day	9.10 a.m., 1.0, 5.15 p.m.	9.5, 11.0 a.m., 3.15, 5.15 p.m.	11.20 a.m., 1.20, 5.10, 7.30
[F]AIRFORD	Cirencester	Daily	10.10 a.m.	3.50 p.m.	6.30 p.m.
[FR]OME	Mere	Mondays	4.0 p.m.	8.0 a.m.	10.30 a.m.
GLOUCESTER	Ledbury	Each week day	3.15 p.	8.0 a.m.	10.20 a.m.
HANDBOROUGH	Woodstock	Daily	9.15 a.m., 5.5 p.m.	8.0 a.m., 4.15 p.m.	8.30 a.m. 4.35
HAVERFORDWEST	St. David's and Solva	Tues. and Sat.	4.0 p.m.	6.30 a.m.	10.0 a.m.
Do. (from P.O.	Do. Do.	Daily, except Sun.	6.45 a.m.	2.25 p.m.	5.0 p.m.
Do. (Van)	Do. Do.	Mon., Thurs., Sat.	2.0 p.m.	5.40 a.m.	10.0 a.m.
Do. (Salutation Hotel)	Fishguard	Daily, except Sun.	2.0 p.m.	7.0 a.m.	10.30 a.m.
Do.	Newport (Pem.)	Do. Do.	2.0 p.m.	5.30 a.m.	10.30 a.m.
ILFRACOMBE	Lynton	Each week day	8.30 a.m.	6.0 p.m.	9.0 p.m.
KEMBLE	Tetbury (Mills' coach)	Each week day	3.0 p.m.	11.0 a.m.	12.0 noon.
KINGSBRIDGE ROAD	Kingsbridge (King's Arms)	Week days	9.52 a.m., 3.53, 7.22 p.m.	7.0, 11.45 a.m., 4.30 p.m.	9.0 a.m., 1.30, 6.30 p.m.
LAUNCESTON	Bude	Mon., Wed., Fri.		1.15 p.m.	5.30 p.m.
Do.	Do.	Tues., Thurs., Sat.	1.20 p.m.		
LLANDYSSILL	Newcastle Emlyn, Cenarth, Llechryd and Cardigan	Each week day	6.55 a.m., 4.30 p.m.	Leaves Cardigan at 7.30 a.m. and 1.25 p.m.(see page 51)	10.20 a.m., 4.10 p.m.
LLANDILO	Llandovery	Sundays	8.0 a.m.	2.50 p.m.	4.25 p.m.
MENHENIOT	Looe	Week days	5.45 p.m.	8.0 a.m.	9.20 a.m.
MINEHEAD	Lynton see page 2)	Do.	9.45 a.m. and 3.25 p.m.	8.0 a.m. and 4.30 p.m.	11.30 a.m and 8.15 p.m.
MORETONHAMPSTEAD	Chagford (Globe Hotel)	Week days	12.48, 6.22 p.m., 9.10 p.m.	3.40 a.m., 2.50 p.m., 5.50 p.m.	10.40 a.m., 3.55, 6.55 p.m.
MOREBATH	Bampton	Each week day	12.30 and 4.43 p.m.		12.0 noon, 4.15 p.m.
MOULSFORD	Wallingford	Sundays only	9.10, 11.0,11.50 a.m.,9.15 p.m.	7.45, 10.15, 11.10 8.15	9.15, 10.55, 11.40 a.m., 8.45 p.m.
NANTYGLO	Brynmawr	Each week day	From all Trains	For all Trains.	
NEWBURY	Speen, Shaw & Donnington	Each week day	After each Train except 9.50 p.m., if ordered		Meets each Train except. 7.50 a.m. & 9.50 p.m. if ordered
NEWTON ABBOT	Ashburton	Week days	6.15 p.m.	9.30 a.m.	11.0 a.m.
PADDINGTON	Bank, via Oxford Street or Strand		From all Trains	For all Trains.	
PENRYN	Helston	Week days	7.5, 9.55 a.m., 1.55, 5.40 p.m.	9.15 a.m.,12.45,3.15, 5.15p.m.	10.45, 12.50, 4.35, 6.55
Do.	Do.	Sundays	7.5 a.m.	3.15 p.m.	4.35 p.m.
PENZANCE (POST OFFICE)	Lands End and Logan Rock	Each week day	9.0 a.m.	1.0 p.m., 3.30 p.m.	3.0 p.m., 6.0 p.m.
Do.	St. Just (Post Office)	Do.	9.0 a.m., 4.0 p.m.	7.30 a.m., 2.0 p.m.	8.30 a.m., 3.0 p.m.
Do.	Helston do.	Do.	8.30, 11.0 a.m., 4.0 p.m.	10.30 a.m., 2.30, 5.45 p.m.	12.30, 4.35, 7.50 p.m.
PENSFORD	Chew, Magna and Stanton Drew		From all principal Trains.	For all principal Trains.	
PLYMOUTH (Royal Hotel)	Kingsbridge	Tues. and Sat.	4.45 p.m.	7.45 a.m.	11.30 a.m. (Royal Hotel)
PORTSKEWETT	Caldicott	Daily	9.2, 10.33 a.m. 2.0, 5.5 p.m.	8.35, 10.5 a.m., 1.20, 4.35 p.m.	9.0,10.33 a.m.,1.45,5.0p.m.
PURTON	Cricklade	Each week day	9.16 a.m., 1.35, 4.45 p.m.	7.45 a.m., 12.0, 4.0 p.m.	8.15 a.m., 12.30, 4.30 p.m.
RADLEY	Abingdon	Sundays only	9.45 p.m.	9.0 p.m.	9.35 p.m.
REDRUTH (Bullars Arms)	Helston	Each week day	4.0 p.m.	10.0 a.m.	12.30
Do. do.	Do.	Mon., Wed., Thurs., Sat.	9.0 a.m.	5.0 p.m.	7.15 p.m.
ST. AUSTELL	Mevagissy and Pentewan	Each week day	5.0 p.m.	10.0 a.m.	11.30 a.m.
Do. do.	Do. do.	Fri. and Sat.	7.30 p.m.	1.30 p.m.	3.0 p.m.
ST. COLUMB ROAD	St. Columb	Week days	7.38, 9.28, 11.22 a.m., 1.32, 5.5, 8.18 p.m.	6.55, 8.45, 10.30, a.m., 12.50, 4.25, 7.35 p.m.	7.25, 9.15, 11.0 a.m., 1.20, 4.55, 8.5 p.m.
SALTASH	Callington	Daily	5.10 a.m., 5.20 p.m.	8.5 a.m., 5.45 p.m.	9.45 a.m., 7.10 p.m.
Do.	Do.	Week days	7.10 a.m.	5.40 p.m.	7.30 p.m.
Do.	Do.	Wednesdays	11.20 a.m.	3.0 p.m.	4.30 p.m.
Do.	Do.	Saturdays	7.0 p.m.	11.45 a.m.	1.30 p.m.
SOUTHAM ROAD	Southam	Each week day	10.15 a.m.,2.20,4.40,7.20 p.m.	8.40 a.m.,12.50, 3.50,6.30 p.m.	9.10 a.m.,1.20,4.20,7.0p.m.
STROUD (George Hotel)	Painswick	Mon. Tues. Wed. Sat.	12.0, 2.0, 5.45	9.15, 10.30, 2.15	
Do.	Do.	Thursdays	2.0 p.m.	10.30 a.m.	
Do.	Do.	Fridays	12.0, 2.0, 5.45, 7.45	9.15, 10.30, 2.15, 4.45	
STRATFORD-ON-AVON	Shipston-on-Stour		5.0 p.m.	9.0 a.m.	
TIVERTON	Witheridge	Tuesday	From Half Moon at 1.30 p.m.		11.30 a.m.
Do.	Bampton	Tues. and Sat.	From Royal Oak at 1.30 p.m.		

Coaching in Lakeland

Coaching in Lakeland is excellent sport,
If your limbs are quite sound and your wind
isn't short

Innominate Tarn on Haystacks, Alfred Wainwright's favourite fell, where his ashes were scattered. Wainwright, who lived 1907 to 1991, mapped walks around 214 Lakeland Fells.

(Michael Graham)

BRIDGING THE PERIOD – THE LAKE DISTRICT

Too many visitors to The Lake District come away with the impression of rain, wind, cold and greyness. In the Good Old Days horse drawn char-à-bancs were required particularly for visitors following the trails of Wordsworth and similar poets but they had a certain rather hapless reputation.

The first two cards of the 1870s clearly show this.

With the third we move into the motor age still with a great degree of bitterness inherent in the caption.

The fourth, a 'real' photograph, shows in real life how grey and wet a summer's day can be near Keswick. Much of this latter scene is lost under the reservoir built to meet Manchester's water requirements.

Coaching in Lakeland
Uphill · Downhill

If to travel through Lakeland by coach you decide, you'll find (when you've all paid your fare)
That travelling by coach is common enough, but travelling in coach is rare

Motoring in Lakeland.

Wise motorists get up betimes, nor long o'er
  breakfast tarry,
They start before the monster cars which so
  much vex and harry;
These clatter on with noise and fuss, and
  hamper cars whose drivers cuss';
But oh! its lovely fun for us, its all right in
  the 'charry'!

MOTORING THROUGH THE ROCK-CUTTING, THIRLMERE

TWO CHRISTMAS GREETING CARDS

Many, many long years ago Christmas Day was one of the two days that were holidays. In the country pre-TV and radio even the arrival of the stagecoach marked the up-coming season.

These are two of a set of engravings reproduced by the Rotary Photographic Company Ltd, both by J.C. Maggs. And Christmas could really be like this, described by my late mother-in-law who entered 'service' at The Big House when 12 years old, as 'crying cold'. Interestingly she used the same cure for chillblains as we did in the 1940s – an almost forgotten way of life they could cripple almost anyone, and what it was like to ride, jammed up, beside the loose-fitting door of a creaking, shaking, unheated stage-coach, with your feet nestling in wet straw I hate to think. That bundle of rags on top could have been one of us...

COACHING IN SOUTH DEVON 1892

The engraving and the slightly melancholy text tell of an age long gone and impossible to re-create. Both are drawn from a pleasantly middle-class magazine entitled "*The Graphic*" – the issue being dated 13 August 1892. Founded in 1869 *The Graphic* echoed the dreams and aspirations of the literate and instinctively curious minds of the Victorian middle class, but at the same time the editors drew attention to the problems of the under-classes and sought to ameliorate them.

This paean of regret echoes Wordsworth and many other writers for the perceived loss of the human touch under the onslaught of the railway; but elsewhere the writers in the Journal speak of progress

It was a sad – if inevitable – end for the magazine in 1932 as the stump bit and pennies counted even among its clientèle.

Coaching in South Devon
BY "TIM"

"A COACH-DRIVE in Devonshire" sounds as familiar to our ears as the "Underground Railway" in London; yet there could hardly be a greater contrast than, after months of toilsome experience in the latter, to find, on emerging from the train after a six hours' journey from London, nothing but an old-fashioned coach as the only means of conveyance to one's destination. The coaches of Devon and Cornwall seem, indeed, as much a part of those counties as the narrow stony lanes, the red earth, and the high hedges, with their luxuriant growth. Often it is most oppressive walking, between these high banks, for the sun beats straight down and hardly a breath of air seems able to penetrate through those leafy walls. But on a coach it is at once a revelation. From thence one can see over the hedges and far beyond into the lovely country all around, and right down among the mossy banks with their countless flowers and ferns, while the soft, sweet air fans one's cheek and seems to welcome us in an almost intoxicating manner.

Clever engineering has been required to make many of the roads in North Devon, but, in spite of sharp curves and precipitous corners, the coaches rattle along at a pace which causes the more timid occupants to shudder in spite of the perfect confidence between the horses and their skilful driver. But on the South Coast it is quite different ; there the scenery may not be so grand, but it is more pastoral, more peaceful: hills there are still and many, but not so steep, and it would seem as if the whole country undulated gently along the many little valleys right down to the sea.

There is one far-famed coach-drive in South Devon between Dartmouth and Kingsbridge. This line of coaches first commenced running in 1872, before which there was no direct communication between the two places except by a carrier, who started always with extreme punctuality, but whose eventual arrival was regarded with much uncertainty. Nevertheless, every one regarded the new coach with mistrust, and it had a hard struggle for existence till a party of casual tourists found it out one summer, when its success was at once assured. A second coach was started in 1884, and a few years later it was found necessary to start even a third, and in 1891 they carried no fewer than 12,852 passengers, besides those passengers' luggage.

The coaches are timed to start from Dartmouth on the arrival of the London trains. Three times a day they go through the process of loading up the coach with people and luggage, the children of Dartmouth taking day by day the same unflagging interest in the proceedings, and staring, immovable and openmouthed, at the heterogeneous gathering waiting to be placed. The honeymoon couple trying to look coldly and indifferently at each other with but partial success; the maiden aunt being driven to the verge of desperation by seeing her favourite bonnet-box tossed up and then secured upside down in spite of her entreaties; the artist with his long spiky umbrellas and portable easels that run into every one, who is "Hail, fellow, well met!" with all, shakes hands with the barmaid, gives drinks all round, and finally climbs up into the box-seat; there are pretty girls and plain ones; an amateur photographer; a fisherman; a clergyman giving bland advice to his wife and the rest of the passengers, while his children embrace the opportunity of abstracting dainty morsels from the lunch-basket left in their care; and there are a host of others. They are all put somewhere, tightly wedged along the narrow seats, and off the coach starts, going slowly at first till it is safely out of the little winding street. You take a last look at Dartmouth harbour on your left, gay with ships, yachts, and boats of all descriptions dancing in the sunlight, as the coach seems to plunge all at once into the cool green lanes. You do not see the sea again till you have passed Stokefleming, and then it seems lying just below the road, and rippling up opalescent into the little Blackpool Bay. The variation of the drive is never ending, but the chief feature of all is still further on, when, after a long ascent, all at once you catch sight of the long straight stretch of sandy beach, more than two miles long, only broken by the yellow sea-poppies which grow in masses together, or perhaps by a party of the Slapton fisherwomen in their picturesque sun-bonnets, hauling in a seine.

Running parallel with the sea, about fifty yards distant, is the famous Slapton Lea, a long, narrow lake of fresh water, the coach-road running between these two in an even, white line till it reaches Torcross. Here the coach pauses to change horses, and, perhaps, more than one-half of the passengers go no further, tempted by the double attraction of sea and lake fishing and the walks to the Start Lighthouse and countless places of interest that abound. But all is businesslike: in an incredibly short time the luggage is down and readjusted, fresh horses are in, and the coach moves on again, turning sharp away at once towards Chillington, so that you can only just catch a final glimpse of the glimmering sea and long stretch of beach as you turn the corner. The scenery now is more or less monotonous till you reach Kingsbridge, the centre for Salcombe Hope Cove and Bigbury Bay. Here the coach stops, but is replaced by another which runs to Kingsbridge Road on the main Great Western line. But the days of this last coach are numbered, as the projected line to Kingsbridge is almost finished; and one trembles to think whether it will cease there, or eventually take the route that we have just come by, and so irretrievably vulgarise and completely ruin for all true lovers of Nature one of the loveliest parts of England.

Coaching in South Devon – Torcross and the road between the sea and the Lea. Running parallel with the sea about fifty yards difference is Slapton Lea, a long narrow lake of fresh water, the coach-road running between these two in an even white line 'til it reaches Torcross. Here the coach pauses to change horses, and perhaps more than one half of the passengers go no further, tempted by the double attraction of sea and lake fishing, and the walks to the Start Lighthouse.

REMINISCENCES OF A BUS CONDUCTOR

A Paper read by Mr George Hart to a meeting of the Omnibus Society held at Tilling's Social and Athletic Club, Park End, Sydenham Park, Forest Hill, on Friday, 10 October, 1930.

Why I became a bus conductor is too long a story to tell now, but it was in May 1895 that I first went to Scotland Yard to get a licence. It was not, however, a conductor's licence that I applied for but a cab driver's. I was put through a test for my knowledge of London. Did I know my London? I thought I did, but when I was asked the route I would take from Scotland Yard to Chalk Farm Road I could not tell them, for I had never been to Chalk Farm in my life. Then I was asked the route I would take to Charing Cross. That's easy I thought, and said "Just outside here into Parliament Street, Whitehall – and there you are," but there I was not, for I should have said Embankment, Northumberland Avenue and so Charing Cross. However, I was given a book and told to study it and come up in a week's time. I was naturally disheartened but on crossing the Yard I saw over a window "Conductors Licences issued here." I went to the window and asked for the form, and was given one. I filled it in giving the names of two householders as references. Waited about a week, received notice to call, paid 5s and received my licence. Now I had to find work somewhere. Applied at the office of the Star Omnibus Company, New Kent Road, near the Railway Arch. Saw Mrs Perry and was told to wait and see Mr Patrick, saw him and was taken on and told to turn up at the Elephant and Castle next morning at 7am. I did spare work for about a month, when I got a service on No. 1, Elephant and Castle and Earls Court route. Out at 7.30am. finishing at 10.50pm. The bus, with the stud of horses, stood under the railway arches in Station Road, Elephant and Castle. I went there every morning to fetch the bus out, sometimes putting the horses in myself. The bus was driven by a man named Rivers, whose brother was employed by Thomas Tilling at Pelican Yard up till a few years ago.

I don't know whether any of my hearers have seen a Star Omnibus. They were peculiar buses, all four wheels being of the same size, and the springs being on the outside of the wheels. I believe the idea was that the gauge of the wheels were the same as the trams. I do know that when we got into the tram lines it was difficult to get out, and when we did we swung all over the road.

My first route was from the Elephant and Castle to Earls Court Tavern, via Kennington Cross, Vauxhall, Victoria, Buckingham Palace Road, Pimlico Road, Sloane Street, Knightsbridge, Cromwell Road, Gloucester Road, Earls Court Road. I am afraid I don't quite remember what the fares were but I think it was sixpence; that is Kennington Cross a half-penny, Vauxhall a penny, Victoria twopence, Sloane Square threepence, Knightsbridge fourpence, Gloucester Road fivepence, Earls Court Tavern sixpence. We had roll tickets, but no punches. We were supplied with a cylinder shaped tin, divided into four sections, which, of course, could not hold all our tickets, in fact, we seldom used it, preferring to keep the tickets in our pockets. There was one inspector and Mr Patrick himself, who used to jump the buses, and they were all over the road, jumping on when one least expected them, although each conductor signed to the bus passing him where he left one of them (or both) by pointing to that part of the bus which had the point painted on it (for nearly every point was painted on some part of the bus, either in the windows, canopy, or staircase). This knowledge may have been very useful to some conductors, although for my part the anxiety of not knowing when they would double on you took away all the help the knowledge was likely to give.

I was only on these buses for a few months, and at that time was living in Thrush Street, Penton Place, Walworth. I used to get up at half-past six in the morning and get to bed about a quarter to twelve at night. I did this for about four weeks without a rest for I could not get one because being first bus out there was never a spare man there in time to take my bus. However, one morning I missed my bus and was told to see Mr Patrick, who gave me a week off. I preferred to draw my bill, which I did, and then went to the Atlas and Waterloo Omnibus Association, in the London Road by the South London Music Hall. I was given a start on William Birch's bus on the same road with the same fares. This bus was a break bus, breaking in all kinds of horses, kickers, shyers, borers and even biters. The bus had a very thick teak plank across the front of it, because of the kickers kicking in the front panels, and it was often the case to see a Dandy Brush (with the bristles outward) strapped to the pole or the splinter bar to stop borers and those horses who liked to sit on the bar and let the other horse do the work. Other horses were fitted with special harness of a skeleton nature, but with a wide leather strap, called a kicking strap over the buttocks. This bus was driven by a man named Turner. A very fine looking man indeed, an ex-sergeant major of the Army Service Corps, and what he did not know about horses was not worth knowing. How he became a Sergeant Major I do not know, for he was most illiterate and more than fond of his beer, but that's another story. I used a pistol punch on this bus, which was put (with the tickets and the waybill) in a small canvas bag. These bags were given out to the conductors by the timekeeper each morning at the Elephant, and when we had finished our days work, we left the bus at the Elephant and went home, where we made up the waybill (deducting the driver's pay 7s and the conductor's 6s) wrapped the money and the Waybill into a parcel, put the total amount on the outside, also name and badge number and gave the parcel to George Dicks (who was cashier for the Atlas and Waterloo Association at that time) the morning after. My wife used to make up my waybill each night whilst I was washing.

I have said after deducting driver/'s wages 7s and my own at 6s. I might say the 6s was never there, for the incidental expenses were many. For instance, morning and night I had to give the horse keepers fourpence, besides purchasing a whisky or two for my driver. Where drivers thought we got the money from I don't know, but if the conductor did not pay up the driver saw that he did not earn much money and he ran the risk of being stood off for low earnings. Tis true one could make a little if he was a considerate and helpful conductor. I well remember a gentleman who rode on my bus every morning, but never had any money, but I was told to call at the end of each week at Cromwell Mansions, and the hall porter would give it to me. When I pulled the bus up outside and went in for it I was always given half-a-crown, and frequently the fares only amounted to eightpence, and the change became my "perks." There was also a lady who would often ride on my bus. She lived in the corner house of Lexham Gardens. She would go to the Oratory or Harrods. I think she was sweet on my driver, in fact, I am sure she was. This lady used to send her servant out (in the winter) with a can (covered neatly with green baize) filled with soup, also some bread in a dinner napkin. The servant would meet the bus, I would take the parcel, go to Earls Court, ten minutes on the stand, where we would devour the supper, and give the empties to the girl, who came out again to meet us on our return.

Of course, we were not supplied with uniforms in those days, still we tried to look as swell as we could. Turner dressed very well indeed. I know I paid Cohen, who supplied all the busmen round the Elephant with clothes, two shillings every week for him, and then he owed pounds. I myself bought my coaching coat off Cohen.

I worked on this bus for a while and the reason I left was that I met a man named Joe Coy, who was a good mile runner (I also was a runner). I had got a day off to do a coaching job as post horn blower for Lavell of the Boro, when I met Coy, and he said "Why don't you try and get on our firm, they want post horn blowers". (I'd been a bugler in the First Surrey Rifles). I said I would try. He told me to see Mr Loveridge at Winchester House, Peckham. Next morning I went to see Mr Loveridge and got the job. I went back to Mr Dicks, told him about it and drew my bill. I had a couple of days off and started for Thomas Tilling Ltd on City and Suburban Day 1897. My first job, if I remember rightly was Lord and Lady Herbert's party from a club in St James Square. A coachman named Skillern drove the coach. I had to pick up the coach at the Windmill Stables, Clapham. My pay as a post horn blower was 10s 6d per day for race meetings. On the occasion referred to I think I had the best days work I had ever done on a coach. My wife was surprised when I took home enough sandwiches to last us for days, half a bottle of whisky, lots of cigars and put £2 in her hand. That was the beginning of my coach work throughout that season. Jack Eagle and I sharing the coach work, he having Alf Tilling to drive him, and I several different men. "Billy do Bad" Hawthorne, Tom Richman and others. In the Winter I went conducting (as I did between the coach jobs) sometimes on the Red Road, Herne Hill and Lord Nelson, sometimes the yellow, Camberwell Green to Gracechurch Street, the green, "Times", Rye Lane to Oxford Circus, the Tower Bridge and the "Plough" Dulwich. Then came the time when a new road opened, Hanover Arms, Rye Lane, to Lee Green. I conducted the first bus from the Peckham end. It was a four-horse bus standing at Bull Yard. I blew the horn. We had a load of passengers (first journey) composed of fellows from Winchester House, which included Ben Baxter, and I think Will Wolsey and Ernie Foster. I set them down at the Tiger's Head Lee Green, and a jolly party they were. I cannot recall how long I was in this road, but one day I was informed by Mr Jim Elsey, the road manager, that I was for office. What for I did not know. I had done nothing wrong, least I hadn't been caught. When I did attend office, I was agreeably surprised when Mr Walter Wolsey promoted me, and I became an inspector. About two years afterwards I left the firm for a short time and went into business again, but it was not a success. I saw Mr Harry Tilling, told him the circumstances and went to work as a clerk in Winchester House, and stayed there until 1917, when I joined up. After I was demobilised I went to the Army Pay Corps, Blackheath and Woolwich. Left there at the beginning of 1921. I then went to the Camberwell Town Hall and was clerk in the Health Department until May that year when I sailed for Canada, and became a road masters clerk on the Canadian National Railway at McBridge, British Columbia. I had an object in doing this, but the story is too long to tell. I came back from Canada, landing in England on 24 May, 1923. I went to see the late Mr Richard Tilling, who sent me to see Mr Walter

Of a pattern issued by the Metropolitan Police during the period 1850-1902, 3861 was certainly in use by the conductor on – to use the terminology of the period – an 'Atlas' horse-drawn vehicle (bus) c.1890.

Wolsey, and he sent me to see Mr Harry Cooper, the commercial manager, who gave me a job. I drove a WH Smith van on the Leytonstone and Whipps Cross journey. I did not like that job, so I again took out a conductor's licence, then I went to see Mr Webb, our traffic manager, and he was kind enough to give me a start, and on June 4, 1923 I started again as a bus conductor at Croydon garage for the "old firm" Thomas Tilling. Today I am working in the traffic office, and there I hope to spend the rest of my business days. But what a different job it is these days conducting to what it was when I first started. Now uniform is found, cash bags and ticket racks provided, and 13s 6d per day instead of 6s, and nothing to pay out of it. No drinks for this one or for that one, eight hours a day, not sixteen, travelling time to pick up the bus and garage allowance for making up your box and paying in. No wonder the bus conductor of today is a different type of man than he was in the old days, yet it is not a skilled job.

So far I have briefly given my career since I took out my first licence in 1895, and apart from a few outstanding incidents I presume my life as a conductor is much the same as the life of other "old timers". It is an extremely interesting job for a person who studies human nature and possesses the right temperament. It is furthermore a healthy life, despite exposure to the elements, and many busmen live to a good old age. (Roger Kidner)

The Folkestone, Hythe and District Omnibus Company's badge has been in my possession for 20 or more years but of late a number of others have surfaced. The omnibus and tramway stories around that area intersect and ultimately fail due to the intransigence of one landowner and his son, the two Lord Radnors, an example of the power held by one family over the travel desires of many.

THE 'BRUMMAGEM' HORSE-BUS

The bulk of reasonably successful horse-buses in Birmingham seem to have been operated under the aegis of the tramway companies. By about 1890 it was clear to the major operators that further tramway expansion would be blocked as tracklaying was entirely in the hands of the Corporation and they had had enough of steam trams, while accepting the physical layout of the city made horse trams quite unviable. New routes would have to be by horse-buses, but even then in the more outlying villages outside the city (King's Norton, Moseley, and Sutton Coldfield among them) there was much opposition to the whole concept; middle-class gentlemen tended to either take the train or a cab. The working class continued to clatter along in their hobnails.

Technically the horse-bus as a machine had evolved into something quite useful, but the old conundrum of building enough strength into the bodywork to withstand the pounding over cobbles without killing the poor animals dragging the whole thing was always in the background. And there are many reports of horses dropping dead in the road from sheer exhaustion, and worse others just fell down unable to continue to await the arrival of the blacksmith or slaughterman with his sledgehammer to give the beast the merciful coup-de-grace.

Ultimately by about 1900 we have a vehicle seating 26 persons, 12 inside in the saloon, 14 outside, but on garden seats, and the lost deadweight of the driver and the conductor (albeit the latter was often a boy), all capable given level terrain of a speed of 8mph (13kph). The late photographs do show a surprisingly elegant vehicle, far from the early crude arrangements. Some idea of the demand in Birmingham can be gauged from a survey carried out in June 1900, which showed that 51 omnibuses per hour stopped outside the Five Ways Tavern on their journey into the City. While in New Street we have even more detail, with 64 horse omnibuses per hour turning around. 16 were bound for the Hagley Road, 9 to Harborne, 2 for Carpenter Road, 16 Five Ways, 4 Ladywood Road, 6 Ryland Street, surprisingly only 8 for the Bristol Road, and 3 down the Pershore Road. But, and it is a big but, even if we allow for 10 passengers in each bus standing or sitting on boys' or girls' laps (as was supposed to be the case) we still have each vehicle carrying no more than 36 souls at most, or in all 2,304 passengers per hour. Any respectable electric tram had a capacity of 60 at least and as soon as the track was laid they were running nose to tail along that area.

Horse-buses here and there (even excluding those preserved) had relatively long lives up to 30 years, in London for all their transport improvements, 63 remained in service in 1914, the last, a Tilling owned car, running out on 4 August that year, when the horses were requisitioned by the army for war service. Photographs exist showing horse-bus feeders still carrying railway passengers to and from a station in the 1930s; but the last in Birmingham seems to have ceased just after the Armistice.

Numerically the number of horse buses and by inference the number of horses used in Birmingham seems rather nebulous, but on 21 July, 1905, when the number had already diminished we find the City of Birmingham Tramways Co., Ltd, had 608 horses to work 45 cars, and the Birmingham & Midland Tramways Ltd, 510 for 74 vehicles. This survey may be taken as accurate for at that time the British Electric Traction Co., Ltd, took over the primary horse bus operators in Birmingham, buying the Omnibus Department of CBT for £42,834, the Omnibus Department of B&MT for £77,166 and although they only had 19 motor-vehicles to their name, £30,000 for the Birmingham Motor Express Co., Ltd. This was all enshrined on paper, if not stone.

As we can see from the photographs until the design evolved these buses were inherently dangerous vehicles – and the conductor's job perched on a step at the back was no sinecure.

Admittedly 'puffed' by the new concern, the Midland Omnibus Company, their prospectus tells us "The glaring misconduct of both drivers and conductors together with the terrifying effect and often fatal consequences arising from careless and furious driving, prevent many (especially females)

Nechells horse bus belonging to the private company the Birmingham General Omnibus Co., who survived from 1878 to around 1885, when they went into liquidation. The obstructive posters in the windows were bitterly complained about.

from availing themselves of those facilities given by the bus."

Accident reports in any of the Birmingham newspapers make doleful reading and unlike trams with their lifeguards there was nothing to stop children getting under them; one surgeon in Birmingham estimated "upwards of 100 amputations of children's limbs were necessitated annually by the lack of any life saving apparatus on the common horse bus". How many children died is anyone's guess.

However, ladies even when they could afford the fares, were virtually forced to ride inside in the saloon as it was not considered decent or indeed practical for them to climb the iron rungs to gain access to the roof, and then to sit back to back facing the road with their legs unprotected by any decency boards was to open them to urchin's chi-yiking, innuendo, and thrown pony-nuts or mud. There are wonderful reports of girls wearing fashionable crinolines having to tilt them to enter the saloon and then being quite unable to sit down or turn around. I wonder how the conductor then squeezed 14 passengers inside – literally perhaps!

Lighting, or the lack of it, ensured that horse-buses, like the steam tram trailers were ideal targets for quicksilver pickpockets (imagine a Birmingham Fagin – there were many); initially candle or colza oil lamps were used, but around the turn of the century acetylene fittings became common, although they could be knocked out by a particularly vicious jolt. A classic London joke tells us of two horse bus operators, the one 'flush with tin', the other not – one had acetylene lamps, the other a set o'lean horses. Eventually the smelly, smutty, smoking delights of paraffin lamps became usual.

Surely looking at the vehicles from this age, the greatest advances came when the BET directors, presumably after trying their acquisitions, decreed that the straw on the floor, placed there to keep boots dry and as feet warmers ('it were better than nowt' said one of our old men, discussing this with me) was to be changed daily, instead of weekly when it was accepted it it would be verminous and stinking from road dirt – much of it horse-muck. These were, after all, short haul omnibuses, not coaches. A few months later a further management decision meant that straw was abolished, being replaced by floor covering – and the buses were to be washed inside as well as out every night! Even 50 years later the smell of Jeyes Fluid which we as much as our predecessors used on bus insides remains a pleasant memory, redolent, too, of school days.

The Illustrations

It has to be said that in many cases the dates on these illustrations are at best problematical. Where they are genuine postcards there are often clues – for example lettering that says 'Stationery supplier to the [late] Queen' or which carry a nice old-fashioned date stamp. Where of necessity we have to use reproductions – some of which are themselves 50 years old, we must hazard an informed guess. We are very grateful to another well-established author, David Harvey, for the loan of his massive collection of Birmingham horse-bus photographs and for providing the locations used in many of the captions. For simplicity's sake the illustrations are presented in rough date order, with a trio of oddments at the end. I must, however, ask forgiveness for the relatively poor quality of some of the images, the murk and dirt inherent in any city before the Clean Air Acts ensured photographers had quite a difficult time.

Presumably, although we cannot be sure, this was a publicity photograph of a very early Birmingham Omnibus Company's machine on the Bristol Road service, the crude iron ladder and exposed seating upstairs are clearly visible; it was unknown for ladies to travel there unless they were coerced ... This company was formed in 1869, with 33-seat buses 'on the latest design', but they only survived until 1871.

This illustration can be dated at roughly 1868 on the basis of the buildings visible in New Street. Back to back (knifeboard) seating was usual at this time.

The "Perseverance" privately operated vehicle, named as many were, after the famous mail coach 'flyers' of yesteryear, is standing at Cannon Hill, Balsall Heath in 1888.

An excellent photograph showing a rather modern vehicle standing at The Swan Inn, Yardley said to be c.1890, but may be later as here we have the proper staircase, garden seats upstairs and full decency advertising boards. The slip board on the side tells us it is operating between Yardley and Sheldon.
(John Whybrow Collection)

Another private owner vehicle, belonging to Charles Winkett who, as one of a seven-strong consortium was to sell out to the Birmingham General Omnibus Co. [BET] 3 April 1897. He had two routes, Dale End to Nechells (where this bus is standing) and Dale End to Castle Bromwich.

July 1897 and a relatively peaceful scene was to be found at the junction of the Hagley Road, and Ladywood Road, Five Ways.

Broad Street, Birmingham, c.1895, with a delightfully tranquil scene. The iron staircase is well visible, as is the destination board. By now ladies regularly travelled in daylight hours.

A truly animated scene c.1896 as the wind whistles along Station Street, and the girls struggle with skirts and hats.

In far-off days when King's Norton was a village, the other form of omnibus waits outside the Plumber's Arms. This, the 'pure' char-à-banc, is surely the precursor of the most swish coach running today.

A pair of photographs, the first (left) depicts a fairly standard late horsebus with proper staircase and garden seats outside. The driver wears his quasi official style of clothing before the advent of uniforms, but I think the second man must be the ostler who has attached the trace horse for the long drag up to Tyseley, Warwick Road on the Acocks Green service. *(Millbrook House Ltd, neg. no.901).* The second of the pair (below) is a real oddity as for example, the driver is wearing a boater and the conductor is incredibly smart. The passengers themselves look rather 'up-market' – was this an official BET inspection? On the Pershore Road, with Priory Road behind the bus. In the days of mail coaches there were a few gentlemen drivers who would in exchange for some 'pot de yin' take the ribbons from the regular man and show their mettle as horsemen. Is this another possibility? The seat covers thrown over the rails upstairs, designed to keep seats dry in bad conditions, are unusual survivors. *(Millbrook House Ltd, neg. no. 901)*

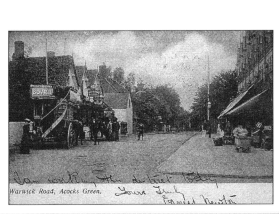

Admittedly, not the best quality photograph, but quite irresistible as depicting such a quiet scene so near the City. Posted to Miss E. Russell, Moat House, Little Bromwich on 4 August 1904 carrying two messages, the one on the front plus: 'Thanks for your p.c. Please save eggs for Friday and oblige'.

Another study, but this time showing the wiggly pattern left by the watercart in New Street 1897. Interesting to see a man standing in the aisle outside while a lady ascends.

At last the conductor has his uniform. A small, lightweight, well lit horse-bus with curved corner glass which ran between New Street and Carpenter Road, Edgbaston (once a very up-market area) during off-peak periods.

THE LAST JOURNEY

This item is drawn from a newspaper entitled the *Town Crier*, 1 February 1890
(Charles Scutt, driver of the Browne's Green bus, died on his box, with his reins in hand,
24 January 1890, leaving a widow and nine children.)

TOLD BY A STABLE HELP

I see as he hoistes isself on the box,
As 'ow he was weaker that day;
But Charlie was always a plucked 'un to work'
And would have his jolly own way.
There was several as noticed as 'ow he was queer –
He'd been badish for more nor a week –
But when you've a wife and nine kiddies at home'
It don't do to "chuck it", so to speak.
Yes, he did take a drop, and I can't deny that,
But temptation came much in his way,
Bein' outside a bus ain't a temperance job,
Whatever the goody 'uns say.
A decentish sort of a feller all round,
He did journeys along with the best;
And he'd sat on that box many winters, he had,

And now he's a takin' a rest.
Yes, he died, as you say, sir, "in harness", that's right,
At his post, with the reins in his hand,
I guess a man can't have a better send off
For a chance in the happier land.

And that's how he made his last journey, poor chap,
Leastways took his seat, sir, up there,
When the 'osses was 'ad out again for 'im, why
He went inside, alone, as a fare.
Beg your pardon, them nine little orphans he's left,
There's one thing we're tryin' to do –
If you could spare a bob it would give 'em a lift,
Which their father, sir, often giv' you.

CHARM OF ANTIQUITY

This is said to be one of the earliest products from the Leyland works. I find it quite a human machine aided and abetted by the photographer. Clearly the latter is under instructions to remove the background but the difficulty of having to work with a glass plate is cruelly exposed. The view through the back window seems to be part of a building – the roof tiles are visible on enlargement, he has 'fudged' the roof rack and left both the telegraph pole (once a commonplace item in English scenery) and that windswept winter skeleton of a tree.

The vehicle is as 'pure' a motor charabanc as we'll ever see and rather delightful for that, but I do wonder what use those curtains would be flapping about in a downpour. The exhaust looks as though it might singe a few toes standing on that running board – cum – mounting step. Presumably the lighting was acetylene and the bus with all its showman's trimmings must have been a joy to see. What colour would you like that paintwork?

THE MOTORS THAT ARE COMING.

Are we within measurable distance of seeing our vehicular traffic transformed by the introduction of the dashing and comfortable motor, and a brand-new commercial industry started?

Those curious thousands who swarmed to see the motor vehicles of many kinds career along Northumberland Avenue and the Victoria Embankment on Wednesday had reason to think so—those who gathered

THE PANHARD 'BUS FOR THIRTEEN PERSONS.

round the festive board at the Métropole at the invitation of the Motor-Car Club may be said by their presence to have shared in the belief that the vehicular revolution is imminent. Mr. Sidney Gedge, M.P., presided over a large company, which included Lord Crawshaw, Mr. Harry J. Lawson (president of the Motor-Car Club), Sir Charles Hartopp, Mr. J. O'Connor, M.P., Colonel Josiah Harris, F.R.G.S., Sir H. H. Bemrose, M.P., Dr. Clarke, M.P., Mr. Guy Pym, M.P., Mr. A. Arnold, M.P., Mr. E. Parker, M.P., Mr. J. J. H. Sturmey, Mr. George Idem, Mr. Thomas Robinson, Mr. J. H. Mace, Mr. E. M. C. Instone, Mr. Baron (Blackpool Motor Company), Mr. Fleming Nesbit, &c.

Mr. Worby Beaumont, President of the Society of Engineers, assures us that the tramways and omnibuses of London alone carry 480,000,000 passengers annually, and these and the Metropolitan Railways together convey 871,000,000 passengers per year. Add to this hanson-cab and other traffic, and the figures rise to at least 1,000,000,000.

There are hundreds of miles of roads and lanes bounded by green fields within a twenty-mile radius of London. To connect these to London by lines of steam motor omnibuses would be a boon. A punctual daily and hourly steam omnibus service would create new towns along the route, and bring cheap land within reach; prosperity would follow as it follows railways and the opening of new lines. In most cases time would be saved. A reference to the suburban time-table shows that to travel from door to door even at slower speed is quicker than the District Railway, because the distance from the railway stations at each end and the waiting at the station form a serious waste of time and a great annoyance, especially when underground. From the Hotel Métropole to anywhere within ten miles can, we are assured, be done more quickly by motor than by ordinary stopping trains if the time is taken from door to door. An easy means of relieving London traffic is to extend the capital to wider and healthier thoroughfares. This cannot be done by horses so easily as by a steam-omnibus service. The omnibus is becoming the favourite conveyance. Shares are increasing in value, and the number of omnibuses employed is multiplied every year. Why, the London General Omnibus Company's takings for last year were £1,334,264 16s. 8d. The number of vehicles owned by the company was 1266, and 14,165 horses, or more than twelve horses to each omnibus. No less than 172,317,192 passengers were carried in one year. The North Metropolitan Tramway Company carried over 107,000,000 passengers, and employed over 4700 horses. The London Tramway Company carried over 98,000,000 passengers, and employed over 4000 horses. The London Road-Car Company carried over 50,000,000 passengers, and employed over 3000 horses. Glance at that startling item in the annual reports under the head of "Horse Renewals." "Horse Renewals," for the London General Omnibus Company is given for six months only as £53,644—positively more than £100,000 per annum for replacing worn-out, maimed, and slaughtered horses in this one company alone. This immense sum is wasted not only once, but every year. The engine saves the whole of it.

Taking the petroleum at threepence per gallon (the price of large quantities), one farthing will carry one person five miles. The journey from London to Brighton would cost twopence-halfpenny per head, and

"If," said the Pioneer of the motor-car industry in this country, "tramcars can be made to work, carrying the same number of people equally well, without the public nuisance of tram-rails, surely it is a matter demanding the attention of the Government at this time, and especially of the London County Council, who will be wasting millions of public money by purchasing a road which is superseded." His contention is that there are five thousand omnibuses now running at a cost of more than double that which ought to be spent upon them. He argued that the Government should take up the motor question, and, after ascertaining the trifling amount necessary for working motor omnibuses and cars, establish works for the manufacture of these vehicles for the supply not only of this country, but of our colonies. India, he pointed out, is particularly suitable for motor traffic, with its beautifully made and perfectly level roads, stretching hundreds of miles. The Pioneer's well-expressed and cogent observations were listened to with the greatest interest, as they deserved to be, for they were practical and to the point, even if tinged by a characteristic optimism.

There are to be steam omnibuses, motor omnibuses, and petrol cabs.

As regards the first, we learn that the steam is created by a slow-combustion stove, which consumes only a very small quantity of coke or petroleum. These omnibuses are of twenty horse-power, to be increased presently to thirty horse-power. One vehicle will, it is asserted, carry twenty-eight passengers, and, where necessary, is capable of being fastened to another omnibus of equal capacity. The cost per passenger is stated to amount to one-fifth of a farthing per mile; speed, from eight to ten miles an hour, to be increased to fifteen miles an hour. The most convenient form of omnibus power is said to be the new London motor omnibus, which neither requires a boiler nor consumes fuel when not working. It makes less noise than other motor vehicles, and has the great merit of not diffusing any sulphur. Then there is the new licensed petrol cab, which, after twelve months' trial, has been licensed as being as safe as horse traffic. This cab will work all day and all night, and will travel upwards of a hundred miles a-day, using only between two and three gallons of petrol, which can be purchased in quantities at 5½d. per gallon. We are told that these three types of vehicles and the motor vans have been fully tested during the past year, and that the French Government has decided to grant special subsidies to the companies manufacturing these vehicles.

result in a handsome profit of one shilling per person.

Steam is thoroughly understood on steam tramcars and railroads, and there is no reason why the profitable employment of steam-omnibus service should not immediately take place in the suburban roads round London for connecting our suburbs with town. It is predicted that lines of steam omnibuses will be the railways of the future. We might all get to the City much more quickly and more cheaply by these early steam-cars and omnibuses.

Lines of steam omnibuses might very well run along the road from London to Brighton, and seeing that petroleum is so reduced in price, and that it is proved that a full-sized omnibus may run seven miles for one gallon, which may be taken at a cost of threepence-halfpenny, or about a halfpenny per mile, it is quite obvious that if twenty-eight persons may be carried for a halfpenny per mile, enough profit could be made out of a farthing per head; that is to say, that London to Brighton might be done for a shilling, eighteenpence there and back, calling at all the small rising towns *en route*, and creating an enormous value to the *terrain* which is now treated as pasture-land.

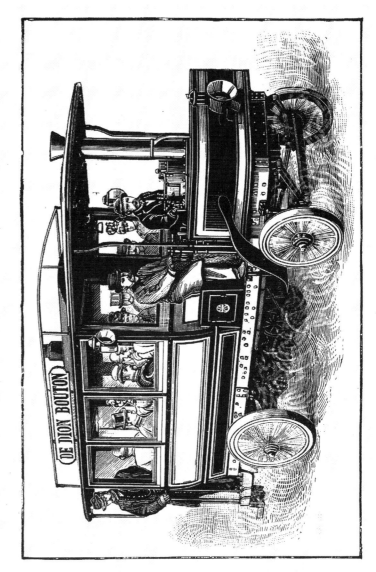

DE DION TWELVE-SEATED 'BUS.

nies to, as it were, fill in the gaps on the Folkestone-Hythe route.

Mechanically, later machines were quite different to the norm and were said to have six cylinder 50hp engines "with a bore of 44 inches and a piston stroke of 6 inches".

"We understand that the original idea of providing such a large engine, besides enabling such heavy machines to tackle the stiff gradients on the country roads at a satisfactory speed, was to eliminate if possible the use of gears, at any rate for anything more than starting purposes. This, however, was not found entirely practicable, and, although most of the driving is done on the top speed, the other gears are, of course, found useful for traffic and other conditions. Four speeds forward are provided, and the gears are made of chrome-vanadium, case-hardening steel. The final transmission is by side chains. At first sight, the size of the driving wheels, which are 21 inches in diameter, would lead to the impression that an unduly large reduction must have been provided in the gearbox, but the compensation is found in the fact that the engine is of such a size as to develop its full horse-power at 900 revolutions per minute. A detail, which we are surprised to find has not been adopted by more manufacturers, is the provision of small rubber buffers, under the spring hangers, which act as auxiliaries to the main road springs, and these buffers effectually damp the oscillations of the long, stiff, road springs that are necessary for vehicles of this class...

During the course of a recent trip between some of the towns already mentioned, our representative was impressed to an extraordinary extent by the easy-riding qualities of these large Thames machines, and he was inclined to ascribe this money-making characteristic to the provision of the huge driving wheels which are such a conspicuous feature of the chassis. The six-cylinder 50hp engine is, of course, quite a novelty with such heavy machines, but the wisdom of the engineer in his choice can hardly be disputed when such hills as those running over Shakespeare's Cliff have to be tackled, at a speed which must compare favourably with the direct line through the cliff by rail, and with the machines carrying a full load of passengers. The ease of riding was quite remarkable, and it is no exaggeration to say that there is no heavy machine unequipped with pneumatic tires that has made such light work of indifferent road surfaces. The last six machines, which are now being delivered, are practically identical with those which have been running for over two years, with the exception that they will be provided with high-tension magneto, and the gearbox will have rather heavier driving shafts...

Mr Cann has a constitutional objection to the use of the word "char-a-bancs", as applied to the vehicles which he controls, and he insists that they be described as patent motor coaches, for he feels, and we cannot do other than admit that he does so with some justification, that there are many char-a-bancs on seaside services which are not much more than toast racks on wheels."

The secret behind these buses, and which distinguished them from the 'char-a-bancs' was that the saloon could be lifted off the seating area for summer use, or could be as here for the spring season and to have both the back portion plus a weather screen and canopy in winter.

[Author's note: Much of the description of Mr Cann's machine is drawn from The Commercial Motor Archives 18 June 1908, and is reproduced with their permission and our thanks.]

A NOTE ON THAMES IRONWORKS AND SHIPBUILDING COMPANY

Once a famous shipbuilders straddling and using Bow Creek with plenty of available labour from Blackwall on the West and Canning Town on the East, the company traced its roots back to 1837 but although successful in terms of work, financially they slipped with the owner C.J. More, becoming bankrupt in 1855, but a rescue plan saw them forge ahead, including taking the contract in 1862 for Westminster Bridge.

In the 1880s they were probably the most successful yard on the Thames, employing over 3000 men, but by 1912 had finally failed leaving only a football club – the Thames Ironworks F.C. drawn from the firm's employees – now better known as West Ham United F. C. – 'The Hammers' from the Shipbuilders took on 'The Irons' from the Ironworks.

Photo: By permission of the Thames Ironworks and Shipbuilding Co., Ltd.
BIRD'S-EYE VIEW OF THE THAMES IRONWORKS SHIPBUILDING YARD, SHOWING TWO WARSHIPS UNDER CONSTRUCTION.

J.W. CANN'S PATENTS

I have some considerable admiration for these Victorian engineers-inventors. In his patent applications, John Walter Cann showed himself to be a "Motor Car Proprietor". Prior to the common usage of pneumatic tyres (and they gave enough problems) solid tyres suffered from a number of difficulties, not least that the relatively poorly treated rubber was quite soft and could creep around the rim or quite suddenly fly off. To combat this, a shaped tyre (roughly figure-of-eight) was introduced, which, using a two part wheel, reduced their evil habits! The word 'clincher' has of course reappeared in a totally different context, that of pneumatic bicycle tyres. We do not have space here to dwell too long on Mr Cann's patents but the relevant four here are:

8289	Accepted	27 July 1905	(Tyres)
8526	Accepted	31 August 1905	(Wheel sprags)
1053	Accepted	5 April 1906	(Tyres)
3757	Accepted	19 March 1908	(Tyres)

The following overleaf is part of the text of patent 8289 together with the relevant drawings:

IMPROVED MEANS FOR SECURING INDIA-RUBBER TYRES TO MOTOR AND OTHER VEHICLE WHEELS.

I, JOHN WALTER CANN, of 17 Copthall Gardens, Folkestone, in the county of Kent, Motor Car Proprietor; do hereby declare the nature of this invention to be as follows.

My invention relates to means for securing rubber tyres to the wheels of vehicles generally, but more especially designed for the wheels of automobiles.

The invention has for object to provide a simple device whereby the tyre may be securely attached, in such manner as to prevent creeping of the tyre or lateral displacement thereof due to side strains, and to admit of the tyre being readily detached and replaced when desired without the aid of a multiplicity of accessories.

According to my invention I construct the tyre (which may be either a solid tyre or a cushion tyre) with a number of recesses entering the tyre at its underside, and disposed radially thereto, each recess terminating in a passage piercing the tyre transversely at right angles to said recess. The tyre is attached by a number of eyebolts or equivalent contrivances, the upper or apertured extremity of each of which is housed in one of said radial recesses and whose lower extremities are screw-threaded and adapted to pass through the rim and the felloe and to be secured thereto by nuts and washers.

A cross-pin adapted to enter the aperture in the upper extremity of an eyebolt is inserted in each lateral passage in the tyre, passing through the eye-bolt when traversing said passage and serving to secure the tyre to said eye-bolts.

The tyre may be provided on the edges of its internal circumference with beads or flanges adapted to be received within a rim having inwardly curved edges (which may be independently attached to the wheel) and to be compressed and expanded when the nuts on the eye-bolts are tightened up so as to fit snugly within said rim and thus ensure greater security when the tyre has been attached to the wheel.

A is the tyre having a laterally enlarged base a and a number of apertures or passages a 1 entering from its underside and disposed radially thereto and adapted to register with correspondingly disposed passages or holes b 1 b 2 in the rim and felloe. Each radial aperture a 1 intersects a passage a 2 traversing the tyre at right angles to said radial aperture a 1.

D is an eyebolt whereof the apertured extremity d is housed in a passage a 1 of the tyre so that the aperture d registers with the transverse passage a 2 in the tyre and b is a cross pin which is adapted to be inserted in said transverse passage and to pass through the same and through the eye of d of the bolt D and serve to attach the tyre to the bolt. The eyebolt passes through the holes b 1 b 2 of the rim and felloe of the wheel respectively and its outer extremity is screw-threaded and provided with a nut c by which it is bolted to the felloe.

The rims are provided with inwardly turned side flanges adapted to receive and fit upon the laterally enlarged base of the indiarubber tyre.

In securing the tyre to the wheel each eye-bolt is passed into the radial passage in the tyre until the apertured extremity of the bolt comes opposite the transverse passage in the

A.D. 1905. April 18. Nº 8289.
CANN'S COMPLETE SPECIFICATION. (1 SHEET)

[This Drawing is a reproduction of the Original on a reduced scale.]

FIG. 1.

FIG. 2.

Malby & Sons. Photo-Litho.

tyre, and the cross pin is then inserted into the transverse passage and passed through the eye of the bolt. The tyre is then applied to the wheel rim so that the threaded ends of the bolts pass through the respective radial passages in the rim and felloe, and the nuts having been screwed on to the bolts are tightened up against the felloe, the consequent indrawing of the cross-pins having for effect to compress the indiarubber tyre and expend its laterally enlarged base below the cross-pins within the inwardly turned flanges of the rim.

By the means above described the tyre is maintained in place with greater security than heretofore, creeping of the tyre is prevented and the tread of the tyre is not liable to become spread and damaged by the rim under excessive load.

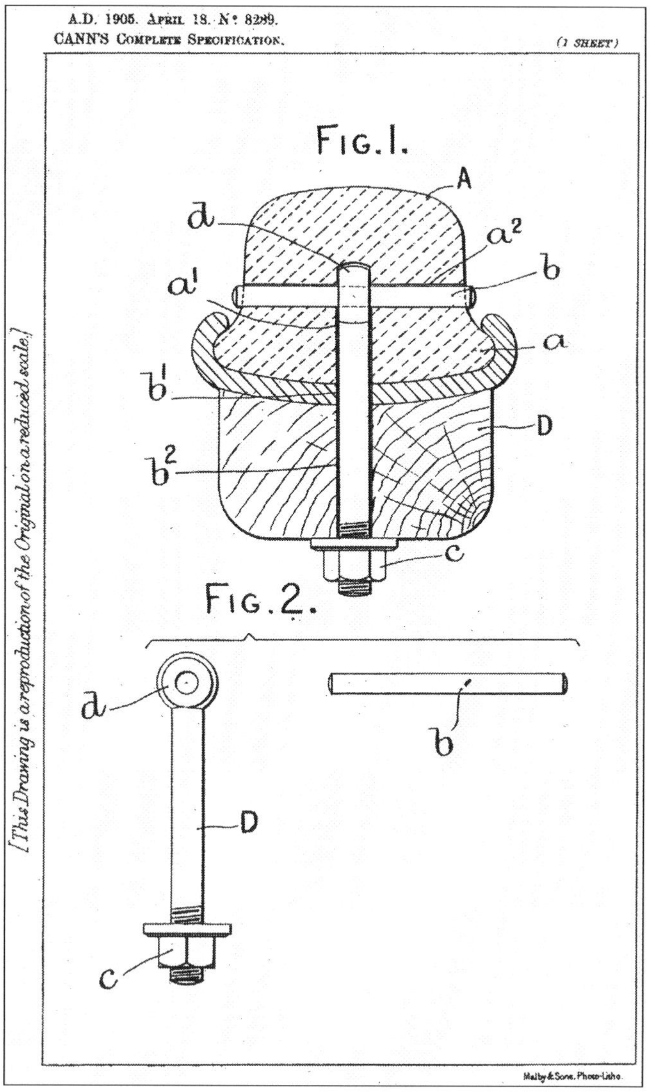

8526 relates to "Driving, Braking and Spragging Motor Cars". Self explanatory really but one of these blind alleys that dogged early motor vehicles; eventually of course, brakes changed from clasp brakes rubbing on the tyres or the rims to acting on the axle. And yet the sprag remained in use on horse carts and was still issued on buses used in hilly territory until twenty years ago.

1053 was to try to secure twin rubber tyres to the rims while remaining separate from one another, as now twin rears were required to allow heavier loads.

3757 seems to have come about due to problems inherent in 1053, mainly in that the whole rubber tyre had to be removed to replace a broken bolt or cross-pin, and that "endless tyres" could not be used. And this is still only in 1908, six years before World War I!

SCOTTISH AC LONG-DISTANCE TRIAL

Official Report on the Performance of the Darracq-Serpollet Omnibus

This is to certify that a Darracq-Serpollet double-deck steam omnibus, having a wheel base of 13 feet 6 inches, and a track of five feet, entered by the Darracq-Serpollet Omnibus Company, Limited, was submitted to a trial, under the supervision and observation of officials of this club, during the period from Friday, 24 to Friday, August 31 1906, both dates inclusive. The makers, in their entry, state that "the vehicle has been made in every way to the requirements of the Commissioner of Police of London; that the carriage body is of the double-deck type and of special design, but is of a very heavy nature, exceeding considerably the weight of an ordinary double-deck body, and that the chain sprockets are of the standard dimensions for city use."

The vehicle weighed unladen 4 tons 18 cwt, and carried loads varying from 26 cwt 3 qrs 2 lb to 12 cwt 1 qr 18 lb, the average load being, approximately, 16 cwt 3 qrs 2 lb - equivalent to 12 passengers of an average weight of 11 stone each. The total laden weight varied from 6 tons 4 cwt 3 qrs 2 lb, the average laden weight being 5 tons 14 cwt 3 qrs 2 lb. In the route, distances between arranged stops, the total mileage covered was 6881 miles, and the running time 47 hr 19 min., equal to an average speed of 14.5 miles per hour. On the Lochna-Craig Hill, Aberfeldy, which formed one of the time-test hills in the Scottish Reliability Trial, 1905, the total distance of which is 2 miles 484 yards, and having a total rise from start to finish of 976.62 feet, equal to an average descent of 1 in 17.6, and with gradients varying from 1 in 10 for 132 feet, 1 in 11 for 128 feet, and 1 in 12 for 1,056 feet, 1 in 13 for 462 feet, and 1 in 14 for 3,630 feet, to 1 in 50; the time occupied was 18 min. 40 secs, equal to 10.5 miles per hour.

The vehicle was ready to run on each occasion in about ten minutes after the lighting of the burner. The consumption of fuel was 153 gallons of paraffin and two gallons of petrol, a total of 155, gallons equivalent to 4.43 miles per gallon of fuel, or 0.2256 gallons per mile, a cost on a price basis of 5d per gallon or 1.128 pence per vehicle mile. The ton mileage consumption works out at 25.4 ton miles per gallon, equal to a cost or 0.197 of a penny per ton mile [unreadable] gallons of water were used during the trial, equal to 2.6 miles to the gallon, or 0.385 gallons per mile of water consumption. With two exceptions, where water was filled in, fuel and water were filled up only before the start and at the luncheon stopping places, printed in italics on the preceding page, each day. There were, as stated, two involuntary stops, which were caused by shortage of water. There was no stop on account of mechanical trouble from start to finish of the trial, and, with the exception of the tightening of a nut on a dust shield, no repairs or adjustments of any kind were made.

The vehicle was under the control and supervision of the Club officials during the whole period, from start to finish, and was locked up, or the engine, boiler, and burner sealed, during each stop for the night. These latter were untouched, and were not examined or cleaned during the entire trial. Messrs Wm Reid and R.L. Stevenson kindly acted as honorary observers.

After the conclusion of the trial, the Club Committee made a special run of about fifty miles on the omnibus. They report an almost entire absence of vibration, excepting that due to the rattling of the windows, etc., of the body, which is noticeable only when travelling in the interior, while from the roadside a few yards distant its running was apparently vibrationless and without noise. It is possible to converse with ease in an ordinary voice in any portion of the vehicle. There was no evidence of either heat or smell.

Under the instructions of the committee special brake tests were made on the level, and on a hill of a gradient of 1 in 9. In every instance the vehicle was held within a few yards of the instructions to stop when travelling at its normal speed, the hill tests being made both on the ascent and the descent. It was started from rest, after the stoppage in the ascent of said gradient, with the utmost smoothness and without any difficulty.

The starting from rest is secured with perfect smoothness, while the ease and smoothness of the reversing of the road wheels and the dirigibility of the vehicle in traffic are noticeable.

On special speed tests on the level, over a measured mile, the rate of speed was well up to 20 miles per hour.

The tyres were solid, "Gaulois" (twin tyres on back wheels) by Bergougnan of Clermont-Ferrand, and at the conclusion of the trial showed very little signs of wear.

*(Signed) ROBERT J. SMITH,
SAC.
59 St. Vincent Street, Glasgow, 6th September 1906*

This item was drawn from the Commercial Motor 13 September 1906; originally we transcribed it by hand for a book published 30 years ago. There were a number of words which seemingly have baffled the Archive reprint.

STEAMING WESTWARD

In 1905 Great Western Railway passengers were offered a ride from Highbridge, Somerset to Burnham-on-Sea and Cheddar on one of these paraffin fired 16-seater steam buses. Although apparently technically successful and with the rarity of windscreens they proved to be uneconomic and were transferred to Bridgwater where they were still in service as late as 1911.

LOST TIMES

Precious little is known about this photograph, but the probability is that it shows either a wedding party or is an end of World War 1 celebration. Apologies are offered for the scratched condition of the photo but it defied cleaning up. Killinghall is a mile from from Ripley in the West Riding of Yorkshire and the steam lorry appears to be unusually well equipped with headlights, the 2-ton trailer being an "optional extra" from the makers. A cloth, perhaps bleached linen, has been placed in the bed of the lorry to keep clothing clean. This 5 ton over-type is from William Allchin Ltd, Globe Works, Northampton was built as wagon no. 156 and delivered 15 April 1913.

ANOTHER RAILWAY STEAM BUS

The larger railway companies used buses as a means of dipping their toes in the water before building a branch line that might, or more probably might not, pay. The London & South Western Railway, already over-extended financially tried this Clarkson steam bus (one of a batch at £877 each) between Exeter Station and Chagford. Technically it was successful but only ran between 3 June 1905 and 4 May 1908.

ISLAND PRECURSOR

Tourist buses are a normal fact of life within some of the Channel Islands, although the days are long gone when beautiful Heaver – or Reading-bodied Albions prowled the lanes; service buses used on Guernsey offered more comfort than many so-called coaches on the mainland. This outing was in a precursor of those buses – a true char-à-banc with rows of seats (albeit door-less)

offering some degree of comfort, particularly as generally people were much shorter before the first world war; the object hanging down to the wheel by the lady with the white head scarf was one of the waterproof tarpaulins that could be stretched over legs should the weather turn inclement. The coachman has the dignified bearing of some of the better of his kind; the gent in the trilby was probably the owner. What I do not know is the significance of that delightful Margarete Steiff model bear being held so visibly.

The card was issued by Albert Smith in Jersey and is said to be dated 1906.

I do not know the date of these illustrations but they seem to be from a Harrod's-type motor catalogue published early in the 20th century. The Germain was rare; this Dürkopp not so, but the price of both is frightening, and given their unreliability I do wonder how many became 'repos'? A practice well enough known today!

The GERMAIN

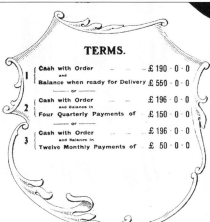

TERMS.

1	Cash with Order *and*	...	£ 190 - 0 - 0
	Balance when ready for Delivery		£ 550 - 0 - 0
	or		
2	Cash with Order *and Balance in*		£ 196 - 0 - 0
	Four Quarterly Payments of		£ 150 - 0 - 0
	or		
3	Cash with Order *and Balance in*		£ 196 - 0 - 0
	Twelve Monthly Payments of		£ 50 - 0 - 0

THE "GERMAIN" OMNIBUS.

DESCRIPTION.—15 h.p. four-cylinder engine, with all the latest improvements, water cooled by honeycomb radiator and fan, four speeds forward and reverse, two or three brakes, acting both forwards and backwards; top speed, twelve miles an hour.   Length over all, 17ft. 5in.   Width over all, 6ft. 8in.   Height over all, 7ft. 8in.   Tare weight, 2 tons 13 cwts.   (Now being used in Durban, Natal.)

The DÜRKOPP

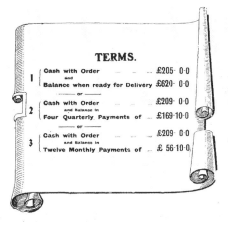

TERMS.

1	Cash with Order *and*	...	£205- 0-0
	Balance when ready for Delivery		£620- 0-0
	or		
2	Cash with Order *and Balance in*		£209- 0-0
	Four Quarterly Payments of		£169-10-0
	or		
3	Cash with Order *and Balance in*		£209- 0-0
	Twelve Monthly Payments of		£ 56-10-0

THE 20 h.p. "DÜRKOPP" OMNIBUS.

DESCRIPTION.—20 h.p. four-cylinder car. Latest improvements, solid rubber tyres, 5in. section. Speed up to sixteen miles per hour.   Inlet valve, double governor to inlet and variable cam, fan-cooled radiator, hind wheels 4in. pneumatic tyres.

THE FALLEN LONDON STAR

The Star Omnibus Company (London) Limited was one of a number (167 at very least) of companies who tried to operate buses in London, and by May 1906 had 18 motor-buses (Milnes Daimler, Brush with Brotherhood engines and Brillie) in service, although it would seem they were withdrawn on the 9th August 1907. But this does not tell a fraction of the story as the original company from 1888 was S. Andrews & Son, renamed on 4 October 1892 Andrews Star Omnibus Company Ltd, which at its peak owned 246 horse-buses serviced by 1,905 horses.

The final name change came on 4 March 1899, with William Alexander Perry as the Managing Director, although the company, following Andrews' death, and the collapse of negotiations with the London General Omnibus Company, was wound up on 21 February 1908.

When the company died, W.M. Perry's brother purchased a number of the horse buses, and three of these after a number of vicissitudes survive in the care of London Bus Museum.

A FIRST FOR WIDNES CORPORATION

When Widnes Corporation ordered their first four buses in 1909 for some reason they went to Commercial Cars of Luton, rather than the local Leyland Motors. The journey must have been exciting taking four days for delivery from Luton to Widnes, especially as they were the first ever buses with enclosed upper decks (themselves a nightmare as the overall height of 16 feet 6 inches (5.03m) meant the men cutting tree branches and avoiding overhanging buildings en route).

Each machine cost the stupendous sum of £844 (the drivers were paid just over £1 per week) but in the first six months April to September 1909 the Town Council should have been pleased as over 15,000 passengers were carried, which even allowing for the novelty factor, really made the exercise worthwhile, especially as the nominal seating capacity was only 34. Two more followed, but the tranche had varying fortunes: Nos 1 and 2 were withdrawn 1915, thriftily the body of 2 was re-used on a later

chassis, 3 and 4 were withdrawn in 1919, and the chassis were converted to truck use, again the body of no 4 was reused, while 5 and 6 both single deckers seating 30 were new in June 1912 and lasted until 1920 – itself saying much for the chassis as a life over five years was almost unknown for such early machines.

The location and date of the photograph from the collection of C. Carter is said to be Irwell Street, West Bank in April 1911.

RETURN OF THE CAMBRIDGE TERROR!

Topical Series—Published by the Cambridge Picture Post Card Co.

CAMBRIDGE TRANSITION

The Cambridge Motor Bus Company died a death fairly quickly being unable to compete with the incumbent (but terminally ill) Cambridge Tramways Company, whose 2.67 route miles remained horse drawn, the locals (gown if not town) having fought off a B.E.T. attempt to replace this with an electric system. Just two tram routes were worked from Senate House to Newmarket Road and Christ's College to near the Cambridge Railway Station. On 1 August 1907 a new bus operator, the Ortona Motor Company owned by J.B. Walford, started operations running in direct opposition to the tramways, but extending their routes not only to the station entrance but over the river to New Chesterton. As both these postcards were dated 1907 it would seem the buses were not without their enemies but the trams are also hardly better. The motor vehicles in the drawings are certainly of interest to us. The single-decker was one of three, registered BN 139, BN 275/6 which were originally purchased in 1905/6 by Lancashire United Tramways but they could not make them pay and returned them to the manufacturers, Scott-Stirling in October 1906, who sold them on very quickly to Ortona. Scott-Stirling had made a relatively successful albeit brief incursion into London traffic but expired in 1908. The double-decker was a 34-seat Maudslay powered by a White and Poppe 35-45hp engine, really up-to-date in having an automatic carburettor but also purchased second-hand. The practice of having passengers sitting by the driver – surely a relic of stagecoach travel – was to long outlast the vehicles.

CAMBRIDGE UP TO DATE!

Topical Series—Published by the Cambridge Picture Post Card Co.

The Commercial Cars, Limited.

A NEW ATTRACTION FOR BUXTON ! ! !

MOTOR TOURS

For Residents and Visitors.

Road and Rail Pleasure Trips by Motor Char-a-banc and Train over the "Toy" Railway running through the beautiful

MANIFOLD VALLEY

Every MONDAY, WEDNESDAY & SATURDAY,

Until September 25th,

A service of well-appointed Char-a-Bancs will run between Buxton and Hulme End. The Cars will run from the Market Place at the times shewn below to Hulme End in connection with the Trains on the Toy Railway through the beautiful and far-famed Manifold Valley.

Char-a-banc Fares Single Journey 2/-, Return 3/-.

In connection with these Tours, Cheap Return Tickets will be issued by the Railway Co. at Hulme End for the full length of the Manifold Valley Line (about 9 miles) to Waterhouses, also to Leek, and Stoke-on-Trent by the Trains and at the Fares shewn.

	From	At				From	At	
			S	**J**				
		a.m.	noon	noon			a.m.	p.m.
Motor Char-a-banc	Buxton (Market Place) ... dep.	9 20	12 0	12 0	Stoke-on-Trent ... ... dep.	...	4 5
	Hulme End ... ... arr.	10 20	1 0	1 0	Leek ... ... "	...	4 45
					Waterhouses ... ... arr.	...	5 15
Toy Railway	Hulme End ... ... dep.	10 35	1 35	1 50	" ... ... dep.	11 30	5 20
	Ecton (Warslow)	10 39	1 39	1 54	Sparrowlee	11 35	5 25
	Butterton	10 42	1 42	1 57	Beeston Tor	11 44	5 34
	Wetton Mill	10 49	1 49	2 4	Grindon	11 47	5 37
	Thor's Cave	10 53	1 53	2 8	Thor's Cave	11 52	5 42
	Grindon	10 58	1 58	2 13	Wetton Mill	11 56	5 46
	Beeston Tor	11 1	2 1	2 16	Butterton	12 3	5 58
	Sparrowlee	11 10	2 10	2 25	Ecton (Warslow)	12 6	5 56
	Waterhouses ... ... arr.	11 15	2 15	2 30	Hulme End ... ... arr.	12 10	6 0
North Stafford Railway	Waterhouses ... ... dep.	11 35	2 30	...	" " ... ... dep.	1 15	6 15
	Leek ... ... arr.	12 5	3 0	...	Buxton (Market Place) ... arr.	2 15	7 15
	Stoke-on-Trent ... ... "	1 E 8	...	...			

E—Saturdays 2 18. S—Saturdays only. J—Mondays & Wednesdays only.

Return fare from Hulme End to Waterhouses	1/3
" " " " " " Leek	1/8
" " " " " " Stoke-on-Trent	2/6

Children under 12 years of age, Half-price.

The Railway Tickets will be available for Passengers to alight from or join the Train at any of the halts on the Manifold Valley Line.

Cambridge Circus, London, W.C., September 1st, 1909.   **The Commercial Cars, Limited.**

HARRY LOCKETT, PRINTER, HANLEY.

This leaflet, a rare survivor, is full of interest, not least because we have a 'Motor Char-à-banc' manufacturer (CommerCars) operating as an ordinary carrier. I would imagine for a courting couple from the Buxton district wanting to see the potteries of Stoke-on-Trent this would make a marvellous day's excursion, with the excitement of a char-à-banc ride for the first stretch, then the polished and really well cared for train to take you through what must have been a beautiful ride, then the train to Stoke and back again. Maybe they would cut out the 'main line' train as it appears many people got off at Waterhouses or Leek and rambled. Incidentally, where did that North Staffs. Railway engine hide for an hour on the Saturdays? (Courtesy Transport Ticket Society, their Historical Document No.11)

DAY TRIPS BEFORE AND AFTER THE FIRST WORLD WAR

Smith and Sons of Wigan were a well known proprietor of wagonettes and other horse drawn vehicles. This is a true four-horse charabanc, and on this Sunday School outing circa 1900 at least thirty bodies are present. Normally a day trip would be limited to no more than twenty miles – this being the horse's endurance, although back then 10 miles sufficed for a total change of scenery in that area. (Courtesy Wigan Heritage Service)

This photograph tells us this is Copps Coaches No. 1 party on 3 September 1906, presumably to or from the Clarence Hotel. Where or which one is another mystery!

Four years later on 16 June 1910, a Colwill's coach party is ready for departure at Ilfracombe.

My wife and I spent some long hours trying to date this photograph of a wagonette and decide what the party were doing. We concluded either cricket or tennis and the motorcycle in the background bottom right suggests the 1920s.

Shown as being near Preston, this delightful family study may be a long way from a charabanc or coach – but I have included it to illustrate the alternative.

Memorandum of Agreement made the 28th day of November 1912 Between THE LONDON GENERAL OMNIBUS COMPANY LIMITED (hereinafter for itself its successors or assigns called "the London General") of the one part and THE WORCESTER ELECTRIC TRACTION COMPANY LIMITED

(hereinafter for itself and its respective successors and assigns called "the Traction Company") of the other part.

WHEREBY IT IS AGREED as follows :—

1. The Traction Company will not at any time directly or indirectly work or be concerned in the working of motor buses within a 30-mile radius of Charing Cross.

This Clause shall not prevent the Traction Company from holding shares or securities of the Company which it is proposed to form for the purpose of holding shares of the Metropolitan Electric Tramways Limited and the London United Tramways Limited or in either of those Companies or in the British Automobile Traction Company Limited or in the South Metropolitan Electric Tramways and Lighting Company Limited or in the London General or in the Gravesend & Northfleet Electric Tramways Limited.

2. The London General may work as they see fit within the said radius but will not at any time directly or indirectly work or be concerned in the working of motor omnibuses outside the said radius of 30 miles from Charing Cross on any of the present tramway or light railway routes of the Traction Company or within a radius of 5 miles from any terminus thereof.

MEMORANDUM OF AGREEMENT 28 NOVEMBER 1912

This document copy, which I obtained in a bundle of papers at a flea market 40 or more years ago must be one of the rarest in my collection, for as can be seen it lays down geographical parameters within which The London General Omnibus Company Ltd and The Worcester Electric Traction Company Ltd could or could not work. The W.E.T. Co. was banned from working motor buses within a 30-mile radius of Charing Cross, and conversely the 'General' were not allowed to work motor omnibuses on any of the present tramway routes of the Traction company. The other clauses are of equal interest.

2

3. This Agreement shall continue in force **for 30 years from** the date hereof and thereafter from year to year unless and until determined by either party by six calendar months' notice.

IN WITNESS whereof the parties hereto have hereunto set their hands and seals the day and year first above written.

The Common Seal of THE LONDON GENERAL OMNIBUS COMPANY LIMITED was hereunto affixed pursuant to a Resolution of the Board in the presence of—

} *Directors*

Secretary.

The Common Seal of **THE WORCESTER ELECTRIC TRACTION COMPANY LIMITED** was hereunto affixed pursuant to a Resolution of the Board in the presence of—

} *Directors.*

Secretary.

BRIGHT IDEAS

It is probably true to say that the great days of Britain were the latter half of the 19th century and the first decade of the 20th. These were also the days of inventors as well as entrepreneurs; as many of the inventions were unsuccessful (if not to say half-soaked) the magazine *"Punch"* found a wonderful field for satire. This appeared in 1912; the derivation from tram cow-catchers (themselves an ingenious arrangement) is obvious and escalators were the latest 'in thing' in London and very posh shops in the provinces.

IT HAS BEEN SUGGESTED IN PARLIAMENT THAT SOME SORT OF COW-CATCHER SHOULD BE ATTACHED TO MOTOR-'BUSES TO PREVENT ACCIDENTS. WHY NOT COMBINE IT WITH A MOVING STAIRCASE?

LONG AGO AND FAR AWAY

HF 115 was first registered with Wallasey C.B.0 in 1913 and had a Daimler CC chassis powered by the 'Silent Knight' 4 cylinder sleeve valve engine developing 40hp. A cone clutch was 'state of the art' at the time, although the chain driven gearbox was to be superseded during the war.

But the most important fact about this advertisement is that it appeared early in 1914 ie before the war to end all wars. It will be seen that the operator never relied on the relatively short touring season but also ran not only a coach booking office, but acted as a London & North Western Railway parcels agent in the days when the railway was the method of transporting everything from tramcar bodies to daffodils.

LONDON GENERAL WITH A DIFFERENCE

Rather than show the usual front ¾ view of B class buses, here courtesy of P.J. Norris, we have three views of the back of a K class bus as built, chosen to show the staircase and seating arrangements. The first fleet number of this class K1 (LU 8231) was supplied in August 1919 and by 1926 including variants the class totalled 1132. Many of them ran contemporaneously with the B model, the K having the advantage of being the first LGOC design to have the driver seated alongside the engine, thus increasing the number of seats to 22 in the saloon, 24 outside; although wooden seats were still de rigeur, as were solid tyres, later a few single-deckers were converted to pneumatics. The two 'industrial' scenes are within Brush Coachworks (although curiously the workman is a different chap in each); the third is on a test run near the AEC works. K1 was built on an AEC 30hp chassis with an L.G.O.C. body, running when new on route 11 ex-Hammersmith Garage a good testing

ground. In all 285 bodies were built by Brush; my presumption is that K1 was sent to their works to show the company what was required. A number of details indicate the bus had seen some service, Brush supplying their first new vehicle in 1920.

The 'K' class, as the first forward-control (driver beside engine) design to be built for use in London, was particularly well scrutinised by the Metropolitan Police before this licence plate was issued. It was at the Police behest that solid tyres, open staircase and top, very tight weight restrictions and most of all a fully exposed driver's cab were retained, this latter until 1932.

ALL IN THE DAY'S WORK : *Some Moments with a Girl 'Bus Conductor.*

Friendly Tips and Advice for the Novice

Before the morning start is made the old hands bestow on her much advice anent the snares and pitfalls that beset her path

Collecting Fares on the Upper Deck

"Sea-legs" are required for this. It is no easy task for a novice to deliver tickets and keep her balance on a swaying 'bus proceeding at full speed

The Retort Courteous

She is an adept at the Parthian shot. "Hussies, I call 'em," says Mrs. Brown

Checking the Way Bills at Victoria

In the station yard at Victoria when the 'buses arrive there is a rush for the hut where the way bills are examined

Guiding the 'Bus in a Fog

In a fog she walks in front and follows the tram-lines, if there are any, and illuminates the way for the driver with her lamp →

A Corner of the Canteen

← Ten minutes' wait at Victoria gives our girl conductors time for a cup of tea at the canteen there and a chat with the drivers

IMPRESSIONS OF LONDON'S 'BUS CONDUCTRESSES

Sketched by D. Macpherson, 1917

CHAPTER 3
THE LAZY, HAZY, CRAZY DAYS
OF SUMMER 1918-1928

As a writer I was surprised to find articles giving some statistics over the number of char-à-bancs. Unlike today, official figures in the 1920s are almost impossible to ascertain, largely because the licensing of motor vehicles (buses or coaches) was entirely in the hands of local councils – mainly guided by their Watch Committees. Since the following item is drawn from *Commercial Motor*, the accuracy – despite the various figures for visitors quoted – is not to be doubted.

VULCANS

A Few Facts About the Daily Invasion of Motor Traffic in Derbyshire in 1920/1

Every day in the season at least 1,000 persons visit Buxton by motor char-à-bancs. This is really a very modest estimate, for when a representative of The Commercial Motor, after obtaining figures of from 1,000 to 3,000 from the local char-a-bancs proprietors, approached the Buxton Information Bureau, he was told that the incursionists would number from 3,000 to 5,000 a day.

There could be no more remarkable testimony of the popularity of the motor coach, and the great pity is that visitors by motor charabancs have not, by their conduct, won the goodwill of the city fathers, who, of course, are out to maintain the tone and dignity, and foster the prosperity of the town of their affections. The director of the Information Bureau told us that, as a result of the unseemly behaviour of charabanc trippers the previous week, no less than 20 residents left the town. We asked the director of the Information Bureau what was the attitude of the local authorities to the motor coach, and their view was expressed as hostile, the reasons given being the way trippers conduct themselves – shouting when passing through the town, general impropriety, and demonstrating to all that they are not Pussyfoots.

Buxton itself has a fleet of about 20 vehicles, about four of which are 30-seaters, the remainder being 15-seaters. It is not often that one finds a town with so big a proportion of small vehicles. This feature, one feels, is intended to make the Buxton coaches distinctive and, to some extent, exclusive by making and encouraging small and select parties. The steepness of the hills may also have been a deciding factor. The smaller coach certainly makes a greater appeal to the eye than the larger one. Most of them have pneumatics on the front wheels and solids on the rear; and at one garage we were informed that it was intended to experiment with the use of pneumatics on the four wheels of the larger coaches.

Amongst the conditions which a motor coach in Buxton must fulfil are: the paintwork and upholstery must be maintained in good condition, the car must be able to ascend a gradient of 1 in 5, and descend, pulling up half-way down. This hill, which is typical of the many dangerous ones throughout the district, is an excellent test. We were told the gradient was actually 1 in 4, and we noticed it has a nasty bend at the foot, where Messrs W.R. Sanders' (1920) Ltd garage is located! The concern, by the way, have a charabanc which is permanently stationed at one of the local hydro institutions. It is a tribute to the efficient state of repair in which the cars are kept when one is informed that hardly a single accident has been known to occur on the Buxton roads during the last 12 months. Safe running – a very necessary precaution where treacherous hills are numerous. The pneumatic-tyred cars always carry spare covers to the side of the coach; whilst Messrs Hodgkinson have theirs neatly fixed at the rear of the body. Daimlers, Vulcan, Lancias, and Karriers are amongst the locally owned fleets.

Messrs Sanders perpetuate the old stage coach colours, having the vehicles finished in primrose and black. The weather; this summer [presumably 1920], has not been all that could be desired from the point of view of motor coach touring – on the day of our visit not a single coach turned out, owing to the inclemency of the weather: Business is very largely dependent on the weather, and bookings for the best part are made singly. Fares work out in the vicinity of between 1¾d and 2½d per mile – quite a moderate figure taking the contour of the country into consideration and the quality of the coaches in the service. Thus we were supplied with the following prices: 30 seater chara, 4s. per mile; 15 seater, 2s 6d. per mile.

Local proprietors have not experienced any of the ill-effects of the resumption of excursion trains.

The modern motor coach made its appearance in Buxton about 1910, and has developed in easy stages since. The 15-seater with pneumatics is a favourite car in the town. From Buxton the principal tours are to the Dukeries, Haddon Hall, Chatsworth, Dovedale, Castleton, Alton Towers, Dane Valley, Miller's Dale, Rudyard Lake, Manifold Valley Monsal Dale, Ludchurch, and also to the famous Cat and Fiddle Inn.

Messrs W.R. Sanders (1920) Ltd, issue a special weekly programme of tours, starting at 10.45am, 2.30 and 2.45pm, the fares for which are between 5s and 10s 6d, which the routes are carefully detailed on their announcements.

Unfortunately, it was axiomatic that the greater the traffic the greater the likelihood of accidents. Few in this period were reported other than locally, although I have found notes of passengers (presumably well oiled) who fell out of char-à-bancs, and of a young girl whose hat had blown off her head, in trying to retrieve it she fell under the vehicle, fortunately, perhaps, dying very quickly. Other entries refer to pedestrians being knocked about with injuries varying from 'minor' to rather serious, especially one poor chap who was forced through a glass shop front by an errant vehicle whose driver did a runner, being caught later and taken to court. Alas, I could not trace the result, but perhaps he had had a jug or two of ale. A 1921 report lays no blame on the char-à-bancs.

However one passenger dying on a char-à-banc was thought to be worthy of note in a local newspaper. The story is tragically simple, but fully understandable to anyone who served in Malaya or Egypt even in the 1950s, as the tablets we were given seemed to have little more effect than make us feel rotten ... some men gave up and suffered from the shakes even into their 50s.

MAN'S FATAL TRIP TO HEREFORD

Died While Riding On a char-à-banc

The story of a tragic char-à-banc trip to Hereford was told at an inquest at Pontlottyn on Alfred Prosser (35), single, of Thomas Street, Pontlottyn.

David John Prosser, brother, said he and deceased were members of a party who went for a trip on Sunday to Hereford. They had dinner and tea, and when about to start on the return journey deceased complained of an attack of malaria.

Deceased was alive when they reached Pandy, but was found to be dead when they reached Pontlottyn at night. Deceased served in the Army and was in Egypt for about four years. He was discharged in February, 1919, but had suffered from severe attacks of malaria since.

Said he Felt "Rotten"

William Stribley said deceased complained to him of feeling "rotten." He could hardly stop shaking.

Louis Gardiner, another member, said deceased rested on him and fell asleep. Witness presumed when he tried to wake him at Tredegar that he was still sleeping, but on reaching Pontlottyn he discovered he was dead.

Dr Jones, who had attended deceased, attributed death to heart failure, accelerated by Malaria, contracted on active service.

The Coroner said there was no suggestion of excessive drinking, and recorded a verdict in accordance with the medical evidence.

[Pontlottyn is just south of Rhymney, within Caerphilly district and was best known in the 1920s for the quality of its high grade coal]

This next accident was one of a number which showed a lack of familiarity with the movements of buses, of particular interest here is the note that the deceased had sat next to the driver on the front seat; a few char-a-bancs had the driver seated in the centre of the front bench seat, although it would be a strange man who was not distracted by having a pretty girl on each side!

SAD FATALITY

Cripple Killed By Motor bus Near Crickhowell

Hedley John Rees (31), a native of the village of Llangrwyney, two miles from Crickhowell, was knocked down by a G.W.R. motor bus on Saturday evening and killed instantly. The tragic occurrence happened only 20 yards or so from deceased's home and caused consternation in the locality.

An inquest was held at the Bell Inn, Llangrwyney on Monday evening before the Coroner for the district (Mr R.H.A. Davies). Chief Inspector James Lidster represented the G.W. Railway Company.

Benjamin Rees, father of deceased, said his son was a cripple, having had a paralytic stroke when a boy. He had almost lost the use of his left side.

William Bobbin, the driver of the 6.10pm motor bus from Crickhowell, said deceased was a passenger by the car from Crickhowell on Saturday and sat by him on the front seat. At Llangrwyney he got down and after exchanging a few friendly words disappeared. Shortly afterwards the conductor gave him the signal to start, but as he proceeded he felt a bump, and got the signal to stop which he did. When he got down from the car he saw the body of the deceased in the road; the left back wheel of the car had gone over him.

Pryce Pugh, the conductor, said that previous to giving the signal to start he walked along the left side of the car to see if the way was clear.

Gladys Edwards, of Charles Street, Tredegar, said she saw deceased standing between the motor bus and the wall. When the bus started he swayed and fell against the side.

W.G. James, proprietor of the Cardboard Mills, Llangrwyney, said deceased was employed as a general hand at the mills. When apparently quite well he would complain of severe pains in the back and almost fell down.

John Griffiths said deceased when working with him unexpectedly fell down on several occasions.

The Coroner said that what the witnesses Mr James and Mr Griffiths had said was probably the solution of the accident.

A verdict of "Death by misadventure" was returned, the driver and conductor of the motor 'bus being completely exonerated from all blame.

From *The Hereford Times*, 24 August 1922

My final accident here is not on a true char-à-banc but involved a Great Western omnibus. In the case of this unfortunate G.W.R. inspector, presumably the handbrake would be a lever without any form of detent or ratchet, on some vehicles (one Seddon I remember for this) the tension on the hand-brake varied according to the load on the machine and it could slacken on its own as the weight came off. The attendance of the G.W.R. officials showed how well regarded Mr Adkins was thought of by the Great Western staff.

THE ACCIDENT

The accident happened with startling suddenness. Deceased and others were standing talking in the road near the station, when a car suddenly moved down the incline, and before anything could be done deceased was crushed practically to death against another car.

He sustained a fractured skull and broken arm and other injuries. He was attended by the ambulance brigade and by Dr. Lewis, but died almost immediately.

The Inquest

The inquest was held on Tuesday afternoon, before Mr W.W. Brodie, Deputy Coroner, and a jury.

Inspector Dalton represented the G.W.R. Company, and Mr A.J. Williams, organising secretary of the N.U.R. watched the interests of the men affected.

George Sidney Reynolds, the driver of the car which ran on and crushed the deceased against a second car standing about five yards lower down on the gradient, said he had fastened it by means of the hand-brake.

While having a conversation with deceased and Inspector Tipping, he noticed the car moving away. He shouted a warning and tried to board it, so as to stop its movement, but was too late.

Driver Exonerated

Inspector Tipping advanced the theory that the pressure of the crowd into the station, and the vibration and the effect of the wet weather on the brake, caused it to slip off.

The jury returned a verdict of 'Accidental Death,' and exonerated the driver; but recommended that further precautionary measures should be taken. Sympathy with the family of the deceased was expressed by Inspector Dalton, Mr. F.D. Beck (stationmaster), and the Coroner associated himself with the expression on behalf of the jury. Deceased lost his wife only last March and she was buried at Penzance. One little girl, seven years old last Monday, is left to mourn her loss.

The Funeral

The funeral took place at Hereford Cemetery on Thursday, the body having been removed thither by rail on Tuesday. The service was conducted by the Vicar of Holy Trinity, the Rev. H.M. Fowler. The mourners were Mr And Mrs Adkins (father and mother), the four brothers – Alfred (and Mrs A. Adkins), Harry George, and Charlie, Mr R. Bridle (brother-in-law), Mr Bullet, chief of the G. W. motor department (Paddington), Mt:

Tipping (Inspector, Plymouth), Mr Dance (head motor driver; Abergavenny) and Mrs Dance, Mr Hatch (Neath), Mr Willett (Slough), Mr Budgford (Slough), Inspector Phillips (representing the G.W.R. at Hereford, and others.

The inscription on the coffin was "Reginald Joseph Adkins. Died August 12. Aged 37 years."

There were wreaths from the bereaved parents and sons; mother; sister, and brother, Penzance; to my dearest daddy from a lonely child, Peggy; from Ted, Nell and children; Mr Alfred Greenland, Hereford; Mr and Mrs T. Bailey and Mr and Mrs Allan Bailey, Hereford; Mr and Mrs Caldecott and family; Mr and Mrs Norman and family, Hereford; Inspector and Mrs Webb, Carmarthen; Mr and Mrs Dance and Mr and Mrs Tipping; Cousin Emily and Henry Jones; Inspector and Mrs Welsh and Mr and Mrs Budgford, Neath; Detective inspector Leybourne, Fishguard Harbour; Inspectors Willett and Hatch, Slough; G.W.R. Staff; Abergavenny; G.W.R. staff, Carmarthen; G.W.R. staff; Ammanford; G.W.R. motor staff, Penzance; G.W.R, motor staff, Neath; G.W.R. headquarters motor staff, Paddington; Mr Davies, Pontrilas; and Mrs Jackson, Abergavenny.   From *The Hereford Journal*, 19 August 1922

COLLINGWOOD TRANSPORT CO.

The Collingwood Transport Co. have four new Daimler coaches, each seating 28 passengers. Since 1 April it has not missed a single day's touring to Blackpool. Not even bad weather has interfered with the unbroken succession of tours and although there have been many days when, perhaps, the number of passengers has hardly justified, on the grounds of economy, the running of the coach, yet the company can justly claim never to have failed in a single contract with the travelling fraternity. This is a feature of which the company might justly be proud, for it is, certainly, no mean accomplishment.

The application of ideals to business is one of those pet theories that is frequently talked about, but rarely practised. The Collingwood Transport Co. is an exception. Since 1 April they have ploughed the lonely furrow and, although it is difficult to assess the success or failure of this branch of the enterprise in the cold terms of s. d. there is no doubt they have established goodwill with their clientele.

Every morning a 1920 Daimler on the Liverpool-Blackpool service leaves Nelson Garage promptly at 9.15am, St John's Lane, Liverpool, at 9.35am, and the "Black Bull", Aintree, at 10am, thence via Ormskirk and Preston to Blackpool. The return fare is 16s 6d, 9s single. When return tickets are purchased the return journey can be made any day, subject to the date being declared at the time of booking. The return journey from Blackpool is made at 6pm sharp.

By a Collingwood coach a Commercial Motor representative recently travelled to Blackpool. There was room enough for everybody and the luggage, to 28lb was allowed free – in the compartment at the rear. In the past, char-à-bancs parties have – sometimes quite unjustly – been associated with indecorous conduct. The fact that the majority of the Collingwood passengers were strangers to each other did not subdue their sociability, and on neither the outward nor return journey was there any incident which could in any way be construed other than to the credit of the service.

Scores of other char-à-bancs, of all makes, from all places, were encountered on the way, several of them outside inns on the wayside, and at Blackpool one could not lift the eye without immediately focussing around half a dozen flitting in all directions. Huddersfield, Lees, Burslem, Manchester, Atherton, Stockton-on-Trent, Halifax, Keighley, Rawtenstall,

Bury; Rochdale, Wigan, Southport, Burnley, Widnes, St Helens, Todmorden and Stockport, they came, some so overcrowded as to arouse one's sympathies for the unfortunate passengers they conveyed. There was more motor traffic on the the the road from Preston to Blackpool than we have ever seen on a single road before, on the return journey particularly.

Picnicking parties out for the day dearly love a splash of excitement and as showing how they spoil for a race with rival coaches on the road, not far from Clifton, where, by the way, there is a dangerous bend in the road, at which in the evening a motor ambulance was situated, we noticed four coaches immediately in front. From the Collingwood machine, which was the fifth, it was possible to observe the gesticulation being exchanged, accompanied no doubt by verbal reiteration between passengers of the two coaches just in front. Our expectations of a race were not fulfilled, coach No. 4 discreetly drawing up by the roadside a little further along the road. Discretion was the better part of valour!

Blackpool was entered near the South Shore and the coach proceeded along the promenade to the garage at the Imperial Hotel in the direction of the cliffs. In every respect the journey is one which would appeal to the man of the work-a-day world, who, one is afraid, has yet to learn of the pleasures of the broad highway for their comfortable, health-giving and not fatiguing travelling, combed with expedition.

The Collingwood trips from Liverpool are really an express service, no stops on the way excepting those already enumerated being authorised. Before the complete success, or failure, of so commendable an enterprise as train-like passenger motors can be adjudged, time must necessarily elapse, but there can be little doubt, now that railway fares are advanced, that the preference for the open road will be accentuated as a congenial, and at the same time, economical alternative.

The promoters of the Collingwood daily service are optimistic as to the results. They are giving it a thorough trial until the end of the summer season, by which time perhaps it will have been proved that the Collingwood Transport Co. have anticipated the need of the public for punctual, regular and efficient travelling by road.

From: *The Commercial Motor Archive*, 24 August 1920

Openbaar gemaakt

PATENT SPECIFICATION

160,871

Application Date: Nov. 12, 1919. No. 27,996/19.

Complete Left: Aug. 12, 1920.

Complete Accepted: Mar. 14, 1921.

PROVISIONAL SPECIFICATION.

Improvements in Life-guards for Motor Buses and the like Road Vehicles.

We, CHARLES WILLIAM MALLINS, of Blundellsands Road West, Blundellsands, near Liverpool, in the County of Lancaster, General Manager, Liverpool Corporation Tramways, and JOHN PAUL BARKER, of 18, Elgin Drive, Wallasey, in the County of Chester, Engineer, do hereby declare the nature of this invention to be as follows:—

This invention relates to life-guards for motor buses, motor-cars and the like road vehicles of all description, and the object is to provide at the front and sides of such vehicles a practically continuous arrangement of guards and fenders, which are adapted to prevent a person who may fall in front of the vehicle from being run over by the wheels.

According to the invention the continuous guard comprises:—

A front guard carried by brackets from the front axle.

Hoods, one for each of the front wheels, of the mud-guard type but extending over the front of the wheel and depending as nearly as practicable to the road, and terminating in a bifurcation which forms a double guard for the rear wheel.

Side guards, one at each side of the vehicle extending longitudinally from the central part of the inside of the front wheel and terminating in a bifurcation which forms a double guard for the rear wheel.

The front guard is shaped at the sides so as to permit the angling of the front wheels in steering and extends laterally sufficiently to project in front of either of the front wheels when turned outwardly so as to leave no gap between the front guard and the wheel hood; the front guard may be provided with rubber or the like buffers to mitigate shock and is arranged so as to leave as little clearance as prac-

ticable between the bottom edge of the guard and the ground.

The front guard is carried by suitable brackets from the fixed portions of the front axle so that it is maintained at a constant distance from the ground.

Each of the hoods in general shape and configuration resembles a mud-guard such as is fitted to cycles but is of course of stronger construction and wider than a cycle mud-guard; the hood extends over the top of the wheel and the front portion depends vertically, very nearly to the ground; the hood is carried by means of stays which may conveniently extend radially from a flange on the stub axle so that each hood moves with its wheel.

The side guards consist preferably of a series of metallic rods or slats suitably pitched so as to extend from the lower slat, which is as near the ground as practicable to the body of the vehicle. The front edges of the slats are just inside the front wheel and extend to a vertical line passing through the axis of the front wheel and are there carried by suitable brackets from the front axle.

The slats extend to, but are just clear of the outside edge of the rear wheel. A second set of slats linable with the slats above described and attached to the latter, are adapted so as to extend in rear and just inside of the rear wheel, their rear ends being carried by a bracket from the rear axle. The rear wheel thus is doubly guarded by the bifurcated portions of the side guard.

In some cases the bifurcated portion of the guard which screens the rear wheel, may be made separate from the side portion of the guard, the rear portion of the guard being made preferably of sheet metal bent to **U** shaped configuration,

---

160,871

the legs of the **U** extending rearwardly on either side of the wheel. The **U** shaped portion is pivotally carried from the vehicle at a convenient point inside the locus of the track—say from one of the arms carrying the usual rear wheel mud-guard—and is spring controlled, in such manner that in event of an obstruction striking the **U** shaped portion of the guard, the latter would be angled outwardly, throwing the obstruction clear of the wheels. In this modification, the side and rear portions of the guard would be so arranged that it would be impossible for an obstruction to pass between the rear portion of the side guard and the front of the **U** guard.

It will be seen that any one colliding with, or being knocked down by, or falling in front of the vehicle is prevented by the front guard from passing under the vehicle, and if pushed from the side of the guard is prevented by the hoods from being run over by either of the front wheels, and is then sheared away laterally by the sloping side guards clear of the

rear wheels, and further, that should a child by any means be passed over by the front guard it would be prevented from being run over by either of the back wheels by the action of the inner branch of the bifurcated side guard.

As the several guards are carried from parts of the vehicles which are maintained at a fixed distance from the ground the distance of the bottom edges from the ground does not vary as is the case where the guards are carried from sprung portions of the vehicles.

The apparatus is neat and effective, does not interfere with the working of the vehicle and has no projecting parts liable to damage by passing vehicles.

The details of construction may be varied in accordance with the design and size of the vehicles.

Dated this 11th day of November, 1919.

SLOAN & LLOYD BARNES,
Chartered Patent Agents,
34, Castle Street, Liverpool.

COMPLETE SPECIFICATION.

Improvements in Life-guards for Motor Buses and the like Road Vehicles.

We, CHARLES WILLIAM MALLINS, of Blundellsands Road West, Blundellsands, near Liverpool, in the County of Lancaster, General Manager, Liverpool Corporation Tramways, and JOHN PAUL BARKER, of 18, Elgin Drive, Wallasey, in the County of Chester, Engineer, do hereby declare the nature of this invention and in what manner the same is to be performed, to be particularly described and ascertained in and by the following statement:—

This invention relates to life-guards for motor buses, motor-cars and the like road vehicles of all descriptions, and the object is to provide at the front and sides of such vehicles a practically continuous arrangement of guards and fenders, which are adapted to prevent a person who may fall from the front of the vehicle from being run over by the wheels.

According to the invention the continuous guard comprises in combination:—

Hoods, one for each of the front wheels, of the mud-guard type but extending over

the front of the wheel and depending as nearly as practicable to the road, and side guards, one at each side of the vehicle extending longitudinally from the central part of the inside of the front wheel and terminating in a pivoted bifurcation which forms a double guard for the rear wheel.

The invention is illustrated in the accompanying drawings, in which:—

Fig. 1 is an elevation, the wheels, which occupy the respective positions shown in dotted lines, being removed to show more clearly the parts behind;

Fig. 2 is a plan, partly in section on the line II, II, of Fig. 1;

Fig. 3 is a fragmentary plan showing the movable guard in its outward position;

Fig. 4 is a part front elevation showing a portion of the front guard and the hood of the near side front wheel in its normal position in full lines and in its outward position in dotted lines.

The front guard A is carried by suitable brackets from the front axle d^1, or from the front of the chassis, and consists

The originators of this Patent (27,996 of 14 March,1921 were C.H. Mallins, the General Manager of. Liverpool Corporation Tramways and of his 'road engineer' John Paul Barker. Tramcars had to have life-guards of one sort or another; the adverse publicity following a series of child deaths had forced this on the tram companies back in steam days, while a dog running between the wheelsets could easily derail the car.

This patent was first propounded back in August 1920 and shows quite an advanced bus for that period, but with their straight high stepping chassis vehicles like this were inherently dangerous to pedestrians, particularly drunks and elderly people unsteady on their feet. The "invention relates to life-guards for motor buses, motor-cars and the like road vehicles of all description, and the object is to provide at the front and sides of such vehicles a practically continuous arrangement of guards and fenders, which are adapted to prevent a person who may be knocked down by, or collide with, or fall in front of the vehicle from being run over by the wheels."

At its simplest we have a 'cow-catcher', a hood over each front wheel which moves with the wheel, side-guards and rear wheel deflectors which as the body bounces from the front, along the sides, effectively push him or her away from the rear wheels. Whether they would then be squidged between the apparatus and the granite kerb-stones is not mentioned.

Rudimentary dog-grates remained in use on some buses and coaches until relatively recently, but of course our pedestrians of today are far more blasé about the presence of motor vehicles.

---

4   160,871

of a lower member a^1 which is just clear of the ground and an upper member a^2 which is bent to the shape shown in the plan view. Bars a^3 connect the members a^1 and a^2 together, the whole forming a fixed guard adapted to prevent any obstruction encountered from passing under the vehicle between the front wheels.

Each front wheel is provided with a hood B, carried by stout radial stays b^2 from a flange b^3 formed on the stub axle so that the hood moves with its wheel. It will be seen that the guard A is so shaped that it extends at each side beyond the inner front edge of the hood B when the latter edge is in its outward position.

There is therefore no gap at any time between either of the hoods B and the guard A.

The inner edge of each hood B is shaped as shown at b^1, Fig. 2.

A pedestrian who may be knocked over by or may slip down in front of vehicles of this class is frequently drawn under the front wheel by the downward motion of the front portion of this wheel. The hood B prevents this and the joint effect of the hood B and the guard A is to support the pedestrian in the recumbent position and so to prevent him from being drawn under the vehicle.

Each side guard C consists of a number of metallic rods or slats such as c^1, c^2, c^3, c^4 and c^5, suitably pitched so as to extend from the lowermost slat c^1, which is as close as possible to the ground, to the body D of the vehicle. At the front end these slats are turned outwardly, and are connected to a vertical bar c^6 which in turn is secured to the fixed front axle d^1. The side guards C are parallel with the centre line of the vehicle.

In the construction illustrated, at the rear end the slats c^1 and c^2 terminate at the vertical bar c^7, which is fixed to the slat c^3, and the uppermost slat c^5 is bent down and attached to the slat c^4, the latter and the slat c^3 being rigidly attached to the flange e^1 on the rear axle E.

F is the rear mudguard which is carried by the radial stays f^1 from the flange e^1.

From the bar c^7 there may be carried outwardly and round the rear wheel, a series of slats forming a rearwardly extending bifurcated portion C^3 of the main guard C as shown in chain dotted lines Fig. 2. Preferably, however, the same result is obtained with some advantages by constructing this bifurcated portion, as shown at G, in the form of a guard pivoted on the vertical rod g^1 and a bracket

---

3   160,871

g^2 carried from the flange e^1 and laterally stiffened by an inclined stay extending to the axle E. The guard has a lower web portion g^3 and an upper bracket g^4 by which it is connected to the vertical rod g^1. The guard G also has a rearwardly extending arm g^5 connected by a spring g^6 to a fixed bracket f^2 carried from one of the stays f^1. This spring maintains the guard in its normal position, but should the guard G meet with an obstruction the spring yields and the guard moves outwardly into the position shown in Fig. 3; in this position the guard G is inclined outwardly and rearwardly and so forms an inclined surface which removes the obstruction clear of the rear wheel.

The front guard and the front wheel hoods thus serve to prevent an obstruction from passing between or under the front wheels, whilst the side guard C prevents an obstruction from passing under the vehicle from the sides, the bifurcated or pivoted guard serving to remove any obstacle from the track of the rear wheels.

The various guards may be fitted with rubber or the like pads to mitigate the effect of shock, and the details of construction may be varied in accordance with the size and class of vehicle to which the invention is applied.

Having now particularly described and ascertained the nature of our said invention and in what manner the same is to be performed, we declare that what we claim is:—

1. The improved arrangement of life guards or obstruction removers for motor buses and the like road vehicles, comprising, in combination:—A fixed front guard, and hoods on the front wheels carried by the stub axles, extending downwardly and in rear of said guard in all positions of the wheels; and side guards carried from the fixed front axle, and the rear ends of which are carried from the rear axle, said guards being parallel to the centre line of the vehicle and each having a fixed or pivoted bifurcation at the rear end extending round the front of the rear wheel; substantially as described.

2. In life guards or obstruction removers as claimed in Claim 1, a spring controlled guard pivotally carried from the rear axle and extending round the front of the rear wheel, and adapted when it meets an obstruction to angle about its pivot into a position in which it deflects the obstruction laterally clear of the wheel; substantially as described.

3. In life guards or obstruction

---

4   160,871

removers as claimed in Claim 2, arranging the spring controlled guard so that it forms a downward continuation of the front of the rear wheel mud guard; substantially as described.

4. The combination and arrangement of parts forming the improved life guards or obstruction removers for motor buses and the like road vehicles; substantially as described and illustrated in the drawings.

Dated this 11th day of August, 1920.

SLOAN & LLOYD BARNES,
Chartered Patent Agents,
34, Castle Street, Liverpool.

Redhill: Printed for His Majesty's Stationery Office, by Love & Malcomson, Ltd.—1921

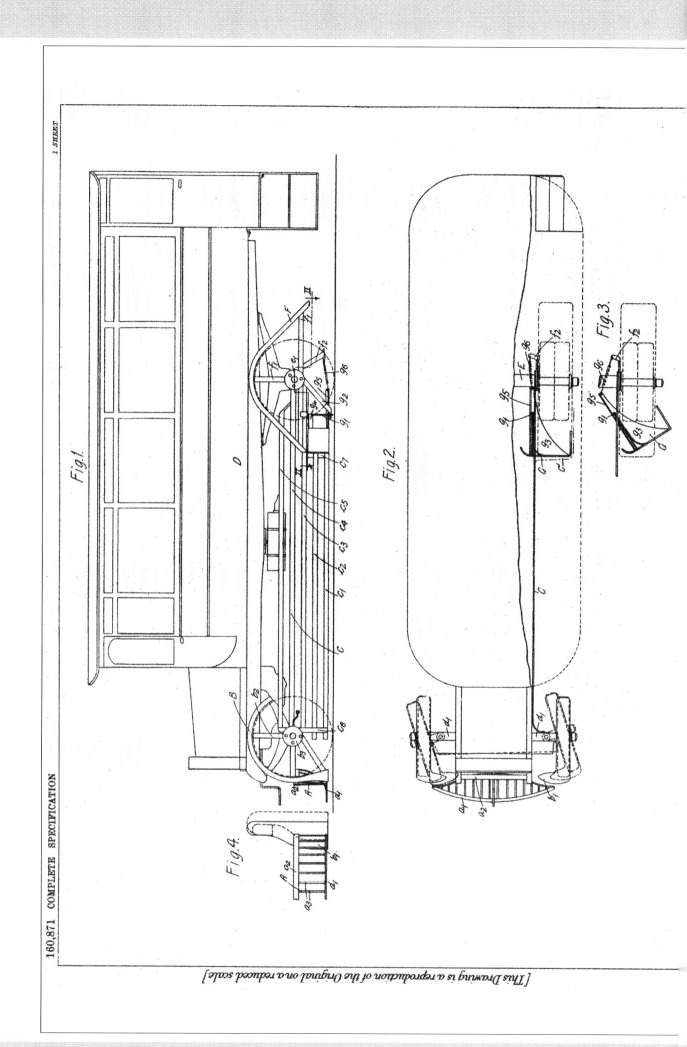

Fig.1.

Fig.2.

Fig.3.

Fig.4.

CLASS CUSTOM

Char-à-bancs Travellers are not Cheap Trippers

No-one who takes the trouble to examine the methods of various charabanc proprietors, and the results obtained, cannot fail to be impressed with the fact that financial success is tremendously dependent upon the class of custom secured and, consequently, upon the measures taken to ensure appealing to custom of a good class. This is true, particularly of the services run at seaside and other holiday resorts.

The holiday maker is often willing to spend money freely. It is not, therefore, so much a question of offering him something at a cheap rate, as of offering an occupation likely to be so enjoyable as to justify the cost. The client of the type that is worth getting wants to know when he will start and when he will get home. He makes his arrangements in advance, and does not merely join a trip on the spur of the moment.

Undoubtedly, the business of many coach proprietors is spoiled by the old and obnoxious system of touting by drivers and conductors. This process eliminates more custom than it secures. Moreover, it is almost always associated with the practice of letting the vehicle start only when it is nearly full. If chance custom is depended on one cannot say when, if ever, all the seats will be occupied, therefore, neither can one say when the trip will commence and when it will finish.

Without a doubt the way to do well out of motor coaches is to keep the vehicles smart and scrupulously clean, to see that the upkeep is so thorough that breakdowns are eliminated, to work strictly to timetable, and to conduct the business in a reasonably dignified manner which will not hurt the susceptibilities of holiday-makers who do not wish to be classified at cheap trippers.

From: *The Commercial Motor*, 20 July 1920.

NEW MOTOR 'BUS SERVICE.

Commencement Being Made This Week.

LINKING UP THE VILLAGES.

The public will be interested to hear that commencing on Wednesday (17th) the Midland "Red" motor omnibus service will be in full swing in Herefordshire.

Seven regular services are announced. The first, No. 86, runs from Hereford (High Town) to Weobley and back, with stops at Credenhill, Mansell Lacy, and Moorhampton. Each week-day, the time table shows a morning and after-noon service each way, two afternoon services on Sundays, and a Saturday evening run to Creden-hill and back.

No. 87 covers the Hereford, Clehonger, and Madley route, there being two services each way Sundays and week-days.

No. 88 goes from High Town to Ross, calling at the Callow, Much Birch, Harewood End, and Peterstow—two services each way Sundays and week-days, except Tuesdays and Fridays.

No. 89 goes to Mordiford and Fownhope, also two services on Sundays and week-days.

No. 90 connects Hereford with Leominster, and, going the Aylestone Hill route, has stops at Sutton, Bodenham, Hope-under-Dinmore, and Ford. There is one morning and one afternoon service each way on Tuesdays and Fridays.

No. 91 is the Ledbury route, with stops at Lugwardine, Dormington, Stoke Edith, and Wallers Green. On this route there are two ser-vices each way, but only on Wednesdays and Saturdays. Each week-day, however, the 'bus will run to Lugwardine and back twice.

The last route, No. 91a, is a Saturday evening service to Widemarsh Common, with five runs each way, between 7 and 9.30 o'clock.

Hereford Mercury 17 March 1920

BUSINESS – MIDLAND RED STYLE

The first world war had been and gone with Midland "Red" as one of the companies who were finding hard graft, clever advertising, and as far as possible reliable vehicles running to proper timetables, brought in the cash, as was shown by their annual returns and by any standard their divi-dend payment was excellent.

Their hunt for accommodation for their 'motor omnibuses' in Hereford, shown in the notice, was successful eventually but when their first three vehicles arrived on 17 March 1920 they had to be parked in the yard of the Black Lion hotel, 31 Bridge Street and itself a one-time coaching inn located just north of the Wye Bridge. This, incidentally, is claimed to be the most haunted inn in Hereford, with parts dating back to 1550. By all accounts conditions for the men and for maintenance were pretty awful; a special request (which being 'Midland Red' must have led to some tooth-sucking) having to be made for a hurricane lamp. This or the candles also in use near the stacks of 2-gallon petrol cans stored in the yard must have made the job interesting. Ten buses finally formed the fleet, together with licensed 15 drivers and 15 conductors.

This advertisement here from the *Hereford Mercury* Wednesday 25 February 1920, was run for at least four weeks, and it seems there was some degree of resistance against these 'Brummie off-comers'. The motor bus service was described in the issue of the *Mercury* on 17 March 1920.

CHARA PROGRESSION

Other than both scenes are in the North East and connected with railway outings these two photographs have little in common but...

The top illustration shows an early char à banc standing at a North Eastern Railway station together with railway servants in charge. The chara's transmission is by chain and more importantly each row of seats has a door on this – the offside – this having furniture typical of railway coaches. And the driver has not one or two passengers sharing a bench with him but three. The single rear lamp underslung from the body is oil fired.

The bottom photograph, also regrettably undated, shows the progression which followed a number of very unpleasant accidents where passengers spilled out of the charas on both sides and were involved in accidents; there were also well authenticated reports of the carriage-style catches being opened by children, so that the law was altered to prohibit openings on the offside. One result was that these doors were sealed up, but also in a few examples (as here) a feature was made of them. The massive headlamp was acetylene fired and the two tone horn was somewhat up-market!

Since acetylene lamps are no longer commonplace the operational method may be of interest. At its simplest calcium carbide is placed in the generator (the lower part of the lamp) and the upper reservoir is filled with water. Via a valve the water flow, and hence brightness of the lamp, is controlled quite easily. A reflector behind the flame enhances the spread of the light; but the difficulties were manifold – especially on a push bike as the water reservoir was tiny and liable to run out seemingly at a whim, whereas on an elderly car a bump in the road could upset the setting and either an enormous and flaring white light or nothing could follow. During the war many and ingenious means were employed by steam lorry operators as dipping or shrouding acetylene lamps was a problem, the heat generated could ignite paintwork very easily indeed.

AEC AND 1921

In 1921 AEC were suffering from the aftermath of the first world war with thousands of ex-WD chassis being released on the market, and without the orders from the London General Omnibus Company there seems little doubt the firm's sales would have been eroded to a point where their existence would be in doubt.

The K models shown here were a slightly desperate attempt by the company to break into the coach market during 1921. The K or 3 type chassis was as up to date as any being of sandwich construction with two 4mm thick nickel steel plates bolted to 36mm filler of prime white ash, which was both strong and resilient. The engine, type A101, was a four-cylinder job with a swept volume of 4,398cc. Built to run at a speed never exceeding 2,000rpm, this was economical on oil (at 700mpg) by virtue of using a splash system (whereby oil is thrown over by dippers) for the big ends although a pressurized supply fed the main bearings. Apparently with 'state of the art' carburettors and magnetos the compression ratio of 3.94:1 power output was 30hp at 1050rpm. Fuel consumption was to the order of 8mpg.

The one, unregistered machine was classed as a "De-Luxe Limousine Bus" and was designed to carry ten passengers in the forward 'smoking' compartment and eighteen in the enclosed rear. I do have to wonder if one or more senior designers had served in France between 1914-1918 as this dual arrangement was commonplace there with the same characteristic of having easily detachable seats in the forward bay to allow for the carriage of freight. Painted bright primrose, the interior was a confection of polished walnut and antique leather, and the whole thing was believed to be built by Eastbourne Aviation.

The batch of tourers on the other hand were on display to show their infinite variety, although none represents the 'pure' char-a-banc with which the whole market was flooded. Slightly later in design to the single car, they were classified as K but also type 501, the main difference lay in the new nominal 45hp engine of 6,785cc, although lubrication methods were identical and the normal rate of revolutions was increased to 1400rpm, at which speed 52hp could be delivered. Unfortunately, sales were still nothing special and reliance on LGOC orders remained.

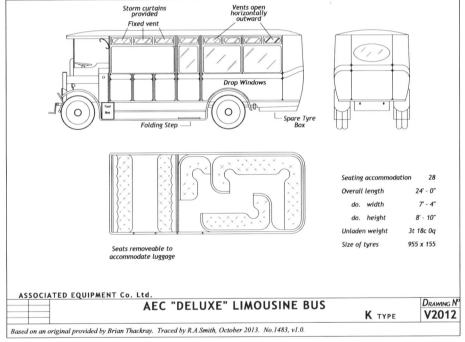

Storm curtains provided
Fixed vent
Vents open horizontally outward
Drop Windows
Tool Box
Folding Step
Spare Tyre Box

Seats removeable to accommodate luggage

Seating accommodation	28
Overall length	24' - 0"
do. width	7' - 4"
do. height	8' - 10"
Unladen weight	3t 18c 0q
Size of tyres	955 x 155

ASSOCIATED EQUIPMENT Co. Ltd.

AEC "DELUXE" LIMOUSINE BUS

K TYPE

DRAWING Nº V2012

Based on an original provided by Brian Thackray. Traced by R.A.Smith, October 2013. No.1483, v1.0.

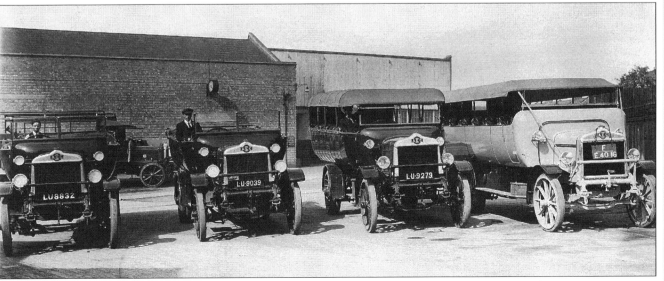

THE BEGINNER

This article first appeared in the East Kent Road Car Company's staff magazine during August 1947 and represents pure 'folk memory'. We cannot recover material like this and we are grateful to the Omnibus Society for permission to reproduce it from one of their 1980 Newsletters. Terence Jones, who was himself the owner of a preserved vehicle at the time, tells us the location is definitely Folkestone and it is a little after World War I, the driver, who is obviously proud of his abilities, presumably learned to drive during the conflict.

The Beginner

I shall always remember my first day as a busman; I went to work with a good heart and I thought to myself, I can drive pretty well anything on four wheels so I've nothing to worry about, but I was soon to learn that a good driver is not necessarily a good busman. I also found that the busman's language cannot be learned in one day.

" RED " 'BUS RECEIPTS.

RESULTS OF PASSENGER SERVICE EXTENSIONS.

The 17th annual general meeting of the Birmingham and Midland Motor Omnibus Company (Ltd.) was held at the Electrical Federation Offices, 88, Kingsway, London.

Mr. R. J. Howley, C.B.E., M.Inst.C.E., chairman and managing director, presided, and in moving the adoption of the report and accounts, said the accounts showed the financial position to be exceedingly strong. The net traffic receipts and other revenues amounted to £103,095, compared with £81,902 for 1920.

The increase had been brought about by the larger volume of passenger receipts, due largely to the extension of the services; and the increased passenger traffic revenue, he was glad to say, had been earned with a smaller percentage of expenditure to receipts than was the case in the previous year.

The amount available for distribution was £90,343, as compared with £59,812. They were paying 10 per cent. on the ordinary shares, with a bonus of 5 per cent., and carrying forward £22,170. The reduced spending power of the public, and the competition of cheap week-end and market tickets on the railways, were becoming apparent in the passenger receipts.

It would interest the shareholders to know that the long-distance services which were worked throughout last summer to Weston-super-Mare and Llandudno were well patronised, and were continued through the season without any mechanical breakdown.

They had in Mr. Power, the traffic manager, and Mr. Shire, the engineer of the company, two officers to whom was due more than to anything else the continued prosperity of the company, and he was sure he was voicing the sentiments of the meeting in conveying to those gentlemen the thanks of the shareholders for the good work they had done.

My vehicle was an old type open affair, gangway in the centre to the entrance half-way along the side. My conductor, Charlie, was an old sweat, a short, stocky fellow with one watery eye and a habit of speaking from the side of his mouth. About 10.00am we were ready for the road. He said "Right-o, take it steady down to the harbour and we'll see what the road's like". We picked up no passengers but he appeared to be making a mental note of the lie of the land with regard to all the other buses. Arriving at the stand, my mate drifted over to yarn to the other busmen leaning against the harbour wall and they appeared to be interested in anything except "bussing". I sat reading the paper and every now and then would hear remarks from them such as "You got a ten minute gap now", "Ain 't no good going up yet", "They got three swingers out today". "I caught a nasty cold on this one yesterday, train was late, a few sparrers 'ad to go right through", "Do'an come up too quick behind me, I'm chucking the anchor out at Woodses", "Give us the beaver if there's anything doing on Dym.

This was all Greek to me and I wondered when we were going to start. Presently my mate came over and said "Pull out quick, and when you git round the corner, drag it". Away we went; I got a perfect second and third gear and was travelling nicely to get a sweet top when my mate shouted out "what the hell you doing? I said 'drag' it; do'an you know what 'drag' means?" I replied "Do you mean go slowly?" I can't quote his reply but that was what he meant. We dawdled up towards the Town Hall and there was the bus that had left a good ten minutes before us, parked on the stand with nearly a seated load. The conductor touted the last passenger on, then looked our way, gave us a broad grin and slowly pulled off. My mate was cursing to himself and if looks could have killed the other conductor would have dropped dead. We stayed on the stand with my mate touting for all he was worth and the 'copper' on point duty glancing up at the Town Hall clock every so often. After about two minutes he nodded in our direction and my mate go aboard, telling me to "take it steady". We only had two passengers on, and as the hopes of an increase died away, the more frantic my mate seemed in his effort to make walkers ride. Finally he abandoned his task and walked up the gangway towards me, sniffing and said "Something burning mate?" I replied that I could smell nothing. He gave me a nasty dig in the shoulder with his elbow and said "something's burning mate, pull up!" Then to the two passengers, "Where d'you want to go?" One of them replied "Central Station". I stopped the bus and then he said to the passengers "Best ketch the one behind; we got something burning and I do'an want no bother". They quickly alighted and I was just going to ask him what the devil he meant, but he spoke first "Drag it to the corner and I'll give you the beaver when the rozzer's got his back to us, then shoot down Shellons Street and we'll lay up at the Library". I parked at the Library while he went to spy out the land. Presently he rushed back and told me to pull away quickly and pip the bloke who was coming up the hill. Before we could get going a Copper stepped out from a doorway and addressed Charlie in no uncertain manner. The conversation went something like this: P.C. "Where are you bound for Charlie?" Charlie: "Just come out; was going to see what the Hythe Road's like". P.C.: "But didn't I see you go by about ten minutes ago?". Charlie: "Do'an think so, we just come out". P.C.: Showed Charlie a notebook. "That's the number of your vehicle; my advice to you is to go down to the harbour and work the road properly, or I shall take a few particulars from you and the driver". Charlie mumbled something to the Copper, then in a vicious tone said to me "git on down the Harbour" and back to our starting point we went. We had a bad day; the takings were poor. Arriving in the garage about 10.30pm, the 'old man' asked Charlie "How was things today?" Charlie replied "What d'yer expect with a fool like that behind a steerin' wheel? He knows nothing about bussin' and strikes me he never will. All he thinks about his gettin' his gears nice and being perlite to everybody. 'E says it isn't right to keep in the middle of the road to keep the opposition back. I do'an want him no more". He never 'ad me no more! Those were the days."

THE PATENTED OMNIBUS

Isambard Kingdom Brunel famously once said there was in existence a patent for everything – that is only true in my field of road transport as, in my micro-collection, I have around 1,000 of these inventors' dreams duly recorded on paper and paid for. Only a tiny percentage were to gain acceptance and sadly quite often the idea was taken up without any acknowledgement – it was a very, very expensive operation for the Patentee to gain recompense.

In an earlier book (Aspects of Buses, Oakwood Press), I included one such patent for folding roofs on double-decked buses, which caught the imaginations of a number of correspondents. So, here are a handful more which, importantly, are not from individuals but companies and their staff.

PATENT 183,341 of 1922

In this particular case we can illustrate the patent with a photograph showing its application. If nothing else this shows how this dire arrangement would end up with the driver sitting among a heap of soggy canvas. The bus, a descendant of the charabanc, is of a type known as a 'torpedo' from the body shape. Type AEC 5D1, built 1920.

Improvements in or relating to Vehicle Bodies and to Hoods therefore

We, Samuel Gage, of 2, Middleton Road, Holloway, London, N.7., a subject of the King of England, and THE LONDON GENERAL OMNIBUS COMPANY LIMITED, of Electric Railway House, Broadway, Westminster, London, S.W.1., a British company, do hereby declare the nature of this invention to be as follows:

This invention is for improvements in or relating to vehicle bodies and to hoods therefore, and has for one of its objects to provide for the more efficient housing of the hood when not in use.

Charabanc hoods are well known which when not in use are housed at the rear of the vehicle. The hoops supporting the hood are slid rearwardly along runners or guides at the sides of the vehicle so as to be received upon hinged end sections of said runners which are subsequently swung downwardly about their pivots to cause the hoops to lie substantially horizontally one upon the other with the material of the hood folded about them. This arrangement for storing the hood when not in use is open to the objections that it increases the rear overhang of the vehicle and is liable to be

damaged when the vehicle is travelling backwards. It also increases the tendency of the vehicle to skid and frequently is the cause of side doors situated towards the rear of the vehicle flying open owing to springing of the rear part of the body shell. Furthermore, the hood when not in use is liable to obscure the driver's view rearwards; it also facilitates cyclists hanging on to the rear of the vehicle and is an encouragement to passengers to misuse the vehicle by sitting upon the hood or filling it with luggage.

It has also been proposed in connection with such vehicles as motor omnibuses to provide a hood for the top deck which, with its hoops, is slid forwardly along guide rails on to hinged end-sections and then swung downwardly with the latter to lie substantially horizontally upon the roof the driver's canopy.

The present invention provides improvements over both of the arrangements described in the foregoing and its primary feature consists of a vehicle body which is shaped at, and adjacent, the position of the dashboard to form a housing for the hoops and other parts of the vehicle hood or cover when not in use.

PATENT 415,217 of 1934

Any enthusiast trying to restore an early vehicle will find one or more lamp holders missing or the metal (mazak*) so corroded as to disintegrate into a white powder. And we found that on other than Plaxton or Duple bodywork finding replacement glasses was akin to finding hen's teeth, this design was to be found from time to time.

(*Mazak – a useful family of zinc-based alloys with elements of aluminium, magnesium and copper. Known commonly in Britain as 'pot metal' or 'white metal' the alloy suffered from zinc pest, due to impurities in the base metals.)

Improvements in or relating to Interior Lamps particularly for Motor Coaches and other Vehicles

We, TAW MANUFACTURING COMPANY LIMTED, a British Company, and LEONARD GODFREY WELDHEN and LEONARD JOHN HUNT, both British Subjects, all of Campsbourne Works, High Street, Hornsey, N.8., do hereby declare the nature of this invention to be as follows:

This invention relates to interior lamps for fixing to vertical walls and other surfaces, particularly for the interior of motor cars, motor coaches, buses, railway carriages and other vehicles.

One object of the invention is to provide a lamp which occupies a minimum of head room.

Another object of the invention is the prevention of rattle under conditions of excessive vibration.

According to the invention a flat pressed metal back plate attached to a vertical surface, is made wedge shaped with its greatest width at the top; the edges of the wedge form are bent inwards to form grooves at each side of the wedge; the moulded glass globe has its back surface similarly wedgeshaped with a projecting edge along each side, and is arranged to slide down into the grooved form of the back plate. When the correct position is reached the sides of the glass globe jamb tight into the grooves formed on the back plate. A small upward movement of the glass globe will disengage it from the grooves in the back plate and the globe can then be easily removed.

A feature of the invention is that the weight of the bulb under conditions of vibration tends to increase the closeness of the fit between the globe and the back plate.

PATENT 532,498 of 1941

It is easy enough to see just what Strachans were thinking of with this patent but 1941 was hardly the most propitious time for its introduction. It is worth noting the No.5 which appears on the drawings overleaf is the spare wheel. Fortunately, in most of our vehicles where a spare was carried it was strapped to the side of the boot, or it lived underneath a false bottom requiring all the luggage to be unpacked for access. In general once we moved on from small Bedfords a telephone call fetched out the van! Locating any spare wheel under a vehicle made a required change a filthy job.

Improvements in and relating to Chassis for Motor Coaches, and other Commercial Vehicles

We, STRACHANS SUCCESSORS LIMITED, a Corporation organised and registered under the Laws of the United Kingdom of Great Britain and Northern Ireland, whose registered address is at Wales Farm Road, North Acton, London, W.3. and ALFRED ERNEST WHITTIT, of 39, Courthope Road, Greenford, Middlesex, a British Subject, do hereby declare the nature of this invention to be as follows:

This invention relates to chassis for motor coaches and other commercial vehicles and has for its object to provide a chassis that will enable the centre of gravity of a motor coach or other commercial vehicle provided with means for stowing one or more spare wheels under the floor, to be brought lower than heretofore.

Two types of overslung chassis for motor coaches and other commercial vehicles are commonly in use. In one (hereinafter called the "high type") the longitudinal members pass in a straight line over the back axles whilst in the other (hereinafter called the "low type") the rear portions of said members are curved downwardly over the forward side of the rear axle so as to lower the portions (hereinafter called the "intermediate portions") of them that extend between the rear and front axles. In the case of the high type of chassis there is sufficient room without infringing existing regulations, to stow a spare wheel under the chassis whilst with a low type of chassis, in order to leave the maximum of space at the rear of the body for the stowage of luggage or for other purposes, the spare wheel has been housed between the chassis members and the floor, thus necessitating the latter being raised sufficiently above the former to provide the requisite space.

Accordingly to the present invention, either or both of the longitudinal side members of a chassis of the low type are provided in one or more positions with portions of a higher level beneath which one or more spare wheels are adapted to be housed at such a level that leaves the necessary clearance beneath the vehicle, and the floor of the coach or other body is adapted to rest directly on the raised portions of said members and upon bearers that rest on the lower portions of said members. In this way it has been found possible to lower to an appreciable extent the centre of gravity of the vehicle for the reason that the difference in the levels of the raised and lower portions of the longitudinal chassis members necessary to permit the stowing of the spare wheel is less than the height it was heretofore found necessary to raise the floor above the level of said members in order to accommodate the spare wheel between them.

Where? When? What?

And truth to tell I have no answers. All that is on the back is "EDE". The most interesting fact, apart from the people standing about, is the vehicle in the rear background. Just about readable on the side is the lettering "Bus To All Parts Of The Town". The rear door appears to read "Private Orders Taken".

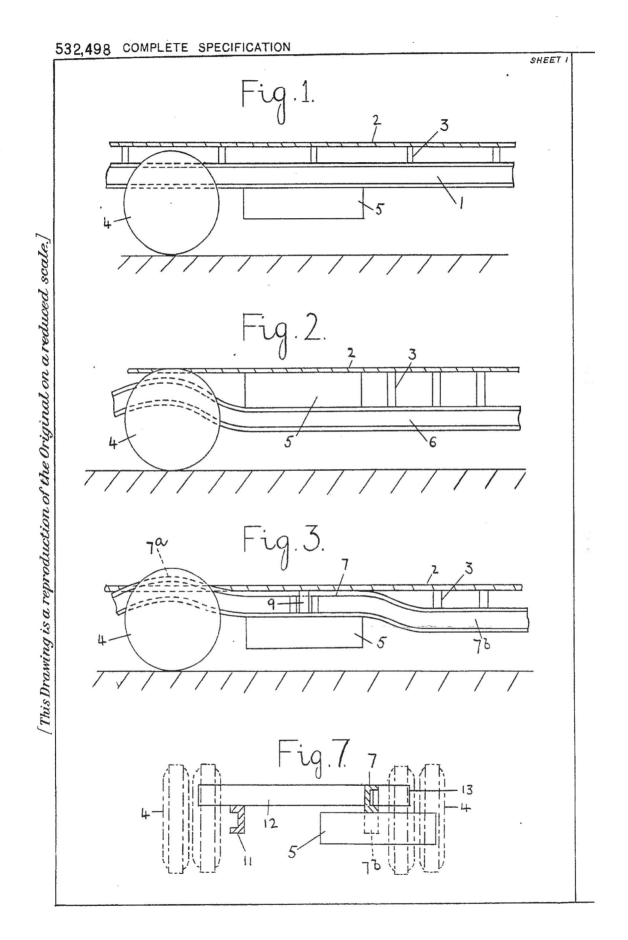

Fig.1.

Fig.2.

Fig.3.

Fig.7.

PACKARD – SURELY THE ULTIMATE RARITY?

Guernsey transport is a story of trials and tribulations, with very narrow lanes, low speed limits and oiks who think that their money gives them right-of-way. Guernsey Motors were both cash strapped and had to fight off rival concerns, but they developed a strong eye for bargains; although even their directors can hardly have thought when they bought a batch of Packard lorries from the War Office 'dump' (the Slough Trading Company) in 1922. that after another war they would still be giving good service. Some of the chassis were fitted with char-a-banc bodywork, and a handful more with ex horsebus bodies, but many including no.24 were fitted with new wheels, pneumatic tyres, electric lighting and new bodywork built in the company's Brock Road works from 1932 onward. The final updating, serving well to hide their origins was the supply of new radiators which as can be seen here carried the lettering 'Guernsey Motors'. Despite all the problems involved in being commandeered by the German forces a number survived, including no 24, until 1948. A memory is of being in Guernsey with my father in 1945 and riding on one of these which was minus all its glass save the windscreen and rear window; the return journey was on a liberated Opel Blitz lorry with rudimentary bodywork.

(Omnibus Society ref 75.1252)

Char-à-Banc For Sale

In general a char-à-banc bought in the first few years after the first world war was based on an ex. WD chassis, probably built as a lorry, and in the case of Leylands carefully recovered by the company from The Dump at Slough or on the Continent and completely overhauled, prior to being fitted with new bodywork. This advertisement appeared the *Hereford Journal* 27 May 1922.

WELSH TRANSPORT IN THE 1920s

One of the most effective restrictions placed on early coach and bus operations was a blank refusal by local authorities, who were responsible for issuing operators local licences (or 'Permits to operate'), to allow any service to run that would lessen passenger ridership on their trams. This attitude is reasonable enough as these trams represented a heavy (borrowed) investment, and one that could easily become a heavy drain on the rates. The problem of restricted access could be got round by the operator only stopping on his own property in the town, and only carrying return passengers who already held tickets. These practices were common, but not forgotten by the Council in later times. South Wales Transport, rather than fight with Swansea, initially terminated their service to Llanelly at the then Morriston tram terminus. By December 1920, these restrictions had gone although protected fares existed between Swansea and Cwmbwrla Tram Terminus (3d, no local pick up points) and Llanelly Town Hall with Bynea Tram Terminus (5d., no local pick up points).

The Rhondda Valley service is a fine early example (undated, but early 1920s) of a single vehicle long distance operation; the late return was unusual in those days of not entirely reliable vehicles and of course without motorways (or much of 'A' class roads of today) trying to maintain the legal maximum of 20mph (32kph) in a mixture of Welsh mist, industrial smog and wandering suicidal sheep must have been interesting for the drivers. Part of the fun of these old timetables is seeing the names of the premises used as booking offices and pick-up points, especially as bus stop signs were almost nonexistent. Local restrictions prevented Rhondda Valley from carrying passengers within the valley sectors.

Keith Turns adds "Rhondda Valley is clearly a Red & White (J.H. Watts Group of Chepstow) subsidiary and is feeding passengers into (and out of) the Red & White London service."

South Wales Transport Company, Ltd.

MOTOR COACH SERVICE

BETWEEN

Swansea, Forestfach, Kingsbridge, Gorseinon, Loughor, Bynea, and Llanelly.

(Park St., Oxford St.) (TOWN HALL.)

Additional Coaches will be run every hour from 12 noon till 9 p.m. each Saturday between Swansea and Loughor.

RHONDDA VALLEY TO CHEPSTOW, LYDNEY, BLAKENEY, NEWNHAM, GLOUCESTER

TIME TABLE

REGULAR DAILY SERVICES — SUNDAYS INCLUDED

READ DOWN	Departing from	Departure Point	READ UP
Dep. a.m.			Arr. p.m.
8 0	TREHERBERT	Mrs. I. Jones, Bute Street	9 45
8 5	TREORCHY	Mr. Richards, High Street	9 40
8 10	PENTRE	Mr. Edwards, Popular Restaurant	9 35
8 25	YSTRAD RHONDDA	Mr. Samuels, Celligaled Road	9 30
8 15	TONYPANDY	Mr. Salter, 21, de Winton Street	9 20
8 30	TONYPANDY	Mr. Davies, Trinity House	9 19
8 26	PENYGRAIG	Mr. Williams, Central Cafe	9 0
8 45	PORTH	Mrs. Morton, 76, Pontypridd Road	9 0
8 51	TREHAFOD	Powell Bros. Garage	8 54
8 54	PONTYPRIDD	New Inn Square	8 51
a.m.			p.m.
Dep. a.m.			Arr. p.m.
9 5	PONTYPRIDD	New Inn Square	8 40
9 10	TREFOREST	Mr. Mantle, 121 The Broadway	8 35
9 55	CARDIFF	Red & White, Wood Street	8 0
10 30	NEWPORT	Red & White, Clarence Place	7 15
11 15	CHEPSTOW	Red & White, Albion Square	6 27
11 42	LYDNEY	Red & White, Newerne Street	6 0
11 52	BLAKENEY	Mr. Richards, High Street	5 50
12 0	NEWNHAM	Mr. Wheeler, High Street	5 40
12 35	GLOUCESTER	85 Northgate Street	5 0
12 40	GLOUCESTER	Red & White, India Road	4 55
1 15	CHELTENHAM	Coach Station	4 30
p.m.			p.m.

FARES — Read down and across

FARES	Fares from Treherbert	Fares from Treorchy	Fares from Pentre	Fares from Ystrad Rhondda	Fares from Tonypandy
PONTYPRIDD	—	—	—	—	—
TREFOREST	—	—	—	—	—
CARDIFF	—	—	—	—	—
NEWPORT	3/- 5/3 3/9	3/- 5/3 3/9	2/9 4/9 3/9	2/9 4/9 3/9	2/9 4/9 3/9
CHEPSTOW	4/6 7/9 5/9	4/6 7/9 5/9	4/3 7/3 5/9	4/3 7/3 5/9	4/3 7/3 5/9
LYDNEY	5/6 8/6 7/-	5/6 8/6 7/-	5/3 8/- 7/-	5/3 8/- 7/-	5/3 8/- 7/-
BLAKENEY	5/6 8/9 7/3	5/6 8/9 7/3	5/6 8/3 7/3	5/6 8/9 7/3	5/6 8/3 7/3
NEWNHAM	7/6 11/3 9/6	7/3 11/- 9/3	7/3 11/- 9/3	7/3 11/- 9/3	7/6 10/6 7/3
GLOUCESTER	8/3 12/6 10/6	8/- 12/- 10/-	8/- 12/- 10/-	8/- 12/- 10/-	7/9 11/9 9/9
CHELTENHAM					

FARES	Fares from Penygraig	Fares from Porth	Fares from Trehafod	Fares from Pontypridd	Fares from Treforest
PONTYPRIDD	—	—	—	—	—
TREFOREST	—	—	—	—	—
CARDIFF	—	—	—	—	—
NEWPORT	2/9 4/9 3/9	2/9 4/9 3/9	2/9 4/9 3/9	3/6 5/9 4/6	3/6 6/- 4/6
CHEPSTOW	4/3 7/3 5/9	4/3 7/3 5/9	4/3 7/3 5/9	4/6 7/6 5/6	4/9 7/6 5/9
LYDNEY	5/3 8/- 7/-	5/3 8/- 7/-	5/3 8/- 7/-	5/6 8/9 6/9	5/9 8/9 6/9
BLAKENEY	5/6 8/9 7/3	5/6 8/9 7/3	5/6 8/9 7/3	6/- 9/9 6/9	6/- 9/6 7/-
NEWNHAM	6/9 10/3 8/3	6/6 9/9 8/3	6/3 9/6 6/3	8/- 9/9 6/3	7/6 9/6 6/3
GLOUCESTER	7/6 11/3 9/6	7/6 11/3 9/6	7/3 11/- 9/3	8/9 10/6 8/9	7/- 10/6 8/9
CHELTENHAM					

Single Fare, 1st Column; LIGHT TYPE. Period Return Fare, 2nd Column, HEAVY TYPE. Day Return Fare, 3rd Column, ITALIC TYPE.

Connections at Lydney with local service omnibuses for Bream, Parkend, St. Briavels, Whitecroft.

Connections at Blakeney with local service omnibuses for Viney Hill.

Children over 3 and under 12 years of age, Half Fare, with a minimum Fare of 2d.

The Company will make every effort to maintain the Services enumerated above, but do not hold themselves responsible for delay from any cause whatever. They also reserve the right to augment, reduce, or withdraw the whole or any part of these Services without further notice.

Passengers are requested to see that they receive a Ticket corresponding with the amount paid, properly punched in the section in which they enter the Vehicle, and to retain the Ticket, and to produce it when requested to the Company's Officials.

Special Terms for Picnic and Private Parties by Motor Charabanc on application.

DAVID JAMES,
Managing Director.

S.M.M.T. DECISIONS OF '22

The whole of the motor industry was in a state of turmoil during the early 1920s and the problems were recorded and repeated throughout the newspaper industry. But then as now quality varied and I have deliberately chosen to quote from the local *Hereford Journal* of 2 September 1922. It was written by a very perceptive and unemotional man well-known within the industry, J.P. Holland, within his column "Motor Notes".

"The decision of the Society of Motor Manufacturers and Traders to pass the Commercial Vehicle Show this year will hardly be a surprise in view of the present state of the commercial vehicle trade. Since the Government saw fit to ignore the wishes of the motor industry in respect to the competition of Slough, the effect has been little short of disastrous to the commercial vehicle industry. The absurdly low prices at which well-known makes of lorries are advertised broadcast, some of them in condition practically as good as new, has literally knocked the bottom out of the market for new machines. Even the additional demand for heavy chassis for charabancs has failed to keep up with the over-plus of supply. And in view of this unfair competition, it is not surprising that the firms engaged in this business (ie, manufacturers) should have decided to forego the expensive luxury of a show, where the possible sales would hardly equal the outlay.

While this decision and more especially the causes leading to it, are matters of regret, it is to be hoped that some means will be found before November 1923, whereby the heavy vehicle industry may have an opportunity of demonstrating to the world of potential buyers the many improvements which have been effected in this class of motor transport within the past year. Such concerns are the A.E.C., Tilling-Stevens and F.W.D. which have not been standing still in the meantime and their latest models would be worthwhile exhibiting.

Solution Wanted

Meantime, the charabanc question looms bigger and bigger every day, and some solution of the problem grows more insistent. The demands of the charabanc companies, as instanced by their attempt to grab the seafront at Brighton or to establish squatters' rights to a public square in London as a terminus for their scheduled trips have aroused public opposition to a degree unprecedented in the history of motoring. Their effect on the road surface of the King's highway has already threatened to double the burden of taxation on all motor vehicles. But worst of all, their unwieldy bulk, so unsuitable to so many of the narrow highways has created a prejudice among other users of the road which cannot fail to have an injurious effect on the future of this class of traffic..."

PARTY TRAVEL

Group or party travel was where the money could be made – this activity had the great advantage that all the operating parameters could be calculated. The clients want to travel from A to B and then seek recommendations where morning coffee, lunch and afternoon tea could be taken. At this point the nature of the party had to be considered as if for example they are rough-and-ready then a pub would often suffice for all three 'necessities', but if it was a batch of nice old ladies then the operator's knowledge was vital – they would not appreciate toilets like some of the filthy things we knew, neither would they want to eat many of the meals that all too often were the best that many roadside caffs could or would offer, but instead they were willing to pay a few pence more for decent restaurants and a good lunch with an hour or so to explore one of the pretty towns that make up Britain.

'Ashington Colliery Welfare Gymnastic Club' says the Daimler charabanc, while its twin on similar duty has on a much more elegant notice, 'Ashington Colliery Welfare Sports Club'. Given the dreadful conditions under which the many colliers laboured, coupled with the long hours, it is a wonder they were fit enough for gymnastics, although our cricket team, mostly miners, were as skilled and tough as any players anywhere. At the time of this excursion around 5,500 men worked in the colliery of whom 4000 worked on the pit faces. Opened in 1867, Ashington by then only employing 350 men closed in 1986 long after these United charas were scrapped.

A school outing from Berwick-on-Tweed with the children quite happy to wear a decent tidy uniform rather than filthy tatty jeans. The driver, too, is uniformed. A nephew of mine last year went to take a photograph of his daughter's outing, but after lining them up he was told by a ditsy little girl teacher that he would need permission in writing from the parents of each child before he could start filming. He ignored her, but the teacher rang the police and caused a kerfuffle – but using his wife's camera as proof he hadn't taken a photograph they went on their way.

The location of this is clear enough although I have no idea of their destination. Although a dull day I would guess from the open roof vent it was quite warm.

Very obviously an outing! But was this the male half of a wedding party? Or a works 'do'? The hybrid style of hood is interesting with fixed glass but a roof sliding along rails.

Take it on the trip

TRAVEL WITH US...OR...US...OR US

When motor transport became acceptable to the public – in fact it was demanded by many would-be passengers – the only means of giving details was through advertisements in local papers. Midland 'Red' were quite clear over their services, although timings for Easter Monday were, shall we say, vague. *Hereford Journal*, Saturday 8 April 1922.

MARGATE

To be accurate the Stanmore Boarding House, Athelstan Road, Cliftonville, Margate, Kent. Unfortunately Margate seems to have re-invented itself as the DHSS capital of Kent and like most 'traditional' B&Bs if the 'Stanmore' still exists physically it is no longer trading. One strange side effect of the town's change is that most bed and breakfast establishments in the area are very shy, having neither email/website facilities or the ability to answer their telephones.

However back in 1923 this was not so, although this photograph throws up a mystery all of its own; assuming the passengers are from the 'Stanmore' just how many slept in each room? Coach-driving in the early 1960s in Blackpool I was offered the 'share' of a bed for the night; there was one double bed and two triple beds – I coiled up on the coach's back seat. I cannot imagine that any respectable 'boarding house' would expect its customers to sleep in such conditions! It is perhaps unfortunate that a high percentage of our chara passengers look quite depressed.

The leading car is probably a Commer with an interesting 'lid', and alas a body which is sagging amidships under the weight of it coupled to the inherent weakness of the traditional charabanc body. The second car would be classed as a limousine with a lightweight car derived chassis; Wolseley and Austin rather specialised in these. Forward of the two standing men at the rear draped over the side of the charabanc is one of the rugs normally provided; one side was a warm woven blanket type material and the other waterproof.

A GOOD DAY OUT WAS ENJOYED BY ONE AND ALL

The travels and travails char-à-banc travellers went through have not been well recorded by 'bus' writers but these reports are a vital part of the weft and woof of transport. In 1924 as this newspaper item shows there was still an element of adventure about the whole outing; tyres, dirty petrol, electrics were all just waiting to go wrong. The father of a friend told me fifty years ago about one trip on a char-à-banc when the driving chain flew off. In the gathering dusk the men (but not the girls) spent around 30 minutes trying to find a lost pin. Found, the chain was then re-assembled and they went on their way ... singing happily!

Even in this successful outing there is a note that "some little engine trouble caused the first delay", from which common sense tells us there were others ... but they were only an hour late.

RINGERS' ENJOYABLE TRIP

Clifford Party Enjoy Bells and Scenery

"Sunday last will be a day long to be remembered by the 30 odd ringers and friend of the Clifford district who took part in their first outing Mr Darling's 'Blue Bus' having been chartered beforehand.

Nine a.m. was the time fixed for departure, and shortly after they were on their way to Leominster. After a visit to the tower and a look round, punctual to time, they left for Ledbury. After a visit to the tower to see the bells (ringing had been refused there) and a look round the interior of this beautiful old church, a start was made for Ross. Much Marcie was to have been visited, as a hearty invitation had been received from the Vicar to try his bells, but, unfortunately, time would not allow.

At Ross and Hereford

Ross was reached a little before scheduled time and the ringers were met by Mr J. Clark, secretary of the Ross district, the ringing master, Mr W. Postons, being unable to get into Ross. Tea was served at the Dairy, High Street, where all enjoyed this welcome meal. The ringers then proceeded to St Mary's tower, where the local foreman, Mr Bushness, was waiting for them. The local band very kindly handed the ropes over to the visitors for an hour before evening service. Rounds and doubles were rung to give all a pull on this beautiful peal, also three courses of Grandsire Triples and an excellent pull brought [church] service time.

Boarding the bus the party were soon on their way to Hereford, where a short halt was made, and here some little engine trouble caused the first delay. However, all's well that ends well and eventually things were righted and they were on their way to Eardisley, where they arrived an hour late, but although tired, everyone voted it a most enjoyable tour, the weather all day being delightful, as was the scenery that was passed through.

Organised Thanks

The first sight of the county's fine hop plantations was observed by several, also the pickers in all their "glory"; in contrast to this was the fields of once gold grain, now nearly black, which was passed all along the route. At tea opportunity was taken of according the organiser (Mr J.P. Hyett) a very hearty vote of thanks for the arrangements he had made, also the clergy of Leominster, Stretton Grandison, Much Marcie and Ross, who had given permission to ring, also to all who had in any way given assistance to make the outing the success it surely was."

From *Hereford Journal*, 20 September 1924

TRAM VERSUS MOTOR BUS

A familiar controversy, upon which many folk hold fixed and very emphatic opinions, was dealt with by the Chief Engineer of the Birmingham Tramways at the Rotary Club lunch yesterday. Mr A.C. Baker was wise not to enter into the realms of prophecy, but he did make out a good case, so far as present-day conditions of city transport are concerned, for the maintenance of tramways. Critics of the system, without knowing, or thinking, overmuch of the problems involved, are rather apt to jump to hasty judgments, and so from time to time the slogan "Scraps the trams!" is raised in newspaper correspondence and elsewhere. Particularly is this the case when any extension of the municipal tramways is under discussion, and we heard the cry very insistently in connection with reconstruction of the Bristol Road and the laying of the new tram route to the Lickey Hills. Those who entertain the suspicion that the local Tramways Committee and its officials are prejudiced against motor buses can hardly fail to be impressed by Mr Baker's statement that Birmingham is the owner of the largest fleet of municipal motor omnibuses in the country – a clear proof that while maintaining, and on selected routes, prepared to extend its tram service, the Committee is fully alive to the advantages of the rival form of transport. On an impartial survey, the fair conclusion seems to be that, while both types of vehicle have their definite advantages and disadvantages, each in turn may be the best fitted for the service required on particular routes.

Familiar objections to the trams are that the lines and overhead equipment involve very heavy expenditure; that the vehicles are obstructive and dangerous to other traffic by reason of their inflexibility and of the risk of skidding which the rails introduce in dirty weather; and that the service cannot be adapted to any temporary or permanent change in traffic demands. The first of these objections needs to be fairly considered, in relation, not only to running costs, which includes interest on and repayment of capital; and Mr Baker argues that, so far from being more costly to run, when all the factors are taken into account, trams are cheaper than buses. In addition it has to be borne in mind the tramways pay £78,000 in rates, thereby relieving the citizens to extent of nearly 4d. in the pound [£1 sterling was 240d.]; that they contribute very large sums to road maintenance which would otherwise have to come out of the ratepayers' pockets; and the adoption of a "scrap the trams" policy would involve throwing away a capital value of about two million pounds. These are potent considerations so far as existing tramways are concerned, but if the case for motor buses were made out on other grounds, they could not be advanced in support of tramway extensions or expensive reconstructions of old routes.

The latter problem was very effectively met on the Nechells line, where the Committee to avoid a re-laying expenditure of £90,000 installed trackless tramways, which are virtually omnibuses run by electric power from the existing overhead wires. But the defence of the tram stands on other grounds. Birmingham's road traffic, probably in common with that of most big towns of wide range, where the majority of the citizens live miles away from their work, is very heavy indeed before 9am and for an hour or two after 5pm. The tram, with its greater capacity, permits of this traffic being handled, in the view of experts, more quickly and more satisfactorily than can be done by motor-buses. This is really the crux of the whole question, and it leads to the definite conclusion that on routes where the demand is heavy the tram is the best vehicle, whereas on less important routes the bus may take its place with advantage. Thus, for some time to come , the local policy will probably proceed along the lines of a delimitation of the respective spheres of tram and omnibus, the latter being used as a supplementary service, for the opening out of new cross-suburban routes such as the Outer Circle, or for districts lying off important main roads, and not presenting such heavy traffic demands. The tram versus bus controversy will go on, yet those who heard or read Mr. Baker's address must at least realise that the Birmingham Committee and responsible officials are not taking a prejudiced standpoint, but are willing to give the newer means of transport its due and to adopt it wherever, in their considered judgment, it appears to offer advantages over the older system. Birmingham Post, April 1924

As time marched on these 'wise men' faded away to be replaced with men who only saw the diesel engine as the way forward. The last Birmingham tram ran in July 1953 and it does seem as though the City Fathers remain lukewarm about even modern trams as their existing one line stagnates. However that said and done in Manchester there has been much discussion over reducing the number of vehicles passing various pinch points. Unsurprisingly in 2010 a local Parliamentary candidate pointed out that 'getting rid' of the 'old trams' would free up space. This in a city where their lines and rolling stock are both advancing and being modernised. Thankfully he was not elected...

WATERSHED

After the first flush of enthusiasm, aided by servicemen's gratuities and factory hands' savings, cold reality began to creep through the population, particularly as many of the young starry-eyed passengers of 1919-1921 now had families and extra rent to pay just at a time when the girl's income was lost. But, as in the late 1940s/1950s, they could not forego their day or two's char-a-banc outings; however, the editor of the Commercial Motor pointed out to operators, they had to make 5/- or 7/6d do where 10/- had gone before and yet the passengers wanted new destinations. Without today's technology, finding a different location where there were 'facilities' and suitable catering establishments was not easy. A relative told us that, many years ago, a teacher's trip in the late 1920s, where it turned out the Council lavatories, supposedly open, were locked up. The driver promptly drove to the Mayor's house and explained the problem. As they were all 'professional' people he made available his own facilities and his wife rang various friends and they laid on a decent meal. The driver arranged for a donation to be made to the Mayor's chosen charity. The coach company lost money but gained immense goodwill. Incidentally, in those days the Mayor was as likely to be a shop-keeper as not – a far cry from today's choices.

We all hear of elderly couples who had gone to Brighton or Worthing for thirty years or more and still loved it, but for every pair like that there were fifty of the type who ambled into the office and booked a week's worth of day trips. And in the 1950s they knew they did not want the 'old coaches' (two year old half cab A.E.C.) but the new full fronted Bedfords (some reckoned it was so they could tell the driver when they needed a pee!) which were perceived as being much newer.

Roger Kidner told us one day how much resistance and disappointment there was when, at their hotel, the operator turned up with a char-à-banc. In reality for the boys it was a better ride in the open air (someone was always going to be sick and in a saloon this was undesirable) and the seating comfortable, but the rival firms' covered Lancia was lusted over; Roger called it a form of snobbery!

But the reality was, as *Commercial Motor* points out, that you either updated or went under – how many lost dreams litter the story of bus and coach work? Too many, I fear.

MOTOR COACHING IN 1925: A PLEA FOR OPTIMISM

Observations on Failures of the Past and Outstanding Needs of the Future.
How to Ensure Success for the Forthcoming Season

"Optimism should be the keynote of the 1925 motor coaching season. In the process of settling down to the more or less uneventful winter trade, backed by the somewhat discouraging returns of last season, there is not much incentive to new and bold enterprises, yet to accept the status quo with an air of finality would be fatal to ultimate prosperity.

What hopes motor coach owners had two or three seasons ago of re-organising their fleets by the inclusion of more of the smaller units, have been deferred fulfilment in some instances by the severity of their experiences, which have been such as to leave undeveloped many plans and ideas for attaining commercial success. The fact has to be recognised that, in the provinces, at least, there has been a thinning out in the ranks of motor coach proprietors – even as the result of last year's traffic – and whether this movement has yet reached the zenith of its course can hardly be determined at this premature stage.

One thing, however, is certain, and that is the industry has not enjoyed a prosperity commensurate with its capital responsibilities. It is not a difficult matter to speculate on causes. They are manifold, and by no means a few of them are directly attributable to motor coach owners themselves. Traffic is their life blood; without it they suffer an anaemic existence with the inevitable consequences.

The ability to transport passengers to seaside and pleasure resorts should be the minimum qualification of the man setting up in business as a motor coach proprietor, but if he be possessed of a modicum of wisdom, he will no doubt perceive that what, in the matter of travelling facilities, satisfied the public two or three years immediately after the war, now falls far short of their expectations. Not only that, for the rates now charged must bear sympathetic relation to current economic standards.

Thus, the motor coach owner is looked upon to provide better service at a lower cost per seat-mile. There is only one way of reconciling these twin factors, and that is to ensure a better continuity in loads. The stimulation of bookings (excepting at the seaside resorts, where the motor coach has an almost ubiquitous existence) in industrial areas is admittedly difficult, and success, in a large measure, depends upon the reputation and goodwill of the coach owner. The better he is known, and the more certain the regularity and dependability of his services, the greater his chance of being remembered when work is in prospect.

At the same time, too much reliance can be placed on such an intangibility as goodwill. The appetite of the public must be whetted by artificial aids, chief of which is the proper employment of publicity, into the technicalities of which it is not proposed to enter in this article.

Only in a comparatively few instances during the past season was an ambitious use made of printed matter. If the public is indifferent to the attractions of the open road, the coach owner must exercise his ingenuity to promote interest and indulge in propaganda on a sufficiently impressive scale to demonstrate that the pleasure-giving possibilities of motor coaching are as real in 1925 as in 1920. Unless the coach owner shows confidence, how can he expect the public to be responsive?

How many coach owners, we wonder, have brought and kept their fleets up-to-date, since first venturing into the business. Comparatively few according to our observations, for the main reason that writing down depreciation on a regularised basis has been exceedingly difficult of accomplishment when revenue has fallen short of expectations. Consequently, many owners have on their hands machines old in age, but with poor mileage to their credit – the young-old.

The man in the street is now more au fait with the conditions that constitute the 'up-to-date' motor coach. He has been taught to appreciate the smaller vehicle running on pneumatic tyres in preference to solids, and giving more roomy seating, and other little comforts which the thoughtfulness of coach-owners has provided. It can hardly be expected that passengers will willingly patronise seemingly old-fashioned vehicles when more modern ones are bookable at the same fees.

Recognising that there are some owners who still claim the 28-seater to be the only sound commercial proposition, circumstances in particular localities do not affect the main argument, which is that the public has been taught to distinguish the comforts of different types of coach and need must, therefore, be given to their preferences.

The outstanding needs of the 1925 motor coaching season are – courage and optimism on the part of vehicle owners, motor vehicles, wisely directed propaganda, and alert administration and enterprise in the organisation and direction of tours, whether for single-seat passengers or booked parties."

MARKFIELD SERVICE

When I obtained this photograph aeons ago I made some mild attempts to find out the location of Markfield and who the operator was. The 'village', for thus it was, had a population of around 1,000 and is located 7.5 miles (12km) northwest of Leicester. The exciting bit came later when I contacted Mike Greenwood, the Archives & Research Director at the Leicester Transport Heritage Trust and after some prodigious research and 'much searching, deliberation and consultation', it was decided that the vehicle was the rarest of rare 'a 20-seater Durant-Mason, possibly NR 6391, new in May 1925, and purchased by W.D. Warner & Sons of Markfield, Leicestershire, in 1928,' from C.S. Peach of Glenfield;

J. Shockley and C.S. Peach being the original purchasers when the vehicle was new.

The Durant Motor Company was incorporated in the USA on 12 January 1921 with this chassis type, probably a Mason Road King, sold as a Durant-Mason until 1926. In all, six of these chassis were sold at the same time (1925), this one being bodied by Willowbrook of Leicester (only later at Loughborough) as a 20-seater. Of course, this raises another mystery of how these lorry/bus chassis from a very obscure and short-lived American manufacturer, ended up in a village in Leicestershire.

M. Greenwood, M.A. Sutcliffe, MBE and J. Bennett.

RFC

The Crossley 20/25 shown here was best known as type 8 or more romantically the RFC (Royal Flying Corps) type. Originally introduced with a four litre (4531cc) engine in 1912, a year later the embryo RFC took delivery of six for use as airfield tenders. So successful were these machines that in various guises and updated models around 10,000 were built and delivered. Such was the speed of the German collapse in 1918 a convalescing relative mentioned seeing dozens of new chassis being driven into fields to await their fates; quite a few were 'borrowed' and not all were accounted for. However this did not preclude Crossley Motors finding their prewar car markets still existed and a modified version of the 20/25 continued to be built until 1925.

With a wheelbase of 11 feet 4 inches and an easy to maintain 30hp engine, cone clutch and silent spiral bevel rear axle plus pneumatic tyres this was a specification that had proved its worth and despite only having brakes on the rear wheels it lent itself to a smart little bus or charabanc, albeit of light construction. The Maltese Cross is just visible on the radiator and the party, somewhere in the Fells, look happy enough except for Granny sitting second from left but one grump-pot out of 14 seems reasonable!

MOTORBUSES WANTED

This little 1925 note of unknown origin has been in my files forever! It seems to me to be somewhat naive; although the advice is good, the nascent company might well find the opposition would drive them off the road. Clearly, if they can see the traffic possibilities, in those unregulated days, beady eyes would watch their every move.

~ THE MEURIG ~
RED BUS SERVICE
Aeron Garage, ABERAYRON.

Summer Time Table.
Commencing April 14th, 1924, and until further notice.

ABERAYRON---ABERYSTWYTH

UP Journey :—	a.m.	a.m.	p.m.	p.m.
Leave Aberayron ...	8 45	9 30	1 0	5 0
„ Llanon	9 0	9 45	1 15	5 15
„ Llanrhystyd...	9 10	9 55	1 30	5 30
Arrive Aberystwyth	10 0	11 0	2 15	6 15

The 8-45 Bus connects the 10-15 a.m. Train at Aberystwyth.
The 9-30 Bus connects the Mid-day Trains at Aberystwyth.
The 5 Bus leaves after the 4-36 Train arrives at Aberayron

DOWN Journey—	a m	p.m	p.m.	p m.
Leave Aberystwyth ..	11 0	3 0	4 45	7 0
„ Llanrhystyd ...	11 30	3 35	5 15	7 35
„ Llanon ..	11 45	3 50	5 25	7 50
Arrive Aberayron ...	12 15 p.m. 4 15		6 0	8 15

The 11 a.m. Bus connects with the New Quay Service and allows 2½ hours stop at New Quay. Also this connects the 1-35 train out from Aberayron.
4-45 p.m. connects with the 6–15 Bus for New Quay.

ABERAYRON---ABERYSTWYTH.
(Via Pennant and Cross Inn).   EVERY MONDAY.

	a.m.		p.m.
Leave Aberayron -	9 0	Return from Aberystwyth	5 30
„ Pennant -	9 15	Arrive Cross Inn -	6 25
„ Cross Inn -	9 30	„ Aberayron -	7 0
„ Llanrhystyd	9 55		
Arrive Aberystwyth	10 45		

Proprietors— D. Meurig Jenkins & Son,
Telegrams—Jenkins, Garage, Aberayron.   Phone No. 8.
Also at 22, Mill Street, Aberystwyth.

Cambrian News (Aberystwyth), Ltd.—

Motorbuses Wanted

"South Coast" writes: "I am taking the liberty of sending you a line to ask your kind suggestion or advice, if you will be so good as to favour me with same, in a business matter that has come under our connection here. Inquiries have been made to me, as to on what basis we should be prepared to run a motorbus service in this district, and which, so far as I can see, ought to be a distinctly profitable undertaking. The point is, we are not prepared to lay out money in buses ourselves, and, therefore, should like to arrange with some firm to go with us in the matter. Can you suggest any suitable firm, who would like to look into it with us and arrange by mileage, or commission, or passengers carried, or any such basis? The journeys are quite short ones, and our facilities here, of course, would be available. Perhaps two or three buses would be employed."

ANSWER: *You could not do better than write to Commercial Car Hires, Ltd of 86, Strand, WC.*

ALLDAYS COMMERCIAL MOTORS

An Attractive Body in the Design of which Special Consideration has been Given to the Comfort and Convenience of Passengers.

Hitherto, the gangway method of body construction for motor coaches has been almost exclusively used for medium and large-size bodies. This feature is not difficult to understand, for the simple reason that, as a certain amount of space is lost in providing a gangway, it is necessary to build a body of such a size that will enable sufficient passengers to be carried to provide a remunerative return at fares which are comparable with those charged on more or less ordinary vehicles. For vehicles which are used on half-day or daily runs the gangway body is unnecessary and it is more suitable for use on vehicles which are intended for touring purposes, and where the comfort and convenience of the passengers must receive primary consideration.

For touring coaches the gangway body has several advantages, notable amongst which are that this method of construction enables a certain amount of passengers' luggage to be accommodated in the body interior, and it also dispenses with the need for a door to each row of seats, a form of construction which inevitably introduces certain fundamental weaknesses in the build of the body. Moreover, the elimination of the doors and the full-width seats enables a reduction in the weight of the body to be effected.

We have recently had the opportunity of examining a small gangway-coach body built by Messrs Alldays Motors, of 78 Jermyn Street, St James's, London, S.W., and fitted to a 50-cwt, Z-type Lancia commercial chassis. The body is built to seat 20 persons, inclusive of the driver. The framing is, as usual, built of ash, and the body sides are panelled in lead-coated iron.

The body is built on most attractive lines, and possesses a symmetry which is pleasing to the eye. It is of the torpedo type. There are only two doors, that on the near-side being for the passengers, and that on the off-side for the driver. They are particularly wide, measuring 24in. in order to facilitate entrance and egress of passengers, and are hung on three coach hinges, each being fitted with double slam locks to reduce the risk of it flying open due to vibration or road shock.

So far as the seating is concerned, three pairs of transverse seats are arranged on each side behind the driver's seat, the full-width seat, to accommodate five persons extending the whole length of the body at the rear. The seat boards are each 22in. in depth, 16in. being allowed for each passenger, and the gangway side of the seats is provided with arm-rests in order to add to passengers' comfort.

The upholstery of the seats is carried out in hand-buffed leather hides, and attention should be drawn to the fact that the spring frames are of special type, in which each cushion has four rows of springs so designed as to withstand hard wear over a long period. The back squabs are provided with two rows of springs. The method of finishing the back of each seat with a pile carpet covering instead of paint, as is often the case, is of note that it is quite a simple matter to brush the carpet.

The inside of the doors and quarters are trimmed in leather, and to give a neat finish to the upholstery a brass beading is employed round its edges.

The method of supporting the seat boards in this Alldays body is, we think, unique – at least, for a coach body – being that more often adopted in bus body construction. The angle-iron supports which are used reduce the weight considerably, but, at the same time increase the rigidity of the body.

Attention should be directed to the sturdy construction of the body throughout, especially the hood rest irons, which, with the object of obtaining better security, are carried right down to the body sides, being held at the top by means of a bolt and nut which passes through the top rail of each body side-member. The hood frame is covered with duck materials, the hood itself being of the Jackson type, in which patent hood-stick separators are employed.

Special thought has been given to the general appearance of the body, and the inclusion of a fascia board, in which oil and petrol gauges are mounted so that the driver may have an uninterrupted view of them while on the road, is evidence of the tendency to favour touring car practice. Other points, small perhaps in themselves, but which indicate the attention given to appearance, include the small detachable curtains inside the scuttle dash, the small screws utilised for fixing the metal beading which is used for attaching the leather upholstery to each seat, the screws and cups employed for fixing the canvas to the hood props, and the heavy-gauge domed wings which, on the nearside, connect the running board, which is covered with linoleum and has brass-edged plates. A nickel-plated windscreen is fitted.

Provision is made for carrying a spare wheel and tyre on special brackets below the off-side of the body, in which position it can be conveniently stowed away and is readily available for use when required. On the vehicle which we inspected, no provision is made for luggage carrying other than that which can be accommodated in the interior of the body itself, but, should it be deemed desirable, luggage boxes could be slung below each side of the body or at the rear of the vehicle.

From: *The Commercial Motor*, 16 January 1923

DERRY'S CLOCK AND THEATRE, PLYMOUTH.

PLYMOUTH c.1925

Some say Plymouth wasn't a bad town but war-time bombing changed the area. Before then we have a very lively scene, with to the left a pair of (almost certainly) Mumford bodied Straker Squire buses, twenty of which were delivered during 1920 and successive years, each of 55hp, seating 34 and used on various routes from Derry's Clock to Laira, Saltash Passage and Mount Gould. The No.4 tram on the right hand side, running on reserved track, was new from Geo. F. Milnes at Birkenhead and was in the opening procession 22 September 1899.

THE MARKET BUS – 1928

It was the market-bus that brought most benefit and pleasure, especially to small-holders and cottagers who had previously been obliged to walk to town on market days.

The bus ride itself was no match for an open-air trap ride on a fine day. It was the company that everyone so enjoyed. Market journeys were jolly, social occasions, rather like day-trips, with friendly, animated country folk laughing and joking and calling to each other across the bus. Everyone was welcome aboard with nods and smiles of greeting and a quip or two from the wits. The drivers were cheerful, willing chaps, ready to carry messages or undertake shopping orders for all and sundry.

Farmers' wives came laden with baskets of poultry, butter and eggs. One particularly inquisitive old dame always wanted to know, of those around her, "What 'ave you got taking today?" On the return journey she quizzed people on what they had made on their produce. Folks tried to ignore her but she persisted until she got an answer. But when she grilled her neighbour on how much he made on his turkeys at Christmas he said he didn't know. "Aye but you do knah," she insisted. "Well I sha' tell ya then," was his brusque reply.

On the return Journey, baskets laden with provisions were stacked aboard, everyone lending a hand. News gathered during the day was shared and lively animated talk echoed around. The eyes of the market-piert were a touch brighter than normal, their loosened tongues additionally entertaining. All passengers alighted to goodbyes, good wishes and jocular advice on how to conduct themselves in the coming days.

In later years city folk on holiday in the district were fascinated by the market journeys. They were mystified when, for no apparent reason, the driver pulled up at a field gate, until they heard him remark, after several minutes, "No sign o' Mrs Jones yet, but she'll be 'ere in a minute, sure to." As she was spotted running and panting with her heavy baskets some might jocularly shout, "Come on, Mrs. Jones, pierten-up or it'll be time to come back afore we gets there." Climbing aboard she might say, "Ow long you bin waitin', Jack ? Our clock was stood and I didna know no aim what the time was." Such a remark would invite a bit of leg-pulling from the men on board and some spirited rejoinders from Mrs Jones. There would probably be further waits at gates or road-junctions, to make sure no one was left behind. Perhaps someone would be waiting to hand the driver a shopping-list, with the request, "Please to bring these few things for me, Jack," sure of a willing response. To city folk it all seemed so friendly and matey and, though unfamiliar with the local parlance, they loved the fun and repartee, and many were forced to revise their previous concept of the countryside as a dull and lonely place in which to live.

JMG

FINALLY THE MAGIC HOUR ARRIVED...

This little story is drawn from a book written by Mona M. Morgan entitled 'Growing up in Kilvert Country' and published by Gwasg Gomer, Llandysul, Ceredigion in1990, and is reproduced with the permission of Mrs Morgan and the publisher. Two points of interest: the distance from Newchurch to Llandrindod Wells is some 13.42 miles (21.59km) and the coach a type known to us as a 'torpedo', which succeeded the char-a-banc inasmuch as instead of individual doors to each row of seats, the folding centre seat reduced the loss of capacity caused by a gangway. The complication arose when someone had a 'call of nature' or was just plain sick from too much candy floss or Knickerbocker Glories.

Excitement tinged with apprehension wakened us early on this eventful morning of 25 June 1926, a morning of gilded mist that heralded a glorious day. For the first time we were to leave the confines of our neighbourhood and travel by motor charabanc to a faraway place called Llandrindod Wells. It was a notable day not only for children but for many adults also, who, until this day had travelled only in horse-drawn vehicles, and few to so distant a place.

Excitement robbed us of our appetites. The minutes passed slowly, the hands of the clock seeming reluctant to move. "Isn't it time yet?" we kept asking. Finally the magic hour arrived when we put on our Sunday clothes and set off across Dol-garn pastures, still heavy with dew, cuckoos calling from every side.

Having wondered for days what a charabanc looked like we turned the Rectory corner to find it, with hood folded back, already waiting at the roadside. Many friends, all in their Sunday best, were already assembled beneath the giant oak that stood at the entrance to the village. The road was chequered with sunshine and shadow; wisps of dust whirled up on a cooling breeze that gently stirred the leaves overhead. Here amongst the grown-ups even the big boys looked small. All remained close to their parents, shy of greeting friends in the company of adults. Suddenly, from the door in the garden wall, the Rector emerged to marshal us on to the lawn, there to present us each with a shilling pocket money.

In the 'chara' the seat in the centre of each row was folded back to allow access to the rear and, as each row was filled, this was replaced and occupied, till the vehicle was filled to capacity. Then we were off, the good wishes of those left behind ringing in our ears.

In places the 'chara' brushed both banks of our narrow roads. Passing even a bicycle would have been impossible except in a few wider parts. Behind us clouds of dust rose from the unsurfaced roads. Our speed, necessarily slow in the narrow lanes, increased when we reached the main road at Walton. Never had we travelled so fast. Before reaching New Radnor a calamity of the first order occurred when a strong breeze carried off Mu's new hat. At that time anyone without a hat seemed only half dressed, so the loss cast a cloud over our day. There was nothing to do, Mother said, but buy a new one as soon as we reached Llandrindod.

From New Radnor the road climbed steadily to the Radnor Forest, where the narrow, hairpin bends were negotiated with interest and excitement. At Pen-y-bont puffs of smoke rose above buildings on our right and soon a train came into view. This, for children living so far from a station, was a rare sight, for some probably their first glimpse of a train. All watched the puffing engine with rapt attention as it ran parallel with the road practically all the way to Llandrindod Wells.

We found the Spa to be a grand place, with wide streets,

huge hotels, boarding houses and neatly kept parks and gardens. There were so many things to see that we hardly knew which way to look first.

While the 'chara' conveyed the main party to the lake we alighted outside the Central Wales Emporium, there to buy the all-important hat. We recognised Mr Thomas, who kept the Emporium, at once, for every year with the return of the swallows he paid us his annual visit. Putting up at the Royal Oak in the village, he trudged from farm to farm with his bundle on his back, inviting housewives to purchase his wares and help to lighten his load. On his arrival we waited expectantly for the pencil or other such welcome gift that he always brought.

Afterwards we accompanied him a short distance on the way to his next port of call, helping to carry his pack. Was it because he was a vegetarian, we wondered, that he broke wind with almost every step, occasioning us considerable difficulty in suppressing the laughter that threatened to explode.

With a suitable hat selected and Mu once more respectable, we sallied forth to join the rest of the party. We found the lakeside alive with folk, some relaxing on seats, some strolling at the water's edge and some in motor-boats, chugging out over the sparkling water. Several of our party hired a boat, which rocked threateningly as we nervously embarked. Soon we too were gliding out over the cool, sunny water. Graceful swans, moorhens and ducks swam lazily across the lake. One brood of small ducklings followed their mother, equidistantly, in a straight line, looking like large, downy beads on an invisible thread. In the wooden shelters dotted along the shore, visitors to the Spa sheltered from the midday heat in the scent of the lime trees that fringed the banks. At the boat-house we paid our first visit to water-closets and were greatly intrigued.

After a picnic lunch on the lakeside common we saw, for the first time, tennis courts and bowling and putting greens. For the first time we walked along well-kept paths and over pretty bridges in a park resplendent with beds of flowers. At the pump-rooms visitors sipped mineral waters whilst enjoying the bracing air.

But all good things come to an end and the day, which in the morning had stretched endlessly ahead, came to a close. We said goodbye to all the fine sights and boarded the 'chara' for home. By now shadows stretched long across the fields and before reaching New Radnor all but the eastern slopes were grey in shadow. It was a quiet party, subdued by exhaustion and drained by excitement, that reached Newchurch on the brooding calm of the summer's evening, our thoughts full of the wonderful sights we had seen. It was difficult to say what had given us the most enjoyment, for all had been so strange and new and unlike anything we had seen before.

A surprise awaited us when we reached home, for there on the table was Mu's lost hat. Ours

was a friendly, intimate world, where people's possessions were easily recognised. The hat had been recovered by a Kington lorry driver travelling in the opposite direction. Like everyone else for miles around he had heard of our outing to Llandrindod and he had returned the hat to Newchurch, where the owner had soon been identified. That day's outing gave us our first glimpse of life beyond our boundaries; our lives were never to be quite so insular again.

Two years later a trip to Aberystwyth afforded all children, and many adults, their first glimpse of the sea, which until the arrival of the motor coach had been beyond reach. Most of the older inhabitants died without ever setting eyes on the sea and perhaps had no clear concept of what it looked like. One old character we met on our way to the coach greeted us with, "I warn you be off to see the big pool.'" Perhaps that's how he visualised it.

That day's outing was not without its misadventures, for the coach fumes proved too much for many, including myself, as did our first boat trip. And during the day one grown-up member of the party found himself adrift from the main herd. The mischief had occurred when he paused to watch the Punch and Judy show and had turned to find nothing but strange faces. Frantically he searched in all directions, without success, till at last, in desperation, he approached a stranger, enquiring, "Ave you sin anythin' of the Newchurch consarn?" The stranger was totally nonplussed and said he was afraid he was unable to help. "Well," promised the lost soul, "if I can once get home to the Missus I'll see I'll never leave 'er again." It was with great relief that he spotted a familiar figure in the distance and he lost no time in making contact with the rest of the party.

The homeward journey was broken to allow passengers their first visit to a fish-and-chip shop. One thirty-year-old passenger, on his first outing from home, eyed with suspicion the packet of chips handed to him by his mother. Noting his hesitation his mother yelled, '"Well, eat 'em, Thomas!" "Taters 'em be!" Soon the packet was empty and Thomas smacking his lips.

I have no idea where this photograph was taken although the dry stone walls give some idea. The point though is that this is a scene any country bus driver will have seen in his (or her) lifetime. My own litany of just one trip included a radiator freezing as we drove along, windscreen wipers giving up the battle against wind and hailstones, frozen and jammed doors and diesel becoming like cheese – towed to a barn we got her going again with a paraffin lamp under the engine and paraffin in the diesel! On another day of giving up because of snow drifts and myself and my handful of passengers spending the night with a generous and kind farmer. That was part of a country bus driver's life. Made a change from overloaded late night cinema services!

THE PULLMAN AND ITS ILK

For some 8-10 years until taxation made it impossible financially, the REO Speedwagon and the later 'Pullman' models were among a number of fast, light and powerful machines to be imported from the USA – others included Studebaker, Willys and Fageol – but numerically the REO sold the most. They seem to have been imported as complete, but bodyless, vehicles and were famed for their reliable 6 cylinder nominally 27.3hp engine, which however was claimed to develop a very strong 67bhp at 2,800rpm.

The origins of REO are interesting inasmuch the firm was set up by R. E. Olds in 1904 after he had been removed from the Board of Directors of his successful firm Olds Motor Works, who as 'Oldsmobile', was later added to the General Motors group. REO originally manufactured cars but sensing a market opening they added commercial vehicles in 1908, offering both lorries and later bus and coach chassis, the latter finding favour with both Black & White Motorways and Yelloway Motor Services in the late 1920s, but for whatever reason both companies later changed to Gilfords. In the USA REO wagons and bus chassis remained available until 1967.

As can be seen from the 1926 advertisement 4-wheel brakes were fitted, but originally the archaic hand transmission brake was still supplied. Although always shown as a parking brake nontheless I have to wonder how many half-shafts were disturbed by a sudden panicky application of this. Seating 23-26 passengers in the majority of cases semi-coach bodies were fitted.

REO – Master of Motor Transport

REO conceived the Law of the Average Load applied to Bus Transportation—

Created the Bus priced in prudent ratio to the investment dollar—

Standardized the production, and

Popularized the type.

No other bus combines these features of the Reo Model "W"

Six-Cylinder Engine
Balanced Crank Shaft
Sub-Frame
Standard Tread
163 Drop Forgings
Four Wheel Brakes
Standardized Bodies
Service in Nearly 2,000 Cities
Low priced Repair Parts
Accessibility of all Units.

REO MOTOR CAR COMPANY   -   Lansing, Michigan

This Reo, described as a heavy duty bus/coach, was supplied to a Belgium firm in 1950 for use as a tourist bus in Brussels. The roof is formed of 'Glassite' sections with a folding centre which could be furled to allow for plenty of air and light. Quite what the purpose of the mini luggage rack on the roof was I do not know but the whole thing must have brought some light to the war battered city.

91

WILLIAMSON'S REOS

Totally lost now and to a very great extent forgotten are the smaller operators who ran worthwhile services that quite often the bigger, railway owned concerns, initially overlooked. To undertake this work the private firms used lightweight, mainly American-built, chassis with local bodies offered at a very competitive price. Quite often a form of hire purchase was involved and when trade slumped or the collieries were found to be overstocked hitherto profitable workings like the transport of both miners to work and their wives to market disappeared overnight.

This photograph showing one of Williamson's Reos with an Eaton body is of particular interest to me as the driver, a Frank White, was apparently some distant relative. The route working within the parameters of the time was more or less successful, Williamsons running on Fridays and Saturdays only from around June 1923 for two years but having built up the traffic he

expanded but with the 1930 Road Traffic Act and the coming of Traffic Commissioners with their penchant for favouring the big boys (Barton, Trent and Midland General) he sold out to Midland General early in 1931; by 1934 no less than 18 other operators had disappeared on the Heanor-Nottingham run. Not entirely coincidentally REO buses ceased to be sold in the UK the same year – but somehow three or four have survived into preservation over 80 years later.

THE BIGGLESWADER

I agree that no living soul is visible in this photograph, but the very name of the vehicle is intended to make the association with the town quite a personal one. Not here the vague Eastern Counties, Midland General, London Transport or First monoliths but a nice friendly local bus.

Mr Watkins ran a motoring Emporium for many years and then finding a demand branched out into local bus operation. NM9197 is a Thornycroft – probably type A2 Long, a 20-seater, typical of its time with an opening windscreen in lieu of a windscreen wiper and a (very) high floor, which however inconvenient for the passengers allowed this bus to be driven over some dreadful roads and through quite deep snow. The manufacturer's option of pneumatic tyres on the rear has been taken up, but solids are still the style of choice for the front wheels.

[My apologies for the poor quality of the photograph – but I have never seen better of 'The Biggleswader'.]

TRANSPORT TO AND FROM A MILITARY CAMP

[This item is culled, with permission, from *Commercial Motor* 22 September 1925, and it is of interest not only as an historical transport note, but as an indication of the post World War One army strength. From a peak of 4,583,300 in 1918 they were reduced (including non-combatants) to 342,200 in 1925, rising back up to just under 5 million in 1945.]

By the maintenance of a Regular Passenger Service into Town during the Period of a Nucleus Occupation, a Good Business has been Created.

When the 12,000-odd troops of the Regular Army who are due, between the present month and the end of the year, to take up their new permanent quarters at isolated Catterick Camp, which is situated on the rolling North Yorkshire moorlands, they will have reason to feel grateful to the road passenger transport industry in general, and to the local firm of Messrs Brand's Garages in particular, for it is only by means of motors that this encampment in the hinterlands is brought into real touch with the outer world. Already, advance parties have arrived at the camp, and it is expected that occupation will go on steadily for the next few months.

Mr A. Brand is responsible for the passenger-carrying business of this enterprising undertaking, which has its headquarters in Richmond (Yorks.), and the zealous manner in which he has devoted his energies towards meeting prospective developments at the camp are now about to bear fruit after almost six years. For the major portion of that period the future of the vast wartime camp has been in the balance and, therefore, the subject of acute speculation locally, for it was only about 18 months ago that the military authorities definitely announced their intention of renovating this once important training centre, which, since the termination of hostilities, has been almost de-peopled.

Therefore, it will be appreciated that Messrs Brand had by no means a very reassuring outlook when, just after the end of the war, they started camp transport facilities. Throughout the intervening period, however, they have maintained services sufficient to meet the requirements of Catterick Camp.

Incidentally, it supplies a noteworthy example of the value of the careful cultivation of a definite district by a motorbus undertaking where there is a likelihood of growth and expansion of population to recompense the operators for their inauspicious, and probably unremunerative, pioneer efforts. The service between Richmond and Catterick Camp was first started in January, 1919, at which time the depot was in a state of partial disuse, and there was then certainly little reason for hope that Catterick would become a permanent army depot, for everything pointed towards its entire abandonment. The service was opened with a subsidy type 26-seater Maudslay saloon bus and a 28-seater motor coach of the same make, and the proprietors at once decided that, in the event of the camp being reconstructed at some future date, quite the best method of firmly establishing themselves for residents since 1919 have comprised, in the main, dependents of men on overseas service, and detachments of special corps, whilst each summer the population has been temporarily increased by visits from a number of Territorial divisions for annual training purposes. In order to provide accelerated services, the fleet was augmented later in 1919 by a further Maudslay and a 32-seater A.E.C., each provided with saloon bodies, and 28 journeys were made daily by these vehicles, a 20-minute service being maintained between Richmond and the centre of the camp, with additional facilities at holiday periods and during the periods covered by visits of the Territorial divisions. By the end of 1920, the fleet had been brought up to eight vehicles by the purchase of one 18-seater Selden motor coach, one 14-seater Vim motor coach, one 32-seater Maudslay and one 14-seater Ford bus...

[The authorities declined to allow a competing firm into the camp]

With the knowledge that the camp was definitely intended as a permanent depot to encourage them, the firm last year commenced upon the task of reconstituting their fleet; in order to ensure their ability to cope with the increased demands of the future, and as a preliminary step, a 2-ton Thornycroft passenger chassis was obtained, fitted with a handsome Bartle body capable of accommodating 26 passengers. The object of the purchase was to ascertain the suitability of a vehicle of this weight and capacity over the undulating highways negotiated daily. In all respects the tests were considered to have resulted most satisfactorily, for the vehicle proved itself absolutely reliable in every way. Fuel consumption, too, was a source of gratification, for this remained steady in the vicinity of a gallon per 11 to 12 miles.

Having found 26-seaters economical to operate and suitable for both light and heavy traffic, Messrs Brand have concentrated upon vehicles of that capacity, and have now replaced the majority of the older and heavier buses. The present fleet still numbers eight units, these being two 30-36-seater Maudslays, three 26-seater Maudslays, one 26-seater Thornycroft, one 14-seater Ford and one 14-seater Vim motor coach.

These vehicles are all mounted on Mackintosh and Henley air-cushion tyres, with the exception of the two 14-seaters and the most recent Maudslay purchase, which are shod with pneumatics. Up to the present there has not been time to make any accurate comparisons between solids and pneumatics, so far as the heavier units are concerned, but, provided results are sufficiently encouraging, it is expected that the latter class of tyre equipment will be substituted generally throughout the fleet.

Messrs Brand Garages have in use a cheap return-fare system, the double-journey fare being 9d. as against 5d. for the single trip, and some time ago they made an interesting departure in the way of tickets at specially reasonable charges for regular passengers. These are issued weekly and enable purchasers of the booklet to make six journeys in each direction for a total sum of 4s., whilst similar facilities have been introduced for the benefit of school children at a charge of 2s. per head per week.

With a fine spirit of reciprocity the military authorities, some time ago, approached Messrs. Brand's Garages with a view to securing a through service between the camp and Darlington, which is the nearest large centre of population providing amusements appealing to the men stationed at the camp. The new service was commenced with commendable promptitude, over a route touching Catterick Bridge, Scotch Corner and Barton, and, in addition to proving of immense benefit to the military, it is, incidentally, now doing much to develop the agricultural neighbourhood traversed. Two buses

– a Thornycroft and a Maudslay – are regularly engaged upon the route, which extends some 15 miles, and together they cover a weekly mileage of approximately 500. When one pauses to contemplate the difficulties formerly experienced in travelling between the two places, the great advantage of the service becomes fully apparent, whilst the cost factor is extremely important.

In the first place, residents of the camp were formerly obliged to travel by bus to Richmond, where they entrained, proceeding in the diametrically opposite direction for four miles, and in consequence paying both additional bus and train fares. The present return bus fare is 3s., which compares most favourably with the existing rail charge of 3s. 10d. from Richmond to Darlington, excluding the bus fare for the double journey between Richmond and the camp, which had to be paid in addition.

Apart from their regular services, Messrs. Brand's Garages now cater extensively for road pleasure travellers during the summer months, and operate attractive tours to all parts of the picturesque Swale valley, and also to a large number of popular seaside resorts on both the east and west coasts, including Scarborough, Morecambe, Whitley Bay, Redcar, Saltburn etc. Another popular venue is the Lake District.

[I have no idea what a "Vim" coach was, but James Bartle was a coachbuilder working between 1919 and 1926, London based, and I would imagine the body was supplied as a part of a package by Thornycroft. Mr Brand was to sell out in 1929 to United Automobile who wanted his Catterick-Darlington route; this sale was one of some 19 independent companies brought about by United that year. At the time, Mr. Brand had nine vehicles in use.]

NORTHERN IRELAND – LAHARNA HOTEL

Like many railway owned hotels, in this case the Northern Counties Committee of the LMS, the Laharna Hotel, Larne, was the place to stay during the 1920s. Built in 1902, following a disastrous fire at an earlier building, after its 1905 up-dating it passed to the railway's predecessors in 1909. In 1935 the cost of a ferry trip Stranraer to Larne was sixteen shillings, with a cabin an extra ten. The hotel by comparison charged 7 shillings and six pence bed and breakfast, but the daily rate including lunch and dinner was only 12s 6d. 'The troubles' were to drag down the hotel (as with most others in the area) as tourists fell from over one million to below 400,000 in two years. At this time the hotel had been sold out by the British Transport Commission and was privately owned by the Hastings Group, who themselves hived it of in the late 1970s, when really it was better known for its dances than much else and even they had declined from the great days of the 1950s and 1960s.

A few of the fleet of McNeil of Larne is lined up ready for day excursions. Henry McNeill was himself a hotelier and for whatever reason had gained the nickname of 'Knock 'em down' McNeill, and back in the 'good old days' presumably not long after the Laharna Hotel was opened, reports spoke of anything up to ten two-horse brakes seating ten inside and ten up top waiting for their passengers. A local gentleman Tommy Shields tells us "I remember all the jaunting cars lined up outside the hotel and the Charabangs. I remember my father driving a Charabang which was a big open bus. You know the type of prams with hoods, well there was one of those came over the top of the bus. Made of canvas. You were frozen to death!"

He goes on to describe the Laharna as beautiful, and how there were always a dozen coaches lined up outside "and they were always full!" Here is a more modest selection of McNeills coaches which comprise, left to right, a four ton Dennis, 32-seater a surely overloaded Ford model T, with its bonnet sides already up! And finally a Maudslay.

The photograph was from the late Reg Ludgate, and the note from Tommy Shields is courtesy of Alison Kane, to whom we extend our thanks.

CHARLES ROBERTS

This photograph which shows one shop, the Road Vehicle Body Shop, of Charles Roberts & Co., Ltd, whose basic existence relied upon the manufacture and leasing of railway rolling stock, everything from coal wagons by the gross to a gloriously over-the-top carriage for some Indian potentate. When this work slackened they were quick to move into the bodying and refurbishment of road vehicles; having a good versatile labour force the company were very competitive. This illustration, courtesy of, and with permission from, the collection of John Wakefield, gives a good idea of their scope and abilities. Clearly the Austin in the foreground has been rebodied, and fabric roof coverings do seem to have been their forté. The skeletons or completed bodies of at least six buses are visible, all mixed up with cars, lorries and raw material. When I worked at a similar workshop (albeit much smaller) we called it The Cathedral and did not like to disturb the peace with anything so vulgar and noisy as an air drill, router or planer! Strangely the foreman thought otherwise!

Licence No. 1015

Barry Urban District Council

Char-a-banc, Hackney Carriage, Wagonette, Brake or Omnibus Driver's or Conductor's Licence.

Badge No. 365

TO ALL WHOM IT MAY CONCERN.

Be it known by these Presents that _William A. Weans_

residing at _18 Thompson St._ is hereby **Licensed**

to be the _Driver_ of a _Motor Bus_ plying for hire

within the Urban District of Barry.

This Licence to continue in force until the 31st ~~May.~~ December

1923, unless the same be sooner revoked.

Given under the Seal of the Barry Urban District Council, this _Eighth_ day

of _October_ 19_23_

_____ Chairman.

Thomas Powus Member.

I.B. Ironoff Clerk.

95

On the face of it this is a fairly ordinary timetable (on opposite page), dated 15 July 1926 which gave an hourly service in weekdays and a slightly confusing Sunday service Garstang to Blackpool, albeit by two different routes. An additional Sunday-only offering was from Pilling to Blackpool, which however gave a good day out.

However the twist in this item is that this sheet was probably a printer's proof, for the reverse, which I have asked to be shown, represents a long forgotten facet of social history. Conversely it may be the 'Poor Law' side is the printer's proof for it has been modified with addition of "Out Relief", the system whereby tramps, or 'Gentlemen of the Road' received an allowance in exchange for labour – somewhat akin to the overnight working of the Youth Hostel Association.

From 1919 to 1929 Poor Law administration was under the aegis of the Ministry of Health. The Workhouse (Wukkus) was long used as a threat – I heard "if you don't attend to your schooling you'll end up in the Wukkus" in the 1970s, and it was also a reality for many. Although the workhouse system was abolished on 1 April 1930, nonetheless as late as the outbreak of war over 100,000 people were accommodated in former workhouses (re-named Public Assistance Institutions) 5600 being children ('bastards'). Until quite recently at least 50% of old peoples' homes were ex-workhouse buildings.

Outdoor relief was normally paid to the 'deserving poor' to keep them in their own homes as being far more economic to the Guardians (ie ratepayers) than housing the bodies in the workhouse (in the 1860s about half the cost). The sad fact is that by the 1920s a tramp turning up at the "Spike" could well have a better diet of cooked meats, or pickled pork, with vegetables, even perhaps a bowl of gruel with dumplings, than one of Mr Smith's drivers or conductors.

Coachbuilders' Products for Olympia

[Extracted from the report in *Commercial Motor*, 20 November 1923]

James Bartle and Co., Ltd. Stand 32

This company has paid considerable attention to the construction of high-class bodies for passenger carrying, and examples of their coachbuilding, which fall under this heading will occupy much space on the stand. There will be two buses and a motor coach on view.

Dealing with the passenger vehicles, the first is a 16-seater single-deck bus body mounted on a Guy chassis, which has Michelin pneumatic-tyred wheels. This vehicle is arranged for operation by one man, the safety door at the front being under the control of the driver. An exit for use in emergency is arranged at the rear.

An 18-seater bus which will be shown is also arranged for one-man control, and in this case the Burford chassis of the forward-dash type is used to carry the body. On both of these buses the upholstery is carried out in leather, and garden spring seats are employed, the cushions being removable. Each vehicle is also fitted with automatic balanced windows, which enable the buses to be employed all the year round without discomfort to the passengers. The 18-seater has been built to the order of the Great Western Railway.

The 20-seater coach body on a Lancia chassis is an excellent example of high-class coachbuilding. The body is of the bulbous type, and it is luxuriously upholstered in antique leather. The special type of Bartle hood is fitted, and it may be recalled that in this patented method, provision is made for the individual hood fittings, which act as supports for the covering, to be folded neatly down behind the seat frames when they are not in use.

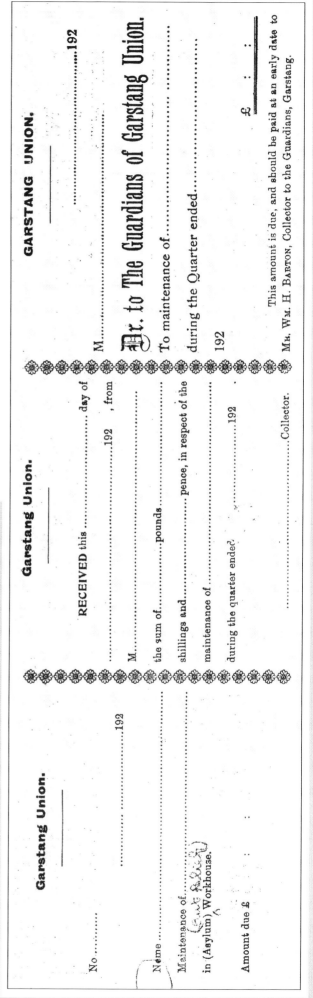

The 'Pilgrim' Daily Motor Omnibus Service between Blackpool, Garstang, Knott End and Pilling.

Good through connections for Lancaster, Preston, Inskip, Catforth and Woodplumpton.

TIME TABLE commencing July 15th, 1926.

Garstang → Blackpool

	am	am	Noon	pm	pm	pm	pm	pm	pm	pm	pm	pm	pm	pm	s	s	s	s	s	s	s	s	s	s	s
GARSTANG	9 0	10 0	11 0	12 0	1 0	2 0	3 0	4 0	5 0	6 0	7 0	8 30	9 30	10 30											
CHURCHTOWN ...	9 10	10 10	11 10	12 10	1 10	2 10	3 10	4 10	5 10	6 10	7 10	8 45	9 45	10 45											
ST. MICHAELS ...	9 20	10 20	11 20	12 20	1 20	2 20	3 20	4 20	5 20	6 20	7 20	8 55	9 55	10 55											
GT. ECCLESTON	9 30	10 30	11 30	12 30	1 30	2 30	3 30	4 30	5 30	6 30	7 30	9 0	10 0	11 0											
ELSWICK	7 50	9 40	10 40	11 40	12 40	1 40	2 40	3 40	4 40	5 40	6 40	7 40		9 25											
THISTLETON	7 55	9 45	10 45	11 45	12 45	1 45	2 45	3 45	4 45	5 45	6 45	7 45		9 30											
SINGLETON	8 5	9 55	10 55	11 55	12 55	1 55	2 55	3 55	4 55	5 55	6 55	7 55		9 40											
SHARD LANE ...	8 10	10 5	11 5	12 5	1 5	2 5	3 5	4 5	5 5	6 5	7 5	8 5		9 50											
POULTON	8 20	10 15	11 15	12 15	1 15	2 15	3 15	4 15	5 15	6 15	7 15	8 15		10 0											
BLACKPOOL	8 35	10 30	11 30	12 30	1 30	2 30	3 30	4 30	5 30	6 30	7 30	8 25		10 15											

Sunday only. To Singleton only. Sat.

(Talbot Mews) Blackpool → Garstang

	am	am	am	Noon	pm	pm	pm	pm	pm	pm	pm	pm	pm	pm	pm	pm
BLACKPOOL		9 0	10 0	11 0	12 0	1 0	2 0	3 0	4 0	5 0	6 0	7 0	8 0	9 0	10 30	
POULTON		9 15	10 15	11 15	12 15	1 15	2 15	3 15	4 15	5 15	6 15	7 15	8 15	9 15	10 45	
SHARD LANE ...		9 25	10 25	11 25	12 25	1 25	2 25	3 25	4 25	5 25	6 25	7 25	8 25	9 25	10 55	
SINGLETON		9 30	10 30	11 30	12 30	1 30	2 30	3 30	4 30	5 30	6 30	7 30	8 35	9 30	11 0	
THISTLETON		9 40	10 40	11 40	12 40	1 40	2 40	3 40	4 40	5 40	6 40	7 40	8 45	9 40	11 10	
ELSWICK	8 15	9 50	10 50	11 50	12 50	1 50	2 50	3 50	4 50	5 50	6 50	7 50	8 55	9 50	11 15	
GT. ECCLESTON	8 20	9 55	10 55	11 55	12 55	1 55	2 55	3 55	4 55	5 55	6 55	7 55	9 5	12 5	11 15	
ST. MICHAELS ...	8 30	10 5	11 5	12 5	1 5	2 5	3 5	4 5	5 5	6 5	7 5	8 5	4 5	8 35	11 20	
CHURCHTOWN ...	8 40	10 15	11 15	12 15	1 15	2 15	3 15	4 15	5 15	6 15	7 15	8 15	4 15	8 45	11 25	
GARSTANG	8 50	10 25	11 25	12 25	1 25	2 25	3 25	4 25	5 25	6 25	7 25	8 25				

Sundays only. Saturday only. Thursday only.

S Runs on Sundays.

Sundays.

	am	pm	pm
GARSTANG	8 30	1 15	5 15
NATEBY CHAPEL	8 40	1 25	5 25
MOSS EDGE	8 50	1 35	5 35
RAWCLIFFE P.O.	9 0	1 45	5 45
HAMBLETON	9 10	1 52	5 52
SHARD LANE ...	9 20	2 53	5 6
POULTON	9 30	2 15	6 15
BLACKPOOL	9 45	2 30	6 30

Sundays.

	pm	pm
	1 05	0
	1 105	10
	1 205	20
	1 305	30
	1 405	40
	1 505	50
	2 06	0
	2 156	15

Sundays.

	am	pm	pm	pm
BLACKPOOL	9 0	11 0	3 0	7 30
POULTON	9 15	11 15	3 15	7 45
SHARD LANE ...	9 25	11 25	3 25	7 55
HAMBLETON	9 35	11 35	3 55	5 58	8 10
STALMINE	9 45	11 45	2	5 3	4 56	5 8	8 20
PREESALL	9 55	11 55	1 53	5 56	1 58	8 30
KNOTT END	10 5	12 5	2 54	56	2 58	40
PILLING	10 25	12 25	2 45	4	2 56	4 59	0

Sundays.

	pm	pm	pm	pm	pm
	1 0	2 45	7 0		
	1 15	3 0	7 15		
	1 25	3 10	7 25		
	1 35	3 30	5 40	7 35	
	1 45	3 40	5 50	7 45	
	1 55	3 40	6 0	7 55	
	2 53	5 04	3 06	10 8	5
	2 54	104	5 06	3 08	25

Sundays.

	am	am	pm	pm	pm	pm	pm
PILLING	8 20	10 40	1 0	5 2	4 57	1 09	0
KNOTT END ...	8 40	11 0	1 25	3 53	5 55	2 57	3 09	20
PREESALL	8 50	11 10	2 0	1 53	5 55	3 57	4 09	30
STALMINE	8 50	11 20	1 20	4 53	2 55	3 57	5 09	40
HAMBLETON ...	9 10	11 30	1 53	2 55	3 55	5 58	0 9	50
SHARD LANE ...	9 20		2 5	6	6 58	20 10	0
POULTON	9 30		2 15	6 158	30 10	10
BLACKPOOL	9 45		2 30	6 308	45 10	20

All enquiries and complaints to be made direct to ERNEST SMITH, Elswick, near Preston.—Telephone: 8 Great Eccleston.

H. Wrightson, Printer, Garstang.

97

SNAPSHOTS

Before today's slick use of various digital devices the taking of photographs was relatively rare and the further back we go in time the rarer it becomes. The cost of a camera, be it a Box Brownie or Ensign had to be budgeted for, as did the cost of film – only eight shots (or at best 12) on a film and then unless you had the knowledge and time to process your own the chemist had to be relied on. There developed from this a number of seaside itinerant photographers who would take a photograph of a seaside charabanc or toastrack tram about to depart with all the smiling passengers, find out how many wanted a print (Guernsey 1950s nine pence, say £1 today) and have them ready on the party's return. A tiny, tiny handful of these prints have survived the effects of a war (bombing, flooding) and age (fading, the dreaded skip etc) and of those that have if we are lucky someone will have made a note on the back of what we are looking at and a few others detective work can help. But they are all, good, bad or indifferent vital social documents showing not only people's fashions but advances in vehicles.

A family record with most of the details clearly visible. The date is 5 September 1922 just three years after the Armistice – and the notation on the back "Annie & Frank on holiday in Germany 1922 or 1923". This was 'Peter's vehicle' and the Elite group a trading co-operative. The international appeal may be gathered from the English notice above the Travel Bureau "Potsdam start here".

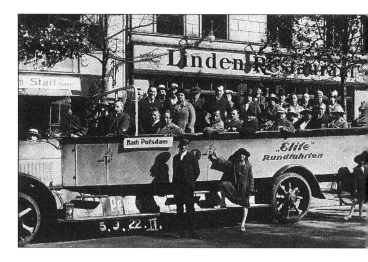

Lewthwaite Brothers of Cleator Moor, near Whitehaven, Cumberland, ran this Ford Model T on outings, mainly in connection with the local Catholic Church. 1925.

Another char-a-banc but this time said to have been mounted on a first world war Rolls Royce chassis (the Spirit of Ecstasy on the bonnet may or may not be real) but we do know that this car was the pride of Pearl White Motors of Barrow in Furness and that the proprietor, Mr E. Johnson was at the wheel.

A rather anonymous card although we know the photographer, a Mr Rigby of Cemetery Road, Southport. It is said to have been a FIAT chassis and the body is a pure char-a-banc with doors to each row of seats. The neat step and grab-handle did little to make entry easy for ladies; my aunt told us one day that her husband was required to give her a discreet push!

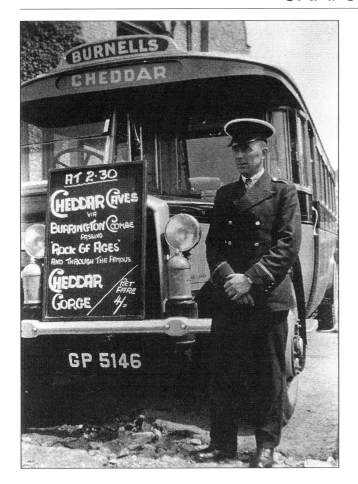

Burnells Coaches were to survive in one form or another until the 1950s when they sold out to Western Engineering & Motor Services Ltd, who in turn passed the coach operations to what is now Bakers Dolphin. This photograph typifies a scene that would be replicated on The Marine Parade, Weston-super-Mare for many a year. The vehicle is a Gilford, new to The Ledbury Transport Co., of Reading (better known as 'Thackrays Way') in 1932, passing to Burnells when hardly run in and staying in the fleet until 1942. The items under the headlamps were Gruss air springs said to enhance the ride.

(Frank White)

If every coach driver was given the photographs that were promised he or she would have boxes full of them. This (borrowed) one made it and bears the endorsement "Mr WALTER JONES. Thanks for the memories of some nice rides – and for keeping me the front seat!" I wonder if the lady really realised how lucky she was as the front seats were prizes not easily given. And the next trip is for Llangollen when it was still a quite quiet town.

"Will you take a photo of us dear?" and the next thing you knew was that an unfamiliar camera (very breakable) was thrust into suddenly sweating hands. As far as I remember this mob were at 'Skeggy' and luckily it was quite a decent day. Just about a paying load; had there been less than 20 they would have been combined with another tour to make up the preferred 44, the ensuing 'spare' driver would receive a guaranteed number of hours pay – three probably – and be told to turn up the next day at 08.00.

Both a 'line' service and a coach outing. Saltburn Motor Services ran a bus service from Saltburn to Loftus from 1928 to their sell-out to Cleveland Transit in 1974, but this service which climbed the fearsome Saltburn Bank was more often than not used as a sightseeing run by visitors – the lady passengers here are mostly wearing summer frocks. This vehicle originally fleet no.22, but later 30, was one of very few to carry the firm's crest on the side. A Guy Arab III, FAJ 174 was delivered to SMS in 1949 with an unusual but luxurious Wilks & Meade 33-seat body. How far the leaks present in this body during 1957 contributed to its short life I do not know but no.30 was withdrawn in 1960. Cleveland Transit were themselves to pass to Stagecoach in 1994 thus ending the last link with SMS.

THE TROLLEY-OMNIBUS

Photographs of chassis in their natural surroundings littered with dunnage are rare, and here is an unusual variant on that rarity: a "trolley omnibus" chassis built by Straker-Squire Ltd, of Edmonton with electrical equipment and (in this case) motors from British-Thomson-Houston of Rugby. The order for the whole machine with Brush of Loughborough bodywork was received by Clough, Smith & Co., from Keithley and supplied in November 1924. In all ten vehicles were supplied, six chassis nos. 20-25, fleet 5-10 were double deck 50 seaters, the balance w/nos 26-29, fleet 11-14 carried 32 seat saloons. All were notable in the use of twin 40 horsepower motors, slung amidships to give a good centre of gravity.

Street scene of Keithley Tramways, the final route to Ingrow. Car 10 on first day, 14 December 1924.
(Keithley News)

RAILODOK OR, I DON'T BELIEVE IT!

A PASSENGER ELECTRIC TRUCK
Source: *The Commercial Motor*, 1 April, 1924

The small accumulator electric truck is becoming increasingly popular for the rapid transit of small but heavy goods in dock-yards, railway stations, and even in works; but it is entirely new to find one of these machines employed for the carrying of passengers. Such, however, will be the case at the British Empire Exhibition at Wembley, where a number of standard Railodok electric trucks, specially adapted for passenger carrying, will be utilised on the 15 miles of roads and paths within the precincts of the Exhibition.

Each car will carry 12 persons and, in addition to the ordinary services, will be available for hire by private parties, the terms for which can be had on application to Railodok Electric Passenger Service, whose office is at the Exhibition.

The garage for these cars will, it is stated, be the largest and most up-to-date electric garage in Britain, and will be fitted with the latest type of battery-charging plant.

These trucks are manufactured by G.D. Peters and Co., Ltd, of Caxton House, Westminster, London, S.W.1, at their works, which are situated at Slough, Bucks.

The faded postcard was issued by the 'Sole Concessionaires' Heelway Press of Holborn, who I hope made enough to cover the stiff charges. There do not seem to be many photographs of these little machines, but what they all have in common is a suicidally inclined driver and squashed up passengers. Technically they were quite advanced having the latest in battery technology whereby a full charge normally taking 50 hours was reduced by a British invention from D.P. Batteries of Bakewell to a mere 15, more or less matching the Exhibition's opening hours.

We are grateful to members of the Provincial Historical Research Group of the Omnibus Society for much of the above information.

EAST AFRICA PAVILION

To Earn an Honest Crust

This is the main body-shop of Northern Counties Coach-builders in 1924. Feast your eyes on all these variants on coaches and buses, then lie back and enjoy the evocative smell of a wood-shop and hear again the sibilant whisper of a plane fettling up a length of timber. Pure nostalgia at its best.

CHAR-A-BANC-DRIVER FINED

Sequel to Collision at English Bicknor

From *The Hereford Journal*, 13 September 1924

"His Good Record

Before the Coleford magistrates, on Tuesday, Walter Philip Hawkins, of 12 King Barton Street, Gloucester, a motor chara-banc driver, in the employ of the Bristol Tramway and Carriage Company, was summoned by Supt. Shelswell for driving a motor-charabanc in a manner dangerous to the public in the parish of English Bicknor on the 17th July. The case was adjourned a month ago owing to defendant's solicitor (Mr Trevor Wellington, Gloucester) being away on holiday.

Mr Wellington entered a plea of not guilty.

Struck His Right Wing

John Collett, postmaster, Christchurch, near Coleford, stated that on the day in question he was driving a motor-car in the direction of English Bicknor, from Lydbrook, about 5.45pm, and as he was negotiating a sharp bend by the Glen Cottage, Stowfield, he noticed a charabanc approaching Lydbrook. Witness sounded his horn; they were only 33 yards apart. Witness said the charabanc was about three feet on its wrong side, and he was forced to shut off his power and steer along the bank, and went up the bank about 18 inches.

"At the time the charabanc was passing me;" he said, the rear part struck my right wing, damaging it; also the screen, damaging the glass and breaking the stay and ripping the hood right back – doing damage to the car to the extent of £45." He (witness) did not hear the charabanc sound any horn. He was driving about five miles an hour, the charabanc could not have been going more than five miles per hour; otherwise, it could not have stopped as it did.

Plenty of Room

He (witness) asked the driver of the charabanc why he was on his wrong side, and defendant said he was not driving fast, and he "wasn't going over that bank." Witness replied that there was plenty of room without doing that.

Cross-examined, witness did not agree that the impact and the sounding of the horn occurred simultaneously. The impact was not caused by the dislodging of three stone steps. He had brought his car to a standstill before the impact.

Mr Wellington: "If you say your car was brought to a standstill before the impact occurred how do you account for the excessive damage done to your car?"

Witness: "There is a great difference in the weight of a charabanc and a Maxwell car." Witness had been driving since 1925.

Clerk: "Was the charabanc loaded?"

Witness: "Yes, sir."

Bound to Occur

Lucy Jane Machen, residing at The Cottage, England Bicknor, said she was in the last witness's car. When nearing The Glen, Stowfield, witness found that the car was pulling right into the bank. She then saw a charabanc and it was quite evident to her that a collision was bound to occur. She quite expected it to have come instantly, but it didn't, though the rear of the charabanc struck the car. It was a terrible evening – pouring with rain. She felt a jar when the accident occurred.

Lucy Margaret Henrietta Crombie, a daughter of the last witness, said Mr Collett was only going at a moderate speed.

The charabanc was on its wrong side, the motor-car being forced right into the bank.

P.C. Smith, of Lydbrook, stated that about 7.40pm on the 17th July he received notification of the collision. In company with Mr Collett, he proceeded there, and examined the spot where the collision occurred. He measured the road, which was about 15ft 9in. in width. On the left-hand side he saw a wheel-mark of a motor-car, which had run into the bank for a distance of eight yards, and he saw wheel-marks for a foot or foot and a half up the bank. On the offside he saw marks of the charabanc, as pointed out to him, for a distance of twelve yards from where the collision occurred. He measured the mark which was only 1ft. 9in. from the bank. There was only one bank on the side of this road.

In reply to the Chairman, witness said the bank was very high, and was the bank on which the wheels of the car had gone.

Cross-examined: Witness agreed that it was an excep-tionally bad night. The rain, however, could not have washed the marks out, the road was very soft.

The Other Side
Defendant Says it was "A Filthy Night"

Mr Wellington admitted that there was a conflict of evidence, but he was in the happy position of having six independent witnesses, who would tell further a different story from that of the prosecution.

Walter Philip Hawkins stated that he had been driving motor-vehicles since 1918 and during the war he was driving for the Mechanical Transport Service. Since 1919 he had been employed by the Bristol Tramway and Carriage Company and had held a clear licence throughout. On the date in question he was driving a party from Gloucester in a charabanc to and from Symonds Yat. The charabanc he was driving was from 40 to 50hp and weighed between four and five tons; its width was about 7ft 10in. It was, he said, a filthy night, rain pouring.

Always Blew Before Corners

As he was going round a corner, he noticed Mr Collett, who was coming in the opposite direction, shoot around another corner very fast. Witness was only travelling about four miles an hour, and pulled right on to the grass. As the complainant was about to pass, he struck a stone, causing the car to swerve into the rear of the charabanc. The car was not stationary, as had been alleged; after the impact it went for a distance of about six yards. The charabanc – which was carrying 26 passengers – was brought to a standstill imme-diately.

Rough Shunt 1924 Style

This little saga encapsulates much of what we know about driving in 1924.

Brakes would be nothing special on either vehicle and the turn was well known as a bad one until very recently. The car driver's evidence is as 'iffy' as it often is, stating "he had brought his car to standstill before the impact" but earlier on he stated he was driving at five miles an hour. Not mentioned in court was what today would be a salient fact, in that neither vehicle was equipped with windscreen wipers and all the witnesses argued it was a filthy night when you either opened the top half of the buses' windscreen to see out and got soaked, or left it closed and peered through the condensa-tion. Similarly, the car driver would not have the best view and the rain would be finding its way under the flapping canvas of his roof. The business of the stone steps is very odd and there must have been some considerable impact between the Maxwell's wheels and the steps to dislodge them. I would have liked to inspect Mr Collett's front offside wheel to see what marks existed. Had he already 'lost it' on a greasy soaking wet road?

The Maxwell car was one that suited the nature of a 1920s postmaster being 'respectable' but the company, founded in 1904, was best known for the massive factory in New Castle, Indiana, but in 1921 they became part of the Chrysler empire and effectively died in 1925, not before, however, building

quite low cost four-seat tourers, a few of which were exported to the UK. I would imagine Mr Collett's car to have been a Maxwell 'Cub' of 1924, to avoid heavy import duly, assembled from knock-down kit at Kew with a straight four-cylinder engine, 3-litre capacity (3046cc) developing 25bhp @ 1700rpm and with a three speed gearbox (direct drive in top). There were a few Maxwell buses recorded but I have not been able to trace many details, although a heavily rebuilt 1922 Detroit 25cwt model charabanc with a four-cylinder 20.9hp engine, brakes only on the rear wheels and a transmission handbrake, is still extant. A 1½-ton 1921 lorry recently fetched US$20,000.

CONCENTRATED CONTRASTS

These two photographs show buses which were first cousins and for their day modern. But the reality was that the Cape cart hood was a shocker to put up in bad weather and the side curtains did absolutely nothing for the paying customer's visibility on a scenic tour. Both bus bodies were of a style which superseded the pure char-à-banc with only one door for entry and egress.

FN 5250 was built on a Daimler Y chassis as long ago as 1922, but by 1925 had been fitted with a second-hand but smart 32-seat coach body, when presumably pneumatic tyres were fitted, but in 1931 it was again updated with a Tilling 28-seat body itself second-hand, but the following year this was scrapped and the chassis sold off.

The registration of the 'enclosed' car is unfortunately a works plate but it clearly is a relative, albeit rather more ornately painted. Still limited to 12mph (19kph) the draughts and noise would have been horrendous and with the best Kent rain pouring down visibility a no-no.

(Both photographs courtesy The M&D and East Kent Bus Club)

SIC TRANSIT?

When the Corporation of Worcester were considering selling their tram birthright for a mess of diesel they asked Alfred Baker, the General Manager of Birmingham Corporation Tramways, for his opinion on their best way forward. Initially he suggested trolleybuses as the power supply, traction poles, feeder cables and so on were in situ, but somewhere along the line his early advice was ignored and instead they 'cosied-up' to Midland Red. Then – perhaps having to some degree cold feet – they once again approached Mr Baker for further advice. This is one of the relevant documents and is an interesting read.

BLIDWORTH BLUE BUS SERVICES

Sparkling new and unregistered

This Tillings Stevens was far from the usual choice of independents partly for reasons of fuel economy and partly because the hill climbing speed of a petrol electric was always slow. The route board reads like a litany – or – requiem for an independent operator. The bus passed to Midland General in the mid 1930s.

Blidworth's Church of St Mary of the Purification has two claims to fame, inasmuch as not only was Will Scarlet (Robin Hood's side-kick) buried in the churchyard but that within the church they hold a Rocking Ceremony during which a baby, born as near as possible to Christmas to married Christian parents from Blidworth, is "rocked" in an ancient cradle on the Feast of the Purification of Mary. These children's names are then recorded on a plaque, but how long this ceremony can survive in this day and age must be doubted.

BIRMINGHAM CORPORATION TRAMWAYS.

Congreve Street,

Birmingham.

2nd September, 1927.

Mr. Alderman W. J. Hill,
        Worcester.

Dear Mr. Hill,

        Referring to the interview I had with you at this Office on Thursday, the 1st. inst. you ask my opinion as to whether it would be more advantageous to the Corporation of Worcester to –

(a)   Complete the Agreement which has already been provisionally settled between the Corporation and the Birmingham and Midland Motor Omnibus Co. whereby the Corporation are to lease to the Company the Omnibus Powers in Worcester upon terms of receiving annually the total net profits (estimated in round figures at £6,300 per annum) the Company undertaking during the period of the Agreement to provide such ordinary and work peoples' services as are necessary to meet the reasonable requirements of the travelling public, and to provide such services and charge such fares as may be agreed with the Corporation, or –

(b)   To lease to the Company upon receiving a fixed guaranteed sum of approximately £4,000 per annum, the Company to be under no obligation with regard to either fares, stages or any kind of control by the Corporation in the operation of the services.

        As I mentioned to you at the interview this is purely a question of policy which your Corporation must decide for themselves – no technical question arises.

        I have, however, responded to your request and in stating my views you will please understand that I am looking at the matter entirely from the point of view of the Corporation. A view which would probably be very different if the negotiations were between two private individuals or trading concerns, no Municipal body being involved.

        Having made this clear I deal with (a)

        The draft agreement provides for adequate services, reasonable fares for both ordinary passengers and work people and it also provides that the Corporation shall take all net profits accruing from omnibus operation in your City and permits the Corporation to have some sort of control.

        The net profits are estimated to be in round figures £6,300 per annum. A sum which is about equal to your annual indebtedness in respect of the purchase of the Worcester Tramways undertaking.

        There has never been any doubt in my mind that given reasonable management this annual sum would be realised.

(b)   The suggested agreement provides for a guaranteed sum of £4,000 per annum to be paid by the Company. The Company is to be under no sort of obligation to the Corporation either with regard to fares, stages or services and the Corporation to have no sort of control whatever.

        This certainly does not appeal to me and I am convinced that it would not appeal to the citizens of Worcester. By placing themselves entirely in the hands of the Company the Corporation would certainly be accused of selling their birthright for a mess of potage, particularly if the operating company were to attempt to pursue the policy of exploiting your ratepayers for the sole purpose of making large profits for their shareholders.

        Let me say however that I am quite sure that the Company as at present constituted would not be guilty of such a policy, but as you know the personnel of companies change and in a few years time the constitution of the present Company might be very different from what it is today.

        Looking at the matter purely from a financial point of view –

(a)   Provides for satisfactory services safeguarded by your Corporation with a (problematical if you like) payment of £6,300 per annum.

(b)   Provides for a guaranteed payment of £4,000 per annum and leaves the Corporation with no control whatever.

        It seems to me that the first duty of your Corporation is to see that a reasonably cheap and satisfactory system of transport is provided for your citizens and to secure this it is necessary for you to have some sort of control, even if the net profits might possibly fall short of the estimated amount. Indirectly your ratepayers would gain.

        Yours faithfully,

        (Sd) "A. BAKER"

BEAUTY IN MINIATURE

An outing in April 1924 being operated by Mr A. Knight of Fivehead Neville. Said to be a Chevrolet, but the disc hides the normal badge, this should be a 14-seater and clearly the number of girls and women in the photograph greatly exceeds this, after half-a-dozen recounts I make it 20 plus the driver and the boy. A reasonable presumption would be that at least a handful are sitting on the offside bodywork or even standing behind this delightful little char-à-banc. Unlike many of the high, clumsy vehicles based on ex-WD chassis Mr Knight's vehicle is a real little gem even to the tidily furled hood, and definitely not one where bodies could be swapped with a lorry platform in winter.

It will be seen that not unusually the driver is sandwiched between two females, one at least quite young. It has been suggested to me that the black bonnets denote war widows – the first world war had only been over for five years – my family had four of these, two of whom never remarried. I have a memory of these aunts, who were often seconded to take us on a bus or tram 'to get they boys out of the way'.

The location is the market town of Blandford Forum; for those with a penchant for exploring the local countryside, beware you do not get 'mazy', as parts of Dorset have a unique, sleepy, charm. Fivehead Neville, around 2 miles from the most pleasant town of Sturminster Newton, is one of three 'Fiveheads', St Quintin and St Magdelen being the others.

G.W.R. ROAD MOTOR CAR SERVICES

For "G.W.R. Road Motor Car Services" read Great Western Railway motor coaches, which in 1927 were kept very busy in the season. This advertisement is from an official tourist publication. The coach entered service in 1925 as fleet no.865, XY 7437. The chassis, a Burford, and bodywork, Buckingham 18-seater, were both from firms that once the GWR stopped buying from them were to expire.

105

THE RED-HEADED MACNABS

I found this item in a 14 March 1946 issue of *Transport World* The original had been marked by someone who, perhaps, knew of the MacNabs. In the 1920s a number of my relatives tried to make a living running mini-fleets of small, easy to maintain vehicles, although if we are realistic their side valve engines probably needed a de-coke and valve regrind every 10,000 miles (if they lasted that long), the brakes required fettling overnight and possibly even an adjustment during the day. Most drivers of my vintage were taught to use the engine/gearbox as the primary brake and then to finish off with the right foot. This though could wear out clutches and the sight of a Bedford OB with a tell-tale curl of blue smoke being brought into the garage was not what we (as driver mechanics) really wanted. Conversely when our hoist had broken itself and another bus was occupying the ramp my mate and I parked a sick Leopard over a roadside ditch and changed the clutch; as the younger one I was the one working underneath and covered in oil while my mate worked the 'Handy Billy' hoist above. No hi-vis vests and no hard hats. Just fags and profanities! In a sense we were the linear descendants of the MacNabs.

Memories of a unique bus service

Those who knew Sussex in the early 1920s may recall MacNab's Bus Service, which ran between Arundel and Lttlehampton as frequently as possible from dawn to midnight during the holiday season. MacNab and his string of red-haired sons and daughters flogged their ramshackle 26-seater unmercifully; and by overloading, hard driving and hurried meals, they made enough money in two years to take the whole family to Australia.

The MacNabs lived in a wayside cottage at Lyminster, and it was here that they relieved one another for meals. The MacNab going off duty would run up the long path between the gooseberry bushes, struggling the while to divest himself of smock and pouch. He would be met halfway by another member of the clan, who would grab the accoutrements and pelt down the garden path, urged by the violent revving of the waiting bus, which was by that time enveloped in blue smoke.

The MacNabs were hard workers. They knew their regular passengers by name and were never unreasonable about transporting greyhounds, push-chairs, pea-sticks or rose bushes in sacks. Young and old were picked up and set down at their doors along the route, and country folk would send a child to the end of their lane to ask the bus to wait, while mother struggled along with her baby and baggage.

The departure of MacNab and his carroty tribe marked the decay of a humanism which is fast dying out of passenger transport. Rough-and-ready, overcrowded and dangerous perhaps, his red bus remains unfaded in memory, symbolising the golden age of independence, when petrol was sold in two-gallon cans and the owner-driver of a bus could run a few miles off the route to do his fellowmen a good turn.

Was it prescience or canny Scots' foresight that sent MacNab and his youngsters to the Antipodes? Sussex roads were quieter and safer after they had gone, but a few will remember with affection the boundless enthusiasm which united the family. Somewhere on the Australian continent there must surely be a little red bus, racing along in a cloud of dust., driven by a red-haired MacNab, with a freckled MacNab of the third generation squeezing between the standing passengers to collect the fares.

REAL PEOPLE HISTORY

Over the years of coach riding, whether in char-à-bancs, buses, horse waggonettes, real coaches or anything that could move and carry passengers many millions of people in the United Kingdom have come and gone with few leaving little trace other than a few bob in the hat for the driver. Where a courier was carried they saw much and said little although I shall never forget the look on our Cynthia's face when after an arduous five-week tour she was handed a very thin envelope. Opened later it contained a very generous cheque indeed – the only time we received such a thing! Most of the riders from the 1920s and 1930s are fading away or have already done so but here and there I have been able to cull reports of travels thankfully recorded in books. The source for each one is acknowledged individually and we (the publisher and I) are grateful to receive permission to use these.

I have interspersed one or two bits of my own travels as they are themselves 50 years old; I may not remember much of travelling before the war (although I am a child of the 1930s) but even up to the hippy revolution of the 1960s old entrenched coaching habits were still commonplace, and we knew that a pleasant leisurely ride with a blind eye turned towards a bottle or two passing around, frequent stops for lavatories and a good noshery for lunch was the recipe for happy passengers and by inference a decent tip. When you started getting named as the chosen driver you knew you had arrived, but a noted thing about the earlier expeditions was that a local operator was inevitably chosen and only later did the big partly railway owned octopi of companies spread their tentacles into the country districts.

These extracts are from Children of Bethnal Green, by Doris M. Bailey published by Sutton Publishing Ltd, in 2005:

I had to get out each morning soon after eight to catch a bus, and what a business this was. No-one then had ever heard of queuing for a bus, so we all stood where we were and hoped the bus would pull up in just the right spot. The young fellows stood around the corner from the bus stop and jumped on as the bus slowed down to round the corner. Sometimes I would stand there too, and pray hard that the policeman would hold the bus up just as it got there, so that I too could jump on, but this wasn't often the case, and sometimes I would get shoved and pushed about for nearly half an hour before I could get on. There was one nice conductor, though, who would let me stand under the stairs, even when the bus was full, and I just loved those mornings. It was easier to get on when it rained hard, because lots of people wouldn't go on top in the rain. But I chanced it, and sat with the canvas cover over my knees and the brim of my hat turned down all round. I think queues were the best thing to come out of the war!

[Later] I loved to boast that I'd been on a covered-top bus. My other favourite bus was a private bus, a bright purple vehicle numbered 525. This did not belong to the General Bus Co., (L.G.O.C.) and the driver would madly overtake all the other buses, collecting all the passengers he could. The conductor would stack us in until we could hardly breathe, and never used the hateful words "Full right up". I was never late for school when he was around.

This section was from 'Where I belong: a Forest of Dean childhood in the 1930s by Joyce Latham and published by Alan Sutton 1993:

It was all very strange at first, but Mam soon made new friends and I was introduced to the chapel Sunday school. Everyone was very kind to me and I thought I was so grown up every Sunday afternoon, dressed in my best, hair curled with the tongs and my little black shoes polished until I could see my face in them. The biggest event of the year was the Sunday school outing, to which we contributed month after month by paying in whatever coppers could be spared. These sums would be entered on to a red card issued to all the scholars, but there was a place for everyone aboard the chara-banc, whatever their annual contribution [Not so elsewhere – in one village if insufficient money had been saved, the youngest child was left behind. My colleague told me it left him with a hatred of the hypocrisy of religion]. It's hard now to describe my feelings before that first trip to the seaside. Of course, I had never seen the sea... I made myself quite ill with excitement long before the great day arrived.

Nobody could afford the luxury of meals in cafés, so the night before the outing all our mothers were hard at work cutting mounds of sandwiches and baking little cakes. These would be well wrapped in greaseproof paper – we saved ours from cornflake packets and stowed away safely in brown paper carriers, along with a couple of bottles of cold tea... [Dad stayed at home] A huge cheer would arise when the chara came into view around the corner, and once we were aboard Mam would make sure I had the best place, next to the window. There would be a roll call then at last we would be away, cheering once more...

We were hardly out of Monmouth, no more than five miles into our journey, when from all parts of the chara could be heard the rustling of greaseproof as hungry children set about their sandwiches. "I be ever so hungry, Mam," I whispered, tugging at her sleeve, and she delved into her carrier bag to pass me a thick slice of bread and dripping, my favourite snack. Our first stop for toilets was Newport, just for quarter of an hour, the driver said. It was more like half an hour before all the stragglers were accounted for, and that was hard to take when all you wanted more than anything in the world was your first glimpse of the sea.

"Ow much further?" was the question on everyone's lips, but at last there would be a triumphant cry of: "There it is! I can see the sea!" We all craned our necks for a glimpse of the dark blue patch honing into view on the skyline, and my heart starting beating so fast I thought it would burst. As soon as the chara stopped, all thoughts of Sunday school etiquette disappeared as the children pushed and shoved towards the door. I was at least as impatient as any of them, but Mam would not budge until the gangway was clear.

"Now then, our Joyce, doesn't get a-runnin' off," she warned me "Thee't get lost an' it 'ud all day to vind tha. This yun't like the Vurest, o'butt." [Vurest = Forest of Dean, Joyce's home]...

[after a number of adventures, mainly in the fairground] ... Many more charabancs had parked since our arrival that morning, rows and rows of them, and it took Mam a while to track ours down. I don't know which one of us was more grateful to clamber aboard and settle down for the journey home. There was of course a wait for the few men who had been brave enough to come along, and who had then made off for the nearest pub. "Thoy drunken devils had better get a move on, or thoy'll vind theirzelves awalkin wum," the driver muttered darkly, pulling out his pocket watch. But they rolled up at last, arm-in-arm and singing their heads off, and the women winced as they scrambled aboard and filled the coach with alcoholic fumes. After a few sharp words they soon settled down, and spent the rest of the journey in loud slumbers. Someone at the back started a chorus of Ten Green Bottles and everyone who was awake and inclined joined in. I snuggled up to Mam, resting my head on her ample lap, and fell asleep with the sound of the sea still pounding in my ears...

These quotations are from Alf Townsend's often amusing 'Cabbie' published by Sutton Publishing Ltd, 2003:

...the little Welsh examiner couldn't possibly fail my driving a four-seater taxi when he had already passed me to drive a forty-nine seater coach! [Alf passed but] ...I was very heavy on the clutch – just like a coach driver!

Plan A had succeeded. I had my PSV licence. Now I needed a job. Grey-Green Coaches of Stamford Hill was my next stop and I was taken on. The new drivers always got the dodgy jobs where there was no 'beer money', like the school run, the service routes and the changeovers. The changeovers consisted of driving the coach on a service run, stopping at all stops as far as Brentwood, in Essex. Then on to Colchester, where you would change over with a driver who had come from Great Yarmouth. He would go back whence he came with your coach and you would do the same, with no 'beer money'. I realised much later, when I was a lot wiser, that it was all about 'bunging' the foreman who gave out the work. The same drivers always seemed to get the cream jobs, like the pub outings and trips to the races with the Licensed Victuallers. A coach driver in those days could more than double his weekly wage with trips like these. I really enjoyed the pub outings and the factory outings to dear old Southend. Again it was a learning curve in life. When you took a crowd of women from a factory in the East End, you needed to be on your best behaviour. They were all out for a good time, but there was a moral limit to their larking about. And if you took a liberty, as in the case of a young fellow driver, you could find yourself minus your trousers and tarred and feathered in the nether regions to boot!... [this tale has been around for a long time, one wonders where the girls would get tar and feathers, but the truth is coach drivers were regarded as seamen, here today, gone tomorrow, and unwanted pregnancy was a real fear among these girls]...

There was one particular job that nobody wanted to do, so it was given out as a punishment and that eventually meant me. I had left behind a young, unaccompanied mental patient at Colchester coach station. Nobody had told me about this young girl, but the management passed the buck to me. So, I was given the dreaded 'Ghost-Train Run' as my punishment. The Ghost-Train was the very last coach to leave Kings Cross at night. I think it was 10 o'clock. It swept up all the late travellers at every stop as far as Colchester. Then on to Felixstowe and back to Ipswitch Garage, which we shared with the Ipswitch taxi-drivers. A few hours' kip on the back seat with a blanket, a wake-up call and a cup of tea from the cabbies and it was heading back to London at 1 minute to 6. [this run suited Alf for as a putative taxi-driver he was able to learn 'The Knowledge' during the day. He duly passed out]... the first thing I needed to do was to go up to Stamford Hill and collect my employment cards from Grey-Green Coaches. All the other coach-drivers gathered around my cab, all taking the mickey out of me and calling me by my garage nickname of "Manningtree". This unfortunate nickname came about when I had to cut through from Felixstowe from Harwich one night in an empty coach. The guys had already warned me about the low bridge at Manningtree and to make sure the sunroof was closed on top. It was late and I was tired, but the loud scraping noise I heard when going under the low bridge soon woke me up. I forced the sunroof shut and continued on my way.

The next day I dumped the coach in the garage and made a speedy exit without telling anyone. It didn't take the garage too long to trace the driver and I was up in front of the big boss once again. Old George Ewer was all right, much the English gent, and he wouldn't even allow a Union in his garage. He suspended me from driving coaches for a month, and I became his personal chauffeur, driving his brand-new Jaguar up and down the Al2 to Colchester and back...

[Grey-Green differed from my employers who made it quite clear that (a) as the 'new boy' you got the worst jobs and (b) you were the first to be laid off when the season ended. Personally I always admired the London taxi-drivers of Alf's generation and as the one-time owner of an FX3 amused myself moving our people from A to B, knowing the police ignored taxies. I was shocked when recently I had to tell the black cab driver the way to the Record Office, Kew – he admitted he got lost earlier on the way to London Airport.]

This item seems to have been set in 1924 or thereabouts and is drawn from Sheila Stewart's 'Lifting the Latch: Life on the Land – based on the life of Mont Abbott of Enstone' published by the Oxford University Press in 1987, with a new edition from Day Books of Charlbury, Oxfordshire in 2003. A superb record of real people full of detail. The Passion-wagon was a Reo – American built, fast and light:

...Our next outing we determined 'ud be on the Passion-wagon.

Adam's Passion-wagon were getting a reputation for matchmaking in the village. It were fundamentally a flat-bedded lorry with no sides. The make, I think, were a Rio. The Adams family used it to cart goods and supplies to and from their farm and their stores in Road Enstone and Charlbury Station. It were a proper meccano job to convert it into a charabong for occasional village outings. First the seats, long box pews, was bolted to the bed of the lorry. They pews went right across. The passengers loaded up from the open end, as in church and latched their own little door across. Once you was cooped up in your pew you was stuck, so it paid to scrawf up next to somebody you fancied. There were no escape.

The roof were a rolled back canvas-effort strapped into a neat bundle across the rear. If it rained it took two chaps, one on each side, to unroll it. It were upheld like the calabash of a covered wagon, by long cane arches, channeled through seams in the canvas, held at either end in special sockets on the end of the pews. The front were held down by fastening the leather straps to the buckles mounted on the front mud-guards. The windows were smoky cracked squares of yellow cellophane stitched to the roof at intervals – no good for viewing the scenery. Who wants scenery in a Passion-wagon? They old windows 'ud wiffle-wuffle, whip-whack in the wind, steamed up with singing and heavy-breathing as the royster-ers, side by side, went "Rolling down to Rio" – or Bognor.

Jim and me, curious to try our luck afresh with the gals, booked to go on the next outing, whatever it might be...

Unfortunately for us hot stallions the next outing turned out to be a tepid all-family outing to the Zoo "starting early in case of accidents". As the Zoo were only Franky Grey's little private menagerie a few miles away, out by they stwum [stone] quarries near Kirtlington, they were allowing a heck of a lot of time for accidents It were women and children first

to board the wagon in the vast queue for potential disaster outside Worth's New Garage. Us called it Worth's New Garage, but it were still only a shed a step up the road from his other shed behind the Litchfield where Dicky Worth – like Mr Morris – had begun his climb in the motoring world by mending bicycles...

Dicky often helped out the Adamses, and were driving the wagon for them on this occasion. Despite loading they pews to the gunnels it were obvious he warn't going to have room for us motley crew of chaps left to the gallant last... [they were loaded into Dicky Worth's Ford taxi] which were built like one of today's iron skips, but with a saloon roof, left-hand drive and a wind-out windscreen in a frame so heavy with chrome it took two chaps to wind out the handle... [seven of them and the driver were squashed in, but] in no time at all we was backing up the next telegraph-pwoost and sailing ass over head, to land upside down in the middle of the road... [no one was hurt apart from their dignity and they walked home]... it were the shortest days' outing 'starting early in case of acci-dents' I ever had.

Almost any city and most towns in the United Kingdom has always been glad to celebrate 'happenings' whether May-day, Bank Holidays, Doggett's Coat and Badge Day on the Thames, or at the other extreme the Henley Regatta, right through to occasions involving the Royal family. And before the days of television for the majority of the population however good the BBC's broadcasts people wanted the sense of being there – belonging – they might not see much but just to say 'I was in the crowd at Hyde Park' or 'near the Abbey' was to become part of the show. But as ever the fat-cats did not want the bother of coping with what they perceived as the 'sweaty masses' and tried hard to make the whole thing elitest. Eventually a groundswell led by the _Daily Mail_ caused considerable relaxation; however 32,000 soldiers and 20,000 police were drafted in to ensure safety along the 6.25 mile route of the stage-managed procession, typically 40,000 children being required to stand on the Embankment and cheer at the appropriate time. An interesting note is that the date, 12 May 1937 should have been the Coronation Day of Edward VIII and his lady consort but as we know he abdicated under pressure from both state and church. But the arrangements stayed in place for George VI and Elizabeth. All the lights and decorations remained up for 23 days giving coach operators time to arrange tours.

12 February, 1937.
CONSENTS FOR CORONATION SERVICES
Reference was again made in the House of Commons to the recent decision of London Transport to grant consents for motor-coach proprietors to operate tours of the decorations and illuminations during May, only on condition that a fare of 5s. per person was charged.

Mr W.H. Green pointed out that the coach proprietors were prepared to run such tours at 2s 6d. per head and that the fixing of 5s. would preclude many Londoners of limited means from participating in such tours; therefore, the Ministry of Transport should ask London Transport to reconsider its decision in this matter.

Mr Hore-Belisha said this was a problem which affected not the Board alone, but street capacity, police control, safety and larger issues, all of which would be taken into account. Incidentally, the London Passenger Transport Act, 1933, placed an obligation on the Board to provide adequate serv-ices.

GOING FOREIGN

In the aftermath of the first World War a number of ex-servicemen – one at least had married a French girl – set up tours to take widows and 'relicts' to see the battlefields and memorials that had separated them forever. Kellyways seems to have been a variant on the theme, and rather ephemeral, I can find no trace of their tours after 1925. However it was the only operator I can trace who particularly emphasized "Amiens" as a town to stay for a night or two.

The battle for Amiens which lasted from 8 to 12 August 1918 marked the end of the war for the Germans. Hopelessly outnumbered both on the land (14 battered divisions against 32, including one fresh American, no tanks against the allies 500+) and in the air, (365 aircraft of all types against 1900+), it was no wonder after an initial stiff resistance they crumbled and broke. However allied casualties were still high (22,000 British Expeditionary Force, 22,000 French) against 25,000 Germans killed or missing, although in the débâcle 50,000+ surrendered, more than half of these subsequently dying from disease, starvation and cold while in captivity.

We must assume that three quarters of an hour in Amiens was both a 'comfort stop' and time for the passengers staying over to be taken to their hotel.

The turbine steamer "Onward", built 1905 for the South Eastern & Chatham Railway and certificated for 1479 passengers, was typical of those used before the war on the Folkestone-Boulogne run although "Onward" was set on fire in 1918 (some say sabotage) and scuttled. Raised she was rebuilt and passed to the Isle of Man Steam Packet Company as their "Mona's Isle" being used for summer work from 1920 to 1939. One of the famous 'Little Ships' of Dunkirk in the course of her three trips she brought back 2,634 servicemen plus a number of refugees, and it was with regret she was finally scrapped in 1948.

36. BOULOGNE-SUR-MER. — 'L'Onward" dans les Jetées.— LL.

BOULOGNE BOAT LEAVING HARBOUR, FOLKESTONE

109

SOUTH WALES TRANSPORT – NEW BUS IN 1926

The company was first registered on 10 February 1914, its first service running from the tram terminus from Ynysforgan to Ynysmendwy, but a later route from Cwmburla to Loughor and then Llanelly made more sense. Expansion seems to have been fast with a route mileage of 38.8 and 26 vehicles by the outbreak of the first world war, with Morriston – Port Talbot and Swansea-Mumbles as two successful services, despite the presence of trams on the latter. In some ways the war must have suited SWT as they were awarded two good contract routes between Llanelly and Pembrey Ordnance Factory and Swansea and Gowerton – a steelworks extension.

SWT seem to have had a bit of a liking for tram or tram connected lines as in August 1920 they took over the services of the Neath gas trams, which by now under Council control had become more and more erratic and irregular, replacing them with new buses. Six new open-top AEC buses were supplied for the Swansea – Port Eynon route, with further deliveries bringing the total fleet to over 100 by 1924, fifteen more in 1925 and twenty-eight the following year including this fine AEC 507 with Brush 54 seat top covered open staircase bodies, but also a batch of Saurers for the Townhill route. The unique part of these low-height vehicles was that the seating upstairs was in a herringbone pattern necessitating two sunken wells and as we can see two possibilities for banging your heads!

LONDON 1926

Both of these photos are drawn from a magazine of 1926 – they appear here as an antidote to the yattering of those who take today's crowds and complain about overcrowding and refuse to believe it was ever thus so.

Tram 1424, showing signs of wear and tear, was a London County Council car of class E/1 built by Hurst Nelson of Motherwell in 1910. The Blackfriars – New Cross Gate was one of the most interesting (in the quiet times!) as it involved not only a tour of part of London but a crossing of the Elephant & Castle. XM 7xxx was from class "S" of the London General Omnibus Company, the first of which entered service on 29 December 1920, seating 54, ours following in 1923. The outside staircase remained a feature of London buses until the late 1940s; I well remember watching the road whizzing away underneath me and despite being with my father feeling terrified.

FAMILY SNAPS

Two family snap-shots, reflecting the spontaneity of a couple of joyful trippers and the bus crew. The sunlight is picking up the side of the bus, an East Yorkshire Motor Services (ex Hull & District) Tillings Stevens. The sheep appear quite unconcerned. Around 1926-7.

This advertisement appeared during 1927 and really marked the last gasp of a successful coach operator. John Harding started working in Penzance around 1910, and commenced operations under the trade name Trelawney Tours Ltd with a single motor coach in 1920, later opening another branch in Newquay, having by the time of the sale of his company seventeen motor coaches of the better kind.

However on 24 May 1928 he agreed to an offer from the National Omnibus and Transport Company for his business, vehicles and premises. One attraction to the National was John Harding's patented invention of which he was justifiably proud was what was known as the "Silent Guide", a mechanical gizmo fitted to the windscreen, which was designed to give the passengers a key to the principal scenic items along their route. Seemingly it worked but disappeared from the National coaches a few years later.

The C.M.U.A. Policy

A note of disagreement from a prominent West of England Motor Coaching Concern

In our last week's issue we drew attention to the contents of the document issued by the Commercial Motor Users Association outlining the 1923 policy of the National Council.

The programme of motor organisations which advocate the same petrol tax (4d or 5d per gallon upon both commercial and private motors) is opposed by the National Council of the Association because this would mean a substantial increase in the price of the fuel to the commercial user. Should there be a reversion to the petrol tax, and such a tax be found to be practicable, the Association announces its determination to fight for the old basis of half the rate of tax per gallon, whilst, should it be decided to retain the vehicle tax, the Association will endeavour to secure various improvements in the method of the issuing of licences, in the granting of one-day licences in the off-season, and in a reduction in the licence fees: This circular has been sent out to members and other persons connected with the road transport industry, and we are in receipt of a letter from the managing director of Trelawny Tours Ltd, who run a large number of motor coaches from Penzance, St Ives, and Newquay, enclosing a copy of a letter sent by the company to the C.M.U.A. It is a system of taxation (or business persecution, to give it its correct description) to which we have been subjected since.

"The present iniquitous measure is in effect, no better than legalised robbery and it has been a matter of astonishment to me that business men have endured the torture of it so long. Why, in the name of British justice, are men who have had the misfortune to invest their capital in perfectly honourable and useful business to be subjected to the treatment we have received?

Take my own case as an example. Why should I be compelled to close down my business on September 30th of each year and keep it closed down until March 29 of the following year, because of some foolhardy regulation? It is the common experience, that the 'Motor Coach Tours' business is that of the summer season; in so far as the close

of it is concerned, is entirely dominated by the state of the weather. If the weather collapses, as it did at the end of last September, our business collapses with it. If, on the other hand, the weather holds good in October as in 1921 – so does our business. Why would we have to speculate on £20 licences, multiplied by the number of our machines, which may not return us as many shillings? Surely business is sufficiently difficult without preposterous obstacles of this nature. Then again, oft-times during the period from September to March, a business chance comes our way. Can we take it? No, because of this unreasonable measure. The bitter experiences I have had (I could quote a long list) have convinced me that rules and regulations won't do. I am going to plump for a Petrol Tax, as the only acceptable alternative offered. Therefore, in view of the expressed Policy above referred to, I regret I must, for the time being, resign membership of the C.M.U.A. until this business is settled. The Association has done splendid work and is worthy of the support of every user in a general way, but, because I so strongly disapprove of the policy decided upon, I feel compelled to take this step."

Yours faithfully. TRELAWNY TOURS LTD
Managing Director
Commercial Motor; 19th January 1923

RAILWAY RAMBLINGS

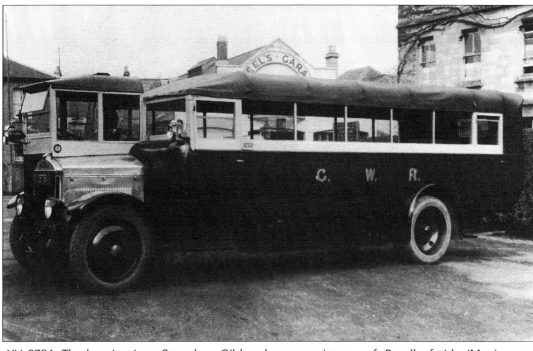

I described this coach to a Great Western Railway 'buff' as being a hen-coop with a fox box for the driver. He agreed and went on to add that Messrs Brunel and Gooch (GWR engineers) could not have dreamed up anything as horrible as this.

The underlying chassis is a Maudslay ML3, the 'lo-line' job of the time. The bodywork, described as an all-weather 32-seat coach, was by Buckingham and the whole ensemble was registered on 30 May 1927, as fleet no.1222, YH 3794. The location is at Stroud station, a well maintained location on the so-called "Golden Valley" line. Opened in 1845, around half-a-million passengers use it annually so the threat of closure has receded for now.

John Buckingham of 333 Mill Lane, off Bradford Street was in the late 1890s one of four coach-builders in that industrious part of Birmingham and at one time in the mid-1920s had a reputation for building high-class bespoke car bodies, one on a 1925 Rolls-Royce 20 hp being still in existence, but the firm had a close tie-in with the GWR producing many of their coach and bus bodies ; hopefully most somewhat more attractive than this.

G.W.R. SPYING ON BUS OPERATORS
27 September 1935

The fallacy has grown up that the Great Western Railways was an honest, decent concern. This is more the truth.

How two Great Western Railway detectives travelled as passengers on a coach trip was revealed when they figures as witnesses in the prosecution of the coach owners, at Blackwood Police Court, for carrying excess passengers. Messrs Albert G. Gibbs, Albert R. Gibbs and Leslie R.

Gibbs, bus proprietors, of Pontllanfraith (Mon), were summoned by the South Wales Commissioners for charging less than the proper fare for excursions from Pontllanfraith to Barry Island.

Evidence was given that Messsrs Gibbs Bros. were licensed to run the excursions at 3s (three shillings) per head, but that, it was alleged, they charged 2s on two occasions. The magistrates found the charges proved.

The partners were also summoned for overloading one of the coaches on 11 August last.

Evidence was given by two G.W.R. inspectors that they travelled on this vehicle, which was on hire to Messrs Gibbs Bros from an Abersychan firm. There were, they testified, 31 adults, 10 children and five babies on the 29-seater vehicle.

The magistrates dismissed the summonses against the two younger partners, but fined the eldest, Mr Albert G. Gibbs, 50s (shillings), plus 10s 6d. costs on each of the two summonses for undercutting and 10s on the overloading charge.

The 70-year-old bus proprietor, Mr W.T. Withers, Pontllanfraith, was also fined 50s (shillings), plus 10s 6d. costs, for each of two offences in respect of excursion fares.

Reported in 'The Commercial Motor' and 'Bus & Coach'

THE WORLD OF RESEARCH

The Cooke family were blacksmiths, farriers and typical fettlers of farm machinery for many generations. In a sense these were the men (and their wives) who provided the agricultural backbone of England throughout the era of horse or steam drawn vehicles.

And yet W.J. Cooke clearly saw the way the future was running (perhaps he worked on mechanical transport during the war) and declared not only that he was an engineer, but that he was capable and willing to build motor car bodies and coaches as well. I do not know if he built any buses or coaches from scratch but it does seem he certainly rebuilt at least two, plus 'vans' – I wonder what he did for the Co-operative Stores of Waltham Abbey?

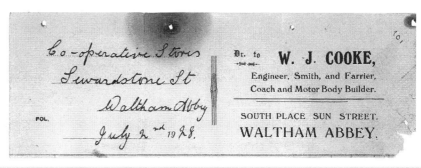

IN THE BEGINNING... HB BUSES

In 1928 the garage and PSV business of Hooper & Berryman trading as H.B. Buses was taken over by Clarence Mumford of Salisbury Road Plymouth, a coachbuilder whose business (as wheelwrights and 'real' coach builders) had existed since the mid-19th century. Mumfords were themselves involved in tour and excursion work in the Plymouth district under the trading name Purple Tours, but deciding that expansion was the way forward they registered the company H.B. Buses on 17 March, 1929, and very quickly set up a subsidiary concern, Cornish Buses Ltd, down in Truro who began a Plymouth-Penzance through service. Not entirely coincidently at the time the only through service from Plymouth to Birmingham, a 12¾-hour marathon, was operated by Red & White Services of Lydney, with their terminal agents in Plymouth, Messrs H.B. Buses, Salisbury Road, Plymouth. Not entirely a part of this story: the Birmingham office was the "West End Candy Stores, Paradise Street", which conjures up images of desperately sucking barley sugar after 12 hours in a Gilford at a nominal 20mph.

Meanwhile, W.T. Coath & Sons were running a service from Plymouth to Hooe, Ivybridge and Totnes under the "Eddystone" name, and Mumfords cast their eyes over this concern resulting in a purchase as recorded in these scraps of paper. The hand-written note signed by Clarence Mumford and J.R. Berryman tells the tale. I have to assume that the sale of the company and its vehicles was carried out separately as £80 was only a nominal amount – presumably the value of the "Eddystone" licences. The dates involved 21 September

This promissory note was given by H. B. Buses of Plymouth for payment to Mr. Coath of Eddystone Motors (also of Plymouth) whose bus service 'H.B' acquired. Signed, Clarence Mumford and J.R. Berryman, directors of 'H.B'.

1929 and 24 June 1931 neatly bridge the setting up of the new Road Traffic Acts. H.B./Mumford then entered battle with Western National on a number of routes, but were eventually forced into a route sharing agreement.

A final note on this saga relates to the name of Mr Coath, as existing records seem to show his name thus but as a countersignatory to the agreement he spelled it: W.T. Coatte not once but twice.

Mumfords carried on their bodybuilding activities as an independent firm until the late 1930s when they were absorbed into the Western Motor Holdings Ltd group but never seemed to recover from their wartime activities, eventually metamorphosing into Lydney Coachworks during 1947 where they rapidly gained a reputation for good quality workmanship, but were forced to close in 1952. The link between the Red & White Group and Mumford activities can be gauged from the fact that Lydney Coachworks was built on R&W's land at Harbour Road, within the Lydney Industrial Estate.

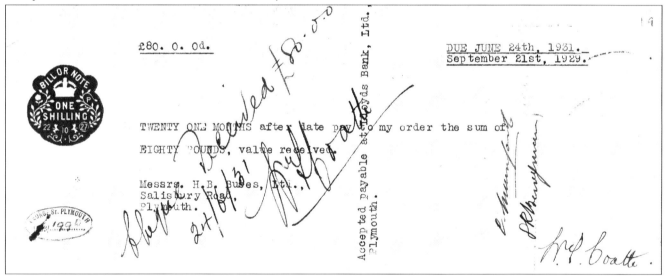

RECTANGULAR

A member of the family when very small looked at this photograph and stated that for purity of line it should have square wheels. I think he'd been studying Le Courboisier at school as had the bodywork builder Christopher Dodson! Seating 32 EF3985, fleet number fleet no.117, had an AEC type 426 chassis and was delivered to the South Shields Corporation in 1928.

FROM GLASGOW TO CLAPTON

That is in part the story of this Leyland Titan TD1 with its Leyland low-height 51-seat body delivered to Glasgow Corporation in 1928 as their fleet no.92. It would be reasonable to expect that on withdrawal from the Glasgow fleet in 1940 this bus like many of the tranche (120 in all) would have gone to scrap. It is true that 42 of them were commandeered as Civil Defence ambulances but a handful survived to see service in some unlikely locations.

William George Harrison was an old fashioned kind of bus entrepreneur and adopted the fleetname "Royal Blue" for his operations out of Clapton near Crewkerne, Somerset, with 'traditional' style market services to Crewkerne and to Axminster, and local excursions from 1924, again of the old-fashioned sort including 'Mystery Tours' where, contrary to local belief the driver was not blindfolded before being given the route.

In 1931 he was authorised to work forward to Bridport and for the summer season to Weymouth. Demand was such for this latter that to cope with weekend would-be passengers our old friend no.92 was purchased and is seen here waiting departure in 1949. A contemporary note is to see how round shouldered the conductress is; not only had she a ticket rack, and cash bag, but at home in 1949 there were no mechanical devices to aid washing so it was all done by hand, and cooking was at best over a gas stove, but quite often on a kitchener. No vacuum for working people until the 'Goblin' came along and then it was both expensive and heavy. Small wonder these working girls often looked exhausted. (Roy Marshall)

BEEN THERE, DONE THAT

Admittedly not working on a Chevrolet but I would imagine that most owner driver/mechanics have had this slightly embarrassing problem at some time. Whether this was Mr Robson of Middleton I have no way of knowing but his 14-seater Chevrolet was due to go to Morpeth and hopefully made it. The engine in this model was nicknamed the "Cast Iron Wonder" and like its Bedford successor was rated at 27hp from its six cylinders.

Letter from Birmingham Corporation Tramways

In 1928 there were some crossed wires between Alfred Baker, M.Inst.T., General Manager of Birmingham Corporation Tramways and an 'expert' on trolleybus working. The letter literally reads as follows:

"Dear Mr Hill,

I thank you for your letter of yesterday's date. Although I marked my letters "Private" I did so simply because yours to me were marked "Private".

I have no objection whatever to your reading them to your colleagues.

Yours faithfully, (squiggle)

I am reminded of a bit of John Locke (English essayist, 1632-1704) that my old Traffic Manager was prone to quote after a driver's peccadillo "it is one thing to show a man that he is in an error, and another to put him in possession of truth".

WHAT'S WRONG WITH THE MODERN COACH?

This article was written by Clem Preece before he attained fame as "Mr Royal Blue" for his unswerving loyalty to that company; Western National and Southern National Omnibus Companies came under Tilling control in 1931 and absorbed Royal Blue Coach Services in 1934. Prior to this Clem Preece was already showing that he had no intention of being browbeaten by anyone.

The experience we have gained from operating coaches with bodies built by no fewer than nine different builders may be of interest to both the builder and the prospective purchaser. Our vehicles are run daily on long-distance services operating between London, Southampton, and Plymouth, and cover a weekly mileage of approximately 1,000 per vehicle. The makers represented are of varying size and reputation, and include some of the best known in the country. The types we have in use include saloons, all-weathers, with and without limousine backs, and both forward and normal steering. For the maintenance of our vehicles we keep a foreman body maker and painter, a carpenter, and a lad.

In long-distance motor coaching nothing plays a more important part in the success or failure of the business than the body. Outside appearance and inside comfort are both equally important, but more important still is the necessity for the body to be free from rattle. In this latter direction there is room for a great deal of improvement in the design of practically all the bodies of our fleet, and only by constant adjustment and repair can noise be kept within reasonable limits. The chief offender in this respect is the normal-drive type, and particularly the all-weather.

Causes of Rattle

The first part to set up noise in a new body is, nine times out of ten, the front door. One has only to examine the lock and striking plate of the front door on almost any coach you will see in the street to realise just how common this complaint is. It is due primarily to weak and badly thought out design. The pillar on which the door is hung is often too weak, and, in addition, is usually boxed out to receive the hinges, cantrail, window channelling and inside fillets, so that in places practically no thickness remains. The hinges are usually much too light in construction and too few in number. In the case of the all-weather coach the trouble is exaggerated still more by the fact that the highest hinge only comes half-way up the door, and in consequence a powerful leverage is exerted on what hinges there are. The weight of a modern door, when complete with glass, fittings, lock, handles, etc, is considerable, and when one considers the intense vibration to which the pillars that carry it are subjected, it is not surprising that rapid wear takes place.

Over and above the rapid engine vibration referred to there is the constant twisting of the chassis, and in consequence the body framing as well, that takes place when the vehicle is in motion. To what extent a chassis can twist can best be seen by following one on test over rough ground. In one particular all-weather we have this movement is so considerable that the front doors fly open of their own accord. Nothing we can do seems to have any permanent effect on this trouble, although we have tried fitting new locks, hinges, and dovetails. If one watches the door while the vehicle is in motion one can see clearly a back-and-forward movement

taking place as the dash and door pillars move in relation to the more rigid body sides. The fitting of dovetails of the usual wedge type has no lasting effect; no dovetail is going to prevent the dash from moving, and in a short time the dovetail spreads, therefore, and things are as before. The hammering that is set up, when the doors are loose, between the metal upper door framing and the surrounding metal head work has to be heard to be realised (Fig. 1 at A).

The top rail (Fig. 2 at B) does not prevent this movement, but transfers it so as to cause distortion, as shown in Fig. 2.

This has been discussed at some length, as on all our all-weathers this same trouble is present in some degree. The proper remedy for this defect lies in making the dash framing sufficiently strong and in so designing the lay-out that distortion and vibration cannot affect the relative positions of the two pillars carrying the hinges and lock respectively. One more trouble we have experienced with doors is, in part at least, due to drivers' carelessness; this is the damaging of hinges and door through slamming, after the draught-flap raising mechanism has broken (this mechanism is usually a most unnecessarily intricate one, consisting of Bowden wires or small chains), thus causing the flap to jamb against the floor of the coach. The mechanism used by Strachans is the most sensible in this respect I have seen, and consists merely of a leather-covered chain attached at one end to the pillar on which the door hinges, and at the other to the draught-flap (Fig. 3).

Second to the doors in noise is the all-metal head work, which sets up a constant clatter maddening in the extreme. The small push buttons by which the hood material is held down usually last but a very short time before breaking away at their base. Although small, they can set up a big noise (Fig. 4). Another frequent source of noise lies in the attachment between the short connecting piece to the windscreen and the top rail of the head work. The bolts at this point are subjected to a rapid alternating load, caused by road shocks, transmitted through the dash and screen (Fig. 2 at C). The metal hoop sticks, after a little use, defy all attempts to keep them tight, and in a short time are contributing their share to the general rattle. The windows, with a little care, can be kept silent even in the all-weather type, although in many types of fitting they will not stay either open or shut. Folding tables invariably rattle after a time, and for this reason we are removing them from those of our vehicles that have them.

The inspection flaps provided in the floor, although fitting tightly when new, after a few months' wear chatter and jump about badly. If made with a practical fastening, no doubt they would last indefinitely; the usual manner, however, is simply to lay them there and leave them. A particular type of fastening, which consists of a threaded plate screwed to the under side of the floor and a screw with folding handle let into the flap, holds the flap down tightly when screwed home, the only point of wear being in the threaded plate.

Sometimes wood screws are provided by the body builders; these, however, soon strip out, and, in addition, for some unexplained reason, fitters have a rooted objection to putting in wood screws.

Figs 5, 5a, and 5b show alternative methods of fixing which would have the advantage of being quick in action. The hinging of one side or end of all flaps, having due regard to seat positions, would seem to have advantages. While on the question of seats, it is a great convenience if the driver's seat is quickly detachable, likewise any other seats over parts of the chassis needing frequent adjustment. The fixing shown in Fig. 6 has proved efficient on the occasional seats in some of our vehicles.

The ordinary fixed seats used by the passengers are, nine times out of ten, extremely inadequate in the legs. Metal frame seats suffer from this a great deal, and, in addition, looseness frequently becomes noticeable between the seat back and the seat pan. To remedy this it is in many cases necessary to lift the upholstery. The wood frame seat, attached on one side to a special rail running along the body side, is undoubtedly the most silent and trouble-free type there is, besides which, when properly designed, it is the most comfortable.

Windscreens and Mudguards

The instrument board, front windscreen, and dash usually rattle or creak through construction being too light or through the designer not having allowed for all the movement that takes place. A most alarming trouble we have experienced on more than one occasion has been the spreading of the side channels of the movable windscreen panels. On one occasion the glass fell right out whilst the car was in motion, nearly causing injury to the driver and thereby endangering the safety of the coach. To obviate any chance of this recurring, we have had metal channels put across the bottom of all hanging windscreen panels (Fig. 9).

The mudguards frequently are a source of noise that, whilst not being always audible inside the body, is a sign of wear, and gives an impression of neglect. In some coaches we have, this trouble is practically nonexistent, whilst in others it is constant. It would seem that if the front end of the front guard is anchored rigidly to the chassis frame, while at the back it is screwed to the running board or body, that the relative motion between the two is bound to cause something to go. The method of fixing Fig. 7) now becoming popular with private car builders is certainly more logical, extremely neat and smart.

Suggested Improvements

Turning now from the consideration of noise let us go into the question of improvements that might be made, particularly from the operator's stand-point. Hood material is a very expensive item if good quality is to be used, and for this reason deserves more care than it receives at present from the body builder. By the stitching and solutioning of leather patches on the under side of the hood on all the corners where friction takes place (Fig. 1 at D) and at any other points where any projections exist, the useful life of an all-weather hood can be trebled, the only need for renewal then being, when the material becomes porous. This method is by no

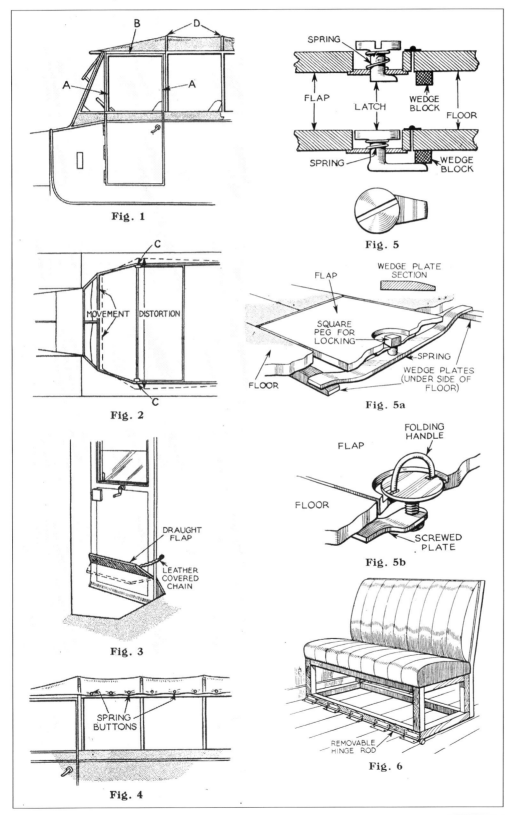

Fig. 1

Fig. 2

Fig. 3

Fig. 4

Fig. 5

Fig. 5a

Fig. 5b

Fig. 6

means unsightly and has been carried out on many of our coaches, with a considerable saving.

When any repairs become necessary to the wiring of the inside lights, it is best to be prepared to take the entire body to pieces. We have found the wiring carried inside the Lincrusta ceiling; we have found it built into the all-metal head-work.

Another common place is between the inside and outside panels. Surely the obvious and proper place for the wiring is under long polished fillets grooved out on their under side into two channels for its reception. By simply removing two such fillets, one on each side of the interior, the entire wiring will be accessible, with the exception of the short connecting pieces leading to the individual lights. The fillets could be carried just above the line of the lamps and could be ornamental (Fig. 11).

Another point in connection with maintenance which builders seem unable to realise is that the body, after leaving the factory, will in all probability be involved in accidents of a minor character causing damage to its panels, mudguards and windows. The body that is designed in such a way as to facilitate repairs will be the most economical to operate, other things being equal. For quickness in panel repairs, all panels should be as small as possible, merely extending from pillar to pillar, the joints, of course, being covered with moulding in the usual way. Where the panels join the back wheel arch they should not be turned under, because this means that in order to remove a panel, the mudguard must first be dismounted, and this not infrequently means lifting several seats as well. The join between panel and wheel arch can be covered with half-round moulding.

The replacement of broken windows of the movable variety is frequently a long job, requiring the removal of seats and lining panels. If the lining panels were made to slide in grooves similar to the window channels and a slight clearance were left between the seats and the panels, removal of broken windows would be a much shorter job. Wh polished facings are employed at the top of the lining par they should be in short lengths for convenience.

The best position for the spare wheel we have found fr experience is on the outside of the body, well to the front the off side. The reasons guiding this choice are fourfold. F it is conspicuous ; the driver, the passenger and the forem all know that it is there and that it is in good condit Secondly, the driver does not have to crawl underneath back of the coach to get it out ; nor can he lose the key of locker. Thirdly, the tyre cannot get chafed through the fit getting loose. Lastly, the wheel cannot drop off in the r without the driver's knowledge.

The accommodation of luggage presents a very diffi problem. The roof rail and flapping waterproof (?) shee certainly not a solution. The type of body designed Mumfords, having lockers inside the roof, is certainly convenient and may well claim to be one solution. The ra floor having lockers underneath is rather awkward, particu if the locks get rusted and the key breaks.

For Luggage

In addition this method has the effect of raising the b slightly. After giving the matter careful thought, the follow would seem to be the best solution and would be li weatherproof, neat and secure. A container built on the fa body principle should be made and attached to the roc the usual position. The sides, bottom and lids should be li with battens to prevent the fabric being punctured. dimensions should be sufficient to accommodate, say, large suitcases standing with handles uppermost. The should be made in halves, hinged to open outwards, where the halves come together in the centre there shoulc a moulding to seal the join. The lids could be secured k strap (Fig. 10).

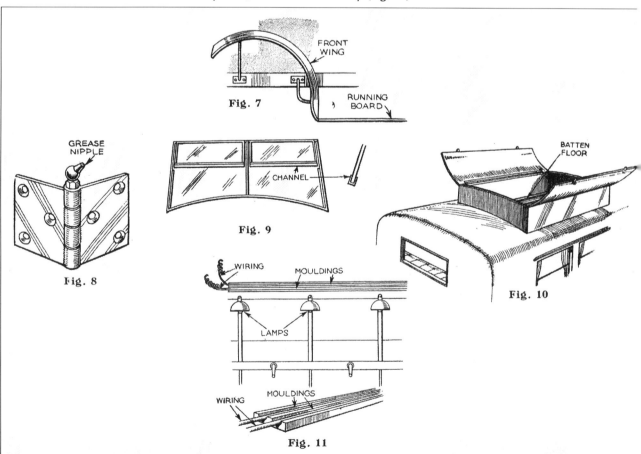

Fig. 7   FRONT WING   RUNNING BOARD

GREASE NIPPLE

Fig. 8

CHANNEL

Fig. 9

BATTEN FLOOR

Fig. 10

WIRING   MOULDINGS   LAMPS   WIRING   MOULDINGS

Fig. 11

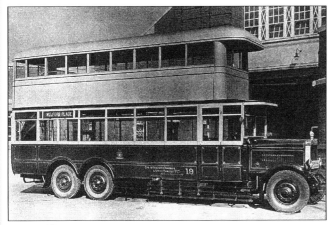

Bus no.19.

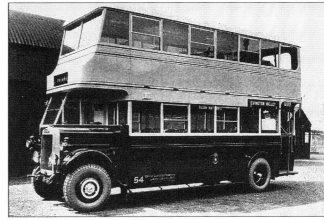

Bus no.54.

The surprising thing about these two buses is that they had the same body builder, Brush Coachworks of Loughborough and were to enter service only four years apart.

No. 19 carries a 56-seat body on a Guy CX chassis registered as RY 4377 in 1927, and purchased as the forerunner of a fleet of eleven CXs delivered that year, and six more two years later, primarily to open and eventually extend a very successful new route Welford Place to Knighton Lane. Leicester seem to have made Guys in both single and double deck formats really work, although Guy Motors never quite caught up with the leading companies. 19, renumbered 219 in 1937 probably did little work between then and withdrawal two years later, by which time she was truly anachronistic.

On the other hand, no. 54 (JF 1530) was bang up to date with its Leyland TD1 chassis, complete with its 90bhp petrol engine and sliding-mesh gearbox, which had it not been for the slow permitted road speeds (20mph), would have been a nightmare for drivers. The Brush body – one of a batch of four – was supplied in 1931 and at 28 feet rather long

AEC Staff Bus.

for the 50 seats it held. The next tranche of Leylands just a year later were of the PD2 class, holding more passengers albeit 2 feet shorter. Renumbered 254 in 1937, withdrawal wasn't until 1946.

July 1928 and a very modern-for-the-period AEC Regent low height bus shows its dimensions. Fitted with a less than 13-foot body by Hall Lewis & Co., this package was designed to allow the passage of a double deck bus under the low bridges which infested most cities. The enclosed staircase was unusual for that period, and led to a rare upstairs layout. Leyland had patented the single sunken gangway plus four seats upstairs arrangement so hated by hundreds of thousands of later passengers so as shown in the drawing Hall Lewis utilised two sunken gangways with the seats in between.

Although beautifully painted in the style of Glasgow Corporation no orders were forthcoming from them and after demonstration work this chassis 661012 and its body became an AEC staff bus in June 1930.

These drawings are reproduced from the original AEC Regent catalogue of October 1929. The body cross-sections were not identified, but probably refer to the Hall, Lewis low-height and normal-height designs of the time.

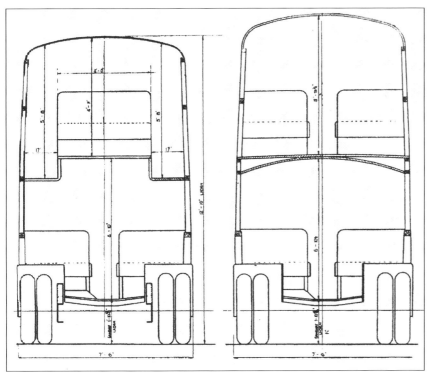

CHANGING TIMES IN WORCESTER

[Unfortunately, this Council report was damaged long ago, and I have never managed to trace another copy. However, it is transcribed as best I can for its great interest. The date can be conjectured as the end of December 1928].

A Satisfactory Position

If they paid interest of 5 per cent, the total amounted to £4,100, and they made a net profit in relation to running of the trams of £1,900. He was in the happy position of being able to state that in the first four months of the bus service – June, July, August and September – the sum they had to receive or had received was no less than £3,400. In other words, during a third of the year, they had received considerably more than half their annual obligation. He pointed out that the figures showed quite clearly that satisfactory traffic receipts were not [part missing] summer weather.

The buses had run some 190,000 miles in four months and carried 2,351,039 passengers meaning they moved the entire population of Worcester 46 times during the period.

There had of course been complaints, some justified and some not. There always would be complaints. He wanted, however, to appeal to the citizens of Worcester to be reasonable and to co-operate with them in running those services with the minimum of discomfort. Of course, it was a new service and, so far as Worcester was concerned, was an experiment. Hitherto it had been so arranged that the buses had stopped anywhere, either to take up or to set down. They were going to amend that to the extent that there would be a certain number of compulsory stops, at which the buses would always stop, and a certain number of stops by request at which the buses would stop when required. The buses would continue to stop anywhere either to pick up or set down. He pointed out, however, that these vehicles were big ones, and they could not handle these buses like they would handle a bassinette.

Fixed Stopping Places

There were four forward gears and one reverse gear, and manoeuvring such a big vehicle was a very big physical effort on the part of the man in control, and they wanted to reduce the number of unnecessary stops and starts. They wanted the citizens to gather at those points which would be indicated in the course of a week or so by plates in suitable places, and to use the services in such a manner so that the number of starts and stops were reduced to the minimum. In conclusion, he remarked that he did not think that the most optimistic amongst them expected that at the end of four months' service of buses anyone would be in the happy position to be able to make such a statement as he had that day. It seemed that they did the right thing when they abandoned the trams, when they introduced the new service of buses, and when they made their contract with the Company.

The Mayor congratulated Alderman Hill. He said that making allowance for people experimenting with rides on the buses at the commencement of the service, there would still be a satisfactory balance at the end of the year.

Mr Hall asked if people were allowed, as in London, to ring the bell themselves as a signal to the driver that they wanted to be set down at a stopping place? He also pleaded for a better light at some picking-up places. How were drivers otherwise to see whether there were people waiting to be picked up?

Ald. Hill said that he thought the matter of the public ringing the bell was a detail of management which they must leave to the bus company. If better lights were found to be needed when the final stopping places were decided upon, he had no doubt that the Watch Committee would provide them.

Mr Roberts asked if there was any hope of a service for people living off the present routes. Residents in the Hylton and Hallow Roads wanted to be taught to ride too!

Ald. Hill said there were hopes. (Laughter.)

These new buses were provided by the Birmingham and Midland Motor Omnibus Company.

BIRMINGHAM TRANSITION

In the 1920s almost all big Corporations were wooed by the manufacturers of both bodies and chassis in the hope that their blandishments would lead to nice juicy orders. It was also the period when all three groups were trying to find their way in modem developments.

295, VP 1159 was a living proof of this having an ADC chassis type 507, one of the fruits of a collaboration between London's AEC and Daimler of Coventry. The politics behind this joint working were complicated and the combined output rather disappointing, but the ADC chassis in this class offered the type 506 as a bonneted version and the 507 as seen here with the cab alongside the engine; two engines were offered, AEC's 45hp four cylinder side-valve design type A115, and a 6-cylinder Daimler sleeve-valve 25hp, the combined chassis and AEC engine costing £880 for the 506 and £915 for the 507; pneumatics seen here added £85 and lighting also extra around the same. The 507 continued to be built up to 1928 when the partnership broke up.

In all the Birmingham Corporation Tramways and Omnibus Department purchased 128, all on pneumatics and 'with lighting equipments' out of the 240 manufactured. 295

arrived in 1928 with a Short Bros. of Rochester body seating 46 which again was a new development having the nearest they could get to low height seating with two sunken gangways upstairs and the seats laid out in herringbone fashion. Given the power of single sunken gangways to attract heads downstairs two must have greatly increased the risk!

In 1932 Roger Kidner 'caught' this ancient Daimler still at work between Pwllheli and Nevin. Even by then it was terribly old-fashioned with the high body perched on top of a straight chassis. At least it had been converted to pneumatic tyres!

UF 5852 Fleet 304. 1930 Leyland Lioness LTDB1. Harrington limousine 20-seat body, serving the passengers well on a Devon and Cornwall tour in 1949. 304 was withdrawn in 1951.

Dreadnaught Motors were located together with another couple of coach firms at the junction of Queen Street and Station Road, Morecambe, conveniently opposite the Ribble bus station and Euston Road railway station. Their heyday reflected that of Morecambe by stretching from the late 1940s to the 1970s, at which time declining passenger figures forced a merger with a rival firm.

The BIRMINGHAM & MIDLAND MOTOR OMNIBUS CO. Ltd.

MIDLAND 'RED' MOTOR SERVICES.

Telegraphic Address:
"OMNIBUS·PHONE·BIRMINGHAM".

Telephone:
BEARWOOD 2020.
BRANCH EXCHANGE.

In your reply please quote

REF. OCP/LEL.

Your ref: H/W.

PLEASE REPLY TO
THE TRAFFIC MANAGER.
Chief Offices:
BEARWOOD,
BIRMINGHAM.

PRIVATE HIRE.

SALOON BUSES & MOTOR COACHES
AVAILABLE FOR
WORKS & STAFF OUTINGS
OF ANY SIZE OR DESCRIPTION.

When telephoning, please
ask for EXTENSION No. 1.

OFFICES & GARAGES		
BEARWOOD	TEL. NO.	
CHIEF OFFICE	2020	BEARWOOD
BIRMINGHAM		
BULL RING	3887	MIDLAND
DIGBETH (GARAGE)	4900	MIDLAND
CARLYLE GARAGE,		
WATERWORKS ROAD	740	EDG.
16, SEYMOUR ST. (PARCELS)	3116	CENTRAL
LADYWOOD (PARCELS)	2066	EDG.
BANBURY		
CANAL STREET (GARAGE)	123	BAN.
BRIERLEY HILL, STAFFS.		
HARTS HILL (GARAGE)	40	BR. HILL
BROMSGROVE		
HIGH STREET (OFFICE)	223	B'SGROVE
THE STRAND (GARAGE)	125	B'SGROVE
COALVILLE		
ASHBY ROAD (GARAGE)	123	COALVILLE
COVENTRY		
6 WARWICK ROW.		
GREYFRIARS GREEN	3536	COV.
DROITWICH		
12 ST. ANDREW'S ROAD	43	DROITWICH
DUDLEY		
BIRMINGHAM ROAD (OFFICE)	2395	DUDLEY
HEREFORD		
52 COMMERCIAL ST. (OFFICE)	2438	H'FORD
FRIARS STREET (GARAGE)	2629	H'FORD
KIDDERMINSTER		
10 VICAR STREET (OFFICE)	108	KIDDER.
NEW ROAD (GARAGE)	295	KIDDER.
KINGSWINFORD		
THE PORTWAY	12	K'FORD
LEAMINGTON		
OLD WARWICK RD.	194	LEAM'N
LEICESTER		
69 GRANBY ST. (OFFICE)	59275	LEIC.
SOUTHGATE STREET (GARAGE)	58268	LEIC.
NUNEATON		
COTON ROAD (GARAGE)	213	NUN'N
RUGBY		
FLINT'S CHAMBERS,		
CHURCH STREET	55	RUGBY
SHREWSBURY		
THE SQUARE (OFFICE)	2485	S'BURY
DITHERINGTON (GARAGE)	2755	S'BURY
STAFFORD		
3 MARKET STREET (OFFICE)	432	STAFFORD
NEWPORT ROAD (GARAGE)	388	STAFFORD
STOURBRIDGE		
FOSTER STREET	487	S'BRIDGE
SUTTON COLDFIELD		
MASONIC HALL BUILDINGS	870	SUTTON
TAMWORTH		
ALDERGATE (GARAGE)	90	TAM.
WELLINGTON		
QUEEN STREET (OFFICE)	239	WELL.
MANSELL ROAD (GARAGE)	167	WELL.

December 11th, 1929.

Alderman W.J.Hill, J.P.,
50, Foregate Street,
Worcester.

Dear Alderman Hill,

Worcester 'Buses.

     I have your letter of the 10th
instant, enclosing a letter which you received from
the Secretary for Higher Education, together with
copy of your reply, both of which I return herewith.

     No one appreciates the necessity
for diplomatic replies of this description more than
I do, but at the same time I will arrange for Notices
to be sent out to our various Garages instructing
Drivers to be as noiseless as possible when passing
the New Secondary School for Girls.

     Thanking you for your
trouble,

     I am,
     Yours very truly,

Enclosure

1929 and an argument has never really been settled. In certain modern circumstances – so called 'executive coaches' – where journeys could be overnight or the clientele well primed with alcohol and unable to last too long – then on-board lavatories made sense. But in the heyday of coaches there were 'facilities' at regular intervals though, I am afraid, they varied between quite decent and dreadful!

Talking to long-distance people, I have recently heard very divided opinions regarding the value of lavatory and buffet equipment. Those 'against' say that passengers, especially women, do not like to use a lavatory on a coach, and much prefer a short break in the journey for refreshments. Other owners are equally emphatic that these objections do not exist, and that the facilities are appreciated. Personally, I favour scheduled halts. Attractive wayside cafes are springing up along all the main roads, and a ten or fifteen minutes' stop at one of these for morning coffee or afternoon tea is an excellent idea, and one that appeals to women especially. Yes, if I were putting a long-distance car on the road, the room occupied by lavatory and buffet would be utilised to give an inch or two extra between each seat.

Statistics show just how crowded some roads are and it is difficult to see just how many of these companies paid their way. For example, London to Brighton in the summer of 1929, there were twelve operators, some, like Southdown, running hourly – all this on a line where the railways contested vigorously. Fourteen coaches ran daily between Cambridge and London. Bournemouth was served by twelve operators each weekday from London, giving, I suppose, 25 separate coaches each holding 24-30 – 600 to 750 seats, at a time when unemployment was just beginning to bite and most would-be passengers that had work were busy toiling in their factories, mills or other industrial plant; whether we like it or not, the majority of coach passengers were, and are, drawn from (what was called) the working classes, students and pensioners.

The relevant sections of the Road Traffic Act of 1930 has been best summed up by Graces Guide, as follows:

Ø   Central regulation of UK coach services
•   Introduction of a 30 mile an hour speed limit for buses and coaches
>   Issue of public service vehicle licences
Ø   Rules regarding the conduct of drivers, conductors and passengers on public service vehicles
>   Limitation of hours of continuous driving

SQUEALING BRAKES AND CRASHING GEARS

On 16 November 1929 came the first salvo in a micro-war between the 'Midland Red' with 'The Faithful City', Worcester. From the Victoria Institute to Alderman Hill, the Corporation Transport's main man "I am directed by the Higher Education Sub – Committee to call your attention to the following extract from a letter received from the head mistress with reference to the bus traffic passing the school". In essence this said that the traffic noise was seriously affecting studies, especially the 'lessons in music' given in the lecture room, this latter being purpose built for the job.

The cause? "In addition" says Ma'am "to the ordinary traffic, the noise of buses starting and stopping" was quite intolerable.

Slightly out of date order it seems Alderman Hill or one of his minions had spent some time recording the effect of bus traffic passing the school. He writes on 10 December:

"I have formed the opinion that the volume of noise is attributable to the general traffic – particularly to the heavy vehicles, such as petrol tanks and oil tanks, and I do not think that any change in the Bus Service is possible at the present time. I am, however, asking the General Manager of the Omnibus Co. to instruct the drivers of the buses to exercise due care in operating the brakes when stopping and the gears when starting their vehicles near the school."

Well bully for him, except that one day later we have the letter on page 122. Incidentally I have included this, lock stock and smoking exhaust to show the BMMO letterhead, some versions of which are in colour.

J. ALDRED

I make no apology for including this photograph as to me it epitomises all that was good about the late 1920 operators. There was an intense pride in their work and their vehicles, partly because many – most – men had been in, and survived the horrors of the war. These were not impersonal concerns run by some faceless Freemason sitting in an office wondering when he is to play his next round of golf, but family men trying to scratch a living. One of the railway-sponsored MPs in 1929 had the temerity to get up and claim these private operators were much more likely to be involved in accidents than the drivers of the big companies, but commonsense will show this is so much hooey as when someone like Mr Aldred had an accident he had to pay for the repairs as well as losing his income while his vehicle was laid up, whereas the big firm,

after sacking the driver (whether or not it was his fault...) put a replacement vehicle on the road.

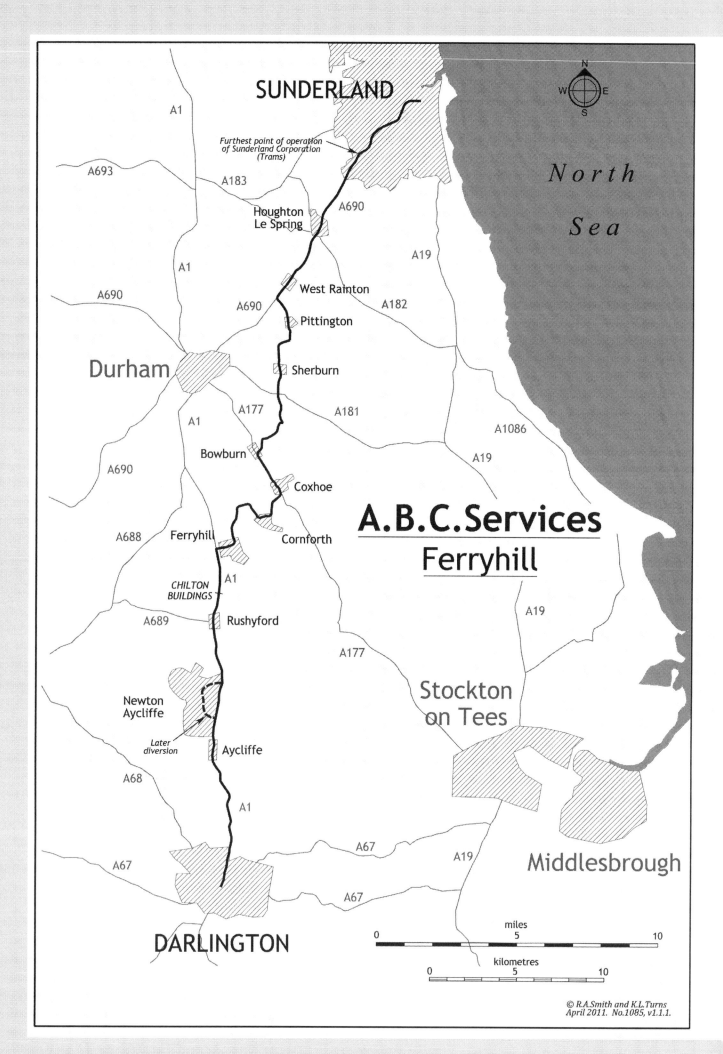

SUNDERLAND

*Furthest point of operation
of Sunderland Corporation
(Trams)*

*North
Sea*

A1

A693

A183

Houghton
Le Spring

A690

A19

A1

A690

West Rainton

A690

A182

Pittington

Durham

Sherburn

A177

A181

A1

A690

Bowburn

Coxhoe

A.B.C.Services
Ferryhill

A688

Ferryhill

Cornforth

*CHILTON
BUILDINGS*

A1

A689

Rushyford

A177

A19

Newton
Aycliffe

*Later
diversion*

Stockton
on Tees

Aycliffe

A68

A1

A67

A19

Middlesbrough

A67

A67

A67

A19

DARLINGTON

miles

0   5   10

kilometres

0   5   10

© R.A.Smith and K.L.Turns
April 2011. No.1085, v1.1.1.

A.B.C. SERVICE

J. Aaron & Sons; R. Binks; P.J. Coulson & Sons

The first on the road with a motor was Coulson in 1915, but in 1928 the tri-partnership, ABC Service was founded, starting in February 1929 to run from Chilton Buildings and Coxhoe, then as permits were given by the relevant councils, extensions via Bowbum, Sherbum, Pittington and Rainton Gate to Sunderland became possible, especially when agreement was made with the Corporation that no local traffic would be picked up or set down between Rainton Gate and Sunderland. Similarly by the end of 1929 they had reached Darlington, albeit no local passengers were permitted from Ferryhill to Darlington. All funds were pooled and although four buses were required two belonged to Aaron, and one each of the others, so presumably the revenue was divided accordingly. Low bridges locally precluded the use of double-deckers.

Ferryhill – Aycliffe was declared free of restriction in 1931, and from Aycliffe to Darlington "for the duration of the war". Extra services were operated by P.J. Coulson to the Royal Ordnance Depot at Aycliffe during the war, and it may be this that decided him to sell out to the other two partners in 1946, although they retained the old trading name. Faced with the threat of quasi-nationalisation by Labour's doctrinaire approach in 1950, the remaining partners sold out to the B.T.C. (better a penny than nothing!). By the late 1950s a basic hourly service was operated by a 'front' company, Durham District Services, plus half hourly on Saturdays, albeit still with the local restriction Sunderland-Rainton Gate.

After the sale of B.E.T.'s transport interests to the state, the purpose of D.D.S. ceased to exist, and the route was merged into United as service 217, becoming hourly each way, each day Darlington-Coxhoe, starting with a short working at 6am Darlington-Ferryhill, with the first through bus ex-Sunderland at 6.35. The through service then ran generally two-hourly to Sunderland, the last from Darlington being at 10.40pm but from Sunderland 9.35pm. Sunday services commenced at 10.40am but there was limited stop working throughout the week between Rainton Gate and Sunderland.

Post deregulation far from being a part of the rat race found elsewhere, the remains, roughly Coxhoe to Sunderland, ran four times a day, operated by S. Blenkinsop of West Cornforth, trading as Scarlet Band. The last relics of the route were finally withdrawn c.2007, roughly eighty years and millions of passengers after it started.

We are grateful to Keith Turns for the company information above. Roger A. Smith worked his usual magic on a sketch map, with the results that can be seen opposite.

This marvellously British vehicle seen here was a Leyland Lion with a 31-seat Leyland body delivered to the partnership in July 1931. Although not clear owing to the film then in use "the main panels of this vehicle are painted in a deep shade of red, the waist panel is green, and the roof supports and roof white". The curves in the woodwork above the windows and the door tops (although almost mundanely so manufactured to increase strength) betray the sure eyes of a top class designer. This LT2 was very much in the modem idiom having a T type 4-cylinder engine rated at 28.9hp (4¼" bore x 5½" stroke) coupled to a 4-speed sliding mesh gearbox with a single plate clutch. Very advanced indeed compared with some of its rivals was the use of an underslung worm rear drive and four-wheel vacuum brakes. In all some 700 of this chassis were manufactured.

DIAMETRICALLY OPPOSED

Diametrically opposed to the philosophies of politicians who had to interfere with what has rightly been called "the natural order of things" was this article by the editor of *Bus and Coach* (subtitled *The Operator's Journal*) in October 1929. It will be seen that he understood the desirability of working with, rather than against, the railway companies. And in the text he states quite clearly "We cannot take seriously the views held in certain quarters that passenger transport throughout the whole country should be one huge municipal monopoly..." of course not, but later the National Bus Company was a giant all-enveloping concern that contained the staffs of many municipalities and led, eventually, to big, highly profitable companies (mainly foreign owned) taking over from local rate-payer owned home-grown concerns.

It has been said, probably correctly, that the municipals were staid in their approach and their committees certainly tended to be timorous when faced with new ideas, but we must remember that, unlike today, they were unpaid and subject to the whims of the electorate who liked the idea of profits being set against rates, but (as now) howled dismally when 'their' almost unused routes were reduced in frequency to save money.

WHAT OF THE MUNICIPALITIES?

Their Place in the Country's Passenger Transport

THE passenger transport industry is a very intriguing study at the present time. What makes it so interesting are the various strategical moves taking place on the part of the railways, the municipalities and the big private interests, all dominated by a desire to have the greatest possible share in the future. The whole aspect of the business will be modified and much will depend on the second Interim Report of the Royal Commission, on which presumably new legislation will be based. Meanwhile, the three parties mentioned are out to consolidate their positions.

So far, the most progress in this direction has been made by the railways and the large bus companies acting together, whilst local authorities with one or two exceptions continue to talk about municipal monopolies throughout the length and breadth of the land and pin their faith in the belief that they have a sympathetic friend in the new Minister of Transport.

The extent to which municipal enterprise should be allowed to develop passenger transport is a matter of political opinion, but the present position is that local authorities have what amounts to a protected monopoly within their cities, and in many cases it has been recognised that outside running within certain defined limits is a legitimate form of municipal trading. It is commonsense that they should be the dominating factors in city transport affairs and that their interests should be protected in whatever schemes for co-ordination the future has in store. We cannot take seriously the views held in certain quarters that passenger transport throughout the whole country should be one huge municipal monopoly and we are becoming tired of the oft-repeated statement about services being run for the good of the public and not for profit. The first would be a gross abuse of municipal trading as we understand it, and as regards the second point, no one gives better service than the high dividend paying companies scattered about the country.

We should like to see municipalities doing a great deal more individually to work in with the private road interests and the railways. Not only is there plenty of room for improvement in within-boundary services, but there is considerable scope for local schemes of co-ordination with private companies and adjoining bus-owning corporations. Surely there is no need to wait for possible new legislation? It has not required any general legislation to reach the happy position found at Birmingham, a good example of a local authority with a monopoly of intra-boundary services working in harmony with a large company which serves the outlying districts. The Manchester and Salford district shows what can be done between corporations and private enterprise. There is no reason why the railways should not come into such plans, as they will through their interests in existing bus companies.

Meanwhile, municipalities should act on views expressed at the recent conference of the Municipal Tramways and Transport Association, and allow managers to be masters of their own houses. Unwieldy and interfering committees are a regular bugbear to many a well-paid tramways manager, who has to spend time waiting on his committee that would be much better expended in looking after the job for which he is paid.

Sell Out

When one of the independents sold out to the BMMO this letter was sent to their Managing Director on 14 September 1929.

"I wish to thank you personally very much indeed for bringing before the Committee the question of honorarium for my services.

It came as a complete and, of course, pleasant surprise to me, and I very much appreciate your kindness and support."

The standard of typing seems to indicate the chap typed the letter himself rather than have it voiced about.

VICTORIA COACH STATION

Victoria will be familiar to almost every coach driver in the land and we must be grateful to our forebears who first came up with the plans, and obtained (with difficulty) permission to build and finally saw it through to completion. This article from *The Commercial Motor* archives first appeared on 30 April 1929 and I have appended two other items which show the amazing number of independent companies operating coach services to London between 1929 and 1931.

A NEW TERMINAL COACH STATION IN LONDON
30 April 1929

We recently had the opportunity for inspecting the new coach station which is now in course of erection and nearing completion at Kennington Oval, London. This coach station, when finished, will undoubtedly be the largest in Great Britain, having a frontage of some 200ft on the Clapham Road, and extending back about 850ft towards Vauxhall. It occupies a most valuable site, accessible both to Victoria and to the junctions of practically all the main roads leading out from London.

The coach station and the station approach have been designed by Mr Edward W. Wallis, LRIBA and every one of the plans has been submitted to and approved by the London County Council, the London Fire Brigade and all other authorities.

The roadway is a new private approach road 100ft in width and 200ft deep. On each side are waiting rooms, buffet bars, tea rooms, booking offices, etc. On either side of the approach and with a frontage on the main road self-contained shops are being constructed, with modern residential flats above them. At the rear of the shops on one side of the approach a large motor works is being built which will be equipped with all the latest devices for effecting quick repairs to coach chassis. Drivers will be afforded facilities for carrying out small repairs to their vehicles and no charge will be made for the use of the benches, tyre pumps etc.

At the end of the private road is the actual coach station. This is entirely covered in and extends 658ft in the direction of Vauxhall. The coach station is equipped with eight arrival and departure platforms, and is so arranged that 40 coaches can be loaded and unloaded at any one time. There is sufficient parking places for more than 250 coaches.

The garage is lit by day with four rows of top lights, plate wire glass and Hope's patent lead glazing being used. Some 17,000sq. ft. of glass are employed in the roof, as well as 40,000 sq. ft. of fireproof asbestos and 100 tons of structural steelwork, the roof being capable of supporting a weight of 400 tons. Over 100,000 bolts and nuts have been used in the steelwork, and the magnitude of the task can be appreciated when one realises that all these bolts and nuts have had to be put in by hand.

The whole of the constructional steelwork, roof, glass and asbestos has been supplied by Smith Walker Ltd, of 16 Caxton Street, Westminster, SW1 and the work is being carried out to the instructions of the owner of the property, who are two directors of Blue Belle Motors Ltd, that well-known Brixton concern which has been so successful in recent years.

The size of the coach station can be better realised when one states that eight long express trains, side by side, could easily be accommodated in the building.

The Coach Owners' Difficulties

Our readers will certainly know that provincial coach owners have to contend with the utmost difficulty in parking coaches in London, and indeed the practice of picking up passengers in the street is rapidly becoming more and more difficult, and might even be prohibited by the Metropolitan Police before many years have passed. Last week's issue of The Commercial Motor included particulars of coach parking places in the London area; these are of considerable service to commercial vehicle drivers who are obliged to park their vehicles for a short time in town, but it is generally recognised that the coach parks available are quite inadequate for the many road services terminating in London, and it is plain that the new London terminal station will fill a long-felt want.

At a recent interview with a director of Blue Belle Motors Ltd, we were informed that large numbers of coach owners had already sought for the facilities and accommodation which the new station will provide. We understand that the scale of charges is not yet fixed, but it is proposed to make a minimum charge of 2s. per day for the use of the station, and a further charge of 4s. per night for garaging; on a weekly basis an inclusive charge of 30s. per week will be made for day use and night garaging. Long-distance operators will also be afforded the opportunity to have their own booking offices in the building, or they may work through the intermediary of the booking agents already established by the station proprietors. Special provisions have been made for the supply of petrol and oils, and graded qualities will be obtainable by coach owners at the lowest rates chargeable to big consumers. A 12,000 gallon storage installation and an equipment of eight of the latest type 5-gallon pumps will be installed by Liquid Measurements Ltd – a company that is better known as the maker of the Hammond pumps.

As a precaution against fire a system of 452 sprinklers of the Hoffmann type has been installed in the roof. This has involved the laying of a 17in. water main and two 6in. steel pipes which run the whole length of the garage; and the entire installation has had to be passed by the London County Council, the Metropolitan Water Board and the London Fire Brigade.

Another feature of interest is the electric lighting system, which has been arranged and installed by Messrs Pruden and Pope, of Westmount Road, London SE9. Over 300 high-powered lamps and four massive bronze three-light lamp standards were required, not to mention searchlights, which are to be used as flood lights for showing the approach and the frontage of the main buildings at night.

Electric Indicators and Clocks

The arrival and departure of every coach will be recorded by electrical devices at the control box situated on the island in the approach road, and special electrical signalling devices are now being constructed which will show the number of the platform and the time when each coach will leave. Electric clocks, operated by a maser clock which is synchronised from Greenwich, are being fitted in the station building, the waiting rooms, the buffet and the booking offices. The main clock in the tower above the entrance to the main building will be some 4ft 6in. in diameter and will be brilliantly illuminated at night time by flood lights.

Hickman (1928) Ltd, of Great Russell Street, WC1, is the principal contractor for the station and has also the contract for the reinforced concrete roadway. It is hoped to have the building ready for use by the middle of June. Inquiries concerning the new coach station should be sent direct to Mr Thomas Boon, of 42 Acre Lane, London SW2.

Within a few years of these reports being published in The Commercial Motor the great majority of these companies had gone, obliterated by a combination of the British Electric Traction's rapacity, railway money and the Transport Acts. I do not doubt that many of the Commissioners did their best to maintain a level playing field, but some of the smaller companies gave up when faced in what was, in effect, a court by the big companies, railway backed, with all the panoply of barristers, and their satellites against a man who only knew how to drive a coach and keep passengers happy. In other cases there was blatant favouritism – one operator wondered aloud if he might have done better had he been a Freemason (then and now pulling many strings) – with old established lines dating back to char-à-banc days being pushed to one side in favour of big operators who swamped the road only weeks before. But, on the other hand, there is no doubt that some of the practices ("like me grandfer did" was one answer to a question on operational methods) which were in themselves reprehensible – if the load was too light it was not unknown for passengers to be thrown out of the coach to wait for a taxi (shades of de-nationalised railway practices!) which is no joke at 4am in an unknown cold and windy bus-stop. And equally as we know from contemporary reports, some vehicles were 'ratty' and the truth was their owners could not even think of replacing them.

Anyway, here it is, the companies who ran from London Victoria to the provinces so very long ago.

PROGRESS OF THE LONDON TERMINAL STATION

More Than Thirty Services Now Utilise This Large Covered Station. Considerable development has been taking place in connection with the use of the London Terminal Coach Station in Clapham Road, London, S.W.9. which appears likely to be very busy in the forthcoming season. It will be recalled that this station was built in the spring of 1929 by Mr R. Toms and Mr T. Boon, and was fully described in our issue dated 20 April of that year. It incorporates an extremely long roofed building extending from the frontage back almost to Vauxhall, which permits of the parking of a very large number of coaches under cover. There is first-class waiting-room accommodation and a full restaurant service, seating for 200 people being provided. Besides the restaurant proper there is a buffet bar, which is open day and night and, in fact, has never been closed since the premises were first ready for service. A comfortable drivers' room is provided, where hot meals are available at specially low prices.

A large workshop on the west side of the forecourt has, by arrangement with the India Tyre and Rubber Co. Ltd, been equipped as that company's chief London tyre-fitting and servicing depot; brake testing and wheel alignment appliances also being available there.

The loading platforms within the station building offer accommodation for 30 coaches, and there is further loading and discharging space for 30 coaches in the forecourt. The established procedure is that coaches arriving with passengers discharge them in the forecourt and then proceed to the rear of the station, where they are filled with petrol, oil, etc., washed and cleaned, being then drawn into their respective bays to await departure times. When leaving again they draw up either at the station platforms or in the forecourt.

A large booking office and an inquiry bureau are situated on the Clapham Road frontage and are open from 7.30am to 11.30pm daily.

The amenities provided by the layout of the premises bordering on the forecourt have, in the experience of the past year or more, proved to be satisfactory from the point of view of the coach-travelling public, as well as to the operators and the management.

Principal Towns Served

Aberystwyth
Baldock
Banbury
Barnet
Barnstaple
Basingstoke
Bath
Bedford
Bicester
Birkenhead
Birmingham
Blackburn
Blackpool
Bournemouth
Bradford
Braintree
Brighton
Bristol
Broadstairs
Canterbury
Cardiff
Caterham
Chatham
Chelmsford
Chesterfield
Chester-le-Street
Clacton
Colchester

Colwyn Bay
Coventry
Darlington
Derby
Doncaster
Dorking
Dunstable
Durham
East Grinstead
Exeter
Gillingham
Glasgow
Godstone
Grantham
Gravesend
Guildford
Hitchin
Horsham
Hove
Ilfracombe
Isle of Wight
Leamington
Leeds
Leicester
Leominster
Letchworth
Lichfield
Liverpool
Llandrindod Wells

Llandudno
Manchester
Margate
Middlesbrough
Newcastle
Newcastle-under-Lyme
Newport
Newton Abbott
Northampton
Norwich
Nottingham
Ongar
Plymouth
Pontefract
Pontypool
Pontypridd
Portsmouth
Preston
Ramsgate
Reading
Rhyl
Rochester
Scarborough
Sheffield
Shrewsbury
Sittingbourne
South Shields
Southampton
St Albans

Stafford
Stamford
Stevenage
Stony Stratford
Stowmarket
Stratford-on-Avon
Stroud
Sudbury
Sunderland
Swansea
Taunton
Torquay
Towcester
Wakefield
Warrington
Warwick
Werrington
West Hartlepool
Weston-super-Mare
Wigan
Winchester
Wolverhampton
Worcester
Yarmouth
York

From: *The Commercial Motor*, 24 February 1931

Armstrong Majestic
Autakoches
Baldock Motor Transport Co.
Bentinck and Ensign
Blue Belle Motors Ltd
Bush and Twiddy
Charlton and Co.
Cliffs Coaches
Corona Coaches
Empire's Best
Ensign Motor Coach Service
Great Western Express Co. Ltd
Greyhound Motors, Ltd
Highways, Ltd
Imperial Motor Services (Liverpool)
MacShane's Motors Ltd
Majestic Saloon Coaches (Newcastle and London) Ltd
Manchester Motorways
Midland Motorways
Orange Coaches (Chatham)
Ovington Motors Ltd
Premier Coaches and Garages Ltd
Queen Line Coastal Coaches
South Yorkshire
Scarlet Pimpernel Cars and Motor Supplies Ltd
Scout Motor Coaches
Solent Coaches Ltd
Standerwick
Thanet Express Coaches
Tourist Motor Coaches (Southampton) Ltd
United Service Transport Co. Ltd
Venture Transport (Hendon) Ltd

LONDON COACH-STATION INTERESTS AMALGAMATED

Commercial Motor. 14 April 1931

The London Terminal and Central London Coach Stations Join Forces in our issue dated 24 February we gave all the latest details concerning the operation of the London Terminal Coach Station in Clapham Road, London SW9, as well as publishing a list of the 30 or more operating companies which utilise the station, enumerating the principal towns which their coaches serve. It is now announced that, as from 1 April, Coach Travels Ltd, the proprietary concern in respect of this station, and the Central London (Road Transport) Station Ltd, of Crescent Place, London WC1, have linked their interests.

From the point of view of the coordination of coach traffic connecting London with distant parts of the country this amalgamation is one of some importance. It may be said that its successful completion is largely due to the initiative of Mr E.P. Lyne, managing director of the Central London concern, and he is to have the executive control of the two companies. Mr Lyne tells us that for a long time he has seen the advantages that would accrue from such an arrangement, the foremost of these being economy in working and the further facilities which, by reason of cooperation, the two stations would be able to give both to the coach-operating companies and the public.

Not all of the practical details of the reorganisation have yet been settled, because, of course, some experience of the joint operation is needed before it can be seen how things will best work out, but it is understood that there is no immediate intention to operate services of what might be called 'ferry' coaches between the two stations, neither is it likely that all the coach services using the stations will be altered to permit calls at both stations.

Nevertheless, by the coordination of departure and arrival times, the public will benefit considerably. As stated above, a full list of the services utilising the London Terminal Coach Station were given in our issue dated 24 February, and the following is a list of the operators using the Central London Station and of the provincial termini served:

All-British Lines, Liverpool
Beaumonts Coach Service, Bedford
Beaumonts Safeway Coaches, Leighton Buzzard
Batten's Luxury Coaches, Clacton, Walton-on-Naze
A.W. Berry and Sons, Colchester
Bird Motor Services, Braintree, Halstead
Smith and Bracewell, Blackpool. Bush and Twiddy, Norwich.
Coachways Ltd, Leeds
Crosville Motor Services, Birkenhead, Liverpool
Ensign Coaches, Aberystwyth
Fingland's Hire Cars Ltd, Manchester
Fleetways Coaches, Grimsby, Cleethorpes
Glenton Friars (Road Coaches) Ltd., Newcastle
Greyhound Motors Ltd, Bristol, Weston-super-Mare, Bournemouth
Happy Days Coaches, Liverpool
Highways Ltd, Southampton, Plymouth, Ilfracombe
Holt Bros (Rochdale) Ltd, Rochdale, Manchester
Huntingdon Coaches, Huntingdon
Imperial Coaches Ltd, Liverpool
John Bull Coaches, Blackpool
London and South Wales Express, Cardiff, Swansea, Llanelly
Majestic Coaches, Manchester
National Coachways Ltd, Edinburgh, Glasgow, Sunderland
Premier Coaches and Garage Ltd, Sheffield
Queen Line Coaches Ltd, Llandudno, Rhyll
Baldock Motor Transport Co., Baldock
Quest Motor Services, Maldon, Burnham-on-Crouch
Red Bus Service, Stroud, Gloucester
Roscoes Motor Services, Manchester, Bolton, Preston
Scout Motor Services, Blackpool
Southern Glideway Coaches, Eastbourne
Strawhatter Coaches, Luton
Thorne's Coaches, Brighton, Hastings, Worthing, Margate, Folkestone
Underwood Express Services, Portsmouth
Varsity Express Motors Ltd, Cambridge, Oxford, Bournemouth
Weald of Kent Transport Co. Ltd, Tenterdem, Rye
Multiways Ltd, Westcliff-on-Sea
Standerwick Ltd., Blackpool
P.W. Watson, Yarmouth, Lowestoft

THE BUS CENTENARY

The following contemporary report is from "*Bus & Coach*" August 1929. L.G.O.C. = London General Omnibus Company, Thomas Tilling were the largest private operators.

The bus centenary was celebrated in proper style, thanks to the L.G.O.C., who had the co-operation of Thomas Tillings. A replica of the Shillibeer (1829) and a knifeboard bus (1850) and a garden seat bus (1880) were in public service from 3 to 6 July, and on the last day there was a procession of buses, old and new, from the Shillibeer up to the modern six-wheeler.

A word of praise is due to the Underground Press Bureau for the part it played in this business. The newspapers were kept well supplied with photographs and matter giving a history of the London bus, in addition to full particulars of the centenary programme. Then there was a most attractive poster at all the stations. Other companies, though not approaching the L.G.O.C. in size, could learn a lesson from their co-operation between the publicity and the operative sides. The moral is: keep the members of the local press fully au fait with developments and let them know anything out of the ordinary.

J.R. TOGNARELLI – A DECADE OF COACHING

Originally Tognarelli, an Italian ice-cream maker, ran char-à-bancs in Bolton starting in 1919 with the usual rebodied lorry chassis, some of which he had previously used in his road haulage fleet during the war, but in 1927 finding a hole in the market he moved into coach work still based in Town Hall Square, Bolton including a half hour interval service to Manchester, where astutely he made use of a private yard for his servicing etc, at the happily named Poet's Corner. His fares dropped until 1s 6d was the normal return which led to his carrying 2,000 passengers in the day (first departure 8am, last 11pm)

Tours to Southport, Morecambe and the Lake District followed, culminating in a direct service via Bolton to and from London, which on the return working left London at 9.00am with breaks both for 'comfort' and to have lunch and tea, which arrived in Manchester at a leisurely 6pm, but we must remember the 20mph still applied, but seemingly speeds of 40+ mph were not unknown... No doubt the passengers would encourage the driver! In Manchester, had you the stamina, a connection was ready to take you overnight to Glasgow giving a 6am arrival. Our predecessors were tough I think.

The photograph shows one of his latest 26-seat Burlingham luxurious bodies that equipped Leyland TS2 chassis. In 1929 he was one of the first victims of the new 1930 Road Traffic Act, and sold out his business for £24,000 on 8 December 1929 to a consortium of local municipalities. This coach, barely run in, became part of Salford Corporation's fleet as their no.2, being rebodied still as a coach in 1938. Such was the quality of this vehicle that it was not withdrawn until 1951.

TRUE TRADITION

I do not know when the practice died out, but once upon a time when you were seated on or in your coach or char-à-banc a roving photographer would take a 'snap' of the party and on your return would be there to greet you with prints for quite a

nominal fee. It could go horribly wrong as we found out when one day the photographer (a friend of ours) had the film jam and could not produce the prints; by some freak another passenger had taken an almost identical image and those that wanted could access this photograph. Conversely many a married man or woman with a – shall we say – different partner must have sweated!

The location here is Stanley Park, Blackpool, and FR 7454 has an S&D Freighter chassis, better known for their very low level dustcarts, but in this case as a 24-seat chara it was in service from 1926 to 1932. The cloche hat was by then going out of fashion but a handful of those visible seem to have strayed from the Wehrmacht!

By the end of March 1929 the Lancashire United Transport and Power Co., Ltd had well over 200 motorbuses and motor coaches in service. The fleet on the motorbus side consisted of 150 vehicles and, as its development had been rapid and continued to be so, the company had to make considerable additions to its garage and repair shop equipment at Atherton, the concern's headquarters. This was located at the very heart of of the LUT system, the 'outposts' being St Helens in the west, Manchester in the east, Wigan and Bolton in the north, and Warrington in the south. This was then a well-developed industrial area, within which LUT pursued an active and and intensive policy of co-operation and co-ordination with neighbouring transport undertakings. Once they had arrangements for passengers to make through journeys between main population centres there was very marked growth in the number carried rising from 6,096,065 in 1903 to 36,352,786 in 1927.

The LUT was one of the very few concerns which operated electric trams (38 route miles) as well as motorbuses and motor coaches, but once the motorbus became viable much of the company's energy and research was expended on these and not electric cars. At the time of the photograph Leyland, Dennis, AEC, and Bristol chassis were in use. Interestingly, Lord Stanley, who had performed the opening ceremony for the tramway side, and by now the Rt Hon. Earl of Derby, was now trotted out to perform the opening ceremony of the new garage and workshops at Atherton, the whole party then enjoying a luncheon in the Midland Hotel, Manchester.

The dimensions of the new garage were 292 feet long by 86 feet wide giving an unobstructed floor area of 25,112 sq. feet. The basic construction was in steelwork, the roof trusses being carried on stanchions at 15 feet, the roof itself being clad in corrugated asbestos, but with four stretches of patent glazing running the length of the roof giving good working light. Three petrol pumps suitably located served this garage, and were fed from underground tanks each holding 13,000 gallons themselves filled via an underground pipe from railway tankers 3,500 feet away.

While the buses are being fuelled the insides were dusted and swept out, they then passing to the wash where relatively old fashioned methods of a hose and brushes cleaned the outsides, it being claimed this whole process sweeping out, dusting, fuelling and washing, took on average six minutes, so that with three washing bays in use three vehicles could be dealt with every six minutes, ferrymen – injured or war veteran drivers – then locating them in the new garage in their morning 'run out' order and location.

The general construction of the garage including the 'Handy Billys' for hoisting engine blocks, gearboxes etc, is self explanatory, the floor space of these eight new pits totalled 8,800 square feet plus there was an equal floor space allocated to the 'overhauling' dock where bodies were lifted off chassis and chassis rebuilt.

Some details of this new garage appeared in *Commercial Motor* on 16 October 1929 and are used with permission.

THE PANTOUM OR THE LONDON 6-WHEELED OMNIBUS

Many years ago a couple of gentlemen-singers, Flanders & Swann, produced a revue called 'The Transport of Delight' with one song referring to the AEC 'Renown' 0663 LT class 130hp,6-wheeled bus. Marvellous machines, they first emerged into daylight in 1929, followed by another 1,227. The Michael Flanders & Donald Swann song really is hilarious and typical of its time, with these three lines typical of all:

> Behind that monarch of the road,
> Observer of the Highway Code,
> That big six-wheeler scarlet-painted London transport diesel-engined 97-horsepower omnibus.

This class of bus and its long ago predecessor are also commemorated in this 'Pantoum', first written in 1929.

18 August 1948, and a survivor of long years of war, LT 494, GO 7187, loads at Clapham Junction on the 37 route, Peckham to Isleworth. A close sister of 561, this bus was withdrawn in August 1949, but the valuable internet site 'Ian's Bus Stop' shows the chassis as being converted to a lorry.

The chassis and mechanical parts are of LT561. The ballast weights are to make it driveable on the run from AEC Southall to the LGOC body building facility at Chiswick. But 561 was fitted with a diesel engine in June 1934, thereafter leading a blameless life until July 1944 when the body was destroyed by a 'doodle bug'. In October the refurbished chassis was fitted with an older 'spare' body, remaining in service until May 1949, when it was 'withdrawn'.

HIRE PURCHASE OVER 20 YEARS

The Worthmore's advertisement appeared at various times in the late 1920s and early 1930s and many vehicles were on offer, from brand new to relatively elderly. They make no bones about their offers. Straight forward Hire Purchase, which led to a flood of repossessions when hard times came after 1930. Firms or partnerships that had bought Gilfords for a quick gallop to the coast or Lions for work across the Pennines suddenly found they were left with a rapidly depreciating asset as last year's model became obsolete with the onward progress in design; the majority of buses or coaches like the Dennis had no more than a two or three year manufacturing life before being superseded. (Typically Dennis E 9/1925 – 3/1929, G 1927 – 3/1930, Leyland Lion LT1 1929 – 1930, LT2 1930 – 1932, LT3 1931 – 1933, Gilford 1680T 9/1929 – 1934 (with different engine from 1932). Couple that for the independents to the loss of their routes and the necessity to buy new tyres, repair lightweight bodywork and probably rebuild the engine it made sense to let the repo man have the machine(s) and hope they paid off the debt.

THE STAR FLYER

A confession. If I had been around as an operator still bright eyed and bushy tailed in the mid to late 1920s I think I would have purchased a Star Flyer. It had prestige, was well made and capable of 50 miles per hour!

The advertisement tells most of the story, that lovely almost unbreakable 3.2-litre seven bearing engine, four speed and reverse gearbox, low straight frame – but therein lay its Achilles Heel, for the Star was very well made indeed and correspondingly expensive, so much so that despite a takeover by Guy Motors of Wolverhampton and a move to a new (already existing but under-used) factory in 1928, four years later it was all over. The Star Motor Company had one endearing characteristic, that of impressing the 'Star' sign (literally a six-pointed Star!) on all the components that could take it – petrol caps, front axle, grease caps and the like.

MAJESTIC MERCEDES

The cachet of owning a Mercedes Benz and seeing the three pointed star at the end of the bonnet must have given a fillip to those operators who bought them. But over the years various attempts to introduce the marque seem to have all failed with sales in penny (low) numbers and this was yet another failure; primarily due to the price at a time when available traffics were falling and the shadow of the slump was falling over operator and passengers alike; price cutting had brought the fast, lean, and economic Gilford down to £595.

Later, of course, the Mercedes 'bread vans' were converted by the hundred but that was to meet a radically different market – very far from luxury. The linear descendant of the luxury Mercedes was the Setra which was (and is for a while) the true dream machine.

THE SHILLIBEER
A PANTOUM
by Horace Wyatt

F.W BEAK

To mark the Centenary of the operation of buses in London, a replica of the original type—the Shillibeer—and actual examples of the Knifeboard bus of the Mid-Victorian period and the Late-Victorian "Penny" bus with garden seats, are being put into service for a few days on their old routes.

"*BENK! Benk!*" THERE *goes the* "*Penny*" *bus!*
THERE *the old* "*knife-board*" *grinds along!*
The Shillibeer is back with us,
Jostling amidst the modern throng.

There the old "*Knife-board*" *grinds along—*
Two-horsed, hard seats, indifferent springs—
Jostling amidst the modern throng.
Compare the new and ancient things!

Two-horsed, hard seats, indifferent springs—
Full-powered, resilient springs, soft seats—
Compare the new and ancient things;
The Chariots of the London streets!

Full powered, resilient springs, soft seats;
Swift, on six wheels pneumatic-tyred,
The Chariots of the London streets,
By full a hundred horse are fired.

Swift, on six wheels pneumatic-tyred,
The grandsons of the Pioneers,
By full a hundred horse are fired
Now, after full a hundred years.

The grandsons of the Pioneers
Hear the Conductor's raucous cry,
Now, after full a hundred years,
As in the days long since gone by.

Hear the Conductor's raucous cry!
"*Benk! Benk!*" THERE *goes the* "*Penny*" *bus!*
As in the days long since gone by,
The Shillibeer is back with us!

"*Benk! Benk!*" THERE *goes the* "*Penny*" *Bus!*
THERE *the old* "*knife-board*" *grinds along!*
The Shillibeer is back with us!
Jostling amidst the modern throng.

NOTE.—The above lines have been written in the old and somewhat uncommon form known as the Pantoum. This is the lyrical equivalent of the wheel or circle. Also, by reason of the constant repetition of lines, the second and fourth of each verse becoming the first and third of the verse following—it conveys an idea of monotony and so illustrates the existence of a bus, constantly travelling out and back, completing its round and finishing at its starting point. This same idea of getting back to where we began is appropriate to the return of the Shillibeer, if only for a few days, to the scenes of its earliest activities.

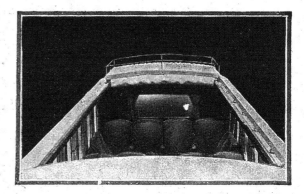

PATENT APPLIED FOR

ALL UP-TO-DATE COACH OPERATORS WILL WELCOME THE "PASSENGER GETTING" SUN AIR SALOON. SO SIMPLE YET REALLY EFFICIENT. OPENED OR CLOSED IN SECONDS, NOT MINUTES. WITH NOTHING TO GET OUT OF ORDER. IT'S THE REAL 1929 IDEA AND WELL WORTH INSPECTING. LIMITED NUMBER AVAILABLE FOR EASTER. (Designed and marketed by Metcalfes, the well-known Motor Body Constructors of Romford, and Ourselves.)

TERMS Pay down say 20% of the cash price and the balance spread over 2 or 2½ years. If this doesn't suit you, make your own suggestion. We can arrange facilities which will surprise and delight you. Why not have Tax and Insurance included for the whole period? It's greatly convenient and appreciated. Worthmores are still ahead, far ahead in supplying Motors on "THE BEST OF TERMS."

"You can do much better at Worthmores!"

WORTHMORE

MOTOR COMPANY,

32, VICTORIA STREET, WESTMINSTER, S.W.1.

Telephone: Victoria 9092   Telegrams: "Rekomendus, Sowest."

Run your Service on Star Flyers

6-CYLINDER LOW-LOADING CHASSIS

"We are considering getting another coach. Certainly it will be a STAR." So writes a satisfied user of a STAR FLYER. He continues his letter:—"The performance of engine, chassis, etc., is everything that can be desired; ample H.P.; very easy steering, quite as light as a small car; gear-changing extremely quiet; picks up very quickly; and at 30 to 35 miles is lovely to drive."

"We had the season's work from it without the least signs of trouble. . . . As you know, we had a splendid body built, and altogether it has been admired very much. Many times we have had our passengers say—'It's the most comfortable car I have ever been in.'"

DESIGNED AND BUILT TO SCOTLAND YARD REGULATIONS

6 - Cylinder - Engine fitted with 7 bearing crankshaft. 4-speed gear-box. 4-wheel brakes. Fully floating accessible rear axle. Pneumatic 32 x 6 twin rear. Loaded height of frame from ground, 21½".

THE STAR MOTOR CO., LTD.
WOLVERHAMPTON
(Associated with Guy Motors, Ltd.)

London Depôt: 24 Long Acre, W.C.2

CHASSIS PRICE **£645**

Also makers of the famous 18/50 & 20/60 Star Cars

The 6 Cyl. which has taken the market by storm at £580

—because

MERCÉDÈS-BENZ

have designed an ideal 20-Seater Vehicle for the satisfaction of users of high class Coaches.

It combines economy with speed and reliability and gives a silkiness equal to the best private Car.

Order now to secure delivery for the coming season.

Demonstration by appointment.

BRITISH MERCÉDÈS BENZ LTD.

37, Davies Street, London, W.1.

'Phone: Mayfair 4148-9.
'Grams: "Cybritimer, Wesdo, London."

MORNING STAR

Morning Star Motor Services of Lawrence Hill, Bristol, ran from Bristol to London via two separate licensed routes – Bath and Reading or alternatively Faringdon and Oxford. Departures were at 08.30, 15.00 and 15.30 via Oxford, and 08.50 (non-stop), and 09.00 via Bath. Normally the journey time was 6 hours, but they were doomed by having to charge higher fares than their main rival, Greyhound Motors, who from 31 March 1928 were a wholly owned subsidiary of Bristol Tramways & Carriage Company, and, worse, were to have a healthy injection of cash from the Great Western Railway.

AT THE END OF A GOOD RUN. A Morning Star Leyland coach arrives in London from Bristol.

139

GREEN LINE – A BRIEF STUDY OF A ROUTE

In some senses London's Green Line coaches began operating in 1929 when the London General Omnibus Company (who ran 'red' buses) started an express coach service from Watford to Golders Green and, by Christmas, another from Charing Cross Embankment to Watford, but Green Line Coaches Ltd were first registered on 9 July 1930. Their services expanded rapidly aided by the London Passenger Transport Board having, effectively, a monopoly of all bus and coach services within their area from 1 July 1933; compulsory purchase increased their fleet and workload to a phenomenal degree.

GREEN LINE ROUTE	AV (21st FEBRUARY 1931)
	Y2 (5th JUNE 1935)
	58 (WARTIME)
	722 (1946)

This service was, in fact, my 'local' for many years and left me with a liking for Green Line services, especially in the innocence of youth when my first love, Beverley, and I would go by the 704/5 to Windsor and then another day to Epping Forest on the 718/720.

WOODGRANGE COACHES

Commencing Monday, December 1st, 1930, a Fast, Frequent Service of Saloon Coaches will operate

between

UPMINSTER & LONDON
(ALDGATE)

via

Hornchurch, Becontree Heath, Green Lane (Goodmayes), Ilford Broadway, Stratford, Bow, Mile End, Aldgate.

A handy Pocket Time Table, giving particulars of Times of Departures, Workmen's, Cheap Mid-day and Season Tickets, etc., may be obtained from any of the following Agents, or Company's Office.

UPMINSTER GARAGE, UPMINSTER
THE CORNER SHOP, 197, RUSH GREEN ROAD, ROMFORD
MAYFIELD MOTORS,
　　　660, GREEN LANE, GOODMAYES, ILFORD

All Coaches will stop if you hail them

Head Office—
28/30, CHAPEL STREET, STRATFORD, E.15.
Telephone: Maryland 2037 & 3634

CLARK, ILFORD.

The first leaflet I have been able to trace for this service. Regrettably no timetable has been unearthed and I am not sure how long Woodgrange lasted as a local company.

Hillman's Saloon Coaches.
(Sole Proprietor, E. Hillman)

Spring 1931

Head Offices: 52b, 52c, Romford Road, Stratford, E.15.
Phone: MARYLAND 4652 (3 Lines).
And at BOW and ROMFORD.

Upminster—London
(ALDGATE)

REGULAR SERVICE

FARES.

The minimum charge is 4d. outside the Metropolitan Area, and 9d. minimum fare inside the Metropolitan Area.

		SINGLE	RETURN
Upminster—Aldgate	.	1/-	1/9
Hornchurch ,,	.	11d.	1/8
Roneo Works ,,	.	10d.	1/6
Becontree Heath ,,	.	9d.	1/4
Chitty Lane ,,	.	9d.	1/4

The remainder of the Single Fares and Return Tickets in the Metropolitan Area are 9d. Single, and 1/4 Return.

Season Ticket Prices and Tickets must be obtained at our Offices.

Our Agent for Upminster is—
UPMINSTER GARAGE.

Phone: UPMINSTER 222.

FOR TIMES, SEE OTHER SIDE.

The Hadden Press, 11, Shrewsbury Road, Forest Gate, E.7.

Edward Hillman was a true entrepreneur of the 1930s. His service almost certainly meant he was regarded as a rival to Green Line, although this timetable dated Spring 1931 shows him to be the incumbent operator and Green Line the interloper. However, on 10 January 1934 he sold out his Aldgate (Bow) services to Brentwood and Upminster, together with 65 Gilford Buses, his Romford garage and 300 staff. The rest of the Hillman bus empire passed during the summer of 1934 to Eastern National. We have to assume Edward Hillman was already a sick and tired man for he died in December 1934 at the ridiculously young age of 45 and with him went the rest of his coaching empire and Hillman Airways.

HILLMAN SALOON COACHES Limited.
(In Voluntary Liquidation.)

NOTICE is hereby given that a Meeting of the creditors of the above named Company will be held at 45, Broadway, Stratford, London, E.15, on Friday the 9th day of March 1945, at 5.15 o'clock in the afternoon precisely to receive the account of the Liquidator showing how the winding-up of the Company has been conducted and its property disposed of; and to hear any explanations that may be furnished by the Liquidator.
　　　　　H. E. THOMAS, Liquidator.

N.B.—This notice is purely formal as all debts have been or will be paid in full.

(041)

UPMINSTER–ALDGATE SERVICE. UP.

		am	am	am	am	am	am	am	am	am	am	am	am	am	pm	am	am	am	am	am	am	am	am	am
Upminster	dep.	3 30	4 30	5 0	5 30	5 45	6 0	6 15	6 30	6 45	7 0	7 15	7 30	7 45	8 0	8 15	8 30	8 45	9 0	9 20	9 40	10 0	10 20	10 40	11 0	11 20	11 40
Royal Oak	,,	3 50	4 50	5 20	5 50	6 5	6 20	6 35	6 50	7 5	7 20	7 35	7 50	8 5	8 20	8 35	8 50	9 5	9 20	9 40	10 0	10 20	10 40	11 0	11 20	11 40	12 0
Ilford	,,	4 0	5 0	5 30	6 0	6 15	6 30	6 45	7 0	7 15	7 30	7 45	8 0	8 15	8 30	8 45	9 0	9 15	9 30	9 50	10 10	10 30	10 50	11 10	11 30	11 50	12 10
Stratford	,,	4 10	5 10	5 40	6 10	6 25	6 40	6 55	7 10	7 25	7 40	7 55	8 10	8 25	8 40	8 55	9 20	9 30	9 45	10 5	10 25	10 45	11 5	11 25	11 45	12 5	12 25
Aldgate	arr.	4 25	5 25	5 55	6 25	6 40	6 55	7 10	7 25	7 40	7 55	8 10	8 25	8 40	8 55	9 15	9 30	9 50	10 5	10 25	10 45	11 5	11 25	11 45	12 5	12 25	12 45

		noon	pm	pm	pm	pm	pm	pm	pm	pm	pm	pm	pm	pm	pm	pm	pm	pm	pm	pm	pm	pm	pm	pm	pm	pm
Upminster	dep.	12 0	12 20	12 40	1 0	1 20	1 40	2 0	2 20	2 40	3 0	3 20	3 40	4 0	4 20	4 40	5 0	5 20	5 40	6 0	6 20	6 40	7 0	7 20	7 35	8 0	8 20	8 40
Royal Oak	,,	12 20	12 40	1 0	1 20	1 40	2 0	2 20	2 40	3 0	3 20	3 40	4 0	4 20	4 40	5 0	5 20	5 40	6 0	6 20	6 40	7 0	7 20	7 40	7 55	8 20	8 40	9 0
Ilford	,,	12 30	12 50	1 10	1 30	2 0	2 10	2 30	2 50	3 10	3 30	3 50	4 10	4 30	4 50	5 10	5 30	5 50	6 10	6 30	6 50	7 10	7 30	7 50	8 5	8 30	8 50	9 10
Stratford	,,	12 45	1 5	1 25	1 45	2 10	2 25	2 45	3 5	3 25	3 45	4 5	4 25	4 45	5 5	5 25	5 45	6 5	6 25	6 45	7 5	7 25	7 45	8 5	8 15	8 40	9 5	9 25
Aldgate	arr.	1 5	1 25	1 45	2 5	2 25	2 40	3 5	3 25	3 45	4 5	4 25	4 45	5 5	5 25	5 45	6 5	6 25	6 45	7 5	7 25	7 45	8 5	8 25	8 30	8 55	9 20	9 45

		pm	pm	pm	pm	pm	pm	pm							
Upminster	dep.	9 0	9 30	10 0	10 15	10 30	11 0	11 30							
Royal Oak	,,	9 20	9 50	10 20	10 35	10 50	11 20	11 50							
Ilford	,,	9 30	10 0	10 30	10 45	11 0	11 30	12 0							
Stratford	,,	9 45	10 15	10 40	11 0	11 10	11 40	12 15							
Aldgate	arr.	10 5	10 35	10 55	11 10	11 25	11 55	12 30							

All Coaches will stop if you hail them.

DOWN.

		am	am	am	am	am	am	am	am	am	am	am	am	am	am	am	am	am	am	am	am	am	pm	pm
Aldgate	dep.	4 45	5 45	6 0	6 30	6 45	7 0	7 15	7 30	7 45	8 0	8 15	8 30	8 45	9 0	9 20	9 40	9 55	10 10	10 30	10 50	11 10	11 30	11 50	12 10	12 30
Stratford	,,	5 0	6 0	6 15	6 45	7 0	7 15	7 30	7 45	8 0	8 15	8 30	8 45	9 0	9 20	9 40	10 0	10 15	10 30	10 50	11 10	11 30	11 50	12 10	12 30	12 50
Ilford	,,	5 10	6 10	6 25	6 55	7 10	7 25	7 40	7 55	8 10	8 25	8 40	8 55	9 10	9 30	9 55	10 15	10 30	10 45	11 5	11 25	11 45	12 5	12 25	12 45	1 5
Royal Oak	,,	5 20	6 20	6 35	7 5	7 20	7 35	7 50	8 5	8 20	8 35	8 50	9 5	9 20	9 40	10 5	10 25	10 40	10 55	11 15	11 35	11 55	12 15	12 35	12 55	1 15
Upminster	arr.	5 40	6 40	6 55	7 25	7 40	7 55	8 10	8 25	8 40	8 55	10 9	9 25	9 40	10 0	10 25	10 45	11 0	11 15	11 35	11 55	12 15	12 35	12 55	1 15	1 35

		pm	pm	pm	pm	pm	pm	pm	pm	pm	pm	pm	pm	pm	pm	pm	pm	pm	pm	pm	pm	pm	pm	pm
Aldgate	dep.	12 50	1 10	1 30	1 50	2 10	2 30	2 40	3 10	3 30	3 50	4 10	4 30	4 50	5 10	5 30	5 50	6 10	6 30	6 50	7 10	7 30	8 0	8 30	8 45	9 0	9 15	9 30
Stratford	,,	1 10	1 30	1 55	2 10	2 30	2 50	3 10	3 30	3 50	4 10	4 30	4 50	5 10	5 30	5 50	6 10	6 30	6 50	7 10	7 30	7 50	8 15	8 45	9 0	9 15	9 30	9 45
Ilford	,,	1 25	1 45	2 5	2 25	2 45	3 5	3 25	3 45	4 5	4 25	4 45	5 5	5 25	5 45	6 5	6 25	6 40	7 5	7 25	7 45	8 5	8 25	8 55	9 10	9 30	9 45	9 55
Royal Oak	,,	1 35	1 55	2 15	2 35	2 55	3 15	3 35	3 55	4 15	4 35	4 55	5 15	5 35	5 55	6 15	6 35	6 50	7 15	7 35	7 55	8 15	8 35	9 5	9 20	9 40	9 50	10 5
Upminster	arr.	1 55	2 15	2 55	2 55	3 15	3 35	3 55	4 15	4 35	4 55	5 15	5 35	5 55	6 15	6 35	6 55	7 10	7 35	7 55	8 15	8 35	8 55	9 25	9 40	10 0	10 15	10 25

		pm	pm	pm	pm	pm	mid't	am							
Aldgate	dep.	10 0	10 15	10 45	11 15	11 30	12 0	12 45							
Stratford	,,	10 20	10 30	11 0	11 30	11 45	12 20	1 0							
Ilford	,,	10 35	10 40	11 10	11 40	11 55	12 30	1 10							
Royal Oak	,,	10 45	10 50	11 20	11 50	12 5	12 40	Romf'd Garage							
Upminster	arr	11 0	11 15	11 40	12 10	12 25	1 0								

For Fares, etc., see other side.

Hillman's timetable shows an incomparable service with the first departure at 3.30am catering for 'The Girls', charladies and other cleaning staff (the backbone of any respectable office in my youth) and a very late night run back FROM TOWN.

Given the rather rapacious actions of the Government-backed Green Line officers the leaflet issued on 27 March 1931 is a lovely sight!

Y1 and Y2

Routes X, Y1 and Y2 were initially unaffected when all other services were withdrawn as they ran back to the garages on 31 August 1939, but they followed a week later. However, on 13 December green double deck buses charging Green Line fares and running as Y2 'Express' re-opened Y2. But as the U-boat blockade of fuel and rubber bit deep they were withdrawn 'for the duration' from 29 September 1942, although ordinary buses were introduced in lieu, the 58 route number being introduced – it is said the letter series would have died anyway as 'ordinary' buses only had purely numerical blinds.

T558c seen here typifies the class of vehicle extensively used throughout the network. 558 was from class 10T10 (AEC Regal chassis, 8.8 litre AEC 'oiler', Chiswick body) entering service seating 34 passengers in May 1938, distinguished as a coach by the provision of heaters, ash trays, lino flooring, roofboard mounts and various other touches.

Requisitioned as a public ambulance in September 1939, 558 was stripped of her interior fittings and adapted to carry stretchers etc., and painted grey. In March 1946, restored almost to her old self, this coach resumed her duties until March 1953, when she was withdrawn, then being sold and exported via the Yugoslav Embassy to the city of Sarajevo; no further records seem to exist. (P.J. Jones)

● GREEN LINE ROUTE AV
UPMINSTER & LONDON (Charing Cross Und. Station)

Via Hornchurch, Becontree, Barking, East Ham, Poplar and Aldgate.

(In operation on and from 28th February, 1931, until further notice.)

For further Coaches between Romford (High Street) and London via Chadwell Heath and Stratford, see Brentwood Service time table.

TO LONDON

MONDAYS TO FRIDAYS.

		a.m.		Then at mins. past each hour.	p.m.		p.m.
Upminster (Thatched House)	dep.	6 16	9 31	41 11	4 31	10 41	
Hornchurch (White Hart)	,,	6 20	9 35	46 16	5 36	10 46	
Romford (Roneo Works)	,,	6 30	9 45	50 20	5 40	10 50	
Becontree Heath (Merry Fiddlers)	,,	6 35	9 55	55 25	5 45	10 55	
East Ham (Town Hall)	,,	6 40	10 10	5 35	6 24	11 5	
Barking Station (L.M.S.R.)	,,	6 59	10 59	29 59	6 59	11 29	
Poplar (Blackwall Tunnel)	,,	7 13	10 13	13 13	7 13	11 43	
Aldgate East Station	,,						
London (Charing Cross Und. Station)	arr.						

SATURDAYS.

		a.m.		Then at mins. past each hour.	p.m.		p.m.
Upminster (Thatched House)	dep.	6 16	9 31	41 11		10 41	
Hornchurch (White Hart)	,,	6 20	9 35	46 16		10 46	
Romford (Roneo Works)	,,	6 30	9 45	50 20		10 50	
Becontree Heath (Merry Fiddlers)	,,	6 35	9 55	55 25		10 55	
East Ham (Town Hall)	,,	6 40	10 10	5 35		11 5	
Barking Station (L.M.S.R.)	,,	6 59	10 59	24 54		11 29	
Poplar (Blackwall Tunnel)	,,	7 13	10 13	13 13		11 43	
Aldgate East Station	,,						
London (Charing Cross Und. Station)	arr.						

Additional Coaches leave Upminster for Romford (Roneo Works) at 10.52, 11.22, 11.52 a.m., 12.22, 12.52 p.m., 12.53 a.m.

TO UPMINSTER

MONDAYS TO FRIDAYS.

		a.m.		Then at mins. past each hour.	p.m.		p.m.
London (Charing Cross Und. Station)	dep.	7 18	9 48	18 48	6 18	11 48	
Aldgate East Station	,,	7 32	10 2	32 2	6 32	12 2	
Poplar (Blackwall Tunnel)	,,	7 40	10 10	40 10	6 40	12 10	
East Ham (Town Hall)	,,	7 51	10 21	51 21	6 51	12 21	
Barking Station (L.M.S.R.)	,,	7 56	10 26	56 26	7 26	12 26	
Becontree H. (Merry Fiddlers)	,,	8 6	10 36	6 36	7 36	12 36	
Romford (Roneo Works)	,,	8 11	10 41	11 41	7 41	12 41	
Hornchurch (White Hart)	,,	8 15	10 45	15 45	7 45	12 45	
Upminster (Thatched House)	arr.	8 20	10 50	20 50	7 50	12 50	

SATURDAYS.

		a.m.		Then at mins. past each hour.	p.m.		p.m.
London (Charing Cross Und. Station)	dep.	7 18	10 37	18 48		11 48	
Aldgate East Station	,,	7 32	10 48	32 2		12 2	
Poplar (Blackwall Tunnel)	,,	7 40	10	40 10		12 10	
East Ham (Town Hall)	,,	7 51	16	51 21		12 21	
Barking Station (L.M.S.R.)	,,	7 56	21	56 26		12 26	
Becontree H. (Merry Fiddlers)	,,	8 6	41	6 36		12 36	
Romford (Roneo Works)	,,	8 11	45	11 41		12 41	
Hornchurch (White Hart)	,,	8 15	55	15 45		12 45	
Upminster (Thatched House)	arr.	8 20	30	20 50		12 50	

Additional Coaches leave Romford (Roneo Works) for Upminster at 6.0, 6.30, 7.0, 7.30, 8.0 a.m. (Weekdays).
7.30, 8.0, 8.30, 9.0, 9.30 a.m. (Sundays).

TO LONDON — **SUNDAYS.**

		a.m.	Then at mins. past each hour.	p.m.
Upminster (Thatched House)	dep.	7 41	11 41	10 41
Hornchurch (White Hart)	,,	7 46	16 46	10 46
Romford (Roneo Works)	,,	7 50	20 50	10 50
Becontree H. (Merry Fiddlers)	,,	7 55	35 55	10 55
East Ham (Town Hall)	,,	8 5	5 5	11 5
Barking Station (L.M.S.R.)	,,	8 10	51 10	11 10
Poplar (Blackwall Tunnel)	,,	8 21	21 21	11 21
Aldgate East Station	,,	8 29	29 29	11 29
London (Charing X Ud. Stn.)	arr.	8 43	13 43	11 43

TO UPMINSTER — **SUNDAYS.**

		a.m.	Then at mins. past each hour.	p.m.
London (Charing X Und. Stn.)	dep.	8 48	18 48	11 48
Aldgate East Station	,,	9 2	32 2	12 2
Poplar (Blackwall Tunnel)	,,	9 10	40 10	12 10
Barking Station (L.M.S.R.)	,,	9 21	51 21	12 21
Becontree H. (Merry Fiddlers)	,,	9 26	26	12 26
East Ham (Town Hall)	,,	9 36	11 36	12 36
Romford (Roneo Works)	,,	9 41	41	12 41
Hornchurch (White Hart)	,,	9 45	15 45	12 45
Upminster (Thatched House)	arr.	9 50	20 50	12 50

P.T.O.

I have two leaflets from Green Line advertising route AV, the first dated 21 February 1931, offering a 60-minute service from The Bell pub in Upminster and terminating at Charing Cross Underground station, their first departure was 7.42am! And the fare was 3d dearer (1s 3d in lieu of 1s). However, this timetable was superseded on 28 February with a different departure point – The Thatched House – and became half-hourly.

● GREEN LINE ROUTE AV
UPMINSTER & LONDON (Charing Cross Und. Station)

Via Hornchurch, Becontree, Barking, East Ham, Poplar and Aldgate.

Every 60 Minutes

(In operation on and from 21st February, 1931, until further notice)

For further Coaches between Romford (High Street) and London via Chadwell Heath and Stratford, see Brentwood Service time table.

TO LONDON — **SUNDAYS.**

		a.m.	Then at mins. past each hour.	p.m.
Upminster (Bell)	dep.	7 42	42	10 42
Hornchurch (White Hart)	,,	7 46	46	10 46
Romford (Roneo Works)	,,	7 50	50	10 50
Becontree H. (Merry Fiddlers)	,,	7 55	55	10 55
East Ham (Town Hall)	,,	8 5	10	11 10
Barking Station (L.M.S.R.)	,,	8 10	21	11 21
Poplar (Blackwall Tunnel)	,,	8 21	29	11 29
Aldgate East Station	,,	8 29	29	11 29
London (Charing X Ud. Stn.)	arr.	8 43	43	11 43

TO UPMINSTER — **SUNDAYS.**

		a.m.	Then at mins. past each hour.	p.m.
London (Charing X Und. Stn.)	dep.	8 48	48	11 48
Aldgate East Station	,,	9 2	2	12 2
Poplar (Blackwall Tunnel)	,,	9 10	10	12 10
East Ham (Town Hall)	,,	9 21	21	12 21
Barking Station (L.M.S.R.)	,,	9 26	26	12 26
Becontree H (Merry Fiddlers)	,,	9 36	36	12 36
Romford (Roneo Works)	,,	9 41	41	12 41
Hornchurch (White Hart)	,,	9 45	45	12 45
Upminster (Bell)	arr.	9 50	49	12 49

Additional Coaches leave Romford (Roneo Works) for Upminster at 7.32 a.m., 8.32 a.m. and 9.32 a.m. Sundays.

FARE STAGES.

	Upminster (Bell)		Hornchurch (Crown)		Becontree Hth. (Merry Fiddlers).		Barking Bdy. or Barking Stn. (L.M.S.R.).		Poplar (Blackwall Tunnel).		Aldgate.	
	S.	R.	S.	R.	S.	R.	S.	R.	S.	R.	S.	R.
Hornchurch (Crown)	4d.	—										
Becontree Hth. (Merry Fiddlers)	4d.	—	6d.	—								
Barking Bdy. or Barking Stn. (L.M.S.R.)	1/-	1/9	6d.	9d.	6d.	—						
Poplar (Blackwall Tunnel)	1/-	1/9	9d.	1/3	9d.	1/3	6d.	—				
Aldgate	1/-	2/3	9d.	1/3	9d.	1/3	9d.	1/3	4d.	—		
London (Charing Cross Stn., Und.)	1/3	—									1/-	—	1/6

CHILDREN'S FARES :—Children under 3 years of age, when accompanied by a fare paying passenger and not occupying a seat, may be carried free. Children of 3 years and under 14 years of age are carried at half the ordinary fare, fractions of 3d. being charged as 3d.

TICKETS CAN BE OBTAINED ON THE COACH OR AT :—

CHARING CROSS	...	Underground Station Booking Hall.
WHITECHAPEL	...	The Hut Booking Office, 3, Mile End Road, E.1. Telephone: East 4042.
FOREST GATE	...	Ray Powell Ltd., 307, Romford Road. Telephone: Maryland 3000.
SEVEN KINGS	...	News & Books Supply, Ltd., 6, Cameron Road. Telephone: Seven Kings 1373.
ROMFORD	...	S. H. Finch, 17, High Street. Telephone: Romford 480.
SUNNYTOWN	...	A. Deer, Post Office, Harold Park. Telephone: Ingrebourne 2.
UPMINSTER	...	Mrs. H. Burry, "The Cosy Corner," The Broadway, Upminster.

ALSO AT ALL DISTRICT MESSENGER OFFICES AND KEITH PROWSE THEATRE TICKET AGENCIES.

Passengers may hail, or alight from, GREEN LINE coaches anywhere en route except between Becontree Heath (Bell House Farm) and Romford (Roneo Works). Passengers boarding Coaches in Upminster between Bell Inn and Bridge House Inn must obtain a ticket from one of the Company's Agents beforehand.

Light personal luggage allowed free. Lap dogs only carried at conductor's discretion. Neither the Company nor its servants can be held responsible for failure to adhere to the scheduled times of the coaches nor can they guarantee the running of the services to be as stated, though every effort will be made to maintain them.

P.T.O.

GREEN LINE COACHES, LTD.,
55, Broadway, S.W.1   VICTORIA 6800

WATERLOW & SONS LIMITED, LONDON WALL, LONDON.

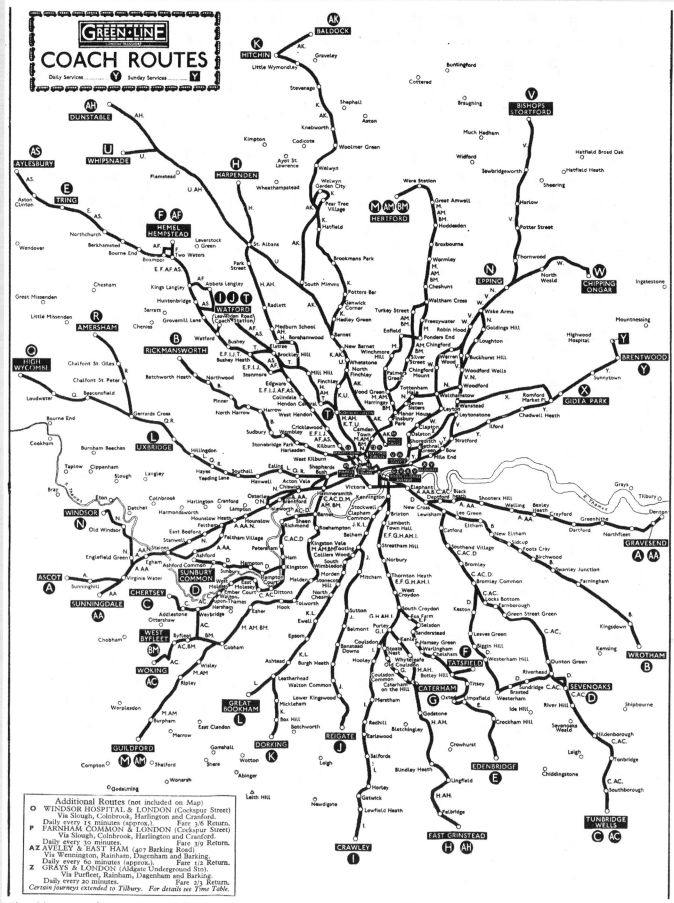

The oldest map of Green Line (London Transport) services I can trace is dated 1933 and noticeable as it does not include route AV or, for that matter, Upminster!

A portion of the 722 summer 1963 timetable shows just how intensive this line had become.

722 UPMINSTER via Hornchurch, Romford, Ilford, Stratford to ALDGATE

MONDAY to FRIDAY

CORBETS TEY *Huntsman & Hounds*	....	5 50	6 20	....	7 10	....	7 40	....	8 00	....
Hornchurch *White Hart*	....	58	28	....	18	....	48	....	08	....
Romford *South Street, Oldchurch Road*	T5 23	6 05	35	7 05	25	7 45	55	8 05	15	8 25
Becontree Heath *Merry Fiddlers*	31	11	41	11	31	51	8 01	11	21	31
Goodmayes *Lord Napier*	36	16	46	16	36	56	06	16	26	36
Ilford *Broadway*	42	22	52	22	42	8 02	12	22	32	42
Manor Park *Broadway*	46	26	56	26	46	06	16	26	36	46
Forest Gate *Woodgrange Road*	49	29	59	29	49	09	19	29	39	49
Stratford *Broadway*	53	33	7 03	33	53	13	23	33	43	53
Bow Road *LT Station*	59	39	09	39	59	19	29	39	49	59
Whitechapel *London Hospital*	6 05	45	15	45	8 05	25	35	45	55	9 05
ALDGATE *Minories Coach Station*	10	50	20	50	10	30	40	50	9 00	10

CORBETS TEY *Huntsman & Hounds*	....	8 20	8 50	Then at these minutes past each hour	20	50	UNTIL	15 50	16 20	....	16 55
Hornchurch *White Hart*	A	28	58		28	58		58	28	....	17 03
Romford *South Street, Oldchurch Road*	8 30	35	9 05		35	05		16 05	35	16 55	10
Becontree Heath *Merry Fiddlers*	36	41	11		41	11		11	41	01	16
Goodmayes *Lord Napier*	41	46	16		46	16		16	46	06	21
Ilford *Broadway*	47	52	22		52	22		22	52	12	27
Manor Park *Broadway*	51	56	26		56	26		26	56	16	31
Forest Gate *Woodgrange Road*	54	59	29		59	29		29	59	19	34
Stratford *Broadway*	58	9 03	33		03	33		33	17 03	23	38
Bow Road *LT Station*	9 04	09	39		09	39		39	09	29	44
Whitechapel *London Hospital*	10	15	45		15	45		45	15	35	50
ALDGATE *Minories Coach Station*	15	20	50		20	50		50	20	40	55

CORBETS TEY *Huntsman & Hounds*	....	17 30	17 55	18 20	18 40	18 50	19 00	19 20	19 50	20 20
Hornchurch *White Hart*	A	38	18 03	28	48	58	08	28	58	28
Romford *South Street, Oldchurch Road*	17 25	45	10	35	55	19 05	15	35	20 05	35
Becontree Heath *Merry Fiddlers*	31	51	16	41	....	11	....	41	11	41
Goodmayes *Lord Napier*	36	56	21	46	....	16	....	46	16	46
Ilford *Broadway*	42	18 02	27	52	....	22	....	52	22	52
Manor Park *Broadway*	46	06	31	56	....	26	....	56	26	56
Forest Gate *Woodgrange Road*	49	09	34	59	....	29	....	59	29	59
Stratford *Broadway*	53	13	38	19 03	....	33	....	20 03	33	21 03
Bow Road *LT Station*	59	19	44	09	....	39	....	09	39	09
Whitechapel *London Hospital*	18 05	25	50	15	....	45	....	15	45	15
ALDGATE *Minories Coach Station*	10	30	55	20	....	50	....	20	50	20

CORBETS TEY *Huntsman & Hounds*	20 25	20 50	21 20	21 50	22 20	22 38	23 38	0 38	....	....
Hornchurch *White Hart*	33	58	28	58	28	46	46	46	....	....
Romford *South Street, Oldchurch Road*	40	21 05	35	22 05	35	53	53	53	....	....
Becontree Heath *Merry Fiddlers*	....	11	41	11	41	....	....	....	....	....
Goodmayes *Lord Napier*	....	16	46	16	46	....	....	....	....	....
Ilford *Broadway*	....	22	52	22	52	....	....	....	....	....
Manor Park *Broadway*	....	26	56	26	56	....	....	....	....	....
Forest Gate *Woodgrange Road*	....	29	59	29	59	....	....	....	....	....
Stratford *Broadway*	....	33	22 03	33	23 03	....	....	....	....	....
Bow Road *LT Station*	....	39	09	39	09	....	....	....	....	....
Whitechapel *London Hospital*	....	45	15	45	15	....	....	....	....	....
ALDGATE *Minories Coach Station*	....	50	20	50	20	....	....	....	....	....

A From Hornchurch *LT Garage* 4 minutes earlier.

T Time at Roneo Corner.

TT.866

ALDGATE via Stratford, Ilford, Romford, Hornchurch to UPMINSTER 722

MONDAY to FRIDAY

ALDGATE *Minories Coach Station*	....	....	....	6 20	....	7 00	7 30	8 00	8 30	9 00
Whitechapel *London Hospital*	....	....	....	25	....	05	35	05	35	05
Bow Road *LT Station*	....	....	....	31	....	11	41	11	41	11
Stratford *Broadway*	....	....	....	37	....	17	47	17	47	17
Forest Gate *Woodgrange Road*	....	....	....	41	....	21	51	21	51	21
Manor Park *Broadway*	....	....	....	44	....	24	54	24	54	24
Ilford *Broadway*	....	....	....	48	....	28	58	28	58	28
Goodmayes *Lord Napier*	....	....	....	54	....	34	8 04	34	9 04	34
Becontree Heath *Merry Fiddlers*	....	....	....	59	....	39	09	39	09	39
Romford *South Street, Oldchurch Road*	5 32	6 00	6 52	7 05	7 40	45	15	45	15	45
Hornchurch *White Hart*	39	07	59	12	47	52	22	52	22	52
CORBETS TEY *Huntsman & Hounds*	47	15	7 07	20	55	8 00	30	9 00	30	10 00

ALDGATE *Minories Coach Station*	9 30	Then at these minutes past each hour	30	00	UNTIL	15 30	16 00	16 10	16 30	16 50	17 00
Whitechapel *London Hospital*	35		35	05		35	05	15	35	55	05
Bow Road *LT Station*	41		41	11		41	11	21	41	17 01	11
Stratford *Broadway*	47		47	17		47	17	27	47	07	17
Forest Gate *Woodgrange Road*	51		51	21		51	21	31	51	11	21
Manor Park *Broadway*	54		54	24		54	24	34	54	14	24
Ilford *Broadway*	58		58	28		58	28	38	58	18	28
Goodmayes *Lord Napier*	10 04		04	34		16 04	34	44	17 04	24	34
Becontree Heath *Merry Fiddlers*	09		09	39		09	39	49	09	29	39
Romford *South Street, Oldchurch Road*	15		15	45		15	45	55	15	35	45
Hornchurch *White Hart*	22		22	52		22	52	B	22	42	52
CORBETS TEY *Huntsman & Hounds*	30		30	00		30	17 00	....	30	50	18 00

ALDGATE *Minories Coach Station*	17 10	17 20	17 30	17 40	17 50	18 05	18 20	18 40	19 05	19 30
Whitechapel *London Hospital*	15	25	35	45	55	10	25	45	10	35
Bow Road *LT Station*	21	31	41	51	18 01	16	31	51	16	41
Stratford *Broadway*	27	37	47	57	07	22	37	57	22	47
Forest Gate *Woodgrange Road*	31	41	51	18 01	11	26	41	19 01	26	51
Manor Park *Broadway*	34	44	54	04	14	29	44	04	29	54
Ilford *Broadway*	38	48	58	08	18	33	48	08	33	58
Goodmayes *Lord Napier*	44	54	18 04	14	24	39	54	14	39	20 04
Becontree Heath *Merry Fiddlers*	49	59	09	19	29	44	59	19	44	09
Romford *South Street, Oldchurch Road*	55	18 05	15	25	35	50	19 05	25	50	15
Hornchurch *White Hart*	18 02	12	22	32	42	57	12	32	57	22
CORBETS TEY *Huntsman & Hounds*	10	20	30	40	50	19 05	20	40	20 05	30

ALDGATE *Minories Coach Station*	Then at these minutes past each hour	00	30	UNTIL	21 30	22 00	22 30	23 00	23 30	....	....
Whitechapel *London Hospital*		05	35		35	05	35	05	35	....	....
Bow Road *LT Station*		11	41		41	11	41	11	41	....	....
Stratford *Broadway*		17	47		47	17	47	17	47	....	....
Forest Gate *Woodgrange Road*		21	51		51	21	51	21	51	....	....
Manor Park *Broadway*		24	54		54	24	54	24	54	....	....
Ilford *Broadway*		28	58		58	28	58	28	58	....	....
Goodmayes *Lord Napier*		34	04		22 04	34	23 04	34	0 04	....	....
Becontree Heath *Merry Fiddlers*		39	09		09	39	09	39	09	....	....
Romford *South Street, Oldchurch Road*		45	15		15	45	15	45	15	....	....
Hornchurch *White Hart*		52	22		22	....	22	....	22	....	....
CORBETS TEY *Huntsman & Hounds*		00	30		30	....	30	....	30	....	....

B Arrives Hornchurch *LT Garage* 4 minutes later.

TT.866

TR35 was one of the non-standard fleet – a Leyland Tiger ex Prince Omnibus Company and used both for Green Line Services and private hire until 1938. Route letters as here (in this case C2 – Tunbridge Wells – Woking via Eccleston Bridge) were used between 5 June 1935 and 4 December 1940. Two other non-standard machines which saw at least a couple of years service were the GMC/Bedford BD5b, operating out of Amersham to Tring; and the Dodge, which although carrying Green Line lettering is in LGOC private hire livery. (courtesy The Omnibus Society)

As an inveterate rider with a girl of Green Line services to Epping and Windsor, I remember mostly the RF class (AEC Regal IV with MCW bodywork) but in comfort and ambience these coaches were easily outclassed by the 1st of the T-type. This beauty (T220) of class 1/7T7/1 was delivered early in 1931 and epitomised all that was good about London Transport-style coaching in the 1930s, even to a sliding door. An AEC petrol engine and 'lazy' springing ensured a quiet comfortable ride. The apple-green paintwork is relieved by the black waist-rail and the white roof.

A wartime photograph by Charles F. Klapper showing the virtually blanked off headlights and white tipped wings, together with the 'target' on the rear of the another T-class coach. These latter two items were supposed to compensate for the lack of lighting; road casualty rates (especially with a combination of American and drunken drivers) made today's almost inconsequential. The location is Eccleston Bridge, the bomb damage commonplace. (The Omnibus Society)

Ebery Bridge Road, 1937. Weymann supplied front entrance bodies for a batch of 50 oil engined AEC Regal chassis in 1936. The last of class 9T9 T452 shows her elegant lines and (by now) two-tone green paint. The non-flashing trafficators were a very modern touch, while the white plate is a 'Scotland Yard' Hackney licence.

A T-class bus-seated 'coach' pressed into use as a private hire vehicle to the Races. Classed 10T10 by the 1950s most of these 1938 built vehicles had been down-graded to Country Bus services.

Most of the TF class of London Transport 'coaches' were incredibly advanced for 1939 incorporating not only an underfloor 8.6-litre Leyland engine with AEC built fluid flywheel and pre-selective gearbox but most were of integral (unitary body/chassis) construction. TF 2-13, however, had beautiful Park Royal bodies with observation panels in the roof and spectacular visibility not only for the passengers but the driver. Classified 2TF3 their lives were short, all but TR9 being destroyed in their Peckham garage during the 1940 blitz. (The Omnibus Society)

The front end of modernised and preserved RF 355, AEC Regal IV chassis, Type 9821LT, introduced with an AEC 9.6-litre underfloor engine and MCW bodywork in 1951. Photographed peering through the boscage in 1989.

The TF class is so well known I thought it as well to show the back of one more-or-less as built in 1951. RF2 shows her smart green and grey original livery but also her Achilles Heel – bus seats. Not really ideal for touring although the rooflights worked well on the river tours; but those were the days when real people worked on and around real ships in a real port.

AN EVOCATION OF THAMES-SIDE PIRATES

The transport historian, the late Roger Kidner, once worked it out that there were 263 separately recorded 'pirate' bus companies in London during their brief flowering from 1922 to 1933, but not all had any permanency. Seemingly one morning in the late 1920s he saw a familiar vehicle with a different name on the side – he gathered the operator had swapped his vehicle for another chap's wife! Furthermore the word 'pirate' is a misnomer where London operators were concerned, for while it is true that they shifted routes to gain the maximum passenger up-take, all vehicles and men were licensed by Scotland Yard. Most stories were, of course, put out by the incumbent operator, LGOC (General); the 'pirates' activities were far less ruthless than those of modern predatory bus concerns whose only ambition (aided by a misguided government) was to destroy municipal fleets, lap up the profits then sit and scream for subsidies to run 'marginal' routes, hitherto covered by the busier services. Our 'pirates' could only stick a bony finger in the ribs of the LGOC who were as a result galvanized into a degree of modernisation. 'Overground' was never a true independent although apparently it was a precursor of today's 'stand-alone' subsidiary companies.

Glen was one of the last of the independents to survive, lasting until November 1933. Owning one Leyland Titan and one LB2 their vehicles ran on routes 36 and 173e. Roger recalls them as being red, not of course picked up by the film emulsion of the day.

Heard Once...

...by Roger Kidner, when he was on a "pirate" bus in London during 1931. It seems both driver and conductor were graduates working the 'Long Vac'; by talking in French a nearby ear-wigging "General" crew had no idea what was planned. "Vous ne les laisserez pas passer, mes camarades". ("You shall not let them pass, my comrades.")*
*General Robert Nivelle at Verdun 1916.

Cardinal used an 'almost orange' livery on their Dennis Lance, which although it was operated by London Transport (D2 class) was too non-standard and prematurely withdrawn in 1937. (The Omnibus Society 8/87)

Nelson was another late survivor, their fleet of two Leyland Titans and one TD2 remaining until 1 November 1933. (Roger Kidner)

Thomas Tilling was not a true privateer but independent of the 'General'. Caught by Roger Kidner in September 1931 the impression of movement is rather fabulous. (Roger Kidner)

Overground chose to have Dennis Lance buses fitted with very modern Metropolitan-Cammell all steel-framed, 49-seat buses. They were beautifully kept and reflected their owners' pride. Delivered between October 1931 and January 1932 but withdrawn in 1937.

There would not have been any pirates among this collection showing the Bank of England around 1936-7 but the photograph was taken by a Pharisee who wanted to record the buildings and not the buses...!

A line-up at Victoria with D1 (as it was to become in LT days) on route 284. A Dennis H type chassis was utilised. (Omnibus Society 8/72)

ECONOMIC

A partnership between two disparate firms, Economic Motor Services Ltd of Whitburn, was to survive for 50 years. Both partners, G.R. Anderson and A.W. Wilson, were employees of Northern General at Stanley when they decided in 1925 to have a go at running a daily service between Stanley and Chester-le-Street, using a 12-seat converted Siddeley Deasy wartime (1914-1918) ambulance (Anderson) and a Reo Speedwagon (Wilson).

The Reo had an accident while on a private outing to Whitburn. It seems Wilson saw possibilities of working between Whitburn and the Sea Lane tram terminus, Sunderland and so in July 1925 the Economic Company was formed. Within a year both partners had purchased first 'Economic' Reo buses and extended the route at one end to Monkwearmouth and the other via the Harton Coal Company's private road and after that the only way was up! But under political pressure and the avowed intention of Tyne & Wear PTE to gobble up all and every independent operator within 'their' patch, Economic sold out on the last day of 1974.

The partners' vehicle policies were radically different with Anderson always preferring Leylands. This 1931 Lion LT2 with Leyland bodywork (UP5356) entered service in July 1931, as one of the last built with a 5.1-litre petrol engine and the "silent third" gearbox with constant mesh helical gears.

The original Leyland notes add "... *this vehicle is painted crimson and white and will be operating between Sunderland, South Shields, Whitburn and Marsden.*"

DEPRECIATION

Many long years ago the Aunt instructed me in the subject of depreciation; The Aunt's operation had been sold to Midland General when her mathematics showed that, while on paper they were operating at a profit, in reality this was a false figure as the family members involved were driving for low wages. The conductresses were wives and daughters (more or less unpaid, although they had a daily meal allowance) and worse, the three buses they had on their one route no longer brought in enough money to meet the losses through depreciation – in other words in 2 or 3 years they would not be able to afford to replace the vehicles. And that, she said, was that!

Uncle eventually became a Trent Inspector, the other two cousins ended up as Corporation drivers. Much is written nowadays about 'the power of women' as though it was new; even 80 years ago it was our women that quietly decided men's fates!

This, then, is a synopsis of the notes on depreciation she handed me; I assume the period was 1929-1932.

It seems the 'proper' practice was to write off each vehicle at the end of five years (this was, of course, a paper transaction) so a decent 'strong' machine costing £1,000 needed to be knocked down at £3 16s 9d per week, week in, week out. On top of this you have tyres (which are often sold as extra on buying vehicles for preservation, we rented ours on a contract). Tyres in 1929 cost £60 and had a life as little as 10,000 miles or if run until bald 24,000. In 'old money' these write-off figures went from 0.90d per mile to 0.60d. Her figures she averaged out at 0.75d which on their normal service mileage equalled £3 10s per week ... per tyre, so six – £21, itself a shock!!

Interest – i.e. what you would have earned on this bus money if left in the bank – 4% per year or 16s a week, counted on the 'loss' side, so far then your bus has cost in lost money £21 16s. With the vehicle running costs and other expenses the total runs out at over £32 per week or £2 14s per mile. But to these amounts have to be added a mixture of intangibles and practical items; office expenses, cost of printing tickets, maintenance or rental of Bell Punch machines or even the racks holding tickets, ticket-inspectors' wages – not entirely applicable but The Aunt was quite capable of checking school parties, rent of the office (as a percentage of the yard) furniture, salaries – this would probably come to £7 15s per bus, less for a large fleet. Assuming you settle for a clear profit of 8s 8d per mile for a 1,200 mile week = £5. In all the minimum revenue of £45 per week per vehicle, or £3 15s per mile, is essential, which roughly equated to 1,800 passengers per week (paying average fares).

Thereafter The Aunt added "*it is all 'if' as passenger numbers are so affected by exterior factors – employment being the main one, but today a few pence on a gallon of fuel impacts on us all.*"

MODERNISATION – TILLINGS STYLE

In 1932 Tillings were anxious to gain increased seating capacity in their Brighton fleet and at the same time replace their Tillings-Stevens petrol-electric buses, which while reliable enough were painfully slow. On 28 November 1916 Thomas Tilling purchased the Brighton, Hove and Preston United Omnibus Company and steadily expanded thereafter. On 26 November 1935 an entirely new company, Brighton, Hove and District Motor Omnibus Company wholly owned by Thomas Tilling Ltd, absorbed the older one, two years later reaching agreement with Brighton council whereby the latter would abandon their tram services and while retaining the revenue from 27.5% of town services would utilise diesel-engined buses and trolleybuses, the B.H & D would handle the rest.

GW 6286 was one of a batch of 46 AEC Regent chassis purchased in 1932, and for the period had surprisingly conservative Tillings-built bodywork. The outline was broken but by and large the blinds and subsidiary destination indicators seem to have been clear enough. The handwork involved to do a decent job by the cleaners must surely have added to the running costs. The conductor seems a military type from his polished boots to his upright stance. The open staircase is all too obvious, but an AEC oil engine type A173 was fitted in July 1937 to improve economy – the majority of the batch were retro-fitted with Gardner 5LW motors. During 1946 6286 was rebuilt by ECW becoming an open-top seaside service bus. The staircase at long last migrated indoors. In November 1955 with two of her half-sisters this bus passed to the Southern Vectis Omnibus Company.

CARNIVAL

Macclesfield, Cheshire, has had a Carnival for (it is said) 700 years, and in the days before the war there were often fête days when money would be gathered for the local Hospital which, prior to the postwar founding of the NHS , relied upon subscriptions from wealthy landowners (so called 'Landed Gentry') local factories and charitable bodies. However even a working man could contribute – perhaps 2d a week – through his Trades Union or his Friendly Society (Buffaloes, Oddfellows or Foresters); I was always told the treatment was the same, but as a subscriber you got free medicine.

As a local employer the old North Western Road Car Company were well aware of their obligations and loaned a vehicle which was 'bulled-up' by the men in their own time, with polished paintwork burnished chrome, and as seen here whitewall tyres. The specially made blind reads "Macclesfield Carnival" and the roof boards "Macclesfield Hospital. All contributions gratefully received". Clearly given that the wheel hubs are garlanded the bus was not going anywhere for a while.

DB 9426 (fleet no.526) was delivered new in 1931, but the radiator rather than saying Tillings Stevens carries 'North Western'. A year later out of a fleet of 383 vehicles 340 were of Tillings Stevens manufacture, but for some reason at this point the company decided their buses would be known as of TSM production. Probably not entirely coincidently their sales fell away at an alarming rate although it has to be said that this model, the B10A2, was by 1934 really outclassed and famous not for its speed, but its ability to plod up hills, famously being overtaken by farmers market bound. A Tilling-built 31-seat body was fitted, although this was replaced by a new ECW body in 1939. In that guise the reliable old beast lasted until 1948.

caught by the photographer but I do wonder why Mr Turner went to Brush of Loughborough rather than a local body-builder – perhaps Brush were short of work and offered a reasonable price for a top-class job.

The Centaur stayed in production from late 1931 to mid 1935; two wheelbases were offered, 10' 6" and 12' 9" allowing for 14 or 20 seats in normal trim, while the power source was a 6-cylinder side-valve engine nominally of 22.6hp, driving via a single plate clutch to a four-speed gearbox and a quiet spiral bevel rear axle. If JL 979 had an Achilles Heel it lay in the Bendix cable operated brakes – although if taken up every night these were probably adequate to stop this sub-3 ton coach in the Lincolnshire countryside, even at the legal dizzy speed of 30mph. One vehicle of this pattern, RB 4757, albeit with Reeve & Kenning bodywork, is in the care of the Golcar Transport Collection, Huddersfield.

It is hard to know exactly what traffics Mr Turner had in mind for his little Brush bodied Commer Centaur as this is a very fine example of a mini-coach with all the fittings on and in its 14-seat bodywork that even a big operator might specify, whether it is the sliding sunshine roof, luggage rack or that nifty little ladder thoughtfully provided for the driver to ascend to the heights. Suitably scaled down louvres are fitted above the drop lights, and curtains to enhance the ambiance while as we can see from the interior views luggage racks took ladies' hat-boxes and the like, while the light-shades were very Art Deco and the bucket seats quite sumptuous. These photographs are all Brush 'officials' and the silver/blue bodywork is well

CLASS OF '31

Dartford September 1931, and the late Roger Kidner caught this animated scene showing what was available for motorised transport in the area.

The double decker in the middle of the road is East Kent's fleet number 75, a Tillings Stevens petrol electric, type TS3A, in which a fairly conventional high chassis was used but propulsion was from a 40hp 4-cylinder petrol engine to a dynamo (generator) and from there by an electric motor to the back axle. Showing the destination 'Sittingbourne' it must have been a relatively comfortable ride for the 50 possible passengers as obviously there was no crash gearbox for the driver to mishandle.

Next to it and looking very sleek is a Gilford of Grey coaches, while behind according to Roger's notes is East Surrey fleet no.7 and a Green Line coach.

Altogether a very satisfying cameo.

And for a contrast in the same year a new Duple bodied

AEC Regal waits delivery to Mr Nevill of Southsea. This body style represented a short lived design; as a hybrid between the older folded canvas-and-hoops and a proper tin-top it had the faults of the one, and being designed for touring it lacked the advantages of the other. The roof was still quite slow to erect, with 17 or 18 poppets to close on each side and draughty when closed, while as a structure it made the bodywork relatively weak, not helped by the use of twin outward opening doors. I have to wonder how many of the windows were droplights – rather superfluous if the roof was used correctly! However there is plenty of photographic evidence that drivers tended to leave the roof closed while touting for passengers on Southsea's Promenade; the material covered (rather than leather) seats would give one an unpleasant ride if a sudden shower came off the sea.

NOT A GOOD YEAR

At around 09.20 on Friday 1 January 1932, a Southdown Tillings-Stevens TS3A coach collided with a similar machine but one owned by Aldershot & District. The Southdown machine had left Bognor Regis at 08.30, and the one witness who came forward, R.F. Day, stated that on this vicious corner the road was greasy and the two vehicles seemed to just slide together, the coaches' front wheels sliding under the cab of the Aldershot bus.

Although no-one was killed, ten people were taken to

hospital including Bertram Etheridge, the driver of the Southdown vehicle, and both Albert Stoner (driver) and George Madgwick (conductor) of the Aldershot & District bus.

Both cabs were reduced to matchwood with the greatest danger being from broken glass, which long before safety glass tended to splinter into flying razor tipped shards.

INSTRUCTIONS TO DRIVERS AND CONDUCTORS

This tiny booklet (6" x 4") was supplied to me many years ago. Printed in 1932 it was apparently brought out in response to the Traffic Act requirements when, for probably the first time, bus crews had their duties closely defined. As long as the bulk of services were run by individuals they and their employees fully understood the common-sense rules of operating bus and coach services at a profitable level. At its simplest, no courtesy, no profit, no employment. And experience has taught me that in small firms by and large the employees' flexibility counted for a lot, not the least when adverse conditions were met.

Larger companies tended to suffer from layers of management, my first meetings with B.E.T. Inspectors tended to be on the fraught side (although we reached a state of neutral acceptance, mostly rotating around "bloody Southerners!") and I had to admit to a certain admiration for their ability to keep services on the road, despite an ever-recurring shortage of drivers and conductors, and having due regard to drivers' hours requirements and, of course, the ever present Union agreements.

One answer to the quandary perhaps lay in the ability of a small local operator to choose his personnel, many being drawn from within an extended family; as a corollary to this if none of the second or third generations wanted to take over the firm then it may well quietly go out of business, whereas a big firm by virtue of its management structure merely imports a new manager from within one of its other tentacles or nowadays when bus and coach work is 'just another business' they will import someone from outside the industry – even a failed banker! Sadly despite in real terms far better wages the vacancy lists seem to grow, and as old hands leave the quality of the drivers seems to deteriorate, particularly in cities, with the hardly surprising result that more Polish and other hard working immigrants are being chosen.

Whether they would understand this booklet is I fear doubtful!

INSTRUCTIONS

TO

Drivers and Conductors of

Public Service Vehicles

BY

W. T. W. WELLS

(41 CHARLOTTE SQUARE, EDINBURGH)

———

Copyright 1932.

Drivers and Conductors are required to study the following instructions very carefully, as their efficiency will be judged by the extent to which they have complied with these in the carrying out of their duties.

Failure upon the part of Drivers or Conductors to carry out any of these instructions will not necessarily make their Employers liable at law for any injury or damage that may result, but such failure will be regarded by the Management as a lapse from the high standard of care Drivers and Conductors are required to maintain as a condition of their employment, the Management being determined that every possible step must be taken to maintain the standard of driving and conducting at such a level that the public may be assured that travel by road is as safe as travel by rail.

This Book must be carried by all Drivers and Conductors when they are on duty.

BY ORDER.

INDEX.

3

B

INSTRUCTIONS
TO
DRIVERS AND CONDUCTORS.

1.—COURTESY, BEHAVIOUR AND APPEARANCE.

A high standard of courtesy and behaviour is expected of all Drivers and Conductors, and the Management will deal severely with any Breach of the following Instructions :—

(a) At all times a Driver or Conductor must be properly dressed and clean and smart in appearance ;

(b) He must be civil, courteous and obliging to passengers, other road users, and any other person with whom he may come into contact ;

(c) He must not enter any public house in the Company's uniform or take intoxicating liquor while on duty ;

(d) He must not smoke in or on his vehicle during a journey or while it has passengers on board ; and never within five minutes of his starting time ;

(e) A Driver must not engage in conversation with his conductor or a passenger when the vehicle is in motion ;

(f) When the vehicle is in motion a Conductor must not distract the Driver's attention without reasonable cause, or speak to him unless it is necessary to do so in order to give directions as to the stopping of the vehicle.

2.—PROSECUTIONS.

A Driver or Conductor must **at once** report to the Management—

(a) if he is warned by a Police Constable that the question of a prosecution for an offence under the Road Traffic Act is to be considered ;

(b) if he receives notice of an intended prosecution ;

(c) if he is served with a Summons.

3.—CITATION AS WITNESS.

A Driver or Conductor must **at once** report to the Management should he be cited as a witness for or against the Driver of another vehicle, or as a witness in a fatal accident enquiry.

4.—STANDARDISED SIGNALS.

(a) One Bell .... Stop.

(b) Two Bells .... Start.

(c) Three Bells .... Full up.

(d) Continuous Ring .... **Stop at once—danger or accident has occurred.**

5.—" AUTOMATIC " AND POLICE SIGNALS.

(a) A Driver must stop **at once** if he is signalled to do so by a police constable in uniform.

(b) Where there are " automatic " signals in operation a Driver must exercise the **greatest** care as he approaches to same. If he sees the " green " light is in his favour and he is following behind another vehicle, he must allow a sufficient distance between his own vehicle and the vehicle in front so

170

that he will be able to stop without running into the back of the vehicle in front *should it be brought to a sudden stop owing to the signal having gone against it* ;

Where a Driver has had to stop owing to the signal being against him, he must not move off when the light changes to " amber," but must await the " green " light.

6.—SPEED.

(a) The **maximum** speed for Public Service Vehicles is 30 miles per hour.

The Company's Time Tables have been drawn up so that there should be no necessity for any Driver to exceed 30 miles per hour **at any time,** and the Management will take a **serious** view should any Driver be charged with having exceeded the speed limit.

NOTE.—It is the duty of a Driver to report to the Management **at once** should he have been on any route where traffic conditions have made him late at any point, **and it is entirely contrary to the instructions of the Management for a Driver to attempt to make up lost time by exceeding the speed limit.**

(b) A Driver must always bear in mind that while he is allowed by law to travel at 30 miles per hour *as a maximum,* **he must reduce speed where traffic conditions require it so as to avoid any risk of his being involved in an accident.**

7.—SAFETY OF PASSENGERS.

The safety of passengers and intending passengers must be the first consideration and depends upon the closest co-operation between Drivers and Conductors.

Experienced Drivers and Conductors are only too well aware that the majority of accidents to passengers are due either to passengers attempting to board or alight from the vehicle **while it is in motion,** or to Conductors allowing passengers to alight **before the vehicle has come to a " dead " stop, or giving the Driver the signal to start before intending passengers have reached a position of safety inside the vehicle.**

NOTE.—**There is no excuse for a Driver to set his vehicle in motion until he has received the recognised signal from the Conductor.**

Special attention must be paid by all Drivers and Conductors to the following instructions :—

(a) As far as lies within the power of a Driver he must not allow any passenger to enter or alight from the vehicle while it is in motion ;

(b) When a Driver receives the signal to start he must let in the clutch **gently** and otherwise take all possible precautions against the vehicle starting off with a jerk ;

(c) When a Driver receives the signal to stop he must draw to a stop **smoothly,** and pull close into the nearside of the road ; **and under no circumstances must he move off until he has received the recognised starting signal** ;

(d) Where the vehicle has a front entrance and any passenger entering or leaving is within the view of the Driver, **he must not move off until he has received the recognised signal from the Conductor,** as he is not in a position to see whether passengers who have alighted have reached a point of safety, or whether there are intending passengers approaching from the rear of the vehicle ;

(e) When the vehicle reaches its destination the Driver must pull close into his nearside and come to a stop **smoothly,** and his Conductor must satisfy himself

that all passengers have alighted and reached a point of safety **before he gives the Driver the signal to turn.**

If it is necessary to reverse the vehicle to enable the Driver to turn to take up the return journey, the **Driver must not move unless he has the guidance of the Conductor,** and the Conductor must place himself in such a position that he will **not** give the Driver the signal to reverse until he is satisfied the reversing of the vehicle will not endanger any pedestrian, other road user, or any property ;

Under no circumstances must a Conductor allow any intending passenger to attempt to board the vehicle until it has taken up its stance for the return journey and come to a " dead " stop ;

(f) At a stance **before** a Conductor gives the Driver the signal to start **he must be at the entrance door and satisfy himself that all intending passengers have been lifted ;**

(g) When the vehicle stops *en route* to set down or pick up passengers a Conductor must place himself in such a position that he can see **clearly** that all passengers have alighted **safely,** and that all intending passengers have **safely** entered the vehicle **before he gives the Driver the signal to start ;**

(h) Whether the vehicle is moving off from a stance or after a stop *en route* the Conductor must satisfy himself—before he gives the signal to start—that there are **no** passengers desiring to enter and who are in a position to grasp hold of the vehicle as it moves off, and either lose their balance and fall on the roadway or retain their hold and be dragged along until the Conductor can give the Driver the emergency signal to stop ;

(i) When the door of the vehicle is closed and any passenger desires to alight, the Conductor must station himself at the door, and after opening the door he must make **every** effort to prevent any passenger attempting to alight **until he personally is satisfied that the vehicle has come to a " dead " stop.**

NOTE.—**This instruction is of particular importance after dusk, as it is almost impossible for a passenger leaving a brilliantly lit vehicle to judge whether the vehicle has actually come to a standstill.**

(j) **Particular attention must be paid to cripples, aged persons, women and children,** and every assistance must be given to such persons whether entering or alighting from the vehicle, and especially where children are concerned **they should be warned not to run round the back of the vehicle after alighting** *and thereby prevented from being run over by another vehicle approaching from the opposite direction ;*

(k) Where the vehicle has both a front and a rear entrance on the nearside the Conductor must satisfy himself that **all** passengers have alighted and **all** intending passengers have entered **in safety** and that both doors (if opening outwards) are closed **before** he gives the Driver the signal to start ;

(l) Where the vehicle is fitted with a bell and the Driver is in a closed compartment the Conductor must **not** give the Driver the signal to start or stop by a wave of the hand, a nod of the head, a blow of a whistle, a shout, a stamp of the foot, a knock on the panelling of the vehicle, or a knock on the glass partition behind the Driver, **and a Driver is expressly forbidden to move off unless he has received the recognised and authorised bell signal** ;

(m) A Conductor—wherever possible and specially after dusk—must call out clearly and distinctly the recognised stopping places when the vehicle is still some distance off ;

(n) When accidents to passengers or intending passengers do occur the Conductor must **not** hesitate. He must give the emergency signal to the Driver to stop, he must give every assistance to the passenger or intending passenger whether or not the passenger complains of injury, he must take his or her name and address, and the name and address of every available witness, *whether on the vehicle or on the roadway* ;

NOTE.—A Conductor must always bear in mind that while the passenger or intending passenger may say at the time that he or she has sustained no injury and that it was his or her own fault, later on they may change their mind and intimate a claim, and if the Conductor has failed to take the names and addresses of every available witness, and has not at once reported the occurrence, **the Management may be placed in a serious difficulty.**

It cannot be **too** strongly impressed upon Drivers and Conductors that a passenger or intending passenger can usually secure the evidence of some passenger or some friend or acquaintance who is alleged to have been in the vicinity or at the scene of the accident, and who will at a later stage be quite prepared to give evidence against the Driver or Conductor.

8.—ACCIDENTS.

The following instructions must be faithfully carried out by all Drivers and Conductors :—

(a) The vehicle must be stopped **at once** ;

(b) Medical aid—and, if necessary, an ambulance must be obtained—should a passenger, intending passenger, pedestrian, occupant of another vehicle, or other road user sustain personal injury ;

(c) Every possible step must be taken to secure the prompt attendance of the Police, and Drivers and Conductors must render the Police every possible assistance and give them any information they may require ;

(d) The exact time and place where the accident has occurred must be noted ;

(e) Where a collision has occurred with another vehicle the Conductor—whom failing the Driver—must take a note of the registered letter and number of the other vehicle—*if it is mechanically driven*—its make, the name and address of the owner and the name and address of the driver, and the exact nature and extent of the damage ;

If the collision has been with a horse-drawn vehicle, similar information must be noted, and if the horse has sustained injury, the exact nature and extent of the injury, the breed, colour, sex, and distinguishing marks must also be noted as likely to prove useful for identification ;

If the contents of a vehicle—whether a handcart, delivery cycle, or a vehicle mechanically driven or horse-drawn—sustain damage, full details must be noted of the nature of the goods and the extent of the damage thereto ;

If a sheep, dog or other animal has been run over or injured, the breed, colour, sex, any distinguishing marks, and the nature and extent of the injuries must be noted, and the name and address of the owner and of any person in charge must be obtained ;

(f) Where a collision has occurred or a pedestrian or other road user has been involved, careful note must be taken of the position of the vehicles involved (1)

just before : (2) at the time, and (3) after the collision and when the vehicles have come to a stop.

Such road measurements must be taken as will enable Drivers and Conductors to give the Management a clear and accurate sketch, and wherever possible Drivers and Conductors must see that such measurements are confirmed by the Police or other independent witnesses ;

(g) WHERE THE ACCIDENT IS A SERIOUS ONE, the Driver should refuse to move his vehicle until ordered to do so by the Police, or until full particulars of the position of the vehicle have been noted and confirmed by independent witnesses whose names and addresses should be taken.

Wherever possible, arrangements should be made to have a photograph of the *locus* taken before the vehicle is moved, as the Management will gladly pay any expense incurred for this purpose.

(h) It cannot be too strongly impressed upon both Drivers and Conductors that they must take the name and address of every available witness, **whether the witness is in their favour or otherwise** ;

NOTE.—The Management will take a serious view of the failure of any Driver or Conductor who has neglected to take the name and address of any witness **simply because such witness is hostile.**

(i) Every accident or incident—however trivial—must be reported to the Management by the Drivers and Conductors involved when they go off duty, and a Report Form completed in ink ;

(j) A Driver must report to the Police within 24 hours any accident in which he has been involved resulting in personal injury to any person, damage

to property or injury to any horse, cattle, sheep, dog, pig or goat ;

A Driver must give his name and address, the name and address of his employer, and the registered letter and number of his vehicle to any person who has reasonable cause for asking for such information ;

(k) A Driver must co-operate with his Conductor to see that there is reported to the Police any accident resulting in injury to passengers or intending passengers, whether or not the injured person states that he or she is all right and that it was his or her own fault.

(l) Where an accident has occurred—whether a collision with another vehicle or otherwise—the Conductor must take a careful note of the number of passengers in the vehicle at the time of the accident, and he must ask each passenger whether he or she has sustained injury or shock and take the name and address of any passenger who has any complaint to make, and the seat he or she was occupying at the time of the accident ;

(m) Under no circumstances must either a Driver or Conductor discuss an accident or give any information relative thereto other than to the Police or an authorised official of the Company.

Should they be asked by anyone—whether a Solicitor or other individual—to give a statement, **they must refer such individual to the Management.**

(n) A Driver or Conductor must **not** visit any person injured or in any way connected with an accident **without the written authority of the Management** ;

(o) Any Driver or Conductor who gives to any person

(other than a responsible official of the Company or to the Police) the name and address of any passenger in a vehicle which has been involved in an accident—whether such passenger has been injured or not—will be **instantly** dismissed.

NOTE.—Drivers and Conductors must remember that careful investigation is made by the Management in connection with every accident that occurs and it is, therefore, in their interests to render every possible assistance to the Management by giving the fullest and frankest statement and securing the name and address of every available witness.

9.—CONDITION OF BODY-WORK.

Claims are intimated by passengers for damage to wearing apparel caused—or alleged to be caused—by protruding nails, screws, bolts, springs of seats, grease or other dirt, defective window or door catches, etc.

Conductors must pay particular attention to the following instructions :—

(a) Before the vehicle is taken out of the Depot he must make a careful examination of the floor, seats, doors, etc., to see that there is no oil, grease, or dirt of any kind which may soil or damage the wearing apparel of passengers. He must also see that there are no nails, bolts, damaged or protruding spring seats or other projections which may cause injury to passengers or damage to their wearing apparel.

A similar careful examination must be made before the vehicle leaves each terminus, or when the Conductor takes over the vehicle from another Conductor.

(b) Should any passenger complain that he or she has sustained damage to his or her wearing apparel,

or such damage be observed by the Conductor, the Conductor must take a note of the name and address of the passenger, the nature and extent of the damage, the exact position of the damage, the material and colour of the damaged article, and if a tear, the exact position and extent of the tear, and the Conductor must satisfy himself as to the exact cause of the damage in order that he can make a full report to the Management when he goes off duty.

10.—CONDITION OF VEHICLE.

(a) A Driver must satisfy himself that the brakes at all times are so efficient that the application of either will bring the vehicle to a stop within a reasonable distance.

(b) A Driver must satisfy himself that the vehicle and all its fittings are in such a condition as not to cause—*or be likely to cause*—injury or danger to passengers or other users of the road.

NOTE.—Any defect in the brakes or other part of the vehicle must be reported to the nearest Depot, and if any defect or breakage occurs either in the chassis or body which makes the vehicle unsafe, **the Driver must stop at once and advise the nearest depot by telephone or otherwise and await the arrival of a relief vehicle.**

11.—DRIVING POSITION.

(a) A Driver must always be in such a position that he has full control over the vehicle, **with a clear view of the road and traffic ahead**

(b) Under no circumstances must a Driver allow anyone to be seated in the front seat *on his right or off-side* ;

(c) A Driver must not take his hand off the steering wheel, or look back into the vehicle, *while the vehicle is in motion.*

12.—VIEW AHEAD.

Where a Driver's view of the road in front of him is restricted by any cause, such as fog, snowstorm, blinding rain, smoke or steam emitted by a Steam Vehicle or Railway Engine, or smoke from a fire on the road embankments, moors, etc., he **must** so reduce his speed that he can bring his vehicle to a stop and avoid being involved in an accident *of any nature.*

13.—OVERTAKING PEDESTRIANS.

When overtaking pedestrians on the road **it is not sufficient for a Driver to blow the horn** ;

If the pedestrian does not get out of the way—he or she may not hear the signal—**the Driver must slow down—and if necessary stop—until he has a clear road ahead** ;

Special care must be exercised where the pedestrians are young children or aged or infirm persons.

14.—CHILDREN AND OTHER PEDESTRIANS STEPPING OFF FOOTPATHS.

A careful Driver anticipates the movements of children and other pedestrians walking on footpaths ;

A Driver must keep a close look-out ahead and be prepared for the child or other pedestrian who steps off the footpath on the driver's nearside **without looking behind.**

Even greater care is required where the child or other pedestrian leaves the footpath on the Driver's offside to cross to the footpath on the nearside. Unless the movement of the person is hidden by other vehicles travelling in the opposite direction, **the Driver should see the person leave the footpath on the offside**, and if there is the **slightest risk** that he or she may not have time to reach the footpath on the nearside before being run down, **the Driver must slow down and allow him or her to pass in front and reach the near footpath in safety.**

15.—OVERTAKING PUSH CYCLISTS.

A Driver must give warning **when still some distance off,** and when actually overtaking the cyclist **give as much clearance as possible** ;

If a vehicle coming in the opposite direction does not allow **the Driver to have at least two yards clearance** on the *off-side* of the cyclist, **the Driver must slow down behind the cyclist until the other vehicle has passed** ;

NOTE.—Experienced Drivers are only too well aware that cyclists have a habit of glancing back over their right shoulder when they hear the approach of an overtaking vehicle, and this movement almost always results in their pulling the front wheel of their cycle towards the off-side, **resulting in an accident if the overtaking vehicle is too close to them.**

Should a driver collide with a cyclist travelling in the same direction when it is dark, **the Driver must take immediate steps to see whether the cycle is fitted with a red reflector. If the cycle is not so fitted, it is the Driver's duty to draw the attention of the Police or other independent witness to the Cyclist's failure to comply with the law.**

16.—TRAMCARS.

(a) Before attempting to overtake and pass a tramcar on its nearside, **a Driver must make sure that the tramcar is not going to stop to set down or take up passengers. If so, the Driver must stop until the tramcar resumes its journey, and the passengers who have alighted have reached the pavement**; he must keep a careful look-out for the passenger alighting *just as the tramcar moves off*, and for the intending passenger *who leaves the pavement at the last moment.* The Driver thereby avoids any risk of knocking down anyone who is about to enter or is leaving the tramcar ;

(b) When overtaking a tramcar in motion on its nearside, **a Driver must sound his horn and be on the look-out for the pedestrian who is crossing in front of the tramcar from the offside.** Particular care must be exercised by the Driver *where there is also a stationary tramcar on the offside tram rails.* Passengers may be alighting who will walk round the rear of the tramcar from which they have alighted and cross in front of the tramcar which is being overtaken on its near side *and the Driver will not see them until they step out from in front of the tramcar he is overtaking ;*

(c) Where circumstances require a Driver to overtake a tramcar on its offside, *special care must be exercised.*

The Driver must not overtake a tramcar on its offside unless he is satisfied he has the acceleration and time to overtake the tramcar and pull in to his near side before any vehicle approaching from the opposite direction has come so close as to make a collision possible.

Even greater care is required if the approaching **vehicle is a tramcar on the offside tram rails. If the action of the Driver of the public service vehicle is such as compels the Driver either of the tramcar which is being overtaken on the offside or of the tramcar approaching from the opposite direction to slam on his brakes and, as the result of the sudden stop, passengers are thrown from their seats and sustain injury or shock, heavy damages may have to be paid by the Employer of the offending Driver ;**

(d) **A Driver must exercise the greatest care** when attempting to overtake tramcars when approaching crossings *either on the near or off-side.* If a tramcar is being overtaken on the nearside close to a crossing the Driver may be confronted **suddenly** with a vehicle, cyclist, or pedestrian who has emerged from the offside, and the Driver will not see any of these until they emerge from the front of the tramcar **right in his track** ;

If a Driver overtakes a tramcar on the offside near a crossing he risks a collision with a vehicle, cycle or pedestrian who has emerged from the crossing on his nearside, and if a collision occurs **such collision will take place when the Driver is on his wrong side of the road** ;

(e) When the tram line is " single " a Driver must not attempt to pass a tramcar **near a " loop."**

Equal care must be exercised when overtaking a tramcar on a " single " line when the tramcar is proceeding in the same direction, where the tram line is on the off side of the road, and there is a " loop " close ahead.

17.—OVERTAKING A VEHICLE OTHER THAN A TRAMCAR.

A Driver before attempting to overtake a vehicle proceeding in the same direction—

(a) must give warning to the Driver of the vehicle in front ;

(b) He must await a return signal *or satisfy himself otherwise* that the Driver in front will not pull out to overtake a vehicle, push cyclist, or pedestrian in front of him, *or for other reasons make a turn to the right ;*

NOTE.—Special care must be exercised if the vehicle in front is a horse cart or lorry, as the Driver may be seated on the nearside of his vehicle or be leading the horse by the head, *and will be invisible to the Driver of the vehicle behind if his cart or lorry is loaded.*

(c) He must not attempt to overtake and pass another vehicle if there is traffic—pedestrian or otherwise—coming in the opposite direction **and so close that he will not have ample time to overtake and pull in to his near side of the road ;**

(d) He must exercise the greatest care and be on the strict look-out when overtaking another vehicle for any pedestrian who may be crossing in front of the other vehicle **from the nearside** and whom he will not see **until he or she is right in his track** owing to his view of the pedestrian being hidden by the vehicle he is overtaking ;

(e) **Under no circumstances must he attempt to overtake another vehicle near cross-roads ;**

(f) In busy streets where there are side streets at frequent intervals, a Driver must use his own judgment as to when it is safe to overtake another vehicle ;

(g) After overtaking another vehicle he must not slacken speed, nor must he pull over to his nearside until he has overtaken a sufficient distance to ensure that there will be no collision with the other vehicle even if it accelerates.

NOTE.—Whenever possible the Conductor should give the Driver the " all clear " signal—Two Bells.

18.—MEETING CATTLE, SHEEP, HOUNDS AND SUCH LIKE.

(a) A Driver must **stop** until **all** the animals have passed the **rear** of the vehicle ;

(b) **A Driver must not start off until he has received the signal from the Conductor.**

NOTE.—It is the duty of a **Conductor** to satisfy himself that the animals **and any dog** in charge are clear of danger **before** he gives the Driver the signal to start.

19.—OVERTAKING CATTLE, SHEEP, HOUNDS AND SUCH LIKE.

A Driver must slow down, give warning to the person in charge, give him or her time to herd the animals to one side of the road, await his or her signal, and then proceed **slowly and cautiously,** keeping a strict look-out not only on the animals, but on any dog assisting the person in charge of the animals.

20.—OVERTAKING AND MEETING " LED " HORSES.

A Driver must always keep the man in charge of a " led " horse **between** the horse and the vehicle he is driving.

If the man in charge of the "led" horse gives a signal to stop **the Driver must do so at once.**

NOTE.—A Driver must always remember the man in charge knows the temperament of the horse of which he is in charge, and any want of care upon the Driver's part may result in the destruction of a horse of great value.

21.—TURNING BENDS IN THE ROAD.

A Driver must exercise the greatest care in turning bends in the road, **especially if the bend is a hidden one ;**

He must on all occasions give warning by blowing his horn, he must keep close into his nearside, and he must slow down to a speed which will enable him to stop instantly should he be confronted with an obstacle round the bend.

NOTE.—The careful driver is prepared for the reckless driver travelling at a high speed from the opposite direction and cutting the corner, but he also anticipates there may be a drove of cattle or sheep or a crowd of pedestrians occupying the whole breadth of the road, and unless he has taken all due precautions a serious accident will result.

Under no circumstances must a Driver overtake another vehicle, cyclist, or pedestrian when approaching a bend in the road.

22.—CROSS ROADS.

(a) When approaching cross-roads—whether main or bye—a Driver must always sound his horn as a warning ; he must keep close into his own side of the road, and have his vehicle under such control, and the speed so reduced, that he will **not** collide with a pedestrian, cyclist, horse, cattle, sheep, or other animal, or any other vehicle which may emerge from the cross-roads either on his near or his offside ;

NOTE.—A Driver must bear in mind that no man in charge of sheep or cattle can prevent their emerging *without warning* either from the road on the nearside or the offside.

(b) If a Driver has to stop to set down or uplift passengers, he must draw in close to his nearside of the road, **and he must stop his vehicle when he is still at least two bus lengths from the cross-roads.**

23.—EMERGING FROM SIDE ROAD ON TO MAIN ROAD.

A Driver must exercise the **greatest** care when emerging from a side road ; he must sound his horn and slow down to such a speed that, when he can see up and down the main road, **he can stop "dead" should traffic be approaching from either direction.**

24.—TURNING INTO A ROAD OR STREET ON THE NEARSIDE.

When turning into a road or street on the nearside a Driver must give warning, keep close into the nearside when turning, **and keep a strict look-out for any pedestrian who may be about to step off the footpath.**

If the corner is a "blind" one the Driver must slow down, and if necessary stop, until he can see he has a clear road.

25.—TURNING INTO A ROAD OR STREET ON THE OFFSIDE.

When turning into a road or street on the offside a Driver must give **due** warning to vehicles behind him ; he must allow any vehicle travelling close behind to overtake and pass him before he makes the turn to the right ; he must give the right of way to any vehicle approaching from the opposite direction, the driver of which does not slow down and give him the signal to turn to the right ; **he must not cut the corner** ; and when about to enter the road or street on the offside **he must keep a strict look-out for pedestrians.**

26.—ENTERING GARAGES, YARDS, ETC.

(a) A Driver must exercise the greatest care when entering garages, yards, or other buildings ; *which necessitates his crossing a footpath ;*

(b) He must keep a **strict** look-out for pedestrians on the footpath *both on his nearside and his off-side ;*

(c) If the garage, yard or other building is on the offside of the road, the Driver must not turn across the road *until* he has satisfied himself that there is a clear entrance to the garage, etc., *and that there is no vehicle travelling in the same or in the opposite direction* **and so close that there may be a collision ;**

(d) When leaving garages, yards or other buildings, the Driver *must* have the guidance of his Conductor or other responsible *employee,* who must be standing *outside* to safeguard pedestrians on the footpath, and the Driver *must* await the "all clear" signal *before he emerges.*

27.—STOPPING AND TURNING OUT OF LINE OF TRAFFIC.

When coming to a stop a Driver must—wherever practicable—give **due** warning to traffic behind.

When turning out of the line of traffic in which he is proceeding or when pulling out from the footpath the Driver must not only give **due** warning, **but he must satisfy himself that there is no overtaking vehicle so close that his pulling out will result in a collision.**

28.—REVERSING.

A Driver must not reverse without the guidance of the Conductor or other responsible employee.

He must bear in mind that it is only by the **closest** co-operation with the Conductor that he will avoid, when reversing, a collision with another vehicle, pedestrian, cyclist, animal, window shade, lamp standard or other obstruction.

NOTE.—It is an offence under the Road Traffic Act to reverse a vehicle for a greater distance or time than is necessary for the safety or reasonable convenience of the occupants of the vehicle or of other traffic on the road.

A Driver who desires to turn on a public highway must carry on until he reaches a suitable opening on the nearside ; he must reverse into the opening with the guidance of the Conductor **and take all due precaution when again emerging on to the main highway.**

29.—TRAVELLING BEHIND OTHER VEHICLES.

(a) A Driver must not drive so close behind another vehicle or cyclist travelling in the same direction that he will run into the other vehicle or cycle **should it come to a sudden stop.**

(b) He must have his vehicle under such control, *and so situate in relation to the other vehicle or cycle in front*, that he will be able to cope with **every** emergency.

(c) Special care must be exercised when the road is greasy or ice-bound, and the Driver must keep such a distance behind a vehicle in front that he will be able to slow down or pull up—*if traffic conditions necessitate*—**without his being involved in a skid or an accident of any description.**

30.—STOPPING.

When stopping to set down or pick up passengers a **Driver must pull in as close as possible to the left or nearside of the road.**

He must not allow his vehicle to remain stationary longer than is necessary to set down or take up passengers, **except at a recognised stance.**

31.—LEAVING VEHICLE STATIONARY.

(a) A Driver must not quit his vehicle unless he has taken every precaution against its being started or moving off in his absence ;

If the vehicle is left standing on an incline, the driver must engage the **reverse gear** if the vehicle is facing *down-hill*, and the **first gear** if the vehicle is facing *up-hill* ;

(b) If a Driver has left his vehicle standing on the road—particularly in a town or in the neighbourhood of houses or schools—**no matter how short a time he may have to be away,** it is his duty, and the duty of his Conductor, to satisfy themselves that there are **no** children under the vehicle or hanging on to any part of it *before it moves off.*

32.—LEAVING VEHICLE UNATTENDED.

Under **no** circumstances must a vehicle be left unattended by its Driver or Conductor, and one of these **must** remain in charge of the vehicle if the other is away for any reason.

33.—STOPPING ENGINE WHEN VEHICLE STATIONARY.

When the vehicle is stationary, otherwise than at an enforced stop owing to the necessities of traffic or when letting down or picking up passengers, **the Driver must stop his engine running.**

NOTE.—It is an offence under the Road Traffic Act if a Driver quits his vehicle without having stopped the engine.

34.—PASSING HOUSES, SCHOOLS, FARM STEADINGS, ETC.

A Driver must exercise the **greatest** care when passing houses, schools, farm steadings and other buildings—especially in country districts—and he must **at all times** be prepared for children running into the road and for cattle, horses, sheep or other animals emerging from farm steadings **without warning.**

A Driver must see that his speed is such, and his vehicle under such control, that he is able to avoid running into children or animals emerging from his near or offside.

35.—NARROW ROADS.

Where a road is narrow and there is little more than room for two vehicles to pass, **a Driver must slow down—and, if necessary stop**—especially if the road surface is bad or there is a camber on the nearside, otherwise he may have a skid which may result in a collision with the other vehicle or result in his colliding with a telegraph pole, wall, fence or bridge on his nearside, or overturning his vehicle should it crash over an embankment, causing serious damage to the vehicle and serious or fatal injury to passengers.

36.—ROADS UNDER REPAIR, IN BAD CONDITION, UNDER WATER, GREASY OR FROST-BOUND.

(a) A Driver **must** consider the comfort and safety not only of the passengers in his vehicle, but of other road users, **and where road conditions necessitate his slowing down he must do so** ;

(b) If a Driver is approaching a decline, and the road is greasy or frost-bound, **he must reduce speed and drop into a lower gear, and thereby avoid having to use his brakes except to bring his vehicle to a stop.**

37.—LEVEL CROSSINGS.

At level crossings—*particularly where there are no gates*—**a Driver must exercise the greatest care and be prepared to bring his vehicle to a dead stop until he is satisfied there is no train approaching from either direction.**

38.—TOWING ANOTHER VEHICLE.

Should a vehicle break down and be towed to the Depot or should it be used for the towage of another vehicle which has broken down, the Driver must see that the tow rope is so adjusted that the distance separating the nearest points of the two vehicles is not more than 15 feet, **and he must take all necessary steps to see that the tow rope is easily seen by other users of the road.**

NOTE.—**No passengers must be carried in the vehicle which is being towed.**

39.—OBSTRUCTION.

(a) A Driver must always bear in mind that it is an offence to allow his vehicle to stand on a road so as to cause any unnecessary obstruction to other traffic or danger to other users of the road ;

(b) Under no circumstances must he leave his vehicle standing close to a bend in the road.

(c) Should a vehicle break down at a part of the road where vehicles approaching from **either** direction will not have a **clear** view of the broken-down vehicle **for some considerable distance,** it is the duty of both the Driver and Conductor to take **all** possible steps to warn approaching traffic, **especially after dark.**

40.—CONVOYS.

Where there is a convoy of vehicles travelling in the same direction, each Driver must keep a sufficient distance behind the vehicle in front to give the driver of an overtaking vehicle room to pull in between should he not have a clear road further ahead.

41.—FILLING PETROL TANK.

A Driver must not remove the cap from the petrol tank until he has stopped the engine.

42.—OVERCROWDING.

A Conductor must not allow more passengers on his vehicle than its licensed seating capacity, **except at " peak periods " or under circumstances in which undue hardship would be caused if he refused to carry passengers in excess of the seating capacity.**

Should a Conductor be prosecuted for having infringed the regulations under the Road Traffic Act in that he has allowed standing passengers, **he must provide his own defence.**

Under **no** circumstances must a Conductor allow standing passengers on the **upper** deck of a " double-decker," or more than **five** standing passengers on the lower deck of a " double-decker " or on a " single-decker " seated for more than 20 passengers.

If the vehicle is seated for **less** than 20 passengers it is an offence under the Road Traffic Act to allow standing passengers **in excess of one-fourth the seating capacity.**

43.—ENTRANCE, EXITS, AND GANGWAYS.

A Conductor must **not** allow any obstruction such as parcels or passengers' luggage to be placed at the entrance, exit, gangways or passage-ways of his vehicle.

44.—PASSENGERS' LUGGAGE.

Where luggage or other articles are placed on the roof of the vehicle **they must be properly secured and protected against rain, high winds, etc.**

Where luggage or other articles are placed beside the Driver the greatest care must be exercised to secure that they will **not** be damaged by any projection, by heat from the engine or the exhaust, or by other luggage or other articles.

45.—LUGGAGE RACKS.

A Conductor must note that luggage racks are for **light articles only** and he must **not under any circumstances** allow any passenger to place on the luggage racks heavy articles or bulky articles which may fall and cause injury to other passengers.

46.—LOST PROPERTY.

(a) A Conductor must search the vehicle at the **termination** of **each** journey for any property which has been left by passengers ;

(b) Should a passenger find property left in the vehicle by another passenger and hand it over to the Conductor, **the Conductor must accept custody of the article** ;

(c) Property found by the Conductor or handed over to him by a passenger must be dealt with as follows :—

If the Conductor is relieved by another Conductor **before** the vehicle returns to the Depot the Conductor who is being relieved must obtain a receipt from the Conductor who is taking over.

The Conductor who has the custody of the article when the vehicle returns to the Depot must hand over the article to a responsible Official at the Depot and obtain a receipt.

The Conductor who has custody of the article on the vehicle must take every practicable precaution for its safety.

If the article has been found by a passenger the Conductor **must** take the name and address of such passenger.

47.—CONDUCT OF PASSENGERS.

Under the Road Traffic Act the following regulations have been laid down, and either the Driver or the Conductor is entitled to remove from the vehicle any passenger who has infringed any of these regulations, or the Driver or Conductor may request a police constable to remove the offending passenger.

NOTE.—Either the Driver or Conductor should request the offending passenger to give his or her name and address, or if a police constable is present the Driver or Conductor should see that he takes the name and address of the offending passenger.

Passengers must not—

(a) Use obscene or abusive language or conduct themselves in a riotous or disorderly manner ;

(b) Enter or alight from the vehicle otherwise than by the doors or openings provided for the purpose ;

(c) When entering or attempting to enter the vehicle wilfully or unreasonably impede passengers seeking to enter or alight from the vehicle ;

(d) Travel in or on the upper deck of a "double-decker" unless they occupy a seat provided for the purpose or in or on any part of the vehicle not provided for the conveyance of passengers ;

(e) Wilfully do or cause to be done with respect to any part of the vehicle or its equipment anything which is calculated to obstruct or interfere with the working of the vehicle or to cause injury or discomfort to any person ;

(f) When the vehicle is in motion distract the Driver's attention without reasonable cause, or speak to him unless it is necessary to do so in order to give directions as to the stopping of the vehicle ;

(g) Give any signal which might be interpreted by the Driver as a signal from the Conductor to start ;

NOTE.—This regulation is of the greatest importance and should such a signal be given by a passenger—even if no accident results—the name and address of the offending passenger—and of every available witness—must be taken.

(h) Spit upon or from, or wilfully damage, soil or defile any part of the vehicle ;

(i) When in or on the vehicle distribute printed or similar matter of any description or distribute any article for the purpose of advertising ;

(j) Wilfully remove, displace, deface or alter any number board, route indicator or destination board, or any printed or other notice or advertisement in or on the vehicle ;

(k) When in or on the vehicle, to the annoyance of other persons, use or operate any noisy instrument or make or combine with any other person or persons to make, any excessive noise by singing, shouting or otherwise ;

(l) When in or on the vehicle throw any money to be scrambled for by any person on the road or footway, or throw out of the vehicle any bottle, liquid or litter or any article or thing to annoy persons or to cause danger or injury to any person or property ;

(m) Attach to or trail from the vehicle any streamer, balloon, flag or other article in such a manner as to overhang the roadway ;

(n) Wilfully obstruct or impede any authorised person acting in the performance of his or her duty upon or in connection with the vehicle ;

(o) Smoke or carry a lighted pipe, cigar or cigarette in or on any part of the vehicle on which a notice is exhibited that smoking is prohibited ;

NOTE.—This regulation does not apply to " contract " vehicles, *i.e.*, vehicles which have been hired for a special occasion and are not plying for public hire.

(p) Sell or offer for sale any article while in or on the vehicle ;

(q) Remain in or on the vehicle after they have been requested by the Conductor to leave the vehicle and have had tendered to them the amount of any fare previously paid, if their condition is such as to be offensive to passengers or the condition of their dress is such that it may be reasonably expected to soil or injure the linings or cushions of the vehicle or the clothing of other passengers ;

(r) Enter or travel in or on the vehicle with loaded fire-arms, or any dangerous or offensive article, or except with the consent of the Conductor bring into or on the vehicle any bulky or cumbersome article or place any such article elsewhere in or on the vehicle than as directed by the Conductor ;

NOTE.—Conductors must clearly understand that it is an offence under the Road Traffic Act to allow to be carried on

a public service vehicle any explosive, highly inflammable or otherwise dangerous substance (other than the fuel and lubricant necessary for the use of the vehicle), unless it is so packed that, even in the case of an accident to the vehicle, it is unlikely to cause damage or injury to the vehicle or passengers carried therein.

(s) Bring any animal in or on the vehicle without the consent of the Conductor, or retain any animal in or on the vehicle after being requested by the Conductor to remove it or place any animal elsewhere in or on the vehicle than as directed by the Conductor ;

(t) Wilfully alter or deface his or her ticket ;

(u) Unless they are already the holder of a ticket in respect of the journey, before leaving the vehicle or immediately on demand, refuse to declare the journey they have taken or intend to take and pay the Conductor the fare for the whole of such journey and accept the ticket provided therefor ;

(v) If requested by the Conductor refuse to leave the vehicle on completion of the journey, the fare for which they have paid ;

(w) Refuse to show their ticket—if it has been issued—when required to do so by the Conductor or other authorised person, or if they fail to show their ticket, refuse to pay the fare for the journey taken or be taken by them ;

(x) At the end of the journey refuse to surrender their ticket to the Conductor or other authorised person if required to do so ;

(y) If they are the holder of a period or season ticket, refuse to surrender the ticket at the expiry of the period for which it has been issued, if required to do so.

J. Bain & Sons Ltd., Printers, 32 York Place, Edinburgh.

A HAPPY PARTY

The coach is a Wycombe bodied Gilford complete with folded back soft top and a completely exposed driver's cabin belonging to "Silver Cars", normally running the 9¼ hour trip from London to Exmouth via Staines, Salisbury, Dorchester, Bridport, Lyme Regis and Seaton.

The card, though, shows the coach as being at Weymouth; presumably on an excursion. The postmark seems to be Saturday 16 July 1932, and in part reads "just a card to see if there is any one you know", but are the fashions not fearfully old-fashioned?

With the exception of the hatless girl in white and the children the rest look truly Edwardian.

WALLACE ARNOLD

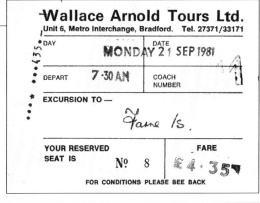
At one time Wallace Arnold services, or at least the company vehicles carried the soubriquet "Wally's Trolleys", in part quite an affectionate title. Their 'main line' fleet was always well turned out, and it was noticeable that they had a very low level of double booking, that bane of a driver's life before the days of mobile telephones.

The bones of the company lay in Robert Barr's acquisition in 1912 of a Karrier which ran as a lorry in the week but gained a charabanc body for weekend passenger work; but it was not until 1926 that the partnership of Wallace Cunningham and Arnold Crowe was purchased, Robert Barr then using the Wallace Arnold name for his coaching activities; freight haulage was developed entirely separately under the trading name of R. Barr (Leeds) Ltd, although in 1937 when a public company was set up – Barr & Wallace Arnold Trust Ltd – to consolidate all the family interests, which by then included a good number of companies that had been taken over – a programme which continued for years afterwards; among others were a coach-building firm, strategically placed hotels, and local bus operators.

Stratford-upon-Avon railway station as it was on 25 June 1992, with a Plaxton 50-seat coach built on a Volvo B10M-60 chassis, H615 UWR, advertising "Come with us to EuroDisney, the World of Make Believe".

KUM 834 was a more typical Wallace Arnold vehicle, having a Leyland PS1 chassis of 1947, being originally supplied with Burlingham half-cab body, but this was superseded in 1949 by another Burlingham 33-seat coach body, as always in this period with a centre door, although this was again modified, modernised if you will, with a 'Seagull' styled front as seen here. Withdrawn in 1957 the next owners were Pilot of Blackpool for a season and then to that home for battered vehicles, Austin Woodseaves as their no. 20, where KUM was last seen derelict in August 1964.

108 EUA has what I have considered one of Plaxton's least happy bodies visually, as I believe the front grills have the look of a sulky girl. Apart from a habit of leaking the rest of the design has the advantage of being well ventilated and extremely well lit with 'panoramic' glass for tourist work. Wallace Arnold Tours standardised on this design which was nominally an 'Embassy' but with 'Panorama 1' 36 feet body shell, and had fourteen including 108 delivered in 1963. Withdrawn in 1973 after a relatively short life, it ended its days as a car transporter.

METAMORPHOSIS

Many long years ago R.F. Mack knowing my penchant for collecting photographs of strange coaching events supplied this one to me.

What we have is on the face of it a more-or-less standard Wallace Arnold half-cab. But the registration dates back to 1946 whereas the body was from the coachbuilders H.V. Burlingham in 1948. And … the chassis in turn dated back to 1933 when it first saw life as a petrol-engined AEC Regal and yet if you stood near enough the rattle and rasp of an AEC 7.7 litre diesel was apparent.

When war broke out the War Ministry sent its minions out to round up virtually every coach and bus they could find – sometimes taking an operator's entire fleet, although some men showed a little sensitivity and left enough vehicles (as few as one!) to run essential services. In some cases the operators hid their vehicles away from prying eyes particularly where their sons and their drivers were called up on the basis the war could not last forever. Little or no compensation was initially paid for vehicles collected and in some cases the paperwork was 'overlooked' so the small operator had no hope of making a claim. One of my uncles – in the Territorial Army (as was) was given no option but to drive his fairly new vehicle to a nearby Army dump and found himself called-up as a driver and held incommunicado – being unable to let even his wife know what had happened. Eventually he was sent off to France and was taken prisoner during the retreat. The first aunt knew where he was took the form of a postcard forwarded from the Germans via the Red Cross. Small wonder they went to Australia in 1946 where he ended up as a Manager for a Queensland bus fleet. But at the end of the war innumerable vehicles were offered to the larger operators, irrespective who was the original owner, and this little gem of WA was one of these. It survived in second-line service until 1954.

The location is itself a long forgotten aspect of coach work, the coach being hired to football supporters from the North-West and is seen outside Leeds United ground as one of 30 plus such vehicles. Alongside can be discerned parts – including bow collectors – of the eight or nine Leeds trams awaiting the crowds of local supporters to take them home at the end of the game. [the late R.F. Mack]

LOST CITY, LOST BUSES

A 'Valentine' postcard photographed in the very early 1930s. One of my landladies used to become quite poetic talking about the Birmingham of her youth, describing the city as friendly and that everything about it (and specifically the thriving markets) was human sized. As we look down New Street we can see how the buildings are varied and in some ways are quite welcoming – even when I started work there was a pride in 'our' office and 'our' company – and, strangely her only grudge against the Luftwaffe was that they damaged 'her' shop and 'made it all messy'. Today's glass canyons may be architects' dreams but I find them quite inhuman with the workers reduced to the status of, at best, worker ants to be disposed of at a financier's whim.

Similarly, buses are quite marvellous today with all their gimmicks but conductors have gone and how long drivers can survive for is debatable; worse still these modern machines are characterless whereas the three buses nearest to us represent the best designers could imagine in 1930 being 6-cylinder petrol engined AEC Regents. In all 167 of these were to be supplied to Birmingham over three years, although local politics was to ensure no further 'foreign' AECs were to be purchased, later bus orders being placed with local i.e. Midlands firms. As can be seen bodywork was of a rather short lived but functional design, the 'piano front' – I was told many years ago the problem was that there was nothing inherently wrong with the shape, but cleaning, rigorously enforced, was very labour intensive indeed compared with later flat fronted vehicles. Brush of Loughborough, Shorts of Rochester, and the local Metro-Cammell all built batches of bodies, pretty well all alike.

NEW STREET, BIRMINGHAM (27)

OVER-WYRE

This timetable is a fine example of a country carriers' operations. As with so many Mr Melling started at a public house, the Kings Arms, and terminated at another, the Black Bull. This was in the purest sense 'traditional' as it was normal practice for horse-drawn wagons carrying the ladies of the village to the market with their butter, eggs, live chickens, vegetables and other produce after unloading to lay up at a suitable pub where the horses could be stabled and a "Shilling Ordinary" lunch could be had, together with a jug or two of ale and a good degree of gossip. Even in motorised days this practice continued, especially where there was no-where for the bus or coach to park in the market place; empty running was totally unproductive and if the driver had nothing else to do a keen boss would send him off with a bundle of excursion handbills to be given to shops.

As can be seen the service was tailored to the traffic on offer; Monday was washday of course, while Thursday and Saturday were market days, and the 10.15pm was the cinema bus, normally grossly overloaded and a true money-spinner. No extra pay for unsocial hours in 1933, but I expect a toffee or two. I assume Mr Melling attended other markets on Fridays, thus keeping his bus busy.

Over-Wyre Motor Omnibus Service between Garstang, Poulton, and Eagland Hill.

Good connections for Lancaster, Preston, Blackpool and Fleetwood.

	Tues., Wed.				Thursday.					Saturday.						Thursdays only. Garstang to Eagland Hill.	
	a.m	a.m.	p.m.	p.m.	a.m.	a.m.	p.m.	p.m.	p.m.	a.m.	a.m.	p.m.	p.m.	p.m.	p.m		
																a.m	a.m.
GARSTANG, Kings Arms	7 45	9 0	1 15	6 30	7 45	10 30	1 45	5 0	9 0	7 45	9 0	12 0	3 0	6 0	9 0		
NATEBY P.O.	7 55	9 10	1 25	6 40	7 55	10 40	1 55	5 10	9 10	7 55	9 10	12 10	3 10	6 10	9 10		
MOSS EDGE	8 5	9 20	1 35	6 50	8 5	10 50	2 5	5 20	9 20	8 5	9 20	12 20	3 20	6 20	9 20	9 40	10 0
RAWCLIFFE P.O. ..	8 15	9 30	1 45	7 0	8 15	11 0	2 15	5 30	9 30	8 15	9 30	12 30	3 30	6 30	9 30		
HAMBLETON, R. Corner		9 40	1 55	7 10	8 25	11 10	2 25	5 40			9 40	12 40	3 40	6 40	9 40	———	———
SHARD LANE C. ..		9 50	2 5	7 20		11 20	2 35	5 50			9 50	12 50	3 50	6 50	9 50	p.m.	p.m.
POULTON. Black Bull..		9 55	2 10	7 25		11 25	2 40	5 55			9 55	12 55	3 55	6 55	9 55	1 0	1 20

	Tues., Wed.				Thursday.				Saturday.					Eagland Hill to Garstang.	
	a.m.	a.m.	p.m.	p.m.	a.m	a.m.	p.m.	p.m.	a.m.	p.m.	p.m.	p.m.	p.m		
														a m	a.m.
POULTON, Black Bull...		11 15	3 15	8 0		11 30	3 15	7 15	10 35	1 35	4 35	7 35	10 15	10 0	10 20
SHARD LANE C. ..		11 20	3 20	8 5		11 35	3 20	7 20	10 40	1 40	4 40	7 40	10 20		
HAMBLETON, R. Corner		11 30	3 30	8 15	9 0	11 45	3 30	7 30	10 50	1 50	4 50	7 50	10 30		
RAWCLIFFE P.O. ..	8 15	11 40	3 40	8 25	9 10	11 55	3 40	7 40	11 0	2 0	5 0	8 0	10 40		
MOSS EDGE	8 25	11 50	3 50	8 35	9 20	12 5	3 50	7 50	11 10	2 10	5 10	8 10	10 50	p.m.	p.m
NATEBY P.O.	8 35	12 0	4 0	8 45	9 30	12 15	4 0	8 0	11 20	2 20	5 20	8 20	11 0	1 20	1 40
GARSTANG, Kings Arms	8 45	12 10	4 10	8 55	9 40	12 25	4 10	8 10	11 30	2 30	5 30	8 30	11 10		

SUNDAY.
June, July and August only.

GARSTANG ...	...	10 0 a.m.		POULTON	... ...	10 55 a.m.
,, ...	...	7 0 p.m.		,,	... ...	7 55 p.m.

JANUARY 1st, 1933.   Enquiries—W. MELLING, West View, Garstang.

1934 A.E.C REGAL KG3612 FLEET NO.268

This rather impressive bus has an AEC Regal chassis with 8.8-litre engine. Delivered early in 1934 as one of a batch of eight with Weymann 32-seat bodywork of, generally, standard B.E.T 'Federation' design, albeit the roof-mounted inter-locked double WW of Western Welsh must have made them stand out on their journeys. Sliding entrance doors were unusual for a bus reflecting Western Welsh's relatively long hauls.

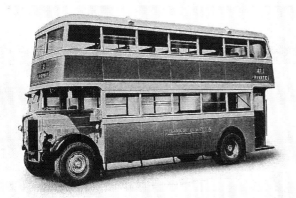
SHORT BROTHERS OF ROCHESTER

This 1934 advertisement shows how modern the clean, long lived, all metal bodywork produced by Short Brothers was. In addition to building coach and bus bodies they also produced a unique tramcar no.842 for Birmingham Corporation Tramways built as a tripartite experiment by Shorts, BCT and Aluminium (II) Ltd utilising aluminium alloys for the framing, roof, and upper saloon floor, with all the panelling in pure aluminium, each party sharing one-third of the cost. Ultra lightweight 842 was doomed to be a one-off but in its 22½ years of service it ran 486,200 miles.

The unfortunate fact for omnibus history was that Shorts backed out of building PSV bodies owing to the pressure of orders from the Air Ministry, moving to Rochester Airport in Kent in 1934/5 where they designed and built the Shorts S29 Stirling bomber, while continuing to build Empire and Sunderland flying boats at their main Medway base.

SUNSALOON

It is curious to remember that even in the just post war period there were still many passengers who had a fear or at least dislike of going 'upstairs' – outside as our charlady called it – reasons were nebulous, the bus might fall over, going up the open staircase was frightening as the road whizzed away underneath, or perhaps something atavistic. It has to be said that wooden seats lingered longer there than in the saloon and the nicotine flavoured condensation was not inviting – working a miner's special one morning I was greeted by cigarette smoke actually coming down the staircase so I ascended, opened the two 'Auster Pattern' quarter-lights at the front and collected the fares amid mutterings in the local dialect and as soon as I reached the stairhead there was a resounding crash as they were closed. Smoky smelly fug was OK!

In theory this patented Sun-saloon head should have been the answer, but even on this 1930s low-height body with its four-a-side seating there were no takers. I would imagine the weakness caused by cutting the roof sticks would be too much for a wooden framed body. They had a niche market in coaches and survived for some years.

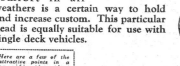

Admittedly there are no people visible here, but think how many people, women as well as men, were involved in the manufacture of this bus. First there would be discussions between the engineering division of Lancashire United and the commercial side over the size and traffic the new machine was intended for. Then company representatives would be called in and quotations obtained ... together with decisions over how payments were to be made. With the chassis and body builders, apart from the draughtsman, anything up to fifty bodies could be directly involved, from the steelworks rolling the chassis frames to the girls in the mill weaving the moquette.

It is rare that the back view of a bus can be very attractive but this is an example of compound, almost sensuous, curves. Curiosities abound clearly marking the period, not the least that single high mounted rear light, a spare wheel carrier was specified and slung underneath in about the filthiest location and the number of ventilators seem slightly excessive for a vehicle that was expected to pass over the Pennines on its prestigious daily run from Liverpool to Newcastle. 'Slip' or destination boards would be carried on the cove-panels. Lining out is rather marvellous and yet somehow expected, together with chromed hub-caps.

A Dennis 'Arrow' chassis, with Roe bodywork seating 30, delivered in 1933, fleet number 235 was one of a tranche of six, the majority albeit slightly updated, including 235, surviving until 1949; a good life for a hard-worked bus of the period. The overall weight as shown was remarkably light at six tons four hundredweight and three quarters, but despite the pneumatic tyres speed was restricted to 30mph although the London Transport equivalent machines were "said to be good for 50 [mph] on a clear road".

TEA FOR TWO?

This photograph of the waiting room in Pier Street, Ryde, Isle of Wight is almost certainly pre-war; but the room offers some degree of comfort while the passengers waited for their coach excursion or steamer. Inexplicably (at least to me) three of the notices seem to show that the "Next Motor Omnibus" runs at 5.30, 6.30 and 8.0 all on the "Circular Route". I have to assume there was some detail we cannot read here. However, it is a memory of days gone.

WAITING FOR BOTH YOU SIR, AND MADAM

This magnificent piece of period layout shows the Southern National waiting room at Weymouth, much railway styling is apparent in the decor and the furniture an uneasy cross between Lloyd Loom's best as supplied by Waring and Gillow and of Japanese minimalism. The flowers are a beautiful touch, and the telephones are elegant enough to fetch serious money today. Charming!

TWO'S & THREE'S ... BITS AND PIECES

In days of old ... this photograph was apparently one of a series taken back in the 1930s and fairly obviously was a proof copy. The presence of a 'proper' fire extinguisher rather than the vehicle issue [Pyrene**] makes it apparent the two technicians are in all probability in the old Experimental Shop, which had a 'fire-proof' parquet floor, rather than the show-room which was concreted. An intriguing illustration of 'bitsa'; today this would be an electronic image, rapidly deleted and lost.

** 'Pyrene' (carbon tetrachloride) extinguishers were very useful for removing stains from uniforms and tended to be empty when checked.

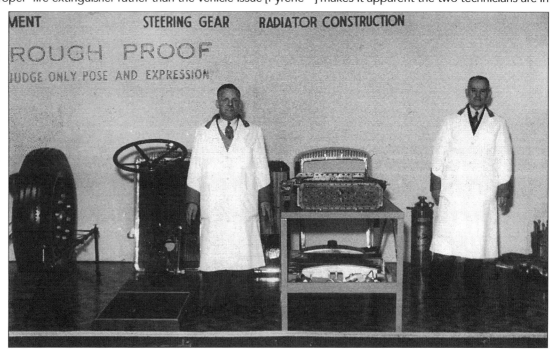

ALLEN'S OF MOUNTSORREL

Gradually over the years a number of 'official' photographs have been released on to the open market by the coach-building side of the Brush works, Loughborough. This enables us to see some aspects of bus design from a 'second-string' manufacturer, whose basic output was for companies in the B.E.T. group.

No doubt this bus, built on a Leyland TS7 chassis was comfortable enough, presumably the deep luggage racks were specified by the owners of Allen's Motor Services of Mountsorrel, for the carriage of weekday shopping and weekend by the seaside paraphernalia. The disadvantage of the design was the necessity for each pair of seats to carry a notice warning the passengers to lower their heads, and probably worse, the three rearward facing seats. Hopefully Mr Allen's customers knew where they were going; that blind arrangement is really quite hopeless. JU 4372 was delivered in 1934 and the Brush Coachworks Ltd body,

one of two supplied at that time with fleet nos 22 and 23, sat 38 passengers.

The company started with three locally bodied Chevrolet buses in May 1922, and was really very successful but the stage carriage services were sold out to B.M.M.O. (Midland Red) in July 1955, following the death of the owner Charles Herbert Allen.

The basic idea behind the AEC Q class was to produce a side-engined single rear wheeled bus or coach in both single and double-decker forms. The theory was that this would be an incredibly modern machine with an increased passenger payload. Two engines were on offer, both designs being canted to fit in the available space, and other than on the proto-type a fluid flywheel and preselector gearbox was fitted. In all 319 Q buses and coaches were built of which 233 went into service with London Transport. As a generality most orders came in dribs and drabs – this particu-lar one, WS 1508, was supplied to Edinburgh Corporation Transport, and is seen when brand new at the coach-builders, Weymann. Personally I feel for the period 1934 this is a most elegant design, although it remained on its own within the fleet. It served Edinburgh for 11 years and was still around with other operators for at least eight more years.

A Brush Coachworks official photo-graph this shows South Wales Transport Company's fleet no 361 registration WN 8261, a normal AEC Q, delivered in late 1935. With both front and centre entrances 39 seated passengers were carried in a remark-ably bare body shell being purchased for work only on local services and more specifically the fairly steep Town Hill route in Swansea. The entire tranche of five vehicles, renumbered 4-8 in 1939, plus a demonstrator added later were withdrawn and scrapped in 1949. The engine and radiator cooling vents, single rear wheels and Manx tail are very apparent in this photograph.

A fascinating photograph showing aspects of vehicles. On the left is an AEC "Q", a side-engined design that almost worked. The last of its type KG 7750 was built for Cardiff Corporation in 1936 with English Electric 60 seat bodywork, passed to Worths of Enstone in 1945, and ran until 1956. The Midland Red vehicle also has an English Electric body seating in some luxury 30 passengers, was new on a home-designed-and-built SLR chassis in 1937 and was scrapped in 1955. Difficult to visualise just how versatile bodybuilders were when one consid-ers both vehicles were planned, laid out and completed within a year of one another.

STOCKTON CORPORATION

THE TRANSPORT WORLD, May 17, 1934　　　　　XXXV

Stockton Corporation ended their tram services in 1931 and a year later started a very busy joint service with Middlesbrough.

6 Leyland TD1 arrived in 1928

11 Leyland TD1 arrived in 1929

6 Leyland TD1 arrived in 1930

1 Daimler CG6 arrived in 1930

5 single Daimler CH6/CG6/CP6/AEC Regent/Crossley Condor arrived in 1931.

These trials led to the choice of Daimler poppet valve with fluid flywheel buses for tram replacement. It was considered these were easier for ex-tram drivers.

6 Daimler CP6 also arrived in 1931

6 Daimler CP6 arrived in 1932.

6 Daimler CP6 with Brush H26/26R bodies arrived in 1934 as shown in the advertisement.

3 Daimler COG5 (diesel engines) arrived in 1936

6 Leyland 'Gearless' TD5c arrived in 1937

12 Daimler COG5 arrived in 1938

6 Daimler COG5 arrived in 1939

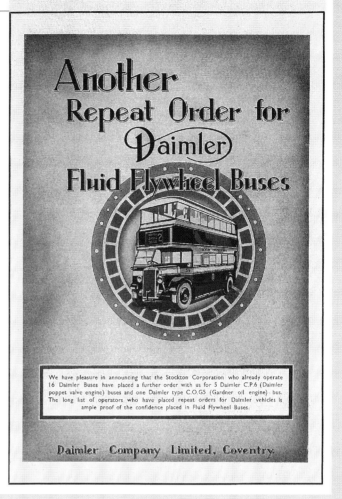

Another Repeat Order for **Daimler** Fluid Flywheel Buses

We have pleasure in announcing that the Stockton Corporation who already operate 16 Daimler Buses have placed a further order with us for 5 Daimler C.P.6 (Daimler poppet valve engine) buses and one Daimler type C.O.G5 (Gardner oil engine) bus. The long list of operators who have placed repeat orders for Daimler vehicles is ample proof of the confidence placed in Fluid Flywheel Buses.

Daimler Company Limited, Coventry

ART DECO

HG 4551 qualifies to be in this book for many reasons. The chassis no.15001 was one of three built after the manufacturers, Gilford Motor Company had ceased trading in November 1935, given that their normal chassis run ended at serial 12280 (although that entered service way out of sequence in April 1938) the suggestion from the PSV Circle that they were built up from spare parts by order of the liquidator seems quite logical – delivery for these three was June and July 1936 to J. & M. Kirkbright (Devonways) of Burnley.

Gilford were really a victim of their own success offering incredibly cheap hire purchase terms, especially when fitted with bodywork by their sister company Wycombe Motor Bodies Ltd, with the greater bulk of their sales coming in the period 1929 (268 delivered), 1930 (594), and 1931 (402) after which date they never again attained three figure sales. At their height these fast low 6-cylinder 20-24 seat coaches were the 'bees knees' with, according to the PSV Circle no less than 88% of all express coaches delivered in 1928 being of Gilford manufacture, and in August 1929 they paid their shareholders the very respectable dividend of 33.33%.

As we know the whole face of buses and coaching changed in the early 1930s with a continuous stream of smaller operators (the ones who particularly purchased Gilfords) being taken over by their larger railway-backed brethren and those who survived being unable to meet their 'deferred payments' due to the slump, which killed off much of the day-tripper traffic.

I am uncertain what happened to 15001, but her sister, 15000 was to survive until 1955 – a remarkably long life for a bin-end job. The bodywork on this tranche of vehicles is a bit strange as although designed and built by Thomas Harrington of Hove it seems a mess with those curious 'Art Deco' louvres or rain-strips above the windows, a lonely chunk of chrome matching no other design factor and a window line which while adhering to the 1930s arrangement of a kicked up last quarter appears very enfeebled. Two doors on the visible side plus one for passengers to board and a sliding roof must have made 15001 a bit of a rattlebones in her old age. (the late R.F. Mack)

187

Obtaining details of wage structures is always difficult. For comparison, in 1952 I received £3 per week and could pay my landlady and have a little over. A five shillings rise enabled me to buy a motor bike (Pride & Clarke ex WD Matchless five shillings a week 'on the drip'). Another five shillings and I could afford to take my girlfriend to the pictures!

Three sets of rates are quoted below; as an ex London Transport trolleybus driver I wanted to get the comparison of routes before and after the war, plus today (2014). One important note is the difference in the basic hours worked; and in fact the drivers did relatively well for this as in 1947; most industries still relied on a 44-hour week.

MEMORANDUM OF AGREEMENT BETWEEN
THE LONDON PASSENGER TRANSPORT BOARD
and
THE TRANSPORT & GENERAL WORKERS' UNION

as to the Rates of Pay and Conditions

of Service of Drivers and Conductors

November 1936

1936

....

PART 1 – RATES OF PAY

1. STANDARD RATES OF PAY.
The rates of pay applicable in respect of a 48-hour week shall be as follows:

	Per Day		Per Week		
	s.	d.	£	s.	d.
On entering service	11	10	3	11	0
After six months	12	1	3	12	6
After twelve months	12	7	3	15	6
After eighteen months	13	1	3	18	6
After two years	13	4	4	0	0

2. SPECIAL RATES OF PAY.
The following special rates of pay shall be paid:-

(a) On Sundays and Good Fridays, time-and-a-quarter.

(b) On Public Bank Holidays and proclaimed National Festivals, time-and-a-quarter.

(c) Christmas Day shall stand by itself for purposes of payment and double time shall be paid with a minimum of four hours' work.

(d) On all time worked voluntarily on an appointed rest day, time-and-a-quarter on the rate prevailing for the day.

(e) On all-night services, an additional 1s. per night or 6s. per week.

3. This part of this Agreement shall be subject to three calendar months' notice on either side, but no notice shall be given before 30th September, 1937.

PART II – CONDITIONS OF EMPLOYMENT

1. NORMAL WORKING WEEK.

(a) The normal working week shall be 48 hours, consisting of six scheduled duties, each carrying eight hours' pay at the standard rate. The scheduled working week shall not exceed 48 hours, including (a) signing off, and (b) travelling time allowances embodied in the duty schedule.

The scheduled daily duty shall not exceed 8 ½ hours, excluding travelling time allowances, nor be less than 7 ½ hours including travelling time allowances.

The average amount of scheduled work on a vehicle, per duty, shall not exceed 7 hours 4 minutes, this average to be based on the sum total of all duties for the whole system, in respect of any complete week.

All daily duties shall have a scheduled relief of not less than 30 minutes.

Not less than 80 per cent of the duties shall be completed within a scheduled spreadover of 8 hours 40 minutes. This percentage to be calculated on a duty schedule basis.

The remaining duties not to be subject to limitation in respect of spreadovers except that the number of duties exceeding 11 hours 59 minutes spreadover shall be limited to 9.1 per cent of the total duties for the week at any one depot, and 4.5 per cent for the whole system.

Thirty minutes was allowed for booking on and off and where possible three shifts (early, middle and late) should be worked within **a minimum of 8 hours' rest between shifts.**

If the shift change occurred around a rest day (as it often did) the 'break' period was reduced to 3½ hours. After 12 months' service, 12 days' holiday with pay was the normal entitlement.

Their 1947 rates.

LONDON TRANSPORT

27th June 1947

....

MEMORANDUM OF AGREEMENT AS TO RATES OF PAY AND
CONDITIONS OF SERVICE OF DRIVERS AND CONDUCTORS

CENTRAL BUSES

....

PARTIES:

THE LONDON PASSENGER TRANSPORT BOARD

and

THE TRANSPORT AND GENERAL WORKERS' UNION

....

PART 1 – RATES OF PAY

1. STANDARD RATES OF PAY

The standard rates of pay in respect of a forty-hour-week shall be:-

	Rate per week		
	s.	d.	
DRIVERS			
First 6 months	114	0	(£5. 14s.)
After 6 months	116	6	(£5. 16s.)
After 12 months	119	0	(£5. 19s.)
After 18 months	121	6	(£6. 1s. 6d.)
CONDUCTORS			
First 6 months	111	6	(£5. 11s. 6d.)
After 6 months	113	6	(£5. 13s. 6d.)
After 12 months	115	6	(£5. 15s. 6d.)
After 18 months	117	6	(£5. 17s. 6d.)

UNIFORMS.

The Board shall provide Drivers and Conductors, free of cost, with uniforms to be worn in accordance with the Board's regulations. These uniforms shall remain the property of the Board and shall be returnable as and when required.

They shall consist of the following:-

TROLLEYBUS DRIVERS

Jacket (every two years).
Serge Trousers (yearly).
Cloth Trousers (every two years).
Overcoat (every two years).
Cap (yearly).
Two White Cap Covers (yearly).
White coat (yearly).

CONDUCTORS

Jacket – Serge (yearly).
Jacket – Cloth (yearly).
Serge Trousers (yearly).
Cloth Trousers (yearly).
Cap (yearly).
Two White Cap Covers (yearly).
Waterproof Cap Cover (as required).

Winter garments to be issued about September and summer garments about March in each year.

Note: During the first six months of the service, women conductors received 90 per cent of the male rate. After six months they proceed to the first rate on the male scale, and subsequently receive the same six-monthly increments as men, reaching the maximum six months later than men.

2. SPECIAL RATES OF PAY

The following special rates of pay shall be paid:-

(a) On Sundays and Good Fridays, time-and-a-quarter.

(b) On Public bank Holidays, time-and-a-half.

(c) On Christmas day, double time.

(d) On time worked voluntarily on an appointed Rest Day other than Saturday, an additional quarter time on the rate prevailing for the day; on Saturday the rate will be time-and-a-half.

Other amendments related to the various overtime rates which were complicated – for example, "on all-night duties on the night of Thursday/Good Friday, an additional quarter time on the Good Friday rate". Few men or women on the buses could easily calculate their wages to the last penny, but we had a chap called "The Ferret" who could, and would, for a fag! He was wasted as a conductor.

(f) For new drivers and conductors in training or learning routes 10s. 10d. per day. (New Women Conductors in training will receive 90 per cent of the male rate, i.e. 9s.9d. per day).

Special allowance for conductors training new conductors on the road, 1s. per day.

Special allowance for drivers training new drivers, 1s. per day.

(g) Special allowance for drivers operating one-man buses, 5s. per week, or 10d. per day.

PART II – STANDARD WEEK

3. The standard week shall consist of 44 hours and of six scheduled daily duties, each carrying not less than 7 hours 20 minutes pay at the standard hourly rate. An employee shall not work two duties in one day.

The shift rosters (rotas) appear to have been tightened up from the previously vague statements.

8. ROTA OF DUTIES

(a) The scheduled duties shall be shown as early, middle and late shifts. Early shifts shall comprise not less than 35 per cent of the scheduled duties. Middle shifts shall not exceed 10 per cent of the scheduled duties.

(b) An early shift shall finish not later than 6.0 p.m. on weekdays and 7.0 p.m. on Sundays.

(c) A middle shift shall finish not later than 9.0 p.m. on any day.

(d) Shifts shall change weekly.

(e) The rotas in weeks containing Public Holidays shall be suspended.

(f) In the case of staff booked for scheduled duties, there shall be an interval of not less than twelve hours between such duties, except upon a change of shift which shall take place between Saturday and Sunday. In such cases, and in the case of spare staff, there shall be an interval of not less than eight hours.

9. SPREADOVER DUTIES

(a) The maximum scheduled spreadover of a daily duty shall be twelve hours on Weekdays, and 10 hours on Sundays, Good Friday and Bank Holidays.

(b) On weekdays not more than 20 per cent of the total duties shall exceed a spreadover of 8 hours 20 minutes, and not more than 10 per cent of the total duties shall exceed a spreadover of 9 ½ hours.

The 'spreadover' details continue for some pages with overtime at the following rates but it could all be aggregated for the week whereupon the rates altered!

8 minutes to 22 minutes - ¼ hour
23 minutes to 37 minutes – ½ hour
38 minutes to 52 minutes – ¾ hour

GUIDE TO PAY AND CONDITIONS FOR TfL DRIVERS

These terms and conditions will only apply to those drivers that were in the Company' employment on or after 1st April 2013

GENERAL

The driver's pay week is from Saturday to Friday, with all work and overtime accrued paid into bank accounts the following Friday. Where possible payments will be transferred to bank accounts a day early on Thursday but this is not guaranteed.

DUTY TIMES

All duties are paid for working time on duty (WTOD).

Drivers will be paid a minimum of 38 hours per week for five complete rostered duties. This guarantee does not apply to drivers who request to exchange duties or rest days. Drivers reporting late for one of the five duties will lose the guarantee. Part-time drivers will be guaranteed hours on a pro rata basis.

HOURLY RATES

GRADE		Hourly Rate
A	Drivers having five year's service AFTER 1st July 2008 (i.e. not before 1st July 2013) and joined prior to 11th April 2012.	£15.08
C	Drivers having completed two years on grade D	£12.44
D	Drivers with under two year's service	£11.69
Trainees	Drivers undergoing training to gain a PVS licence	£7.10

No enhancement is paid for overtime.

A daily allowance of £2.22 will be paid for shifts signing on before 06:00 or signing off after 22:00.

---

16 ANNUAL AND PUBLIC HOLIDAYS

(a) On completion of 12 months' service, staff shall be entitled to an annual holiday of two consecutive weeks, with two weeks' pay at the standard rate. The holiday shall be deemed to include two rest days.

(b) One additional day's holiday with pay shall be given in respect to each public holiday on which staff are required to work, or are rostered as available for work. An employee who absents himself without justifiable cause on any of these public holidays shall not be entitled to a day's holiday in lieu.

Public Holidays for this purpose shall be deemed to be Good Friday, Easter Monday, Whit Monday, August Bank Holiday, Christmas Day and Boxing Day; and the additional holidays to which staff become entitled by virtue of this clause shall be taken in the year following that in respect to which they accrue.

Finally, for these early years there was a reality -- an awareness of change -- within both the Union and L.T.E. Management.

OPERATION OF NEW SCHEDULES DURING SHORTAGE OF MAN-POWER

The Board and the Union recognise that, in the present shortage of man-power, it will not be possible to find additional staff required to work the new schedules, and it has been agreed that arrangements will be made to cover the new schedules by overtime and rest day working, until the man-power position permits of the recruitment of the additional staff needed.

To round off this story, the Training Manager for Metrobus Ltd., an operator not only in London inside the Transport for London 'family', but also operations outside the City, gave permission to quote rates as at February 2014, and it is my pleasure to acknowledge the assistance of this friendly company.

MEAL BREAKS

Drivers will not normally be paid for meal breaks and will be guaranteed a minimum of 40 minutes break. Those drivers agreeing to an early resumption in order to avoid delays in service will be paid in compensation at time plus ¼ for the balance of their scheduled break. This will not count towards the weekly build up of pay.

EARLY MORNING CALL-OUT PAYMENTS

Drivers who offer their services for an early call-out, who are telephoned before 07:00 and report to work that day by 08:00 will receive a payment of £6.85.

SICK PAY

This will apply to all drivers after twelve months service. The rate of sick pay will be:

Grade	Daily Rate
A	£87.94*
C	£70.93*
D	SSP

*Inclusive of Statutory Sick Pay

Holiday entitlement is as follows:

GRADE	1 day per week	2 days per week	3 days per week	4 days per week	Full Time
A	5 days	10 days	15 days	20 days	25 days
C & D	4 days	8 days	12 days	16 days	20 days

HOLIDAY BLOCKS

The following holiday block systems are in use at Orpington and Croydon Depots

- Drivers employed before 31st December 1991 are not subject to holiday blocks.
- Drivers employed between 31st December 1991 and 7th August 2003 will have one week blocked.
- Drivers employed after 8th August 2003 will have four weeks blocked.

Holiday blocks will be broadly allocated as follows:

Holiday Allocation
1st January – 31st March   1 week (5days)
1st April – 30th September   2 weeks (10 days)
1st October – 31st December   1 week (5 days)

BANK HOLIDAYS and NEW YEAR'S EVE

Drivers who would have worked but are not required will be paid the following hours while resting on bank holidays, subject to conditions explained below:

Permanent staff	Hours paid for Bank Holiday
1 Day	1.6
2 days per week	3.2
3 days per week	4.8
4 days per week	6.4
Full time	8.0

Drivers who would have been resting on a bank holiday will receive a lieu leave day paid at the prevailing rate.

Drivers who work on bank holiday (meaning duty begins on the bank holiday) will receive a payment of £160.00 for each complete rostered duty worked which sign on time was on the bank holiday. Where working time on duty exceeds eight hours such additional hours will be paid at normal rates. They will additionally receive a lieu leave day paid at the prevailing rate.

Drivers who work on Boxing Day (meaning the duty begins on Boxing Day) will receive a payment of £200.00 for each complete rostered duty worked which sign on time was on Boxing Day. Where working time on duty exceeds eight hours such additional hours will be paid at an enhanced rate based upon normal rates plus £4.27 per hour. They will additionally receive a lieu leave day paid at the prevailing rate.

Boxing Day working is allocated on a voluntary basis followed by "juniority". Other bank holidays will have duties allocated in accordance with local arrangements. Where drivers wish to avoid an allocated bank holiday duty, the mutual exchange procedure will apply as with any other shift.

NEW DRIVER MENTORING

Those drivers mentoring new drivers will be entitled to an enhancement for the duty worked of £10.00.

NORTHERN – A B.E.T.TER COMPANY

Although the British Electric Traction group kept an eye on their subsidiary companies, up to 1954 it seems the concerns were free to develop and manufacture vehicles suited to their locality, provided overall they made a profit which could become a dividend for the BET shareholders. The obvious example is 'Midland Red' (BMMO) who not only built vehicles of their own designs at Carlyle Works, but supplied them to other BET group companies, including Northern.

Northern General Transport Company Ltd trod their own path ending up with a group of coaches and buses that were unique in the UK. A handful of these are illustrated, but the story is intriguing. At one time and another NGT swallowed up many of the ex tram operating companies including the Sunderland District Omnibus Co. (never to be confused with Sunderland Corporation and their proud fleet) Wakefield & District, Tyneside Tramways & Tramroads, Gateshead & District, Jarrow & District, and Tynemouth & District. In the early 1920s Bensham Depot near Gateshead became the Headquarters and the Central Engineering Depot was erected, probably as funds became available after the London & North Eastern Railway took a shareholding.

The problems that Northern faced were many faceted but the main ones were the number of low bridges which constrained the use of high-capacity double deck vehicles, that as war preparations moved into high gear so did the demand on shipbuilders and their requirements for men, the coal mines were busy and, with 'more brass in the can' housewives wanted to buy better and more food during the day. All this meant that Northern had to have more seats available on more routes. In the early 1930s vehicle length for a two-axle omnibus was set at 27 feet and 6 inches overall, although a third axle could take this out to 30 feet. London Transport used this clause quite extensively during the 1930s with the LT class vehicles, but for whatever reasons the NGT decided to design and manufacture their own variants. In all 67 side-engined buses and coaches were to emerge, in bus mode each sat an incredible, for the period, 44 passengers.

The chosen engine was an American Hercules six-cylinder job, petrol driven mounted as can be seen by the vents aft of the set-back front axle and in front of the driven axle. Their lives were as complex as their origins, and it is necessary to note that 31 of the chassis came from AEC at Southall, probably as a deal arising out of patent infringement. The final 25 of this pattern of vehicle reverted to two axle seating 40, and at least one of the three axle buses was converted to have only two, officially becoming the first two-axle 30 feet long bus in the UK, but the economy of the diesel was such that the last batch of twins had a 'special' AEC engine designed to run at an angle of 30°. Steve Stevens-Stratten told me that a rather clever economy used by NGT was to purchase redundant diesel engines designed for 'Matilda' tanks which were paired. Those with auxiliaries mounted on the offside of the engine proved to fit the space vacated by the Hercules (for which getting spares was impossible, anyway) whereas the other 'handed' engine prolonged the lives of the SOS (Midland Red) chassis in the fleet.

Fleet nos. 651-6 were delivered in 1935, and were coach bodied by Short Bros. With a capacity of only 28, in total luxury. Dimensions overall for these, then giant, machines were:

Wheelbase 14' 9" + 9"
Overall height 10' 0"

Overall width 7' 6"
Overall length 30' 0"

For a very non-standard design 652 and the others in the batch were quite long lived, this coach being 17 years old when it went to the dealers.

655 has a variant on the body style and livery. The luggage capacity must be negligible for long tours.

654 has the touring bodywork but may well be seen postwar as those rather crude air intakes were cut to cool the diesels. The radiator, although front mounted, was not initially man enough for the job, and a comparison of 655 with 654 will show a difference between the 'Odeon' grill and the plain rectangle.

1153 FT3478 was originally sold to Tynemouth & District and was one of the first built in 1935, still of class SE6 (side-engined 6 wheels) and was fitted with a Short Bros. body seating 45 – the rise and fall of the seats over the hump of the mid-engine is quite clear. 1153 was to remain in service until 1954.

AUP 590, fleet no.701 is seen when new and although still having a side mounted engine this is the AEC 6.6-litre oil engine. Hardly any dimensions, other than width are common to the SE6, with the wheelbase at 16' 3" overall height 8' 6" and length 27' 6". Bodywork was by English Electric with seating capacity reduced to 40 very thin indeed seats. 701 was another survivor until the cull of non standard vehicles in 1954.

This represents a more standard product of 1935, an AEC Regal. No. 677 with a 7.7-litre diesel (oil) engine seems to have been a dual purpose machine, the rather square bodywork coming from Weymann but only seating 36 in reasonable comfort. Whether there were problems with these bodies or maybe wartime took its effect but in 1946 the batch of six were rebodied by Pickering of Wishaw, being taken out of service in December 1955. However, this is not quite the end of the story for all but one of the set were exported to Enterprise Bus Service, Jamaica, West Indies in the following year.

653 CN6612 is seen postwar in Edinburgh. This particular photograph shows the cooling vents very clearly indeed. The contrast with 654 is interesting – my own feeling is that this relatively fussy body must have been a nightmare to keep clean.

UP STEPS NOT STAIRS

In my introduction I mentioned the use of luggage porters or (locally) 'hufflers' who were paid by hotels or coach operators to help load or unload baggage on and off the roof rack. Even in the mid-1950s this was, thankfully, an almost extinct practice. The method was simple, carrying a bag or package you climbed up the steps inset in the rear of the coach, and then stood on top while another man threw up the other 20 or 30 pieces of baggage that a party would need. No real problem in decent weather but a shocking and dangerous job in the face of wind driven snow – and trying to spread the tarpaulin over the top to protect the cases against the weather and to retain it all in place was an unmitigated nightmare.

DUC 906, LT30, was a three-axle Duple 43-seat bus belonging to the City Coach Company of Brentwood, based on a Leyland 'Tiger' TS7T chassis, and one of 36 bought between 1935 and 1937 for the very busy London (Wood Green) to Southend service which, despite cut price rail fares, ran full every fifteen minutes. Seen here in the Spring of 1952, at Laindon Station, LT30 as one of the tranche not rebuilt after the war was working out her last year on a local service.

The Leyland TS7T (T=trailing third axle) was an interesting machine with a relatively high capacity, the Scottish firm Western SMT being particularly proud of their Leyland bodied variants which were 'pure' coaches fitted not only with the roof rack but a sliding 'sunshine' roof, the epitome of mid-1930s coaching luxury. In all cases the Leyland 8.6-litre diesel engine was fitted, with a constant mesh gearbox, the 18' 10½" wheelbase allowing for a 30-foot long body, as opposed to a two-axle version carrying a maximum 27' 6" body.

With permission from: Essex Bus Enthusiasts Group, Frank Church collection.

NUMBER 1000

On the face of it, a very simple photograph, but one full of detail. The chassis is a relatively rare animal, the TS7D, the D indicating double drive as both rear axles were powered. There were six in this batch supplied to Southern National in 1937, who had 44 seater Beadle of Dartford bodies fitted, their primary use being on services to the Portland area, where the well known winds made it highly unsafe to operate double-deck vehicles. The strongest available diesel engine was fitted in the form of the 8.6-litre version, although the constant mesh gearbox would reduce many modern drivers to gibbering. The problem inherent in any three-axle vehicle of the period is that of tyre scrub, the front tyre on no.1000 does appear to be reaching the end of its life; today's VOSA or TrafPol inspectors would wet themselves at the sight.

The main stamping ground of this tranche of vehicles (six in all) was to be between Upwey and various points on the Isle of Portland, although during the war they were loaned elsewhere for the movement of factory workers; stories abound of 60-70 passengers being carried! But it does say much for good old British workmanship that each of these buses ran in excess of one million miles before their withdrawal in 1954.

Route 22 was one that itself mutated over the years, with variants reaching as far as 22M, while the famous destination Statue refers to the King's Statue in Weymouth, served at various times by the 22C, D to F inclusive and G-K plus M. Behind the rear quarter of 1000 can be seen an unusual variant on a spelling: BUSs ONLY rather than the more orthodox BUSES. Obscured by the fuel pump the forequarters of a Bedford OB – that maid of all work – can be seen.

TWO PRE-WAR BEAUTIES

Stockton Corporation fleet no.15 with the body-work outlined in the latest streamlined idiom. Underneath that high class paint job Cravens Railway Carriage and Wagon Company had produced in 1935 pretty much of a battleship on an almost indestructible Daimler COG5 (Gardner powered) chassis which made its way along some rough old roads, often – especially during the war – grossly overloaded, until withdrawal in 1949.

Streamlined again as befitted a bus for the twin seaside towns, carrying a quite different clientèle to the Stockton vehicle. In this case an AEC Regent III chassis underpinned what was to be fleet no.45 registration CTF 861. Oil engined, albeit with an AEC 7.7-litre power unit, premium 56-seat bodywork was by Park Royal Vehicles and which was assembled in 1937 in time to be an exhibit at the Commercial Motor Show in November 1937, and after some degree of demonstration work was not registered into the Morecambe & Heysham fleet until April the following year. A notable feature of this class of vehicle was the by now rare fitting of a folding roof, but somehow it befitted a seaside omnibus! 45 remained in service until 1959.

THE DUNLOPILLO TYPIST

Remember typists? An almost extinct species, often known generically as 'Sectries' [secretaries] but coming in three or four sub-species. Our firm had shorthand-typists, famed for their Pitman training, audio-typists, capable of translating the Gaffer's maundering into a letter, copy typists who could read our writings and more importantly could be relied upon to tabulate figures, and 'The Pool', girls who could produce a document and then 'Gestetner' [duplicate] it.

In this advertisement which first appeared in *The Transport World* 16 May 1935, we have a typist of the better sort with neatly trimmed finger nails given a very responsible task, that of ordering the requisite quantity of Dunlopillo. Those typewriter keys were a devil to keep clean but most of that Qwerty board is the same as today's computer keyboard.

FROM HULL TO ... BLACKPOOL

Delivered new in March 1936 (as can be seen from the wintry backdrop) East Yorkshire's fleet no.295 (BKH 476) has a Brush 52-seat body on a relatively rare Leyland TD4c chassis – the 'c' indicating the fitting of a torque converter, in effect an automatic gearbox with a manually engaged 'top gear', an 8.6-litre Leyland diesel engine providing more than enough power especially in East Yorkshire's home territory of Hull. EYMS and Hull Corporation had reached a form of 'Polo mint' traffic agreement whereby the centre of Hull was entirely the fiefdom of the Corporation, the middle zone joint and outside this area entirely in the hands of East Yorkshire.

The whole vehicle is a fine advertisement not only for the bodybuilders and their coach-painters but also for one of the company's best traffics – Hull to Blackpool for your holiday – hopefully though not on those longitudinal seats over the rear wheels on no.295!

A STUDY

The bus, JG 7027, fleet no. 974 was on its normal run to Canterbury when this accident occurred; apparently it was side swiped by a lorry. A normal Leyland TD4 with Brush of Loughborough bodywork, 53 seated passengers were possible when it was new in 1936.

The position of the vehicle enables us to see items that would normally be decently hidden. The front tyre tells a tale on its own, as does the starting handle necessary to wake up the 8.8-litre petrol engine, although the little 'Pyrene' fire extinguisher was more use for cleaning oil stains from uniforms than to prevent serious combustion. A constant mesh gearbox is fitted, and the cylinder for the servo hydraulic system appears to have caught the attention of the gentleman in his clean suit, albeit the Sheltie dog thinks it is all a new game. One final item, commonplace enough then if normally unnoticed are the floor boards of the upper deck. Forbidden or not by management normal practice was a for a conductor to stamp twice on the floor above the cab as a signal to go. I can confirm that sometimes in hot dry weather the dust went down the driver's neck and left him itchy as well as sweaty.

JG 7027 was recovered in due course and it says much for Brush bodywork that new glasses and other minor repairs sufficed to allow the bus to live out a normal life, not being scrapped until December 1950.

UNITED WE STAND

Helmsley, North Yorkshire some time in the late 1930s. Three "United" vehicles are about the only Life in the Market Place, two buses, and a coach. The tilt over the lorry's cargo area will bring back memories to many of wet flapping canvas and broken finger nails; the latter catching everything until you can borrow a pair of scissors or a sharp knife. One lonely 'slow' road sign, otherwise peace and tranquility.

GEAR-LESS

This 1933 scenario is one that is becoming inconceivable nowadays. In general few men could drive and even fewer had cars. A surprisingly high number had driven trams and understood the basics of finding their way through crowds and having the patience to work with conductors. But, the average bus had a 'crash' constant-mesh gear box which, in some models, seemed to have a few excess gears trying to get in the way of a clean change. Add to this the fact that our tram-man had to steer nearly 10 tons of metal ware and there is a recipe for disaster.

Someone at some time within Leyland must have put two and two together developing a functioning variant on the Lysholm-Smith patent semi-automatic torque converter which by 1933 was offered on their main chassis range, the Tiger, Titan, Titanic and Lion.

This rather clever 'bit of kit' was in effect a fully automatic gearbox apart from having to manually engage top or direct drive.

No clutch was necessary and instead of the usual gear-lever (gear shift) there was a four-position control reading (on the one I tried) direct-converter-neutral-reverse. The owner explained I had to engage converter up to 20mph or so, then direct which put us in cruising mode. The converter in use acted as an infinitely variable drive and solved a problem.

Unfortunately as was the case with many early automatics the drive slipped internally and as energy equals heat coolers or radiators had to be fitted on the chassis to absorb this. This in turn cost more initially but municipalities, especially those operating in 'elite' districts liked the arrangement – finding the inherently high fuel (diesel) consumption to be of little account when for the comfort of their people the costly petrol engine was the alternative.

Sheffield, despite its hills, made the converter work, running them until 1957. Technically the chassis type was always signified with the addition of a lower-case letter "c". This machine is apparently a T.S.8c.

The owner of a preserved model has found with modern specialist oils and (expensive) super-seals his Titan is as good as any on the road and very relaxing on a long run.

ALAS, POOR YORICK

I always find that scenes of abandoned and scrap buses and coaches to be rather melancholy as all of these machines have at some time carried mums with new babies, men to and from work – perhaps for promotion , or alas redundancy – courting couples full of dreams, married couples shopping, widows, widowers, priests, police, nurses, happy, sad, quiet, noisy,dreamers, writers and just people. But all these memories are lost as the breaker's men dismantle the vehicles.

Chesterfield's trolleybuses had a short life on their one route from the 'Terminus Loop' in the town, initially to Stephenson Place and later to New Whittington, opened on 25 May 1927, and dying three days early on the 24 March 1938. Their first vehicles nos 1-12, 14,15 came from Clough Smith & Company, who also installed the overhead and other electrical gear. Bodied locally by Reeves & Kenning at Pilsbury, the chassis was from Straker-Squire, Edmonton, London and the electrics from British-Thomson-Houston. Next in 1931 were a couple of double-deck trolleys from Ransomes, Sims and Jeffries, which numbered 16 and 17 and sat 48 passengers in their RSJ

bodies rather than the 32 of the older cars. Finally in late 1935 the corporation purchased the entire fleet of the City of York's operation, numbering them 18-20. These to add variety had Karrier chassis (Straker-Squire having gone bankrupt) and C.H. Roe bodywork.

Cast aside without a thought the majority of Chesterfield's fleet lie awaiting their fate, memories dying with them.

Yeast-Vite is still available today (2016) in tablet form containing modified yeast reinforced with vitamins B1 (thiamine) B2 (riboflavin) and B3 (niacin). The presence of caffeine assists in its 'boost affect'. Seemingly the product first appeared in 1929, and was at its sales peak from the 1930s to the late 1950s using imaginative advertising. In 1952 for example: "JUST LIKE THAT! Listless, Headachy, Depressed? Then snap out of it with Yeast-Vite." One feels a drum roll should accompany this statement!

This 1936 advertisement is fascinating although I have some doubt over the reality of Mr Blossom as a driver – he has no PSV badge visible and worse, no cap badge, the omission

of which could drive any garage inspector to tell the man to be gone out of his sight

However STL 622 was real enough being delivered as AYV 788 in December 1934, AEC chassis number 06613037 with an L.T.P.B. Chiswick built 56-seat body. This was one of the first production oil-engined STL buses, with an AEC indirect injection 7.7-litre engine and an AEC/Wilson pre-selector gearbox, the whole ensemble being classed as 9STL5. Testing completed 622 was allocated to Merton garage. After the usual war-time adventures the wood framing of this bus was suffering from loose joints and it was withdrawn from Merton in January 1950 and sent for scrap the same month.

Willmotts Motors of Hammersmith, London W6 was one of many pre-war (and just post war) builders of coach and bus bodies. Due to the seasonal nature of the industry designers moved around from, for example, Hall Lewis (Park Royal) to Willmotts via Duple, all of whom were within a tram ride of one another. As a result almost any model of PSV or commercial vehicle body will show influences from those of a rival design, not helped in the case of small companies by their reliance on

bought-in components (windows, seats, and interior lights among other items) coupled to the use of identical chassis.

The majority of models illustrated in their catalogue York (26-seater Luxury Coach), Epsom (26-seater Super Luxury Sunsaloon Coach), Goodwood (26-seater Super Luxury Coach), were on Bedford WTB chassis, while the awkward looking 32-seater bodies were on Dennis Falcon Mk. 1 chassis, and undercut Duple's equivalent by £10 for the "Lincoln" bus.

Bedford Chassis.
Willmott Coachwork.

"THE GOODWOOD MODEL"
26 Seater Super Luxury Coach

Bedford Chassis
Willmott Coachwork

"THE YORK MODEL"
26 Seater Luxury Coach

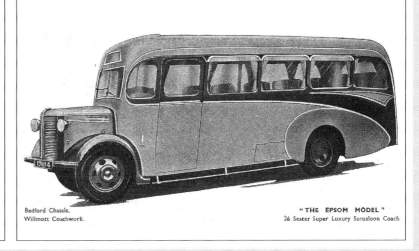

Bedford Chassis.
Willmott Coachwork.

"THE EPSOM MODEL"
26 Seater Super Luxury Sunsaloon Coach

HERE IT IS! THE BEDFORD WTB (EVERY OPERATOR'S DREAM)

In the far off days of the 1930s it was expected that not only could a mechanic do the job properly, but could read and understand a diagram. Sadly, in my experience, not all could do this even recently. The fact is that Bedford, as part of the General Motors combine, realised many of these neat little 20-26 seat buses and coaches would be sold to owner/drivers who would probably pin this diagram on the garage wall, or put it in his book of useful bits and obey the instructions as long as possible. Sadly, wartime meant higher mileages, shortage of even oils and greases plus the rationing on men who were probably by now elderly. Many of the coaches were requisitioned by the armed services and instead of a gentle 250 miles a week, were hammered by enthusiastic amateurs.

The 500-mile requirements were interesting – the Stauffer grease cup No.2 if overlooked, could lead to the fan departing at speed amid horrible noises! The wiring diagram for the same vehicle is gloriously basic, with the bodybuilders expected to add the internal lights and wiring. It makes an interesting contrast with the Metroliner's wiring, which will be partly shown in Volume 2 of this series.

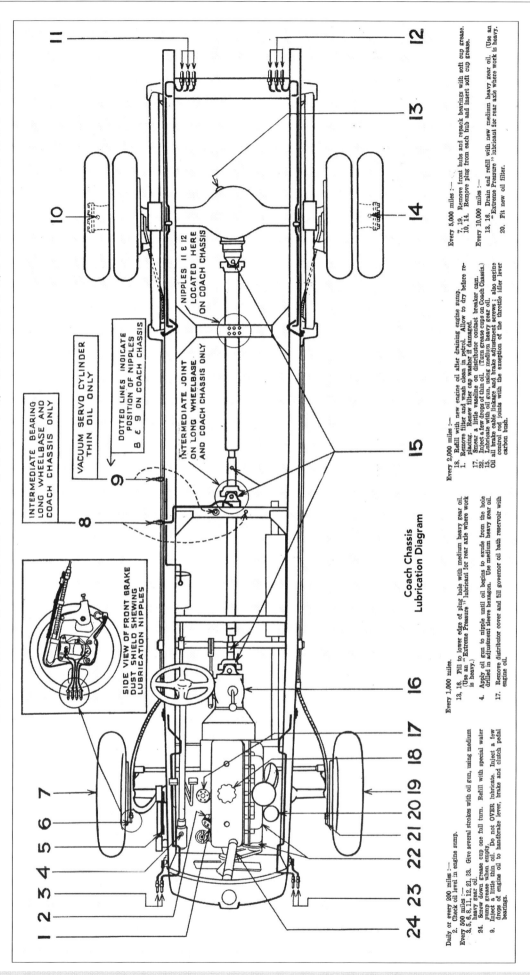

INTERMEDIATE BEARING
LONG WHEELBASE AND
COACH CHASSIS ONLY

VACUUM SERVO CYLINDER
thin oil only

DOTTED LINES INDICATE
POSITION OF NIPPLES
8 & 9 ON COACH CHASSIS

NIPPLES 11 & 12
LOCATED HERE
ON COACH CHASSIS

INTERMEDIATE JOINT
ON LONG WHEELBASE
AND COACH CHASSIS ONLY

SIDE VIEW OF FRONT BRAKE
DUST SHIELD SHEWING
LUBRICATION NIPPLES

Coach Chassis
Lubrication Diagram

Daily or every 200 miles :—
2. Check oil level in engine sump.

Every 500 miles :—
3, 5, 6, 8, 11, 12, 21, 23. Give several strokes with oil gun, using medium heavy gear oil.
24. Screw down grease cup one full turn. Refill with special water pump grease when empty.
9. Inject a little thin oil. Do not OVER lubricate. Inject a few drops of engine oil to handbrake lever, brake and clutch pedal bearings.

Every 1,000 miles.
13, 16. Fill to lower edge of plug hole with medium heavy gear oil. (Use an "Extreme Pressure" lubricant for rear axle where work is heavy.)
4. Apply oil gun to nipple until oil begins to exude from the hole drilled in adjustment sleeve hexagon. Use medium heavy gear oil.
17. Remove distributor cover and fill governor oil bath reservoir with engine oil.

Every 2,000 miles :—
18. Refill with new engine oil after draining engine sump.
1. Remove filter and wash clean in petrol. Allow to dry before replacing. Renew filter cap washer if damaged.
17. Smear a little vaseline on distributor contact breaker cam.
22. Inject a few drops of thin oil. (Turn grease cups on Coach Chassis.)
15. Lubricate with oil gun, using medium heavy gear oil. Oil all brake cable linkage and brake adjustment screws; also engine control rod joints with the exception of the throttle idler lever carbon bush.

Every 5,000 miles :—
7, 19. Remove front hubs and repack bearings with soft cup grease.
10, 14. Remove plug from each hub and insert soft cup grease.

Every 10,000 miles :—
13, 16. Drain and refill with new medium heavy gear oil. (Use an "Extreme Pressure" lubricant for rear axle where work is heavy.)
20. Fit new oil filter.

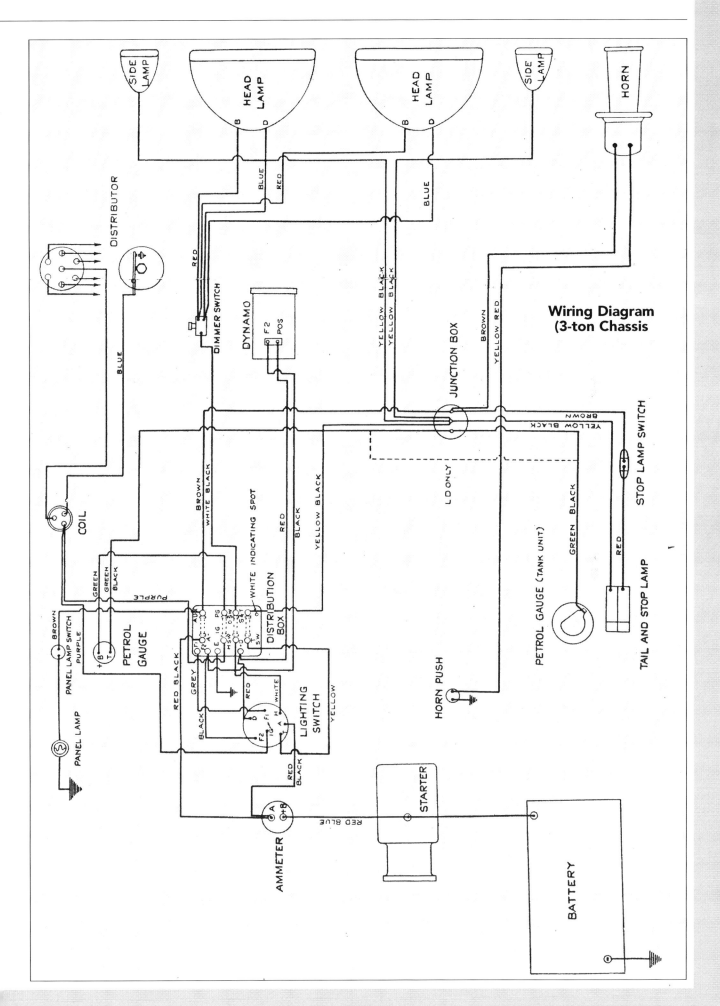

Wiring Diagram (3-ton Chassis)

203

VIEWS OF EXPORTS

One of the great success stories of British chassis and body manufacturers was their ability to produce vehicles which suited local markets whether Australia, Hong Kong or some remote part of Africa. It was helped by the ownership of many of the foreign operators being British – or at least the directorship – but where the firms failed to meet market requirements they soon lost ground. Towards the end strange things happened, like Sydney docks having tons of spares arrive before the buses, and an argy-bargy then ensuing with the Customs who impounded the lot.

The buses arrived in dribs and drabs, entered service but no spares were then available, so parts stripping from new vehicles ensued. In Ceylon, someone forgot the termites; teak framed bodies by A.V. Roe were termite proof, and on MCW all metal bodies only the 'Hairlok' sound proofing got attacked, but composite bodies were delightful meals on wheels for the insects.

Top photograph: However, back in 1932 two beautiful examples of Duple Bodies & Motors Ltd workmanship were ordered, both being supplied in May1933. The top photograph is of one of two AEC "Ranger" long distance coaches to the special order of Mr Cyril Cooper, President of Canadian American Coaches Ltd, Windsor, Ontario. Described as having "all the refinements of British body-building practice" the deep backed seats with headrolls, marvellous light fittings, curtains and mirrored interiors were rather special as was the toilet in the rear.

Centre photograph: The second illustration is an interior view looking forward also in a normal control AEC Ranger, with its easily accessible 120hp engine, and showing some of the 29 reclining seats fitted (35 when the toilet was dismounted). This pair were to the order of Gray Coach Lines, a subsidiary of The Toronto Transportation Commission. Rather plainer, the left hand drive position is obvious as is the simple instrument binnacle; but with no provision for air conditioning that fan on the left of the driver may well have been vital.

Bottom photograph: Very much a 'Colonial' machine, this is a combined passenger and mail vehicle with first class (by inference European or Eurasian) customers in the front, and others with their belongings in the rear. The wire mesh at the windows is redolent of the heat expected with roll down curtains against the sun. Although the interior is nicely furnished, the paucity or indeed total lack of lighting is strange to European eyes. Described as "for country services" the whole bus was supplied by John I. Thornycroft's agent in Cape Town, South Africa. Said to be 1928.

Winter holds no terrors for a "Nulac" Finish

ROBERT KEARSLEY & CO., RIPON, YORKS

PAINT SHOP

The competition between paint manufacturers was always high with very imaginative advertising designed to appeal not only to the major manufacturers but to the small fleet owner as much as a local body-builder. I find the particular entry for Kearsley's paints which first appeared in the *Passenger Transport Journal* 10 February 1939 to be entirely matter-of-fact and yet attractive.

Docker Brothers were famous the world over and yet they too seem to have had an enterprising advertising agency; the use of a negative to catch the eye and then to offer the positive solution was a well known, but here in *Transport World* 10 March 1949, a cleverly applied trick.

YOU CAN'T WRAP IT UP!

But you can apply a protective film.

Modern Passenger Transport demands the finest surface protection. Paintwork must withstand the vagaries of weather, the wear of traffic, and contact with grease and oil.

It must retain its fine appearance under the most arduous conditions. That is why still more Transport concerns are using Dockers' Transport Finishes.

DOCKERS' TRANSPORT FINISHES

SYNTHOLUX · SPEED SYNTHOLUX
DOCKERS' T.C.S.

DOCKER BROTHERS
Ladywood. Birmingham. 16.

MAKERS OF PAINTS, VARNISHES &
LACQUERS FOR EVERY PURPOSE

CARS TO BUSES – CROSVILLE

All good fairy stories start "Once upon a time". In the Crosville story the fairy godmother was the London Midland & Scottish Railway, but before that we had the combination of Georges de Ville of Paris, and a wealthy son of a Yorkshire mill-owner, George Crosland Taylor, united in order that they might jointly at the Crane Works Chester build a super new car; the date was 6 May 1906. For whatever reason the car plans failed but the Crosville Motor Company adroitly turned itself into a general mechanical repair shop, but adding their first motor-bus service Chester to Ellesmere Port to their portfolio in 1910, expanding thereafter with some speed.

There is a tale that in the 1920s a practice grew up of sending a bus, probably a 40hp Leyland saloon, complete with driver and guard to go forth to the more remote parts of North and Mid Wales as far south as Aberystwyth (Aberwristwatch once to a lost London-based 'National' driver) and set up a route, using the proceeds in the conductor's bag to pay for oil and petrol. Presumably the crew's food would be covered and they would be expected to sleep on the bus. If they were unsuccessful it is said they looked for new employment on their return.

By whatever means expansion was rapid and there is no doubt that with a good financial basis the apples that fell off the PSV tree could easily be harvested but in 1929 the company was sold to the LMS railway although Claude Crosland-Taylor, the son of the founder, remained as manager. Whether the LMS found this bite at the bus industry too rich to swallow is not clear – there may even have been murmurings about the appearance of a monopoly, which was politically unwise, but within a year the combine of Thomas Tilling and B.E.T. (The Tilling & British Automobile Traction group) purchased half the concern from the railway, although again the Crosland-Taylor family were to remain as very efficient and strong managers.

In 1942 the TBAT alliance (itself a rather unholy combination of personalities and methods of working) broke up, and the constituent parts were placed with either BET or Tillings, Crosville Motor Services Ltd going to the latter, only to follow Tillings in 1948 in falling into the hands of the British Transport Commission. In all Crosville only had 19 years of truly independent bus operation, and it says a lot for the family that their story still has echoes today.

One result of their rather sparsely populated countryside operations was that they had to squeeze the utmost out of their vehicles but by purchasing top-notch chassis, however antediluvian the body may look, the bus would huff and puff its way over the hills (and more importantly stop at Mrs Lewis's cottage half way down the hill!) while maintaining the running time. I have tried to reflect some of this variety in this selection of photographs – mostly these were the Crosville buses of my youth!

KA 252 and KA 258. (LFM 328 and 334). Although in white coach livery these bodies were classified by their manufacturer, Weymanns of Addlestone, as dual-purpose when delivered in March 1950. Conversely at least the chassis were to coach standard being Leyland PS1/1, although the entire tranche of 35 vehicles were originally ordered by the Midland General Omnibus Company and arrived in bus livery. It will be Eastern Counties won the 'contest' making life impossible for the independents. They were withdrawn in 1964. Alongside LFM 328 is a more Tilling-style vehicle with a full set of blinds – KG 117 (KFM766). It' a Bristol L5G chassis with an E.C.W. 35-seat bus body new in March 1950, withdrawn in 1967 but it became a company towing vehicle G117.

A 'pure' coach, EFM 642, KA 188 ex K116, was delivered to Crosville at not the most propitious of times, March 1940. A rather marvellous machine it had a full luxury Burlingham 33-seat body with a sliding door and just one destination blind in the canopy. The chassis was a rock-solid Leyland TS8 – said by one aficionado to be the finest Leyland ever built with an 8.8-litre petrol engine and constant-mesh gearbox – today's drivers might debate that gearbox as the finest ever after trying AEC's offering! In December 1946 Crosville re-engined this coach with a relatively noisy but cheap to run Leyland 8.6 'oil' engine. It survived in service until 1957 and then became a workers' hack-cum-bothy for a contractor, McAlpine, finally going for scrap the following year.

Although another 'pure' coach, seen here late in life in dual purpose livery, BFM 132 (K41 later KA182) was delivered in June 1937 with a Harrington of Hove 32-seat body on a Leyland TS7 chassis. In 1948 K41 was refitted with a Leyland 8.6 'oil' engine for reasons of economy, but was scrapped in 1953, by which time this body pattern was positively archaic!

LFM 754 (KW173) arrived in the Crosville fleet during July 1950. E.C.W. bodywork with 31 dual-purpose seats was supplied on an Bristol L6B chassis, but the shell was upseated by one to DP32 in 1953. Withdrawal as ELB173 was in 1962, but she passed to Bleanch's Coaches, Helton-le-Hole in September, then to a dealer and so to scrap in December 1964.

Seen at Welshpool not far from the narrow gauge railway is FM 8139 (GA8) which is not far off being the fabled Irishman's broom. The chassis is that of a 5.1-litre 4-cylinder petrol engined Leyland LT5A with sliding mesh gearbox delivered with its Eastern Counties 32-seat bodywork in May 1934. In 1949 it received a new bus pattern Burlingham body, with 34 seats but given that massive dome and blind box to power this ensemble a standard Leyland 8.6 litre diesel (or as Crosville insisted 'oil') engine was supplied in which shape it was to survive until 1961.

FM8138 (GA7) led an almost exactly similar life to FM8139 although withdrawn slightly earlier but passed into the hands of a contractor: H.O. Andrews Ltd, Leeds. Clearly by the time of this photograph GA7 was sick having been dragged to the site on tow. Broken windows and torn and ripped panelling tell the story of any contractor's vehicle.

LFM 810 (KW229) arrived into the world of Crosville during December 1951 with a Bristol LWL6B chassis and with an E.C.W. 39-seat rear entrance body. Apart from the 1958 reclassification from KW229 to SLB229 this bus seems to have led a fairly uneventful life, not being withdrawn until 1970, when it passed to a Scout troop.

This rather rare machine in a standardised fleet like Crosville's, JC 9949 arrived with the rest of the fleet belonging to Mrs M. Ellis, (Ellis Blue Motors) of Llanllechid in February 1952. New in May 1949 JC9949 was a Guy Vixen with bodywork by another relatively rare make, Barnard. Seating 29 this little bus had pottered up and down on school and excursion work plus on the Ellis's line service from Gerlan and Rachub to Bangor. Numbered SG1 (Small Guy, I suppose!) in the Crosville fleet it was not withdrawn until 1958, when it was in the state seen here. After a time in London, it passed to the Coventry Hospital Management Committee in October 1961 and was used for transporting nurses and other staff.

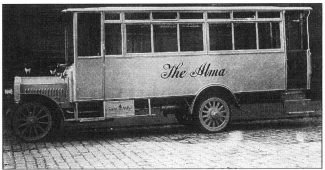

'The ALMA' was not in the Crosville fleet. A Dennis 23-seat machine with an Eaton body, it was to Crosville's design with a Parisian style open rear, normally in service from Chester to the Ellesmere Port area, but also available for private hire. Another of the Crosland Taylor quirks was that the two banks of side windows were removable so that customers could enjoy the breezes from the Dee Estuary. 'The Alma' (FM387) was sold on prior to the first world war.

Wrexham Bus Station 18 July 1992 and this forlorn sign shows only dereliction to the rear. Clearly an attempt was made to titivate the place with flowers but this is sadly a case of how far the mighty had fallen.

When World War 2 broke out thousands of combatants in WW1 must have had an awful feeling of déjà vu. Here are two aspects of that war later to be repeated. In the early days of World War 1 censorship seems to have been very lax, this photograph being reproduced in a London magazine, under the heading "A missing Londoner". Sent to the front D219 (one of 310 Milnes-Daimlers in use in London in 1908) was captured during the retreat to Antwerp when "some raiding Uhlan patrol managed to cut in and ambush ... the bus, whilst returning after discharging its soldier 'fares'".

A part of the Marschlied (marching song) of the German WW1 'Greif Division' reads:
Wenn einst wir geschlagen die letzte Schlacht   Rough translation: When once we've fought the last battle,
Geht's wieder der heimat entgegen.   We will go back to our homeland.
The battle was lost, but these lucky men returned home in a sort-of bus.

PLEASE NURSE THOSE TYRES

In Britain we do not have a natural source of rubber or even latex so tyres were a problem, particularly when one considers all the areas where rubber was involved, wire insulation, intermediate sections in tank tracks, aircraft tyres and fittings plus anti-flare in the fuel tanks being just a few, but each army lorry needed a minimum of seven tyres, and a coach like the one shown here six plus the spare. So even in 1943 a little Government homily crept in. The wartime headlight masks and white painted wings date the machine although the clothing seems not to reflect the necessity for coupons to obtain the smallest item.

The second page is a blatant advertisement and leaves nothing to the imagination but I must confess a wry smile at the bottom line!

A.R.P.

This article appeared in *"Passenger Transport Journal"* in the issue dated 10 February 1939 and is worth quoting in full.

The Southport A.R.P. (Air Raid Precautions) officials have taken the initiative in providing one of the first mobile first-aid stations in the country for dealing with civilian victims of air-raids. The station has been ingeniously devised by Captain F. C. Poulton, A.R.P. Officer to Southport Corporation, and has been constructed from an old Leyland second-hand double-deck bus of the "Titan" low-bridge type. We understand that the bus was bought for the nominal sum of £50.

Despite nine years of municipal service, the original Leyland body, stripped of interior furnishings, has been retained, and it has been adapted so that hinged extensions mounted on the sides of the bus fold out to form two separate compartments, each extending on either side of the bus for a distance of 10 feet. When both compartments are extended the bus is 30 feet wide.

In the event of war the unit will be used for decontamination, and the general treatment of gas casualties. It will work in conjunction with a further unit of a similar type which will shortly be built, and which will deal with non-gas cases.

The normal lower saloon of the bus has been equipped with an operating table, medical supplies and bins containing clean clothing for 65 men and 65 women. In the upper saloon is the staff rest-room, and this is fitted with bunks, bath, stove and water tanks. The extension on either side of the bus body is identical; the offside one is reserved for men, and is divided into two main compartments, a dressing and undressing room,

partitioned by wood pulp walls fitted with mica windows. All the necessary decontamination equipment is housed in the compartments, that for women being more or less similar to the equipment installed on the men's side.

It has been estimated that two of these mobile units would serve all the functions of a standard Ministry of Health fixed first-aid post, the Government estimate for the cost of which is about £3,000. So far the cost of the unit we have just described, including the medical equipment, amounts to only £700, and if, as is likely, it is fitted with an air-conditioning and filtering plant, the complete outfit will cost less than £800.

CP 7675 was new to Hebble Motor Services in 1929 fleet no.69. All Leyland chassis and body, withdrawn 1938.

Clearly wartime, the bus having both white painted bumper and wing tips plus heavily shrouded headlights. The girls' clothing is distinctly 'utility' with the length of skirts governed by Ministry of Supply edicts). With services heavily cut back to save fuel overcrowding in public transport was a fact of life, particularly so in rural districts where the three times a day bus had become twice a day. Churchstoke was then in Montgomeryshire; Mr Hailstone's Bedford WTB bus operating from Shrewsbury with a specially narrow body built by Victor Greenhous just for work in narrow twisting and 'blind' lanes. The driver is the proprietor, Bill Hailstone, himself. Photo courtesy Keith Turns

ASPECTS OF WARTIME

Three different advertisements, each telling a wartime tale.

"But for the buses" appeared in both trade and 'popular' magazines during 1942/3. This variant appeared in *"Picture Post"* and certainty typifies the house of the period with the front door opening directly on to the pavement, the wife in Utility clothing, which was compulsory for ten years 1942-1952, but her hair has been washed and 'permed'. Earlier illustrations showed an infantry man like this with his rifle, perhaps this regulation no longer applied.

"Buses at War" is a curious July 1943 advertisement, but this time for its appearing in the *West Briton* newspaper, Cornwall, which is far from a land of towering coal mines and their associated slag-heaps, albeit derelict tin and copper mines dot the countryside.

And the strangest of all is this Liberty Shoes Ltd of Leicester advertisement. Founded in 1877 providing high quality footwear for Ladies (and women!) they closed less than 20 years after this notice appeared; 'Utility' shoes were made down to a Government imposed quality often involving the use of compressed cardboard, leather being required elsewhere. If you add in the fact that many of the machinists left to enter other more lucrative occupations, clearly even Liberty shoes were going to suffer a drastic fall in quality, but this hardly excuses such an inept piece of copy-writing; the clearly superior 'Madam' would never walk anywhere.

BUT FOR THE BUSES · · ·

'Seven days' leave', 'forty-eight hours', 'late pass', are just so many precious minutes to Service men and women—minutes to be made the most of.

The network of bus services which now covers the countryside has provided ready-made transport for the forces going on leave to and from even the most remote places. Contrast this with the road passenger transport available to the troops of the last war and one realises the progress made in this important public service by private enterprise, in twenty-five years.

But for the buses, short leaves would be shorter still.

BRITISH BUSES

ISSUED BY THE BRITISH OMNIBUS COMPANIES PUBLIC RELATIONS COMMITTEE

CVS-8

The effects of wartime stoppages lasted long after the conflict. Notice lower right is from a 'Midland Red' (BMMO) conductors Fare Alterations booklet dated 19 July 1948. Some 31 pages of tiny type but (topical today) including "Special fare table no.132 for Shrewsbury Town during floods". The importation of paper was subject to all manner of controls; one of my publishers told me of his rambles around eastern Europe buying up what was available – printing was never a problem but anomalies occurred where half the book would be on white paper and balance on cream, or on rapidly browning stock.

Every effort today is being made to produce more coal, the essence of all war munitions.

So that this effort is not wasted, every worker must be on time, and bus operators see to it that vital industry is kept supplied with manpower—on time, although peacetime comfort often has to be sacrificed to this end.

THE SOUTHERN NATIONAL OMNIBUS COMPANY LIMITED

Walk with Liberty

Let the bus go. With Liberty Shoes on your feet, you need not wait. Comfort-giving, ankle-supporting Liberty will get you there quicker and you will enjoy the walking. People will notice your smart, exclusively designed shoes as well as the graceful carriage that comes from perfectly shod feet. The difficulties of war-time affect Liberty delivery, but you do not have to wait very long. You can walk with Liberty tax free in the new Liberty Utility Shoes.

Send Card for Liberty Styles

Liberty SHOES LTD. LEICESTER

PAPER SHORTAGE.

IMPORTANT INSTRUCTIONS TO CONDUCTORS.

1. It will not be possible to reprint the Fare Book for some time; but occasional changes in fares will be notified by means of slips which must be carefully affixed to the appropriate pages, thus keeping the book up to date. On no account must pages of the fare book be detached, and

2. Fare Books must be handed in by Conductors on termination of their employment with the Company, for the use of their successors.

THE 661T TROLLEYBUS

This trolleybus is included for a number of reasons. Bradford's 605 was originally built in 1934 with an AEC/EE type 661T chassis of 15ft 6½ in. wheelbase and designed to carry 50-52 seated passengers plus the ubiquitous five standing. The 661T because of its manoeuvrability was quite a popular choice among trolleybus operators.

In 1944 this vehicle was rebodied to the 'relaxed' wartime utility style by Brush Coachworks of Loughborough, still retaining only those two side opening windows, masked headlights (and presumably bulb-less fog light), full visibility white paintwork albeit on a grey background, but with refurbished soft seats instead of wooden slats, and glass in the upper-deck emergency door. The lack of panel-beaters work is visible at both ends of the roof, but on the other hand this austere appearance

seems to suit the bus. The lining-out would not, in theory at least, have been approved of a couple of years earlier, although it seemed to happen.

Weighing around 7tons l0cwt seating was increased to 58.

OOF! OR MORE ACCURATELY EUF 204

Once the pride of Southdown and later Brighton Corporation fleets EUF 204 was a 1938 Leyland Titan TD5 chassis which was rebodied after the war by Park Royal. When photographed on 27 April 1990 it was fairly apparent that this bus had fallen on hard times, and it was only thanks to the collection we knew as "Winkleigh" (now West of England Transport Collection) that it has survived at all, although the British Bus Preservation Group funded its recov-

ery. Rather than show the whole vehicle this is the part of the bus that must have been seen at one time or another by holiday-makers, soldiers off to war and their girl-friends, lovers, school children, even American servicemen with their GI Brides, these latter often to get a terrible shock when they reached the USA, plus literally millions of people who entered and departed the vehicle.

Seating was simple and reflected the age of the vehicle, although five standing were permitted, plus all the others who sat on one another's laps to get home after the last 'flick' and before Daddies time edict – perhaps as late as 11pm. Below the basic load figures was the box so favoured by schoolboys who busily collected tickets trying to get a complete set – if they were very very lucky the conductor might open the little flap at the bottom of the container and let an acquisitive hand take all it could in one handful. This was a great favour, and it is only due to the activities of such boys (and adults!) that we still have bus tickets of 70 or 80 years ago available to view and occasionally buy.

There was a downside of this activity of course, inasmuch if Mother found the carefully hoarded and sorted ticket collections they went on the fire or in the bin as they could spread all manner of diseases. Father, more realistically, might let them be kept in his shed...

Adam Gordon Books

Battery Trams of the British Isles. David Voice, B5, softback, 56pp, £12

Bibliography of British & Irish Tramways. David Croft & Adam Gordon, A4, softback, 486pp, £35

British Tramcar Manufacturers: British Westinghouse and Metropolitan-Vickers. David Voice, B5, softback, 110pp, £16

British Tramway Accidents. F. Wilson, edited by G. Claydon, laminated hardback, 228pp, £35

The Life of Isambard Kingdom Brunel. By his son, reprint of the 1870 edition, softback, 604pp, £20

Treatise upon Cable or Rope Traction. J. Bucknall Smith plus some other literature on that subject, 434pp., all reprints, card covers, limited print run of 125, £45

The Definitive Guide to Trams (including Funiculars) in the British Isles, 3rd edition. D. Voice, softback, A5, 248pp, £20

The Development of the Modern Tram. Brian Patton, hardbacked, 208pp, profusely illustrated in colour, £40

Double-Deck Trams of the World, Beyond the British Isles. B. Patton, A4 softback, 180pp, £18

Double-Deck Trolleybuses of the World, Beyond the British Isles. B. Patton, A4, softback, 96pp, £16

The Douglas Horse Tramway. K. Pearson, softback, 96pp, £14.50

Edinburgh Street Tramways Co. Rules & Regulations. Reprint of 1883 publication, softback, 56pp, £8

Edinburgh's Transport, Vol. 2, The Corporation Years, 1919-1975. D. Hunter, 192pp, softback, £20

Electric Railway Dictionary, definitions and illustrations of the parts and equipment of electric railway cars and trucks. Reprint of 1911 publication by R. Hitt, huge number of figures including numerous very detailed scale drawings, 350pp; hardbacked in buckram, limited print run of 125, £45

Electric Tramway Traction. A. Greatorex (Borough Engineer and Surveyor, West Bromwich), reprint of 1900 original, 92pp, hardbacked in buckram, limited print run of 125, £25

Fell Mountain Railways. Keith Pearson, A4, hardback, 362pp. £45

The Feltham Car of the Metropolitan Electric and London United Tramways. Reprint of 1931 publication, softback, 18pp, £5

Freight on Street Tramways in the British Isles. David Voice, B5, softback, 66pp, £12

The Age of the Horse Tram. David Voice. A4, laminated hardback, 208pp, £40

Hospital Tramways and Railways, third edition. D. Voice, softback, 108pp, £25

How to Go Tram and Tramway Modelling, third edition. D. Voice, B4, 152pp, completely rewritten, softback, £20

A History of Kingston upon Hull's Tramways. Malcolm Wells, 364pp, laminated hardback, lots of pictures and superb plans compiled by Roger Smith, £50

Huddersfield – The Trolleybus Years. Stephen Lockwood, A4, 232pp, laminated hardback, colour, £50.

London County Council Tramways, map and guide to car services, February 1915. Reprint, 12" x 17", folding out into 12 sections, £8

Manx Electric Railway Saga. Robert P. Hendry. A4. Full colour. 144 pp, hardback. £38.80.

Metropolitan Electric, London United and South Metropolitan Electric Tramways routes map and guide, summer 1925. Reprint, c.14" x 17", folding out into 15 sections, £8

Modern Tramway, reprint of volumes 1 & 2, 1938-1939. A4 cloth hardback, £38

Monorails of the World. D. Voice, A4 softback, 96pp, colour, £25

My 50 Years in Transport. A.G. Grundy, 54pp, softback, 1997, £10

Next Stop Seaton! – 55 Years of Modern Electric Tramways Ltd. Second revised and enlarged edition, D. Jay & D. Voice, B5 softback, 142pp, coloured covers, £20

Omnibuses & Cabs, Their Origin and History. H.C. Moore, hardback reprint with d/w, 282pp, £25

The History and Development of Steam Locomotion on Common Roads. W. Fletcher, reprint of 1891 edition, softback, 332pp, £18

The History of the Steam Tram. H. Whitcombe, hardback, over 60pp, £12

A History of the British Steam Tram, Volume 1. David Gladwin, hardback, coloured covers, 176pp, 312 x 237mm, profusely illustrated, £40

A History of the British Steam Tram, Volume 2. David Gladwin, hardback, size as above, coloured covers, 256pp, £40

A History of the British Steam Tram, Volume 3. David Gladwin, hardback, size as above, coloured covers, 240pp, £45

A History of the British Steam Tram, Volume 4. David Gladwin, hardback, size as above, coloured covers, 256pp, £45

A History of the British Steam Tram, Volume 5. David Gladwin, hardback, size as above, coloured covers, 256pp, £45

A History of the British Steam Tram, Volume 6. David

Gladwin, hardback, size as above, coloured covers, 256pp, £45

A History of the British Steam Tram, Volume 7. David Gladwin, Includes a complete reprint of Some Remarks on Working Street Tramway Lines by Steam Power with Description of Various Engines. By Leonard J. Todd, May 1874. 1008pp in 2 parts, hardbacked, limited print run of 400, £95

Last Rides, Funeral Trams Around the World. David Voice, A4 softback, 53pp, £10

Around London by Trolleybus, Part 1. Hugh Taylor, A4 hardback, 184pp, £32

Pontypridd Trolleybuses. David Bowler, A4 hardback, 224pp, £40

Portsmouth Trolleybuses. David Bowler, A4 hardback, 393pp, £48

Railways of Scotland. W. Acworth, reprint of a scarce title of 1890, softback, £15

Shocking Solutions to a Current Problem. how tramways tried to find an alternative to overhead current supply, by David Voice, softback, 125pp, black and white, £16

Street Railways, their construction, operation and maintenance. C.B. Fairchild, reprint of 1892 publication, 496pp, hardback, profusely illustrated, £40

Toy and Model Trams of the World – Volume 1: Toys, die casts and souvenirs. G. Kuře and D. Voice, A4 softback, all colour, 128pp, £25

Toy and Model Trams of the World – Volume 2: Plastic, white metal and brass models and kits. G. Kuře and D. Voice, A4 softback, all colour, 188pp, £30

Trackless to Trolleybus – Trolleybuses in Britain. By Stephen Lockwood, A4, hardbacked, small colour section. £50

George Francis Train's Banquet, report of 1860 on the opening of the Birkenhead tramway. Reprint, softback, 118pp, £10

My Life in Many States and in Foreign Lands. G.F. Train, reprint of his autobiography, softback, over 350pp, £12

Tram and Bus Tokens of the British Isles. David Voice, B5, colour, softback, 66pp, £20

Trams Across the Wear: Remembering Sunderland's Electric Trams. Stephen Lockwood. A4, laminated hardback, 160pp, £35

Trams, Trolleybuses and Buses and the Law before Deregulation. M. Yelton, B4, softback, 108pp, £15

The Tram Driver. by David Tudor, hardbacked, 72pp, £20

Tramway Reflections. David Voice, softback, A4 landscape, all colour, 111 pages; the theme is similar to the Past and Present railway series, showing locations in tramway times and then the same today, £25

Tramway Review, reprint of issues 1-16, 1950-1954. A5 cloth hardback, £23

Tramways and Electric Railways in the Nineteenth Century, reprint of Electric Railway Number of Cassier's Magazine, 1899. Cloth hardback, over 250pp, £23

Tramways – Their Construction & Working. D. Kinnear Clark, reprint of the 1894 edition, softback, 812pp, £28

Life of Richard Trevithick. two volumes in one, reprint of 1872 edition, softback, 830pp, £25

The Twilight Years of the Trams in Aberdeen & Dundee. All colour, A4 softback, introduction and captions by A. Brotchie, 120pp, £25

The Twilight Years of the Edinburgh Tram. A4 softback, includes 152 coloured pics, 112pp, £25

The Twilight Years of the Glasgow Tram. Over 250 coloured views, A4, softback, 144 pp, £25

The Wantage Tramway. S.H. Pearce Higgins, with Introduction by John Betjeman, hardback reprint with d/w, over 158pp, £28

The Wearing of the Green, being reminiscences of the Glasgow trams. W. Tollan, softback, 96pp, £12

The History of Worcester's Tramways. David Voice, A4, softback, 108pp, £25.

Works Tramcars of the British Isles. David Voice, B5, softback, 238pp, £25

TERMS OF SALE

RETAIL UK – for post and packing please add 10% of the value of the order. Orders £100 and over post and packing free. Payment by cheque, cash or Paypal.

RETAIL OVERSEAS – postage will be charged at printed paper rate via international standard service mail, unless otherwise requested. Payment please by sterling cash or cheque, Paypal, or direct bank to bank by arrangement.

SOCIETIES, CHARITIES etc. relating to tramways, buses and railways – a special 50% discount for any quantity of purchases for resale is given provided my postal charges are paid.

ADAM GORDON BOOKS
Kintradwell Farmhouse, Brora, Sutherland KW9 6LU
Tel: 01408 622660   E-mail: adam@ahg-books.com   Website: www.ahg-books.com